Socializing Metaphysics

Socializing Metaphysics

The Nature of Social Reality

Edited by
Frederick F. Schmitt

ROWMAN & LITTLEFIELD PUBLISHERS, INC.
Lanham • Boulder • New York • Oxford

ROWMAN & LITTLEFIELD PUBLISHERS, INC.

Published in the United States of America
by Rowman & Littlefield Publishers, Inc.
A Member of the Rowman & Littlefield Publishing Group
4501 Forbes Boulevard, Suite 200, Lanham, Maryland 20706
www.rowmanlittlefield.com

PO Box 317
Oxford
OX2 9RU, UK

British Library Cataloguing in Publication Information Available

Library of Congress Cataloging-in-Publication Data
Socializing metaphysics : the nature of social reality / edited by
Frederick F. Schmitt.
    p. cm,
Includes bibliographical references and index.
  ISBN 0-7425-1428-5 (hardcover : alk. paper) — ISBN 0-7425-1429-3
(pbk. : alk. paper)
  1. Social sciences—Philosophy. I. Schmitt, Frederick F., 1951–
H61.15.S63 2003
300'.1—dc21

                                                            2002154805

Printed in the United States of America

∞™ The paper used in this publication meets the minimum requirements of
American National Standard for Information Sciences—Permanence of Paper
for Printed Library Materials, ANSI/NISO Z39.48-1992.

In Memory of
Peter Winch

Contents

Acknowledgments

I would like to thank Margaret Gilbert for her help and encouragement in the course of this project. Thanks also to Ed Witherspoon and Gary Ebbs for their help. Hugh Chandler has offered inspiring conversation on these topics over the years. In recent years I have taught seminars on topics in social metaphysics at the University of Illinois at Urbana-Champaign, and the participants in these seminars have given me more to think about than I have been able to absorb. Reza Lahroodi has helped my thinking on these topics. Jonathan Sisk of Rowman & Littlefield has long supported new studies on social issues relevant to metaphysics and epistemology, and I would like to take the opportunity to thank him for this important contribution to philosophy. Eve DeVaro deserves praise for her editorial work and not least for her patience as I missed one deadline after another. Reza Lahroodi assisted me in early stages of production, while Kevin Kimble assisted in the late stages. Kevin and I coauthored the bibliography.

I would like to acknowledge the following for permission to quote material:

Quotes from Ian Hacking, *The Social Construction of What?*, pp. 6–99, are reprinted by permission of the publisher: Cambridge, Mass.: Harvard University Press, Copyright © 1999 by the President and Fellows of Harvard College.

Quotes from Ludwig Wittgenstein, *Philosophical Investigations* (New York: Macmillan, 1958), sections 241–261, are reprinted by permission of Pearson Education, Upper Saddle River, New Jersey.

Quotes from Peter Winch, *The Idea of a Social Science,* 2nd edition (London: Routledge, 1990), pages 32–101, are reprinted by permission of Routledge.

1

Socializing Metaphysics: An Introduction

Frederick F. Schmitt

In the last decade, philosophy has seen a burgeoning interest in the social world—in the nature of social relations, social entities, and sociality itself. There has been much discussion in metaphysics of social norms, conventions, rules, and roles. A good deal of attention has focused on the nature of collectivities—social groups, associations, and corporations. Epistemologists have worried about the dependence of knowledge on social relations. And ethicists and political philosophers have explored collective responsibility and group rights. The chapters in this volume address issues in the metaphysics of sociality.

Virtually all of the discussion in the metaphysics of sociality has turned on how individual human beings figure in social relations and collectivities. The key question is whether a social relation amounts to something significantly over and above the nonsocial relations and properties of the individuals related and whether a collectivity amounts to something over and above its members standing in nonsocial relations. *Individualists* deny that social relations and collectivities amount to more than the associated individuals and nonsocial relations, while their opponents—*holists* or *collectivists*—affirm the contrary. Some of the chapters in this volume contribute to the debate between individualism and holism. Underlying the debate between individualists and holists is an assumption, questioned long ago by some philosophers influenced by Ludwig Wittgenstein—notably, Peter Winch (1990)—that we can understand individual human beings independently of social relations and collectivities. This assumption has been denied on the ground that individual human beings are already bound up in social relations and collectivities merely in virtue of having such attributes as thinking, acting, and speaking a language. Two chapters in the volume address the assumption that

1

thinking, acting, or speaking a language can be understood independently of social relations and collectivities.

The debate between individualists and holists has tended to assume that our naive classification of common items as social or not is roughly on track. But *social constructionists* have argued that aspects of the world naively taken to be nonsocial, such as race or gender, turn out on inspection to be socially constructed. There is a question how far sociality extends into the apparently nonsocial world. There is also a question whether social constructionist accounts of these phenomena are genuinely incompatible with naturalist accounts. Two chapters in this volume discuss social constructionism.

In this introduction, I review the basic structure of important issues in the metaphysics of sociality. I begin with the question whether social relations and collectivities add something to the world over and above individuals and their nonsocial relations.

ONTOLOGICAL INDIVIDUALISM

It is nearly uncontroversial that social relations and collectivities are *determined* by individuals and their nonsocial properties in this sense: social relations and collectivities *supervene* on nonsocial properties of individuals. In particular, they *globally* supervene: any two possible worlds in which individuals have the same nonsocial properties (and bear the same relations) will exhibit the same social relations among individuals and the same collectivities.[1] We cannot specify in advance of the discussion just what properties of individuals count as nonsocial, but I take it that they include no more than the following: the physical and biological properties of individuals and the singular—that is, nonjoint or noncollective—actions and attitudes of individuals.

We reach controversy with the doctrine of *ontological individualism*, the view that there are only individuals, their nonsocial properties, and admissible composites of these. The opposing view is that social relations and collectivities are something over and above individuals, their nonsocial properties, and admissible composites of these. (The notion of an *admissible* composite of *X*s here is the inverse of the notion of something over and above *X*s. A conjunction of properties of individuals, or a set or a mereological sum of individuals, would presumably be admissible composites here.) Ontological individualism comes in two versions. *Reductive* ontological individualism holds that social relations and collectivities like groups are identical with individuals, their nonsocial properties, or admissible composites of these. *Eliminative* ontological individualism denies that there are any social relations or collectivities. I begin with a discussion of reductive ontological individualism.

In the case of social relations, reductive ontological individualism is the view that social relations are admissible composites of individual nonsocial properties. (I drop "reductive" for the time being.) These nonsocial properties prominently include properties recognized by traditional psychological theories of individual motivation, such as singular desires and intentions. According to ontological individualism, the social relation of friendship, for example, is a conjunctive property—being disposed to act in certain ways and to have certain thoughts toward one's friend and others. Ontological individualism for collectivities like groups or corporations is the view that collectivities are admissible composites of individuals and nonsocial properties. The identities claimed by ontological individualism do not by themselves provide an account of the conditions under which an item is a group. Thus, ontological individualists must offer such an account in addition to the identities they propose.

I will focus here on ontological individualism for *collectivities*, rather than for social relations. I do so for two reasons. First, many, if not all, social relations entail collectivities. For example, if A and B are friends, it follows that they engage in joint activities and hence form a pair—a collectivity. A's being a mayor entails that there is a municipality of which A is the mayor, and a municipality is a collectivity.[2] And so on, for many, if not all, social relations. Thus, if collectivities amount to something over and above their individual members, the nonsocial properties of their members, and admissible composites of these, social relations must also amount to something over and above nonsocial relations and properties. In other words, if ontological individualism holds for social relations, it must also hold for collectivities. Ontological individualism about social relations is no more plausible than ontological individualism about collectivities. Second, similar issues arise for individualism about social relations and about collectivities; accordingly, a review of the issues for collectivities may stand in place of a discussion of the issues for social relations.

Collectivities are not mere populations of individuals with common properties like race, ethnicity, religion, or class. They are distinguished from mere populations of individuals by their capacity to *act*. This distinction matters because, at some level in the explanation of human behavior, agency has a central role to play: many generalizations of theoretical interest will generalize about agents. In treating collectivities, I will follow other writers in taking the *social group* as the paradigm of a collectivity. By a "social group" here I mean, roughly, a collectivity capable of action in the manner of a corporation or association.

Is ontological individualism for social groups plausible? Most contributors to the debate on the ontology of groups have assumed that a group has a unity that binds its members together. (It is a further assumption that this unity binds the group members into a *single* entity, the group. I discuss this assumption below.) The most basic question confronting ontological individualism is whether it can capture the unity of a group. Perhaps the simplest account of unity is offered by an individualist *identity* account of groups. According to this account, a group is nothing but its members (Baxter 2001, 2002). The unity of the group is simply its identity with its members. One might reply that a group has no one member and thus the account inconsistently identifies one item, the group, with each of several distinct items. A defender of the identity account might respond, boldly, that each member of a group is identical with each other member. But few philosophers will be eager to accept that an item can be identical with each of several distinct items. This view runs afoul of a standard view of identity, on which, if *A* is identical with *B*, then *A* and *B* are not distinct things.

   An alternative to saying that the group is identical with its members is to say that the term "the group" refers *plurally* to its members. Consider the term "Russell and Whitehead" in the sentence "Russell and Whitehead wrote *Principia Mathematica*," where this sentence means that they jointly wrote the work.[3] This term clearly refers to Russell and Whitehead. Equally clearly, this sentence does not translate as "Russell wrote *Principia Mathematica*, and Whitehead wrote *Principia Mathematica*." The "and" in the former sentence cannot be captured by the "and" of the latter sentence; it cannot be captured by the "and" of classical, singular logic, the meaning of which is given by truth tables or rules of natural deduction (e.g., the rules of simplification and conjunction). To explain why this is so, it is natural to deny that "Russell" in "Russell and Whitehead" refers to Russell and "Whitehead" refers to Whitehead. Nor does "Russell and Whitehead" refer to a single entity. Rather, "Russell and Whitehead" refers to two individuals, Russell and Whitehead, *as two individuals.* In other words, the term is noncomposite and refers to Russell and Whitehead *plurally.* In the case of a group term, "the trade union" refers to its members *as plural*, rather than to a single entity. This *plural reference* interpretation of the reference of group terms avoids the implausible consequence that a group is identical with each of its members. The interpretation is individualistic in permitting an ontology that consists only of individuals, their nonsocial properties, and admissible composites of these.

   However, the interpretation does not offer any account of the *unity* of groups (nor any account of what makes a population of individuals a group).[4] Moreover, the interpretation is open to the following objection.[5] The reference of "the group," on the plural reference interpretation, cannot be the group itself, even if my use of the term "the group" in the metalanguage in which I am writing is understood as referring plurally. For distinct groups can have the same members. To use an example of Margaret Gilbert's (1987), the Library Committee can have the same members as the Food Committee. But then, on the plural reference interpretation, "the Library Committee" and "the

Food Committee" refer to the same individuals. This means that, on the plural reference interpretation, what "the Library Committee" refers to (its members) cannot be the Library Committee, even if the latter metalinguistic use of the term "the Library Committee" is understood as referring plurally. For if the term did refer to the Library Committee, then the Library Committee would not be distinct from the Food Committee, contrary to intuition. This shows that the reference of "the group," on the plural reference interpretation, is not the group. And this consequence of the plural reference interpretation is surely hard to countenance. These reflections lead to the conclusion that the plural reference interpretation is incorrect.[6]

A second alternative to saying that a group is identical with its members is to say that it is the *set* of its members. But this *set-theoretic* view of groups faces several objections. It succumbs to an objection analogous to the one just mentioned against the plural reference interpretation: distinct groups can have the same members, while distinct sets cannot. Sets are individuated by their members; groups are not. Moreover, a group acts but a set does not; sets are abstract entities and thus causally inert. In addition, a group has different *counterfactual existence conditions* from the set of its members. A set of individuals exists just when the individuals exist, but a group need not exist when its individual members exist. What is more, the Rotary Club could have different members from the ones that it in fact has, but the set of its members could not have different members from the ones that it has.

Similar objections tell against the *mereological* view that a group is the mereological sum (or fusion) of its members.[7] (The mereological sum of a population of individuals is an item that has as its parts all and only the parts of the members of the population and mereological sums of these parts.) Distinct groups can have the same members, but the mereological sums of the same individuals are identical: the mereological sum of individuals *A* and *B* is identical with the mereological sum of *C* and *D*, if *A* is identical with *C*, and *B* is identical with *D*. Moreover, a group has different counterfactual existence conditions from the mereological sum of its members. The Rotary Club could have entirely different members from the ones it has, but the mereological sum of its members would presumably have to have, as parts, at least some of the parts of its members.[8] In addition to these points, a group is necessarily a group, but the mereological sum of the members of a group is not necessarily a group; the mereological sum would exist if the individuals who in the actual world are members of the group existed, even if these individuals did not form a group.

David-Hillel Ruben (1985) has noted yet another problem for the mereological view. If *A* is a member of the trade union, then, on the mereological view, *A* is part of the trade union, because the trade union is the mereological sum of its members. But the trade union, as it happens, is a member of the Trade Union Congress, hence, on the mereological sum view, part of the

Trade Union Congress. But the "part of" relation is transitive. Hence, it follows from the preceding premises that *A* is part of the Trade Union Congress. This is implausible. In fact, *A* is not even a member of the Trade Union Congress. In other words, one can maintain the mereological sum view only at the cost of denying the uncontroversial assumption that the "part of" relation is transitive, or otherwise accepting the counterintuitive conclusion that *A* is part of the Trade Union Congress.[9]

None of these objections to versions of reductive ontological individualism rules out one last, *structuralist* account an individualist might find attractive: a group is an instantiation of a structure in which individual members are constituents. On one such structuralist account, a group is an instantiation of a functional structure in which individuals play roles. This version of structuralism does face the objection that groups have such attributes as thinking and acting; yet it is not entirely clear how an instantiation of a structure can think or act. But there seems to be no more difficulty in the claim that an instantiation of a structure can think or act than in the analogous claim about individuals (i.e., an individual is an instantiation of a functional structure), a popular claim. There is, however, an objection to structuralism in general: an instantiation of a structure is not clearly an *admissible* composite of individuals, as the reductive ontological individualist requires. In the philosophy of mind, the functionalist view that an individual human being, person, or mind is an instantiation of a functional structure is not regarded as a reductive physicalist view. It is not a view on which the mind adds nothing to what is already recognized by physics and neurophysiology, beyond an admissible composite of the items so recognized. Talk of the mind, on the functionalist view, is talk of something significantly more than physical items, their properties, and innocuous composites of these. Similarly, the structuralist view of groups on which a group is an instantiation of a structure is not plausibly regarded as a version of reductive ontological individualism. It is not a view on which talk of the group is talk of nothing more than individuals, their nonsocial properties, and admissible composites of these. So structuralism is not a reductive ontological individualist view.

In the face of these objections to various versions of reductive ontological individualism, a determined ontological individualist might resort to the radical posture of *eliminative ontological individualism* about groups. The eliminative ontological individualist denies that there are groups and maintains that only individuals and their nonsocial properties and admissible composites of these exist. One cost of this view is that it rules out taking our casual talk of groups to be literally true. We do not hesitate to affirm "The trade union existed from 1900 to 1910," or "The Rotary Club encouraged people to enter the competition." The literal truth of these sentences is inconsistent with the eliminativist denial that there are social entities. Eliminative ontological individualism must reject the literal truth of these casual claims. This is a high cost. Whether we should be willing to pay it depends on two questions. One question is whether it is plausible that there are groups in a sense that commits one to more than individuals, their nonsocial properties, and admissible composites of these. To answer this, we must look closely at what such entities would have to be like. The other question is whether such talk must be literally true if we are to employ concepts of collectivities to do explanatory and predictive work. In my contribution to this volume, I argue for negative answers to both of these questions. In this way, I clear the ground for an eliminative ontological individualism.

I note that eliminative ontological individualism treats "the group" as a *putatively* referring term but denies that the term *succeeds* in referring to anything. The plural reference interpretation, by contrast, treats "the group" as a putatively referring term and maintains that the term does succeed in referring, though it does not refer to any single entity, only to a plurality of individuals. An alternative to these approaches is a nonreferring eliminative individualism that denies that "the group" even so much as *putatively* refers to anything(s). This view is perhaps most palatable when coupled with the view that talk of groups and their properties is really disguised talk of individuals and their nonsocial properties. Group talk analyzes into talk of individuals, their nonsocial properties, and admissible composites of these. The latter idea may be called *conceptual individualism*. I observe that this nonreferring eliminative individualism does not succumb to the objection I raised to the plural reference interpretation of group talk.

CONCEPTUAL INDIVIDUALISM

According to conceptual individualism, talk of groups (or of social relations) is analyzable as talk of individuals, their nonsocial properties, and admissible composites of these.[10] Roughly, talk of groups analyzes into talk of individuals, and attributions to groups of properties like acting and thinking analyze into attributions of nonsocial properties to individuals and composites of these. Conceptual individualism per se is consistent with all versions of ontological individualism listed above, both reductive and eliminative. I take it that conceptual individualism entails ontological individualism. If talk of groups is analyzable as talk of individuals, their nonsocial properties, and admissible composites of these, then groups, if they exist, are individuals, their nonsocial properties, or such composites. (The converse, however, does not hold: both reductive and eliminative ontological individualism could be true even if talk of groups is not talk of individuals.) Conceptual individualism per se is, I take it, independent of whether the term "the group" *putatively* refers or not, of whether it succeeds in referring or fails to refer, and of whether it refers singularly or plurally. Conceptual individualism is consistent with saying that "the group" is a putatively referring term and refers singularly or plurally, and it is also consistent with denying that "the group" is a putatively referring term. It is consistent as well with saying that "the group" succeeds in referring, and also with saying that "the group" fails to refer.

Is conceptual individualism about groups plausible? I begin by discussing a collectivity notion that seems to have as good a chance as any of being individualistically analyzable—the notion of joint action. I will mention here one individualist analysis of joint action and refer the reader to my contribution to this volume for a broader discussion of the issues. The analysis I mention employs a device for aggregating individual actions and another device for relating each individual action to the motivation (or end) for which each agent performs the action.[11]

I have in mind Seumas Miller's (2001a) view that a joint action is constituted by *interdependent interpersonal actions* under a certain kind of *common end* (Miller calls it a "collective end"),

> *A*'s individual action *x* and *B*'s individual action *y* constitute a joint action only if *x* depends on *y*, and conversely; *A* and *B* have a common end for which each performs the relevant action; and this end cannot be realized by one of the agents without the action of the other. (paraphrase, pp. 57–58)

We may understand dependence here as *counterfactual dependence*: if *A* didn't do *x*, *B* wouldn't do *y*, and conversely. The requirements of interdependent action and a common end for which the individual actions are performed together bind *x* and *y* into a joint action. Two strangers walk in opposite directions along a path and by accident meet at a log strewn across the path. Each spontaneously lifts his side of the log, the two heave the log from the path, and each continues on his way. Their individual actions of lifting a side of the log constitute a joint action of heaving the log from the path. These actions constitute a joint action because they are interdependent actions, and each individual performs his action for an end in common with the other—namely, removing the log from the path. This is an end that neither individual can satisfy without the aid of the other.

Perhaps the most important difficulty for this account is that it lacks the resources to answer a number of important questions we want an account of joint action to answer. The account does specify when two given individual actions constitute a joint action, and also when there is a joint action. So it answers these questions. But it lacks the resources to tell us just what the constituted joint action is. In particular, it affords no account of the *persistence* conditions or the *counterfactual existence* conditions of the joint action. It does not tell us how the joint action might change over time, nor does it tell us how the joint action might differ in character from the way it actually is. Moreover, it does not specify which individual agents might have participated in the joint action, nor which individual actions might have constituted the joint action. We want an account of joint action to answer these questions, just as we want an account of singular action to answer analogous questions about singular actions.

Let us consider, for example, the question of which agents might have participated in a joint action. Suppose I go for a joint walk with ten others. Suppose we do so for the common end of getting some fresh air in the company of at least ten others. We might be joined by a twelfth person near the end of our walk. This very description of our walk presupposes that the walk we began continues even with the addition of the twelfth person. If this presupposition is correct, then, plausibly, the same walk might have occurred with these twelve people participating from the start. Moreover, any twelfth person might have joined our walk at the end, and thus any twelfth person might have joined our walk at the beginning. Could the account answer the question which individual agents might have participated in the walk by saying that the walk could occur with any participants who have our common end—the end of getting some fresh air in the company of at least ten others? But it is not obvious that having this common end—the common end we in fact have—is necessary for our taking *this* walk. Among the characteristics that determine whether we are taking *this* particular walk, the trajectory of the walk, its geographical location, and its timing all seem at least as important as our common end in taking the walk. We might have taken the same walk for a different end. The account seems to lack the resources to answer these questions about counterfactual participants. More generally, it lacks the resources to answer questions about persistence and counterfactual existence. Yet answers to these questions ought to follow from a satisfactory account of whatever binds individual actions into a joint action. What binds individual actions also makes the joint action a unity, and the unity of the action determines persistence and counterfactual existence conditions. I develop this and several other objections to the interdependent action account of joint actions (as well as to an alternative individualist account) in my contribution to the volume.

CONCEPTUAL NONINDIVIDUALISM

These reflections force us to take seriously conceptual nonindividualist accounts of groups and joint actions. According to these accounts, talk of groups and joint actions cannot be analyzed in terms of individuals, their nonsocial properties, and admissible composites of these. A nonindividualist account analyzes the unity of groups and joint actions in terms of relations among group members that cannot be characterized by the nonsocial properties of members or composites thereof—for example, cannot be characterized by the psychology of individual motivation (ends) or conation (intentions).

I will take here as an example of a nonindividualist account of groups Margaret Gilbert's account in *On Social Facts* (1989).[12] Gilbert's account is inspired by a suggestion of Georg Simmel's for understanding the unity that binds members of a group: "the consciousness of constituting with others a unity is all there is to this unity" (p. 75). As Gilbert interprets this suggestion, "a social group's existence is basically a matter of the members of a set of people being conscious that they are linked by a certain special tie" (pp. 148–49). (This assumes, of course, that the existence of a group is a matter of the unity that binds its members.) Gilbert's own account, however, differs significantly from Simmel's suggestion in proposing something other than consciousness as the basis of unity: a group consists of individuals who are ready to share in an action or attitude as a body, in so far as this is possible.[13]

It is perhaps easiest to approach Gilbert's account through her view of the formation of a group. On her view, group formation involves two steps.[14] In the first step, the individuals who will become the members of the group are what Gilbert calls *quasi-ready* to share in an action or attitude as a body, and each expresses this quasi-readiness. In one sense, I cannot be ready, independently of others, to play tennis. But in another sense I can be ready. Gilbert calls this second sense *quasi-readiness*. Each individual is, independently of the others, quasi-ready to share in an action (or attitude). Some commentators have understood Gilbert to say that each individual's quasi-readiness is a *conditional* readiness to share in the action (or attitude) as a body in this sense: each is ready to so share if other individuals are similarly conditionally ready to do so and express this readiness (Velleman 1997b). (I return in a moment to whether this conditional readiness is what Gilbert intends.) Each individual expresses this quasi-readiness. This first step of quasi-readiness and its expression is described in individualistic terms (up to the content of the attitude of quasi-readiness, which refers to sharing in an action as a body—about which more in a moment). The second step, however, cannot be individualistically characterized. Provided that each individual is quasi-ready and expresses this readiness, the individuals are *jointly ready* to share in an action or attitude as a body. This joint readiness is all that is needed for there to be a group. It might be described as what constitutes the unity of the group. Once the members of the group are jointly ready to perform an action, their joint readiness amounts to a joint espousal of a goal. The individuals jointly act if and only if each acts in light of their joint espousal of this goal (Gilbert 1989, p. 197).

One might object to this account on the ground that it is circular. It characterizes joint readiness and joint action in terms of individuals' quasi-readiness to share in an action (or hold an attitude) as a body. The content of each individual's quasi-readiness is: to share in an action as a body. And one might charge that this employs collectivity notions twice over—the notion of sharing in an action (or of participant action) and the notion of action as a body (or joint action). Thus, joint readiness and joint action are characterized in terms of sharing in an action and joint action. Now, Gilbert's specification of the content of each individual's quasi-readiness avoids overtly employing the notion of joint action by speaking of each individual's readiness to share in an action *as a body*, employing a notion of action as a body that is indifferent between an individual's action and a joint action. Moreover, the reference to "sharing" in an action can perhaps be avoided by simply speaking of "engaging" in an action.[15] However, it does not seem that Gilbert can avoid overtly employing the notion of joint action. Evidently "action as a body" must mean *joint action*. For suppose each individual is quasi-ready to engage in an action, but it is left unspecified whether the relevant action is an individual action or a joint action. This does not seem to suffice for quasi-readiness to engage in the relevant action—a *joint* action. So it is not sufficient for joint readiness to engage in a joint action. When the account refers to an individual's quasi-readiness to engage in an action as a body, that must mean quasi-readiness to engage in a joint action. So, one might insist, there is a circularity after all.

It is not clear, however, that these remarks really do establish that Gilbert's account is circular. For it is not clear that in *On Social Facts* Gilbert proposes to *analyze* joint readiness in terms of individuals' quasi-readiness. She might be making the different proposal that individuals' quasi-readiness suffices for joint readiness, even though the concept of joint readiness is nonindividualistic in a way that the concept of individual quasi-readiness is not. Each individual's quasi-readiness is a singular state of the individual that can be characterized in individualistic terms, with the exception of the content of the state (if that content employs the notion of sharing in an action as a body). But joint readiness cannot be individualistically characterized. One might say that an ingredient in the concept of joint readiness is missing from the concept of each individual's quasi-readiness. What is missing is the effect of the presence of every other individual's quasi-readiness on each individual's quasi-readiness—an effect that converts the mere quasi-readiness of each individual into the joint readiness of all. The concept of joint readiness is, on this view, a primitive concept, even though the quasi-readiness of each individual suffices for joint readiness. The fact that quasi-readiness cannot be characterized without employing the notion of joint action does not render the account of joint readiness circular.

A second objection to Gilbert's account of groups assumes that, on Gilbert's view of group formation, an individual's quasi-readiness is a *conditional* readiness. The objection is that each individual's quasi-readiness or conditional readiness, even in the presence of the quasi-readiness of others, does not suffice for an *unconditional* readiness to share in a joint action. As Gilbert develops the objection in her contribution to this volume, a conditional readiness to do x can be understood either *externally* or *internally*. To say that A is externally conditionally ready to do x on the condition C is to say that if C obtains, then A is unconditionally ready to do x. To say that A is internally conditionally ready to do x on the condition C is to say that A is unconditionally ready to perform a conditional action: x if C obtains. The objection to Gilbert's account is that, on the one hand, a set of externally conditional individual (or singular) readinesses to share in an action does not amount to any *unconditional* readiness to share in the action—as required if the quasi-readiness of each individual is to suffice for an unconditional joint readiness to act jointly. But on the other hand, a set of internally conditional individual readinesses to share in an action j does not amount to any unconditional readiness to share in *this action j*, rather than merely to engage in a *conditional* action *different from j*. So neither externally nor internally conditional individual readinesses to share in an action suffice for an unconditional joint readiness to act jointly. In reply, one could defend Gilbert's account by conceding the point about internally conditional readinesses, while rejecting the point about externally conditional readinesses: the conditions of the externally conditional readinesses are in fact satisfied (each other individual is externally conditionally ready to share in the action), and when these conditions are satisfied, the externally conditional individual readinesses to share in an action suffice for unconditional individual readinesses to share in the action. However, even granting the success of this reply, Gilbert's account would still face the question why these unconditional *individual* readinesses to share in the action suffice for an unconditional *joint* readiness to act jointly. The answer to this question, I take it, is that these unconditional individual readinesses to share in an action are all there is to the unity of a group. Nothing else is needed. Each individual's unconditional readiness to share in an action in the presence of the others' conditional quasi-readinesses to share in the action suffices for the unity of the group and thus for the group itself.

In her contribution to this volume, Gilbert develops an account of groups that differs from her earlier (1989) account in employing centrally the notion of an unconditional personal readiness to enter a joint commitment (in particular, a joint commitment to act jointly or to hold a joint attitude), rather than an individual's quasi-readiness to share in a joint action (or joint attitude).[16] On this view, to form a group it suffices that each individual who will become a member of the group expresses a personal readiness to enter a joint commitment, with the understanding that, provided that others express their like personal readiness to enter a joint commitment, a joint commitment is formed. This condition suffices for forming a group because it suffices for entering into a joint commitment.

I have not yet mentioned a fundamental element of Gilbert's account of groups. On her view, there is a kind of obligation that attaches to group membership in virtue of the joint commitment entailed by group membership. This is an obligation to follow through with the joint action members are jointly committed to perform. A member must obtain permission from other members not to follow through with this commitment. The obligation does not derive from the demands of etiquette or the moral demand to avoid disappointing the expectations of others, but from the joint commitment itself. Moreover, a commitment generates reasons to act. To hark back to Gilbert's discussion in *On Social Facts*, the obligation that derives from joint commitment generates reasons for an individual member to act that are not merely *singular* or *personal* reasons but *participant* reasons for doing one's part in a joint action. Participant reasons are, from the standpoint of the descriptive psychology of motivation, as basic as personal reasons: one can have a participant reason for doing one's part without having any personal reason for doing it, thinking only of what "we" should do and not of what "I" should do. What is more, participant reasons to do one's part in a joint action in general override personal reasons for not doing one's part in the joint action. One important point of group membership and joint activity, on Gilbert's view, is to bind individuals to follow through in cooperative activity even when it becomes personally burdensome for them to do so.

In his contribution to this volume, Abraham Roth discusses *practical intersubjectivity*, a phenomenon that parallels participant reasons. Practical intersubjectivity often occurs in a joint activity. If you and I are driving together to Las Vegas, I may take your intention to drive the second leg of the trip as a rational constraint on my practical reasoning about what I am to do that functions in much the way my own intentions do—as settling a matter for purposes of deliberation about what I am to do. I cannot rationally intend to drive the second leg of the trip once I take your intention to do so as a constraint on my reasoning. Your intention in effect functions as my intention, though not of course my intention to perform an action of my own. Roth argues against an individualistic account of practical intersubjectivity on which the work of your intention is really performed by an intention of mine (e.g., my meta-intention to coordinate my intentions with yours). Note that your intention functions in my cognitive economy in something like the way my participant reason to favor joint goals does. Both your intention and my participant reason have a rational bearing on what I am to do, a bearing that can be at odds with my singular intentions and reasons for doing things. However, practical intersubjectivity is not in itself a phenomenon of joint intention, nor need it occur in a joint activity. Possibly, participant reasons in joint action are a special case of a more general phenomenon of practical intersubjectivity.

In his contribution to this volume, Raimo Tuomela distinguishes an individual's attitudes and actions in the *I-mode* from those in the *we-mode*. Intuitively, I have a goal in the we-mode relative to a group *g* when I am a member of *g* and I have the goal *as* a member of *g*. If I belong to a group that aims to help the poor, I may have the we-mode goal of helping the poor, even if I do not personally care about helping the poor. This distinction parallels Gilbert's distinction between singular reasons and participant reasons for doing one's part in a joint action. Tuomela gives a detailed account of the difference between I-mode and we-mode attitudes. The we-mode is understood, in the intuitive formula I have given so far, in terms of my having the goal (or other attitude) as a member of the group. The notion of having the goal as a member of the group needs explication. Tuomela accordingly defines the we-mode in terms of the member's functioning in the group. To simplify his story,

> *A* has the goal that *p* in the we-mode relative to group *g* just in case *A* is a member (and functions as a member) of *g*, *A* has the goal that *p*, *g* collectively accepts the goal that *p*, and *A* is committed collectively to the goal at least in part for the use of *g*.

This is a nonreductive analysis of we-mode attitudes, as far as it goes, because it employs the notions of being a member of the group, the group's collective acceptance of the attitude, and an individual's collective commitment to the attitude. Tuomela argues that there being a group entails that some members have we-mode attitudes. He also argues that we-mode attitudes and actions are necessary for success in a variety of actions. For example, in groups, some individuals must sometimes act for the group, and this requires we-mode actions. Moreover, there are essentially collective actions, such as playing tennis, and these require we-mode actions. In addition, we-mode cooperation is sometimes required for rational individual actions. This is true in the Centipede, a sequential prisoner's dilemma.

Both Tuomela and Gilbert employ a notion of collective commitment to an attitude in characterizing collective notions—in Tuomela's case the collective notion of a we-mode attitude, in Gilbert's the notion of a group. On Gilbert's account of groups, individuals form a group when each expresses a personal readiness to enter into a joint commitment. This condition suffices for the individuals' joint commitment to act jointly or hold an attitude jointly. One might object that this condition is not necessary for a group. In particular, one might object that it suffices for a group that individuals act jointly; it is not also necessary that individuals express personal readiness to enter into a joint commitment. One might offer that spontaneous mobs or chanting crowds act jointly without expressions of personal readiness to enter into a joint commitment, and even without any joint commitment. One might go so far as to maintain that wolf packs and elephant herds act jointly even though these animals lack the conceptual apparatus to express readiness, to be ready, or to enter into a joint commitment. One might similarly object to Tuomela's account on the ground that a we-mode attitude or action does not require an individual's collective commitment to the attitude. Wolves can form a group and act jointly, and thus have whatever we-mode attitudes are required for these things, without a collective commitment.

What, on such an inclusive view of joint action, could make it the case that individuals act jointly? A natural answer is: the same thing that makes it the case that a single individual acts singularly. Call this answer *conceptual supraindividualism*.[17] (The view is sometimes called *holism,* but this term is used in so many ways that it is perhaps best to introduce a neologism.[18]) On this view, to say that a population acts jointly is to attribute a property analogous to the one we attribute when we say than an individual acts; and to say that a population is a group is to attribute a property analogous to the one we attribute when we say that an individual is an intentional subject.

According to conceptual supraindividualism, when we speak of a group, we are speaking of an intentional subject. This subject has a body consisting of a coordinated composite of the bodies of its members. The subject has intentional states like joint beliefs, ends, and intentions. On one view, an intentional subject is simply the bearer of a system of intentional states. The point of attributing a system of intentional states to an individual is to explain the systematic, coordinated behavior that we observe in a certain portion of the physical world, the individual's body, which then counts as a unity in virtue of its connection to this system of beliefs and desires. There may be an analogous point in attributing a system of intentional states to a population of individuals. We may have reason to attribute a system of beliefs, intentions, and other intentional states to a population to explain the systematic, coordinated behavior that we observe in a portion of the physical world consisting of diverse bodies of individuals. When we do so, we attribute joint intentional states to a group, according to conceptual supraindividualism. On this view, talk of an individual and talk of a group are on a par. Of course, to say that *talk* of groups is to be understood this way is not yet to say that there is an adequate basis for affirming that populations of individuals *really do* form intentional subjects. Conceptual individualism is a view about the content of group talk. It does not entail *ontological* supraindividualism—the view that the entities that we are talking about when we speak of groups, according to conceptual supraindividualism, in fact exist.

In his contribution to this volume, Philip Pettit defends ontological supraindividualism. He argues that social integrates, or populations that collectivize reason in a certain way, are intentional subjects in the sense that

they exhibit rational thought and action over time. Pettit allows that the attitudes of social integrates can be characterized by an individualist account of
shared cooperative activity like Bratman's (1992, 1993a). That is, he concedes a conceptual individualism. But he maintains that what makes social
integrates intentional subjects is their coherent and constant rationality. He
adds that they are not only intentional subjects; they are also persons in the
sense of intentional subjects who are held responsible for being rational. Pettit addresses the question whether in the psychology of an individual member of a social integrate, the individual's attitudes or the group's attitudes
control reasoning and action. He holds that the individual's attitudes have
priority: the individual chooses whether to enter or exit groups; the individual receives credit or blame for his or her institutional behavior. This contrasts with Gilbert's (1989) view that participant reasons for action operate on
a par with and independently of singular reasons for action.

In my contribution to this volume, I express sympathy with ontological
supraindividualism but argue that actual human populations meet the requirements of intentional attitudes and actions only to a pale approximation.
I do, however, defend conceptual supraindividualism by arguing against
conceptual individualist accounts of joint action.

CONVENTION

What is it for a convention to obtain in a population? We tend to think of conventions as in some way social. We often speak of "social conventions." It is
natural, then, to ask whether conventions are necessarily social phenomena
and in particular collectivity phenomena, and whether, even if they are social phenomena, we can nevertheless understand them individualistically, in
much the manner that, according to ontological and conceptual individualism about groups, we can understand groups individualistically.

On the face of it, there are different kinds of conventions, distinguished by
content. Some conventions prescribe *actions*. These have the content: "An
agent of kind K is to do an action of kind X in circumstances of kind C"—for
example, "Everyone with wealth is to give alms to beggars," and "Each guest
at a dinner party is to send a thank you note to the host." There are also *symbolic* and *linguistic* conventions, such as conventions of syntax and meaning. A symbolic meaning convention has the content "Symbol s is to mean
m." I return below to the question how symbolic conventions are related to
action conventions.

Must conventions be social? One question here is whether, in the everyday sense of "convention," a convention must involve more than one individual. An individualist about convention in this sense would claim that
a single individual can establish (or maintain) and be governed by his or

her own convention without the participation of any other individuals. One could reject individualism of this sort in either of two ways: by denying that a lone individual can *establish* a convention or by denying that a convention can *govern* just one individual. On the first rejection, one insists that a convention must be social in the sense that it takes at least two individuals (standing in social relations, or belonging to a collectivity) to establish (or maintain) a convention. On the second rejection, one insists that a convention must be social in the sense that it governs more than one individual—or more plausibly, that it governs (one or more) individuals by a *general description*, rather than by name. The second rejection is plausible. Everyone might jointly accept that Napoleon is to live on St. Helena (and might even do so on the ground that this is what is to be done apart from any practical or moral considerations for doing it), but it seems inapt to call this a convention. A convention must govern individuals under some *general* description, some description that can hold on more than one individual. However, the first rejection is less obviously true. It seems that, in the everyday sense of "convention," a single individual can set up (or maintain) a convention. If I declare to myself that I am to brush my teeth each morning, and as a result come to accept that I am to do this, I thereby establish a convention (Gilbert 1989). At least, nothing in the concept of convention rules out saying that I have established a convention. I return below to the question whether individualism about convention of this kind is plausible.

Even if conventions had to be social in both of the senses specified, this would not yet settle just what is involved in the sociality of conventions. In particular, it would not rule out understanding this sociality *individualistically*. To examine the question of individualism about convention, we may begin by asking what it takes for a convention to be established (or maintained) in a population. David Lewis (1969) has proposed an individualist view of the matter—a *regularity* theory of convention. On such an account, a convention is a behavioral regularity in a population. A convention that S is to do action x in circumstances C obtains in a population just when members of the population behave in conformity with the convention—do x in C. On Lewis's version of the regularity theory—what we might call an *expectation* regularity theory—a convention obtains just when members do x in C *because* members of the population *expect* them to do so. Lewis's theory is not the only regularity theory of convention. Relying on his individualistic account of joint action mentioned above, Seumas Miller (2001a) has proposed a joint action theory of convention on which conventions entail regularities. And Ruth Garrett Millikan (1998) has proposed a *reproductive* regularity theory: a convention (that S is to do x in C) obtains in a population just in case members of the population do x in C because members of the population *have done x* in *C in the past*.

An important objection to the regularity theory of convention is that a convention can obtain in a population even though members do *not* regularly conform to the convention (Gilbert 1989, ch. 6). Similarly, a convention can obtain even though members do not *expect* conformity. It can be a convention in a population that one is to place the salad fork to the left of the other utensils when setting the table, even though no one conforms to that convention or expects anyone to conform to it. At best what is required for a convention is that when asked whether there is a convention, people give answers like, "Yes, there is. One is to put the salad fork on the left, though no one actually does so." There remains the question whether a convention requires that there was regular conformity *at some time in the past*. One might modify Millikan's proposal by saying that what is required for a convention is lip service to the convention deriving from past regular conformity to the convention. But it does not seem that there need ever have been conformity to the convention. We can imagine a static society in which people have always paid lip service to the convention in the manner described above, yet no one has ever conformed to it. This seems enough for a convention.[19]

A second objection to the regularity theory of convention is that it is inconsistent with the *normativity* of convention (Gilbert 1989, ch. 6). Conventions entail norms, but regular behavior, whether caused by expectations or by past regularity, does not entail norms. If it is a convention in a population that S is to put the salad fork on the left, then there is a reason for S to put the salad fork on the left, and S ought to put the salad fork on the left. The mere fact that there is regular behavior from expectations does not make it the case that people have a reason to put the salad fork on the left, or ought to do so. True, it is imprudent to disappoint people's expectations. But, as Gilbert argues, this does not seem to be the sort of reason people have to conform to a convention. Suppose there is a convention to send a thank you note. It might be that guests regularly do so and hosts expect guests to do so. But suppose your host is aware that you do not in fact engage in this practice. Your host forms no expectation that you will do so. Suppose you are aware of this. Then you have no reason to send a thank you note deriving from your host's expectation. Still, you do have reason to send a thank you note deriving from the fact that there is a convention to do so. Similar remarks apply to the reproductive regularity theory. In short, the regularity theory is inconsistent with the fact that conventions entail norms.[20]

Gilbert (1989, ch. 6) has proposed a *joint acceptance* theory of social convention: there is a social convention in a population P that S is to do x in circumstances C just in case members of P jointly accept the principle that S is to do x in C.[21] Joint acceptance is to be understood as joint belief. Gilbert's view entails that there is a convention that p in a population P only if members of *P* form a collectivity with the psychological attribute of accepting the principle that *p*. Gilbert claims that her account, unlike the regularity theory, explains the normativity of convention. The explanation is that when there is a convention that *S* is to do *x* in *C*, members of *P* jointly accept that *S* is to do *x* in *C*. Joint acceptance of a principle carries a (joint) commitment to reason theoretically and practically from the principle.

Gilbert does not argue in full that her account explains the normativity of convention. To make the case, she must argue that a joint acceptance carries a commitment that generates a reason to do *x* in *C* and an obligation to do *x* in *C*. Perhaps the argument would go like this. Consider first the individual analogue of joint acceptance. Suppose I accept the principle that one is to put the salad fork on the left. Plausibly, my acceptance of this principle commits me to reason in the future, both theoretically and practically, on the assumption that the principle is true. In particular, I am committed to reason practically as follows when setting the table: one is to put the salad fork on the left when setting the table; I am setting the table; so I am to put the salad fork on the left. Thus, I am committed to the conclusion that I am to put the salad fork on the left. This gives me a reason to put the salad fork on the left. Gilbert might make the analogous case for joint acceptance. If members of the population jointly accept that one is to put the salad fork on the left, then the members are (jointly) committed by this joint acceptance to reason (jointly) practically to the conclusion that one is to put the salad fork on the left. And this gives any member a (participant, not singular) reason to put the salad fork on the left.

This argument could be challenged on the following ground. My being committed to the conclusion that I am to do *x* in *C* gives me a reason to accept this conclusion. But my having such a reason does not by itself entail that I have a reason to do *x* in *C*. My commitment to a principle gives me a reason to accept that I am to act on the principle in *C*. But it does not follow that I have a reason to act on the principle in *C*. At least, this does not follow merely from my being committed to the principle. Perhaps I do (typically or always) have a reason to act on my principles. Perhaps my reason derives from a demand that I preserve my integrity or the consistency of my acceptances and actions. But this reason to act on my principles does not follow from my mere acceptance of my principles. So it is not the sort of reason for acting entailed by convention. There being a convention that *S* is to do *x* in *C* entails that *S* has a reason to do *x* in *C*, quite apart from any reason to do *x* in *C* imposed by the demands of integrity. So we do not have here an argument that on Gilbert's joint acceptance theory of convention, a convention entails a reason to conform to the convention. Indeed, the same points seem to show that a joint acceptance of a principle does not by itself entail that one has a reason to conform to the principle of the kind required by a convention.

INSTITUTIONAL FACTS

John Searle (1995) has offered an account of institutional facts that has certain points of contact with Gilbert's joint acceptance account of social convention. His account is embedded in a broader theory of social facts, which
I summarize here. Searle distinguishes brute facts of nature from other facts.
The latter include functional facts and institutional facts. Searle maintains that
functional facts are not natural facts but are observer-relative in the sense
that they depend on a prior assignment of value to objects. The assignment
is a collective intention or other collective mental state. (Searle [1990] rejects
an individualist account of collective intentions.) Thus, functional facts derive from a collective assignment of value to objects. For example, that the
function of the heart is to pump blood depends on a prior assignment of the
values of life and survival.

Searle divides functional facts into *agentive* and *nonagentive* functional
facts. The fact that the function of the heart is to pump blood is a nonagentive fact; it is not imposed by our intentional use of the heart but rather by
our valuing. The fact that this stone is a paperweight is an agentive fact; it is
imposed by our intentional use of the stone. We *discover* nonagentive functions, whereas we *create* agentive functions.

Searle further divides agentive functional facts into *causal* agentive functional facts and *status* functional (or institutional) facts. An object has a causal
agentive function if it has a function (imposed by our collective intentional use),
but it can be used to do what it functions to do without our imposing that function. For example, a screwdriver can be used to drive screws even if we do not
impose that function. Typically, objects with causal agentive functions have
physical features that suit them to perform their functions.

Status functional facts differ in this regard from causal agentive functional
facts (1995, p. 41). An object has a status function only if it has a function that
it can perform only in virtue of our imposing that function. A wall has a causal
agentive function in separating two tribes. It can perform the function of separating the tribes even if the tribes do not impose that function. If the wall de-
cays, the few remaining stones may continue to serve as a border between the
tribes. The stones no longer have a causal agentive function, since they cannot
be used to separate the tribes without the tribes imposing the function of separation. Rather, the stones perform their function only because the tribes impose this function: the tribes intend to use the stones as markers or symbols of
separation and to behave in a way that respects these markers, so that the
markers perform the function of separating the tribes. The status functional
fact is imposed entirely by the collective intention to behave in a certain way
and, in particular, to conform to certain rules. Status functional facts exist
within systems of *constitutive rules*, rules that constitute an activity or item (as
contrasted with *regulative* rules, which merely regulate an antecedently exist-

ing activity or item). A constitutive rule characteristically has the content "*X* counts as *Y* in context *C*"—for example, "This stone counts as a border" and "This move counts as checkmate." General status functional facts ("A piece of paper with a picture of George Washington counts as a dollar bill") are constitutive rules, and specific status functional facts ("This piece of paper is a dollar bill") are instances of constitutive rules. It is plausible to think that constitutive rules are a species of convention, as we used that term in the preceding section.[22] "*X* counts as *Y* in *C*" is equivalent to "There is a convention (in population *P*) that *S* is to treat *X* as if it were *Y* in *C*."[23]

Searle proposes that the constitutive rule "*X* counts as *Y* in *C*" is equivalent to there being a collective acceptance of the form "We accept (*S* has power [*S* does *A*])." The relevant powers are of two kinds: positive powers, or enablements, and negative powers, or requirements. So the collective acceptance can take either of two forms: "We accept (*S* is enabled [*S* does *A*])" and "We accept (*S* is required [*S* does *A*])." For example, "A piece of paper, *X*, counts as a five dollar bill" comes to "We accept (*S*, the bearer of *X*, is enabled [*S* buys with *X* up to the value of five dollars])." Constitutive rules, then, are equivalent to a collective acceptance that *S* is enabled or required to do *A*. Searle argues that all status functions are at bottom imposed by collective acceptances of deontic propositions of this sort. For example, a *symbolic* status function like a sentence *s*'s meaning that *p* is imposed by the collective acceptance that we are enabled to use *s* to perform speech acts in which *s* means that *p*.[24] *Specific* status functional facts are instances of constitutive rules. These instances are presumably collective acceptances of instances of the content of a constitutive rule, or they are commitments to acceptance of instances of constitutive rules. Institutional facts, on Searle's view, are very close to social conventions, on Gilbert's view of social conventions. A social convention, on Gilbert's view, is a joint acceptance of a deontic principle of action ("*S* is to do *x* in circumstances *C*"), just as an institutional fact on Searle's view is a collective acceptance of a deontic principle of enablement or requirement.

In his contribution to this volume, Searle offers an account of political power as deriving from status functions and hence from deontic powers. The power of an occupying army rests on brute physical force and coercion. Subjects conform to demands out of fear and prudence. Political power, by contrast, rests on the collective acceptance of enablements and requirements. Such acceptances can be induced by coercion as well as persuasion.

THE SOCIAL IN THE INDIVIDUAL

The approaches to collective phenomena that we have canvassed so far assume that we can comprehend individual human beings independently of collectivity phenomena. For example, individualist approaches to the analysis of collectivity concepts assume that collectivity notions are analyzable in terms of individuals, their nonsocial properties, and admissible composites of these. Nonindividualist approaches to collectivity concepts assume that we can speak of the joint commitments of individuals and thus that we understand individuals independently of joint commitments. Supraindividualists treat collectivity phenomena as parallel to individual phenomena, and they feel free to employ talk of individuals and their properties in characterizing collectivity phenomena. As we can see, all parties to the recent debate about collectivities assume that we can comprehend individual human beings apart from collectivities. If, as seems plausible, social relations entail collectivities, then the present assumption implies that we can comprehend individual human beings apart from social relations.

The opposing view is that we cannot comprehend individual human beings and their nonsocial properties independently of collectivity phenomena. Peter Winch (1990) has claimed that, as a matter of conceptual truth, "meaningful" individual behavior is possible only for agents who have had experience of society—a claim discussed by Edward Witherspoon in his contribution to this volume. Society is naturally understood as a collectivity, but in any case it involves social relations, and these plausibly entail collectivities. So Winch's claim implies that individuals' meaningful behavior involves experience of collectivities. Winch has also claimed that, as a matter of conceptual truth, individuals' intentional attitudes (beliefs, intentions, and desires) depend on society. More exactly, what makes an intentional attitude have the intentional content that it does depends conceptually on society. The latter view is inconsistent with the *intentionalist* program for characterizing collectivity phenomena to which individualists, nonindividualists, and even supraindividualists about groups subscribe (Gilbert 1989). According to this program, collectivity phenomena like groups, joint actions, and joint attitudes must be characterized in part in terms of intentional attitudes and their contents. This is incompatible with the claim that intentional attitudes and their contents depend conceptually on collectivities. For the two together give rise to a circularity in the characterization of collectivity phenomena.

According to Winch, "all meaningful behavior must be social" (1990, p. 116). In particular, anyone whose behavior is meaningful must at some time have had experience of society (p. 33). I am not concerned here to find the correct interpretation of Winch but simply to consider the plausibility of his claim on two interpretations. (For fuller discussion of Winch, see Witherspoon's chapter in this volume.) These interpretations differ in how they disambiguate the ambiguous term "meaningful behavior." I take it that Winch's term "behavior" is a technical term that encompasses not only bodily actions but mental actions like concept applications (or generating a sequence of numbers by a rule) and mental attitudes like beliefs and intentions as well. In speaking of meaningful behavior, one might have in mind either of two senses of the "meaning" of behavior. In one sense of "meaning," the meaning of behavior is what it *signifies* or symbolizes. In this sense, tipping one's hat often means respect or deference. Mental attitudes always signify their intentional contents, whatever else they may signify (such as Freudian meanings). On this first interpretation, Winch is claiming that an action signifies or symbolizes something, and an attitude has content, only if the subject has had some experience of society. In an alternative sense of "meaning," the meaning of an instance of behavior is its *action type*, or in the case of an attitude, its mental type. For example, my running is of the type running. My belief is of the type belief that p (for a specific proposition p). On this interpretation, Winch is claiming that an action or attitude is of a type only if the subject has had some experience of society. Since the mental type of an attitude includes the type of its intentional content (that p) where it has content, the two interpretations of the claim agree in the requirement that attitudes have intentional content only if the subject has had some experience of society. The interpretations differ, however, in what they say about actions. On the first interpretation, the claim applies only to actions that signify something. But intuitively, not all actions do signify something. So on the first interpretation, the claim does not encompass all actions. It says only that actions that signify something require some experience of society. Yet all actions *are* of a type. So on the second interpretation, the claim does apply to all actions: all actions require experience of society. The claim on the second interpretation is therefore stronger than on the first.[25]

There is a *conventionalist* case for Winch's claim on the first, "signifying" interpretation. Troilus's behavior toward Cressida has a certain significance only because it is governed by conventions of courtly love. Conventionalism holds, plausibly, that there is a sense of the "significance" of an action in which its significance is endowed by conventions. It is plausible that Troilus's behavior is significant, in the sense of counting as being of a certain kind, only in virtue of a convention. (Searle might say that significance in this sense is endowed by constitutive rules determined by collective acceptances of deontic principles.) Suppose now that conventions are social in either of two senses—in the sense that the agent of an action governed by a convention must be party to the convention, or in the sense that an action's being governed by the convention requires the agent to be socially related to others governed by the convention. It follows from this supposition of the sociality of conventions that an action is significant only if the agent has had some experience of society—Winch's claim on the first interpretation. The difficulty with this argument for Winch's claim, however, is that the supposition that conventions are social in one of the two senses specified is mistaken. As we saw earlier, conventions are not social in either sense. A convention does not require more than one party to the convention. Nor is it true that an action is governed by a convention only if the agent is socially related to others governed by the convention. A tourist without experience of a society is nevertheless governed by the convention of putting the salad fork on the left. So the supposition of the sociality of convention used to derive Winch's claim is false. Even if actions get their significance from conventions, it does not follow that the agent of a significant action must have had experience of society.

We may add to these points Witherspoon's observation, in his chapter in this volume, that not all actions can get significance from conventions, on pain of a regress of conventions. For conventions depend on prior actions or attitudes. A convention is a condition in a population constituted by actions or attitudes of certain types. This is so on both Lewis's regularity theory of convention, according to which a convention is constituted by actions or attitudes of individuals, and on Gilbert's joint acceptance theory of convention, according to which a convention is constituted by a joint acceptance of a deontic principle of action. Since any convention is constituted by actions or attitudes, if an action gets its significance from a convention, there are prior actions (or attitudes). If these prior actions are significant, they must get their significance from a prior convention. To avoid a regress of conventions, there must be either significant actions that do not get their significance from a convention, or actions that have no significance at all. Thus, Winch's claim on the first interpretation cannot cover all actions; it does not entail that all actions require experience of society. But as we have already noted, it is not plausible that the claim on the first interpretation does cover all actions, since not all actions have significance.

Is there any case for Winch's claim on the second interpretation: an action or attitude is of a type only if the subject has had some experience of society? Here we may focus on the claim about attitudes. For the best case for saying that action-type depends on experience of society is that action-type depends on attitude content: actions are typed by the type of attitude that gives rise to them, since they are typed by the intentions that give rise to them, and in particular by the intentional contents of those intentions. Thus, we may focus on the claim that attitudes are of a type—and particular attitudes have a certain intentional content—in virtue of the subject's experience of society. Let us take the case of concept application—for example, generating a sequence of numbers by a numerical rule "2n - 1." What makes it the case that the subject's concept applications have one content rather than another? In the example of generating a numerical sequence, the question is what makes it the case that the subject is generating the sequence by one rule rather than another rule coextensive with the former rule up to the numbers already generated? One might argue for Winch's claim in this way. If the subject has in mind one rule rather than another, there must be something that makes it the case that the next number is correct or incorrect. There is something that makes this the case only if there is a norm that governs the subject's sequence-generating behavior. But behavior counts as incorrect only if there is a way of correcting it. And there is such a way only if there is a way of sanctioning the behavior when it is incorrect. A sanction might take the form of verbal correction or of punishment. There is a way of sanctioning the behavior when it is incorrect only if someone can apply the sanction. And the person who applies the sanction must differ from the subject. So generating a sequence of numbers requires that there are others to whom the subject is socially related.

In reply to this argument, we may doubt the premise that there is a way of sanctioning the behavior when it is incorrect only if someone other than the subject is able to apply a sanction.[26] There are two sources of doubt about this premise. First, the difference between correctness and incorrectness does not obviously require that some *actual* person socially related to the subject can apply the sanction. It seems that the most that is required for the behavior to be incorrect is that some *possible* person socially related to the subject can apply a sanction to the behavior.

The second source of doubt about the premise is that even if some actual person socially related to the subject must be able to apply the sanction, it is not clear why the *subject* cannot fill the role of potential sanctioner. Suppose she has a capacity for correcting certain forms of behavior, including her own. She has, we may suppose, the same capacity for correcting her behavior as others do. This capacity is a capacity to correct these forms of behavior, regardless of whose behavior they are. It is not clear why the requirement that some actual person can apply a sanction cannot be satisfied just as well by the subject as by others. Why can't an individual with no experience of society develop, or for that matter have innately, a capacity to sanction herself? Of course this capacity entails that the individual has the capacity for certain attitudes—for example, the capacity to think "The preceding behavior was incorrect." And a capacity to think this requires that the behavior of the individual be governed by further norms of correct behavior. But this shows only that the subject must have further capacities to think. Perhaps this requires an infinity of capacities to think, but it does not require infinitely many actual thoughts. It seems plausible enough that human beings have an infinity of capacities to think, even if we do not have infinitely many actual thoughts. In any event, the requirement that someone other than the subject can apply a sanction also has the consequence that some other subject has an infinity of capacities to think, so long as there are only finitely many other subjects. The regress of capacities is no more an obstacle to a solitary self-sanctioner than to a finite society of other-sanctioners. If all this is in order, then there is no case that an individual's correct and incorrect behavior requires an actual or possible other with the capacity to sanction.

Someone might admit that an individual without experience of society could have the relevant capacities but deny that such an individual would be much like a human being. Such an individual would instead be a concentration in a single mind and body of capacities distributed through an entire society. A reason for saying this is that the individual's capacities for sanction must entail a capacity for *perfectly accurate* judgments of correctness and incorrectness. If a subject is to generate a sequence of numbers under a rule, the capacity for sanction in virtue of which she does so must depend on a capacity to judge whether an instance of behavior falls under the relevant norm and to judge this with perfect accuracy. For the generating rule is determined by the judgments that arise from the capacity. So the capacity has final authority and cannot yield an erroneous judgment about correctness or incorrectness. Yet actual individual human beings have no such capacity. Only the combined capacities of all individuals in a society could yield error-free judgments. Of course this is consistent with allowing that it is possible for an individual without experience of society to have a capacity for error-free judgment. It's just that such an individual would be a god, not a human being. As it happens, only the capacities for sanction of an entire society are error-free, as required for a norm of correct behavior.

In response, I find it plausible enough that individual human beings do have a capacity for error-free judgments for many concept applications. Or more cautiously, and more to the point, individuals have such a capacity *if* it is true that all individuals in society in combination have such a capacity (as the objection requires). Individual human beings have the capacity to judge accurately whether a given instance of behavior conforms to a norm associated with a specified numerical rule if all individuals in combination have such a capacity.[27] Individuals depend on the capacities of others only where specialized expertise is required to make an accurate judgment. Individual human beings have a capacity for error-free judgments for many concept applications if everyone together has such a capacity.

There remains the question whether a subject could, on her own, set up a norm of correct behavior without the aid of sanctions applied by others. As a first step toward an affirmative answer, we should note (what is no doubt obvious) that capacities for sanctions cannot wholly determine correct behavior in generating a sequence. The mere fact that others can sanction my behavior cannot make it the case that I am engaged in generating the sequence $2n - 1$. First, a capacity for sanctions could determine the content of my generating behavior only if the sanctions *appropriately* applied to my behavior. But what could make the sanctions apply appropriately except that my generating behavior and the judgments that guide the sanctions have the same (or commensurable) content? But of course the account cannot appeal to sameness of content, on pain of circularity. Second, even if the sanctions appropriately apply to my behavior, they suffice for my behavior's being incorrect only if the sanctions are *correct*. And what could make this the case? Clearly not other actual or possible sanctions of these sanctions, since these other sanctions would be subject to the same difficulty. Perhaps uninterpreted sanctions can determine whether my behavior is correct. To take the case of applying the concept *dog*, if people look cross at me when I say "dog," this may suffice to determine that I have incorrectly applied the concept. But this can make my concept the concept of dog only if there is something that makes looking cross correct—the presence of a dog. Sanctions can determine that I apply the concept of dog only if they are related in a certain way to the presence (or absence) of a dog. These points suggest that external conditions must enter into the determination of the correctness of my concept applications or generating behavior. But there is no more difficulty relating external conditions *directly* to my application of the concept than there is relating them to the *sanctions*. So sanctions seem to be unnecessary for the correctness of my concept applications.

A *correlational* view of content happily avoids the implication that content requires that someone can apply a sanction to the relevant behavior (Dretske 1981, 1986; Fodor 1992). On a correlational view of content, the content of an attitude is determined by the properties that correlate with attitudes of this type. Along similar lines, whether a subject applies the concept of F is determined by the subject's capacity to apply this concept to objects that are F. A subject applies the concept of a dog to a given object just in case the application manifests the subject's capacity to apply this concept to all and only dogs. Similarly, which rule a subject has in mind in generating a sequence of numbers is determined by the subject's capacity to go on generating more numbers in the sequence.

It has been questioned whether there is any determinate sequence of numbers a subject has a capacity to go on generating, and whether there is any determinate class of possible objects a subject has a capacity to tag with "dog" (Kripke 1982). Jerry Fodor (1992) has answered this question by proposing that there are laws of the form, "A number's having the property F causes the subject to token the numeral for the number"; "An object's having the property of being a dog causes the subject to token 'dog.'" In the case of the latter law, the subject's concept expressed by "dog" is the concept of dog, while under the former law the subject's rule is the rule: generate numbers having F. One might respond that such a correlational approach does not explain the normative character of concept-application or rule generation. But perhaps concept-application need not be normative. Perhaps concept-applications are correct or incorrect in a normative sense of "correct" only when subjects are sophisticated enough to have reasons to avoid incorrect applications, to make judgments about correctness, and to apply sanctions. One makes a mistake in reading back into concept-application in general features that are specific to the sophisticated concept-applications of mature human beings.

The correlational view of content has numerous difficulties, but there are plausible enough responses to these (Fodor 1992) that we should countenance the possibility that sanction need not be among the determinants of attitude contents. If this is so, then there is no case that attitude contents require experience of society. They are not collectivity phenomena.

OTHER ARGUMENTS THAT THOUGHT
AND LANGUAGE ARE SOCIAL

Winch claims that it is impossible for an individual with no experience of society to act and think. I have questioned the force of an argument for this claim. One can also question the claim itself on the ground that a solitary agent and thinker—a congenital Robinson Crusoe—seems possible (Gilbert 1989, ch. 2). Granting the possibility of a congenital Crusoe, however, is consistent with a final, albeit slim, requirement of social relations for action types and attitude contents. One might maintain that a congenital Crusoe can act and have thoughts—for example, use "corn" to refer to corn—only if *possible*, rather than actual, others are able to learn from Crusoe's use of "corn" to use the term as Crusoe does, to refer to corn. Certainly it is true that in the case of "corn," possible others could learn Crusoe's use of "corn": if there were others, they could observe Crusoe using the term in the presence of corn. But one might insist that this must be true in the case of *any* term. One might deny that it is possible for a subject to use a term to refer (even putatively) to items of a kind without possible others being *able to learn* from the subject's use of the term how to use the term to refer to items of these kinds. In other words, one might deny the possibility of a private language of sensation.

It is tempting to reply to one who denies this possibility by insisting that a subject could use a term to refer to his or her own sensation states of a certain phenomenal kind, even though others could not learn to use the term to refer to states of this kind. To deny the possibility of a private language is to deny that this is possible. If it could be argued successfully that it is impossible for a subject to use a term to refer to such a state, this would establish a sense in which language must be social, albeit a sense considerably weaker than the claim that a congenital Crusoe is impossible. It would establish that language is social in the sense that the use of a term must be learnable from the subject's use by possible others, rather than that language is social in the sense that the use of it depends on actual others' ability to sanction. Crusoe's use of "corn" is inconsistent with the claim that language is social in the latter sense, but it is consistent with the claim that language is social in the former, weak sense, since possible others could learn the use of "corn" from Crusoe's use. But I do not try to evaluate here whether language must be social in the weak sense that a private language of sensation is impossible. Wittgenstein (1958) is usually interpreted as having argued against the possibility of a private language of sensation. In his contribution to this volume, Edward Witherspoon proposes an alternative interpretation, on which Wittgenstein is denying that there is clear content to the dispute between those who affirm and those who deny the possibility of a private language.[28]

Tyler Burge (1986) has argued that for many beliefs, the individuation of belief contents makes essential reference to social circumstances. This is a weaker claim than Winch's claim that having attitudes depends on having had some experience of society. It is also weaker than the conclusion of the private language argument that a subject can use a term to refer to a kind only if possible others can learn this use from the subject. Burge does not claim that having just any belief entails standing in a relation to society. Rather, he claims that for a subject who uses a communal language, what content the subject's attitude has depends, in many cases, on the subject's relation to the communal language. This is consistent with allowing that for some beliefs of such a subject, what contents the beliefs have does not depend on social circumstances. It is also consistent with a congenital Crusoe.

In his contribution to this volume, Gary Ebbs argues (to a first approximation) that whether an individual's kind term (e.g., "gold") refers to the same kind as a subsequent historically related community's kind term does not depend only on the dispositions of the individual to apply the term to objects of a specified kind but on the subsequent community's judgments of sameness of denotation as well. Suppose a jeweler applies "gold" in 1650 to both gold and platinum, but the subsequent community comes to limit the application of the term to gold. Does the term refer to the same kind as the subsequent community's term "gold"? It might seem that the answer must be No, because the jeweler's disposition to use the term differs from that of the subsequent community. But Ebbs argues that if the subsequent community judges the jeweler's use to refer to the same kind as its own, then the earlier use does refer to the same kind. If the subsequent community had instead persisted in applying "gold" to both gold and platinum and judged that the jeweler's use has the same denotation, then it would be true in this case as well that the denotation is the same. Thus, whether the jeweler's use is the same turns on subsequent judgments of sameness of denotation and not merely on the sameness of dispositions to apply the term. Assuming that Ebbs is right about this, the denotation of a kind term in a use depends on the user's relation to a subsequent historical community. Contingent subsequent developments in the use of the term, together with the community's judgments of sameness of denotation, affect whether the earlier use is the same. Although Ebbs does not do so, one who finds his argument convincing might go farther and claim that just which kind the jeweler's use of the term refers to—whether gold or the disjunctive kind platinum or gold—turns

on the jeweler's relation to a subsequent community. These are claims to the
effect that linguistic reference is socially sensitive in a nontrivial way.

SOCIALIZATION AND INDIVIDUAL AUTONOMY

Even if one thinks that we can comprehend individual human beings independently of social relations and collectivity phenomena—that being an individual, acting, and having thoughts are conceptually independent of social
phenomena—one can still worry that social relations of the sort people actually or typically have are incompatible with certain desirable characteristics
of human beings. In particular, one can worry that human autonomy is incompatible with the fact that people are products of socialization. In his contribution to this volume, Seumas Miller addresses this worry. Miller allows
that in special conditions socialization is a threat to individual autonomy, but
he argues that socialization need not be a threat and that social conventions
and norms are indeed necessary for certain shared ends essential to individual autonomy. As he puts it, the only coherent notion of autonomy is one
that takes an historically established framework of social norms as a background condition for individual action.

SOCIAL CONSTRUCTIONISM

Social constructionism has been understood in several ways. It has taken the
form of an *ontological* claim, that kinds of objects, in particular, kinds that have
seemed not to be social (electron, gender, race), are socially constructed—
constituted by social relations. It has also taken the form of a claim about
causal explanation. In one version, it is the proposal that our classifications of
things and people into kinds are caused by social conditions, rather than by
nature ("idea constructionism"). In another version, it is the claim that human
differences (gender, race) are caused by social conditions (e.g., evaluation)
rather than by natural ones.

For natural kinds, idea constructionism seems a more plausible view than
ontological constructionism. (I use "natural kind" here to mean "naturally occurring kind," a sense that contrasts with "artifactual kind" rather than with
"socially constructed kind.") It is more plausible that our *classifications* of
subatomic particles are socially caused than that distinctions among kinds of
subatomic particles are socially constituted. However, ontological constructionism has plausibility for human kinds such as gender and race, as Sally
Haslanger argues in her contribution to this volume. The causal-explanatory
constructionist claim that human differences are caused by social conditions
rather than natural ones would seem to depend for its plausibility on onto-

logical constructionism about those differences; for it is more plausible that human differences are socially caused if they are socially constituted than if they are not so constituted.

Ontological social constructionism about a kind says that, for things of that kind, their being of the kind is (in part) a matter of their being treated by human beings in a certain way. For artifactual kinds, ontological social constructionism is certainly true. For to be a screwdriver is to be intended to drive screws. This follows from Searle's account of causal agentive functions discussed above.[29] Thus, ontological social constructionism about artifactual kinds has a causal agentive functional basis. There is, however, no such basis for ontological social constructionism about natural kinds like mountains: to be a mountain is not to be intended for human use.

Even so, there is some plausibility in a different version of ontological social constructionism for certain natural kinds. For example, one might maintain that what counts as an electron depends on scientific activity (Rouse 1987). To be an electron is to be a particle like those physicists manipulate in laboratory experiments. For to be an electron is to be a particle that falls under the extension of the term "electron," and this term gets its extension by reference to experimentally treated or created particles in laboratory conditions.[30] Whether this view amounts to ontological social constructionism turns on just how the view is formulated. If the view is that what it is to be an electron is to be like a particle of a certain kind, where the kind is merely *accidentally* that of the laboratory particles, then it does not amount to a version of ontological social constructionism. But if the view is that what it is to be an electron is to be like a particle of a kind *essentially* defined by laboratory manipulation, then the view entails counterfactual dependence. I have conceded that there is some plausibility in this view, but the view certainly has some bizarre consequences. For example, it entails that whether there were electrons a million years ago depends on whether human beings perform certain experiments. And it entails that there would be no electrons, if there had been no human experiments, even though there would still be particles that are intrinsically, and in all respects relevant to physical explanations, just like electrons.

Ontological social constructionism is highly plausible for human kinds, such as race, gender, and class. In her chapter, Haslanger explores just what such a claim of social constructionism comes to. She proposes that social theorists discover that kinds that might have seemed natural, or only thinly social, are really thickly social—amount to social relations in a rich network. Haslanger suggests that we understand our everyday talk of human kinds on the model of the Putnam-Kripke treatment of natural kind terms—we use our terms to refer to kinds, in ignorance of the real social nature of these kinds, deferring to experts for the relevant information.

It is worth observing the logical limits of ontological social constructionism for human kinds. A broad enough ontological social constructionism will be inconsistent with individualism about groups, as well as with nonindividualism and supraindividualism. In particular, if being an individual is said to be ontologically socially constructed, and this means that individuals depend on collectivities for their individuation, or for the individuation of their attitude contents, then groups cannot be understood as individuals, their nonsocial properties, or admissible composites of these, contrary to individualism.

Let us turn now from ontological social constructionism to the *causal-explanatory* view that human differences are caused by our treatment of people (as contrasted with the view that the explanation of our ideas of race, gender, and so on are caused by our treatment). As Ron Mallon observes in his contribution to this volume, social constructionists have sometimes claimed that the causal explanation of, say, gender differences among human populations lies in the social roles of the individuals who exhibit the behavior, rather than in human nature defined by biology or in natural environmental conditions. These social constructionist explanations of difference contrast with *naturalistic* explanations. For example, evolutionary psychology offers naturalistic explanations of differential patterns of behavior that appeal to biological properties of individuals, such as their sex. Evolutionary psychologists have explained alleged differences in sexual jealousy between the sexes by appeal to alleged differences in reproductive strategies. Explanatory social constructionists, by contrast, strive to explain differences in behavior between genders by appeal to differences in social roles correlated with genders.

Naturalistic explanations of difference have been thought to have an advantage over social constructionist explanations: they can explain the *stability* of the target differences by appeal to the stability of features of human nature. By contrast, the social roles to which explanatory social constructionists appeal have been thought to be unstable and so incapable of explaining the stability of the target differences. Reacting to this apparent advantage of naturalistic explanations, explanatory social constructionists have insisted on the instability of the target differences. They have explained this instability by appeal to the claim that social regularities are caused or constituted by unstable intentional states of agents. As Ian Hacking (1999) suggests, the point of calling some kind K socially constructed is often to undermine our assumption that K is a natural kind, thereby making it more plausible that K is optional, and that it is within our power to change or get rid of K, than we might have thought when we viewed K as a natural kind. Social constructionists want to encourage us to see gender or race as optional kinds, susceptible to rational alteration. But as Mallon argues, the fact that a kind is socially constructed rather than natural need not make it any more controllable than a natural kind. For social kinds are often enough caused by stable social roles. This defends causal-explanatory social constructionism, though at the cost of raising the question whether the political ends of social constructionists are achievable.[31]

NOTES

1. Note, however, that *social laws* do not supervene on the *laws of individual psychology*. As Philip Pettit has observed, the social law "Unemployment is followed by a rise in crime" may hold in one society and not another, despite the fact that the laws of individual psychology are the same in the two societies (Pettit 1993, pp. 129ff).

2. However, there is an important objection to ontological individualism for social relations that has no analogue for groups—David-Hillel Ruben's objection from *multiple realization* (Ruben 1985). Social relations are multiply realizable—realizable by quite different nonsocial properties of individuals. What amounts to friendship varies enormously from one culture to another. There may be certain universally necessary conditions that can be formulated in individualist terms—for example, friends are expected not to act in ways detrimental to one another's interests, and friends are expected to come to one another's aid in times of crisis. But there is no reason to think that any set of universally necessary conditions like these will suffice for friendship. Just when nonfriends are expected to act in these ways depends on social customs and norms that vary greatly across societies. And nonfriends are also expected not to act in ways that are detrimental to one another's interests and are expected to come to one another's aid in times of crisis. There does not seem to be a universal set of individualistic necessary and sufficient conditions for friendship, at best a societally indexed set of conditions.

3. I borrow the example from (Yi 2002).

4. Note, too, that the plural reference account offers no clue about the counterfactual conditions in which "the group" refers plurally to these individuals rather than those or in which this joint action is performed by individuals other than those by which it is actually performed.

5. Here is another objection. Groups have attitudes and perform actions. But it is impossible for a mere plurality of individuals to have attitudes and perform actions, by the very nature of having an attitude or performing an action. An item or items that have the attribute of thinking must compose a single thing; they cannot be a mere plurality. Peter van Inwagen (1990, pp. 118–19) has claimed that in this regard thinking contrasts with, say, supporting a weight. It is possible for a plurality of things to work together to support a weight without composing one thing. At least, nothing in the nature of supporting a weight prevents this. But the nature of thinking entails that any items that work together to think compose one thing. On this objection, reference to the group cannot be mere plural reference if talk about groups that attributes thinking is literally true. (Strictly speaking this claim may be consistent with the plural reference interpretation. For it may be compatible with saying that the term "the group" refers plurally, even though the sentence attributing thinking to "the group" is true only if the plurality to which the group refers is not a mere plurality but composes a single thing. However, this latter view is at best strained. It is natural to suppose that if "The group thinks" is literally true, and the predicate "thinks" applies to a plurality only if it composes a single thing, then the "the group" refers not to a plurality but to this single

thing. Indeed, this natural supposition follows from the plausible assumption that if "*a* is *F*" is literally true, and "*F*" applies only to an item of type *G*, then "*a*" refers only to an item of type *G*.) In reply, I find it less than obvious that, by the very nature of thinking, items that work together to think must compose one thing. So I do not find this objection to the plural reference interpretation persuasive.

6. Note that there is no comparable objection to the idea that a *population* term refers plurally to individuals in the population. For unlike groups, populations are individuated by their members. I have no objection to using plurally referring terms and plural quantifiers for purposes of formulating claims about social ontology. These terms can be conveniently used to refer plurally to populations of group members. I make no judgment here about whether plural reference is indispensable for formulating social ontology.

7. Let it also be noted that a group is not an *aggregate* in the sense characterized by Burge (1977). Burge's notion of aggregate is a notion of a sum in which a population of individuals not only uniquely determines a sum, as in the case of a mereological sum, but the sum uniquely decomposes into what Burge calls its *member-components*. Mereological sums do not uniquely decompose into parts. For example, the parts of the individuals that compose a mereological sum also compose that sum. But the parts of an aggregate do not compose the aggregate, in the relevant sense of "compose." The parts of the member-components are not necessarily member-components (or perhaps even parts) of the aggregate, as the parts of individuals are parts of their mereological sum. Burge's aggregates thus resemble sets in respect of unique decomposition into member-components. However, these member-components differ from members of a set in being parts of the aggregate. Unlike a set, the aggregate is a concrete object, has causal powers, and has a spatiotemporal location; it is located where its member-components are located. The Pleiades galactic cluster is an aggregate. It is not a mereological sum of stars. The proposal that a group is an aggregate does not succumb to the objections from the transitivity of the "part of" relation that tells against the mereological identity view. However, it does succumb to the point that distinct groups can have the same members. It also succumbs to the point that a group could exist without one of its members because aggregates depend on all of their members.

8. This objection appeals to a weak mereological essentialism about sums: a mereological sum could not exist without having as parts some of the parts of its members. This follows from the mereological essentialist thesis that an individual could not exist without having some of the parts it in fact has.

9. A similar point tells against the idea that the "member of" relation for groups can be understood as a "part of" relation. Any "part of" relation is transitive, but the "member of" relation is not transitive. We can also see that being a member of a group does not entail being part of the group. For my leg is part of me. And I am a member of the Philosophy Department. But my leg is not part of the Philosophy Department.

10. Versions of conceptual individualism are developed in Tuomela and Miller (1985), Bratman (1992, 1993a, 1993b, 1997), Kutz (2000a), and S. Miller (2001a).

11. Individualists tend to assume that joint actions are unified in the sense that the individual actions involved in a joint action are bound together. Joint actions are shared. Perhaps the strongest account of unity here would be identity. Each individual partner in a joint action performs numerically the same action. One objection to

this view is that numerically the same action cannot be performed by distinct agents. It cannot be that the joint action of lifting the sofa is identical with Joe's lifting the sofa and Josephine's lifting the sofa, since actions are individuated by their agents. A weaker and more plausible account of unity is that joint actions are shared only in the sense in which diners share a table when they eat together. On this view, each individual performs some part of the joint action.

12. Another version of nonindividualism is Velleman (1997b).

13. Gilbert proposes that in one central sense the pronoun "we" refers to a set of people each of whom is ready to share with oneself in some action or attitude (1989, p. 168). In this collective sense, "we" means "we together," contrasting with the distributive "we" meaning "we both" or "we each." The collective "we" applies when members are ready to share in an action or attitude. It does not require that members actually perform a joint action or hold a joint attitude. Gilbert offers the example of a married couple who upon completing the wedding ceremony may correctly refer to themselves as "we" in the collective sense before undertaking joint action (170). A group, one might say, is in this sense a standing possibility of joint action. An appropriate use of "we" in the collective sense in "Shall we do *A*?" requires "that each of the people referred to has in effect expressed to the others his willingness to share with the others in doing *A*" (p. 179). Gilbert argues that both the willingness itself and its manifestation are necessary for a group. Manifestation matters to us because it fixes willingness—it makes willingness robust. (One might say that manifestation is needed to bring about commitment—at least a joint commitment.)

14. To simplify discussion, I have to leave out of account here epistemological aspects of the expression (such as openness) and conditions of mutual or common knowledge.

15. But does this maneuver work? What an individual is quasi-ready to do, it appears, is share in a joint action, not *engage* in a joint action. I cannot be, independently of others, ready to do something jointly, only to share in a joint activity.

16. Gilbert employs the notion of joint commitment centrally in Gilbert 1996 and 2000.

17. Versions of supraindividualism are developed in French (1972, 1984), Brooks (1981, 1986), Clark (1994), and Rovane (1997).

18. See Gilbert (1989) for a discussion of holism.

19. Of course, this possibility tells against Millikan's original proposal as well as the modified proposal.

20. Could the proponent of a regularity theory say that you have a reason to send a thank you note, not because it would disappoint your host not to, but because others have such expectations and they would take a dim view of your nonconformance? But what if others are aware of your behavioral dispositions and thus have no such expectations?

21. See Tuomela (2002a) for a collective acceptance approach to social practices.

22. I am using "convention" here in the sense in which Lewis and Gilbert use it, not in Searle's sense. Searle distinguishes rules from conventions. As Searle uses these terms, the powers of the king in chess are a matter of rule, not convention, but the shape of the piece is a matter of convention (1995, p. 49). However, both would count as conventions in Lewis's and Gilbert's sense. For Searle, the distinction between rule and convention is relative to an enterprise, conventions being optional in

the enterprise. For Lewis and Gilbert, whether something counts as a convention is not relative to an enterprise.

23. Perhaps Searle's account of institutional facts escapes the objection to Gilbert's joint acceptance account of social convention that an acceptance of a principle does not by itself entail that the subject who accepts the principle has a reason to conform to the principle. Searle can maintain that, unlike social convention, institutional facts do not give one a reason to conform to a principle.

24. Gilbert actually rejects this view of symbolic status functions, proposing instead that a group's having a language involves members jointly accepting, not any deontic proposition, but that words mean such and such (1989, p. 390). On her view, accepting that words mean such and such does not entail that anyone is to use words with this meaning. So a semantic convention is not a social convention in her sense. I think we should grant that what members must accept is not that any member of the group is to speak the language and use words with such and such a meaning. For a group can have a language even though no member is required to speak it. Nevertheless, it seems plausible that members must accept the conditional deontic proposition that if *S* is a speaker of our language, then *S* is to use words with such and such a meaning.

25. Winch speaks of behavior being intelligible (1990, p. 81). I assume that by "intelligible" Winch means "makes sense." Talk of making sense is, however, ambiguous between the two senses of "meaning"—signifying and being of a type. So talk of intelligibility does not decide between the two interpretations of Winch's claim.

26. Another difficulty with the argument is the assumption that behavior counts as incorrect only if there is available a means of correcting it, and this in turn requires a sanction for the behavior. It is not obvious that this is so, if conventions are the source of correctness. To see this, return to Gilbert's point that a convention can hold even if no one follows it. Suppose that people jointly accept that one is to put the salad fork on the left. Yet no one follows this convention, and after a while everyone forgets their acceptance of the principle. Suppose someone asks whether there is such a convention. I take it that if people discovered an old book in the library in which the acceptance was recorded, this would answer the question affirmatively. People would allow that the convention still holds; after all, it was never rescinded. Now, I suppose that so long as this book is available in the library, correction is available in the sense Winch requires. But suppose the book were destroyed before anyone could read it. Then correction would no longer be available. Still, it seems that the convention holds. It is hard to credit the idea that whether the convention still holds turns on whether the book has been destroyed. Presumably the convention remains in effect until abrogated by a joint rescission. So if conventions are the source of correctness, it does not seem that whether behavior counts as correct or incorrect can depend on the availability of a means of correcting it.

27. Of course, this capacity is learned from others, and one's justification for such judgments may well depend on reasons possessed by others. But the question here is whether mature human beings have a capacity for accurate judgment without help from others, and the answer to that is: we do.

28. For discussions of the private language argument, see McDowell (1989, 1991), Wright (1991, 1998), Moser (1992), and Schroeder (2001).

29. Searle's account of nonagentive functions also entails ontological social con-

structionism for natural functional kinds (e.g., the heart's having the function of pumping blood).

30. A strong version of this view is that there were no instances of the kind electron before laboratory experiments. The weaker version is that electrons exist in nature, before laboratory experiments, but what makes them electrons is their similarity to experimentally treated particles. Even the weaker version has the bizarre consequences mentioned below.

31. Mallon leaves open the question of "methodological" individualism—whether the explanation of the effects of social roles need appeal only to individual psychology (to beliefs and actions of individuals recognized by individual psychology—e.g., individual beliefs involved in the conception of the role) or must appeal to features of the social role defined in social terms (e.g., joint beliefs involved in the conception of the role).

2

The Structure of the Social Atom: Joint Commitment as the Foundation of Human Social Behavior

Margaret Gilbert

INTRODUCTION

The Question

Imagine that you have a bird's-eye view of a particular city. Along one street, a lone woman walks northward at a strolling pace. Some distance north of her, on the other side of the road, a man leans against a wall, smoking a cigarette. Looking southward, he idly takes note of the woman, then looks away and takes another puff. Soon after this, she notices him. A slightly anxious look comes over her face and she begins to walk more quickly.

So far one might reasonably see these people as nothing but discrete individuals, going about their own business. True, the man has observed the woman, as she has observed him. True, the woman appears to have performed what the sociologist Max Weber would refer to as a "social action" in relation to the man. She has, in Weber's terms, "oriented her action" in a certain way on account of the behavior of another person. These things, however, hardly seem to detract from the discreteness of the two individuals.[1]

Suppose now that as the woman draws near to the man, she turns and calls out to him: "Nice day today!" He turns toward her, catches her eye, and responds "Yes, indeed!"

Are the two parties still "nothing but" discrete individuals? Surely once she calls out to him and he acknowledges her and her call a significant connection has been established between them.

One might go further. They are surely now *unified* in a way that they were not before she called out and he responded. One might speak of them, somewhat fancifully perhaps, as now constituting a *social atom*.

What moves them from their status as discrete individuals to their status as constituents in a social atom? What is it to be so unified? What, in other words, is *the structure of the social atom?*

Related questions abound. Is this kind of unity only available to people in twos and threes or other smallish populations, or are some such units quite large? Is there any limit on their possible size? Must the people involved have encountered each other or know of each other? How precisely do these units come into being? And how do they cease to be? These questions give rise to an epistemological one: where are the answers to be found? One obvious place is through examination of the thought and talk of ordinary people as they engage in interactions such as the one described. This has been my approach to the questions at issue.

I should note at the outset that I have focused and shall here focus on the sociality of human beings as opposed to nonhuman animals or other creatures. There are, I think, good reasons to allow oneself to do this, which is by no means to discount the interest of the other cases.[2]

Methodology

Some contemporary philosophers evince a negative stance toward the examination of everyday thought and talk in pursuit of an understanding of how things are. They argue that there is no reason to trust such thought and talk with respect to reality.

Max Weber and Emile Durkheim, commonly regarded as the founders of sociology, evinced a similar stance. While disagreeing quite radically as to what made a phenomenon a social one, they both expressed some degree of skepticism with respect to the role of everyday concepts in a scientific sociology.

Durkheim emphasized that everyday concepts were formed for purposes other than scientific description (Durkheim 1982, ch. 2, section 2). Weber claimed that certain everyday statements about groups were metaphysically suspect. Contrary to the implications of such statements, he averred, there is no such thing as a "collective personality which 'acts'" (Weber 1987, p. 102). The scientifically minded sociologist, therefore, must not think that there is.

Weber also asserted that sociologists could not afford to *ignore* the concepts in terms of which people lead their lives. These are, after all, the concepts that inform their bodily movements. I take this to be uncontroversial. To cite an example drawn from a famous poem of Stevie Smith's, if we see a man in the sea moving his arm up and down, we may not yet know something crucial: is he *waving* or *drowning?* In order to understand what people are doing, we need to understand their intentions. And intentions embody concepts.

The various arguments against the use of everyday concepts for scientific purposes are not conclusive. In particular, it remains possible that the careful examination of everyday thought and talk may yet reveal metaphysically respectable concepts that have a role to play in both interpretation and social scientific description.

My Proposal

What emerged from my own investigations of everyday thought and talk was this. A range of central everyday concepts relating to the social world—including the concept of an agreement and a central concept of social group—have at their core the general concept of what I call a *joint commitment*. This concept is articulated in some detail in due course.[3]

My proposal is that to understand the structure of joint commitment is to understand the deep or underlying structure of the smallest carrier of genuine sociality—the social atom. People have the concept of a joint commitment and are constantly creating—and dissolving—such commitments. These joint commitments play a major role in organizing their behavior, including their reactions to one another. It follows that social scientists cannot afford to ignore the concept of a joint commitment for either interpretive or descriptive purposes. This concept is of fundamental importance for all who seek to understand human behavior in both general and particular circumstances.

In the first section of the chapter I return to the imagined scenario with which I began. I associate it with a broad class of social phenomena and make an observation concerning this class that calls for explanation. The presence of a joint commitment would provide an explanation, as is clear when one fully understands what such commitments amount to. In the central section of the chapter, the nature and genesis of joint commitments is explored in some detail. In the final section it is argued that understanding joint action in terms of joint commitment throws light, among other things, on an issue that has been of interest and concern to many: the possibility of collective moral guilt and its implications for individuals.

ACTING TOGETHER

What unified the woman who called out "Nice day!" and the man who responded "Yes, indeed"? To broaden the question, one can associate that fleeting, small-scale scenario with a range of others, all of them involving cases of what I shall call *acting together*, and discuss that class as a whole.

People often refer to themselves as "doing things with" another person or persons, or as "acting together" in some way: *having a picnic together, doing an experiment together, running a business together,* and so on. In addition, some common descriptions seem to incorporate the idea that a form of acting together is at issue, without any use of the terms *together* or *with*: *quarreling,* for instance, or *playing tennis.* Again, some descriptions that may at first appear to relate to the independent acts of one party, seem on closer inspection to imply the active participation of another and, indeed, a type of acting together. I have in mind here such terms as *greeting, telling, questioning, answering,* and *observing to another,* as in the woman's "Nice day!"

So: what is it to do something with another person, to act together with them, or, in other terms, to participate with them in a joint activity? I start with an observation on a relatively persistent form of joint activity: going for a walk with another person.[4]

The Permission Point

Consider two people—call them Bill and Jane—out on a walk together or, for short, walking together. By hypothesis, Bill and Jane understand that they are out on a walk together, and, indeed, this is common knowledge between them.[5] Now suppose that, without warning, Bill suddenly stops and says, quite pleasantly, "Well, I'm splitting!" He then walks off, leaving their walk.

One can imagine that Jane will be surprised. She may not be disappointed. She may even be pleased. Absent a specifiable circumstance, however, she will understand that Bill has *done something wrong.* I am not construing this thought in terms of specifically *moral* wrongness—whatever precisely that is—but more generally. To put the point another way: she will understand that Bill is *open to criticism.*

Jane will understand that Bill would *not* have been open to criticism in the way in question if, before leaving their walk, he had asked if she minded his leaving. He should, that is, have *obtained her permission* for leaving the walk.

She will understand that all this is true by virtue of what it is for people to be out on a walk together. If you like, she will understand that it follows directly from the fact that they are walking together.

In short, if Bill and Jane are walking together, then, in withdrawing from their walk, and solely by virtue of what it is to be walking together, Bill does something wrong if he has failed to obtain Jane's permission so to withdraw. To generalize: if certain persons are engaged in a particular joint activity with one another, it follows directly from that fact that a participant who withdraws from the joint activity does something wrong if he (or she) has failed to obtain permission from the other members so to withdraw. I shall call this general observation *the permission point.*

On first considering it, some people may resist the permission point.[6] As to the example in the text, they would say that Bill does *not* need Jane's permission to leave the walk. There are plausible ways to explain such a reaction without giving up the permission point.

Those who are initially inclined to dispute the point may well not *like* the thought that those with whom they do things have the kind of power over them it implies.[7] Given a relatively strong desire that something not be true, one's judgment on the point is liable to be affected, at least as far as one's initial reaction is concerned.

Another possibility is that those who resist the permission point have been affected by observations and experiences that, taken out of context, appear to refute it. Once their context is revealed, however, it is clear that they do not refute it. There are at least three types of context that could have this effect.

In one type of case, things proceed along lines similar to the following. Jane asks Bill if he'd like to walk round Horsebarn Hill with her. Bill says he isn't sure he wants to go for much of a walk today. Jane then says, "Look, if you want to stop at any point, that's fine—by all means do so. I'll be happy to continue on my own." Bill responds: "Fine. Let's go, then." Later, feeling tired, Bill wants to leave their walk. He says to Jane: "I think I'll stop here." Jane comfortably responds, "Bye, then," and they go their separate ways.

Taken out of context, Jane's comfort with Bill's decision to leave their walk might seem to refute the permission point. Taken in its context, however, it clearly does not refute it. Indeed, the fact that Jane might speak as she does initially in this example suggests the permission point is true. Jane is, in effect, *giving in advance her permission to Bill* to leave their walk if and when he wants to. This suggests that her permission is required in order for his doing so to be unexceptionable.[8]

In this first type of case, one party explicitly grants to another advance permission to opt out of a particular instance of a joint activity. This may be labeled a case of *ad hoc agreement*.

An example of another type of case is this. Bill and Jane know each other well and enjoy walking together. Both know, however, that Bill finds it deeply uncomfortable to have to ask anyone's permission for anything. They may, therefore, have developed an understanding that, whenever they are out on a walk together it is up to Bill how long he continues to participate in the joint activity. In this type of case, Jane has, in effect, given her permission in advance to Bill with respect to his ceasing to participate in any given walk if and when he chooses to do so. For the sake of a label, I shall say that this case involves a *private convention*.

In yet another type of case, Bill and Jane may both be parties to a society-wide convention that when a man engages in a joint activity with a woman, he may withdraw from the activity without her permission. In this scenario also Jane has, in effect, given her permission in advance to Bill's ceasing to participate in their walk if and when he chooses to do so. I shall say that this case involves a *societal convention*.[9]

It is possible, then, that in particular cases the relevant permission has been given in advance, as a result of an ad hoc agreement or prevailing conventions. Observations of apparently acceptable withdrawals without contemporaneous requests for permission do not, of course, refute the permission point when they are made in the context of such agreements and conventions.

It does not appear that such agreements and conventions are the norm. When engaged in what are understood to be joint activities, such as going for a walk together, people often speak and act in permission-requesting and permission-granting ways, however subtle. Thus one person might say, "I'm getting tired," and the other might respond "Well, why don't you go back, then. I'll go on by myself." Or one might say, "I'm going to have to stop," and the other might reply "That's fine. I'll come back with you."

The prevalence of phrases such as "have to stop," implying some kind of *necessity* or *compulsion,* is suggestive, insofar as if one person really "has to stop" or "can't go on," the other cannot reasonably withhold permission to stop. Is the granting of permission to stop still needed? The second exchange, above, suggests that it is. The second party's response is plausibly interpreted as a matter of granting permission not to continue with the joint activity, and it is made in face of a declaration of presumed inability.[10]

Often, the person who says that they "have to" stop, or whatever, does not really have to. They may just want to stop. However, their simply wanting to stop is nothing like as compelling a reason for granting them permission to stop as is their being incapable of not stopping. If they really *can't* go on, there is no chance that the other party or parties can negotiate their going on. So they say that they have to stop. The other parties may leave it there, or they may seek to discover precisely what degree of incapacity, if any, is present.

To summarize the discussion of the permission point so far. People often act and talk in ways that suggest its truth. That is, in the context of joint activity, they speak and act in permission-requesting and permission-granting ways when withdrawal from the joint activity is at issue. Though the permission point may be resisted, there are reasons for viewing such resistance with caution. People may reject the point because they do not want it to be true, or because, without realizing it, they are focusing on observations and experiences that occur in the context of agreements or conventions whose function is, in effect, to provide the needed permission in advance.

Another reason someone may be disinclined to accept the permission point is this. He or she may find puzzling the idea that the need to obtain permission—or what I shall now refer to as *the permission requirement*—follows directly from the fact of acting together. The problem might be put this way: the permission requirement seems to be something of a different order from acting together. The latter may seem natural, relatively primitive, a matter of "brute fact," whereas the former seems artificial, relatively so-phisticated, a matter of norms or values.

Such thoughts may give rise to the following suggestion. Might it be that though those who act together are indeed subject to the permission require-ment, that requirement does not follow directly from the fact of acting to-gether? Might it depend, rather, on background understandings standardly associated with acting together? Were this so, people could still, if they wished, initiate special permission-granting agreements and conventions to operate in the context of these understandings.

Suppose we assume, for the sake of argument, that acting together does *not* in and of itself ground the permission requirement. Why, in that case, should background understandings that do ground it develop?

One proposal might be that these understandings would develop in order to prevent behavior that could be hurtful to others. Perhaps, in particular, they would develop in order to prevent rudeness.[11]

Now precisely what rudeness amounts to is not altogether clear. In a cen-tral type of case, however, someone who acts rudely in relation to someone else violates a *right* in the person to whom he is rude. In other words, in a central type of case, the kind of hurt involved in rudeness is that associated with the violation of a right.

An understanding that grounds the permission requirement is, indeed, well tailored to forestall this kind of hurt. For suppose that Anne has a right against Ben to his doing X. If he obtains her permission not to do X, she is unlikely to find his subsequent failure to do X hurtful.

A construal of the first proposal in terms of a "rights violation" conception of rudeness may suppose that when there is joint activity, each participant has a right against every other to his or her continued participation in the joint activity. This supposition may well be correct—I think it is. That does not mean, however, that we have here a satisfying solution to the puzzle of the permission requirement. For this proposal solves that puzzle only by in-troducing another with a similar flavor: the puzzle of the grounds of the rights associated with joint activity.[12]

A second proposal might be that background understandings grounding the permission requirement would arise because many people reasonably develop expectations that the joint activity in which they are participating will reach an appropriate conclusion: a tennis game will go on until one per-son wins or loses, a two-hour hike will last two hours, a trial will be com-pleted. Many of these people—reasonably, again—will form plans in light of these expectations, and it may well be costly for them if the expectations are not fulfilled. A background understanding that any given party must get per-mission from the others to break off from the joint activity before it is com-pleted would, evidently, be a safeguard against the nonfulfillment of rea-sonable expectations of continued participation, and related problems, should the party in question be tempted not to continue participating in the joint activity.[13]

It can hardly be doubted that many participants in joint activity form reasonable expectations of the completion of their joint activity, expectations upon which they reasonably place a fair amount of reliance. This point, however, leaves open the question of the source and justification of the expectations in question.

In this connection it is worth noting that, once it is in place, the permission requirement would help to justify and, for that reason, *generate* expectations of continued participation and reliance upon such expectations. Given common knowledge that each of us is subject to the permission requirement, I know that you know you are required to obtain my permission before ceasing to participate our joint activity. This does not, of course, *guarantee* that you will not suddenly cease to participate. Nonetheless, there is a clear and commonly known constraint on your doing so.

In contrast, suppose we have common knowledge only that—as of now—you and I both personally intend to continue to act so that by means of our combined forces a certain log is moved.[14] Unless either of us has entered some relevant agreement, your intention is yours to change, as is mine. Your intention may be something to go on. However, given common knowledge of your freedom to change your mind, it is hard to see that it can amount to much.[15]

It is quite plausible to conjecture, then, that the connection between the reasonable expectations and reliance associated with acting together and the permission requirement is the opposite of that suggested in the second proposal. The permission requirement may well help to give rise to the expectations and reliance rather than the other way round.

Is there a plausible account of acting together such that it grounds the permission requirement? In the following section I sketch the account of acting together that I have developed. On that account, the permission requirement follows from the nature of acting together.

Collectively Intending and Acting Together

A standard model of a single person's action—or, more strictly, a single person's *intentional* action—is roughly this. The person in question intends to do something and, being guided by that intention, behaves in such a way as to fulfill it.[16]

Supposing that a plausible model of joint action will run along similar lines, we have the question of what it is for *us* to intend. Without arguing for it here, I present my own proposal on this question. In terms I shall explain shortly, I understand what we may refer to as a *collective* intention as follows: Persons *A* and *B* *collectively intend* to do *X* if and only if *A* and *B* are jointly committed to intend as a body to do *X*.

Following on from that, we can understand the case of two people walking together roughly as follows:

> Persons *A* and *B* are walking together if and only if they collectively intend to walk together and each acts in light of this collective intention in such a way that it is in the process of being fulfilled. More precisely, each acts in light of the joint commitment to intend as a body to walk together.

There are several aspects of this account that could usefully be further elaborated. In particular, the nature of *joint commitment* must be explained. This is done shortly.

One aspect of joint commitment should be noted, if not explained, at once. It can be argued that when two or more persons are jointly committed to intend as a body to do *X*, then if either wishes to act contrary to the intention, they will need to get the permission of the other parties to the joint commitment so to act, or they will be—in one respect—at fault. Hence the permission point will stand for those who are acting together according to this account.

That is, I take it, a significant virtue of the account. It is beyond the scope of this chapter to pursue a full defense of it.[17] It is now time to explore the key concept of joint commitment.

JOINT COMMITMENT[18]

It will be useful to preface the discussion of joint commitment with consideration of some related matters. Suppose, then, that Janice decides to have lunch at Café Earth today. I take it that she is now in some sense committed to having lunch at Café Earth today. She can, of course, change her mind. But as long as she does not do so, she is committed.

A personal decision creates what I call a *personal commitment*. By this I mean a commitment of a person *A*, such that *A* is in a position unilaterally to make and unilaterally to unmake or rescind it.

I shall not attempt fully to characterize the general notion of *commitment*. I take the following, at least, to be true of any commitment. A commitment has what philosophers refer to as *normative force*. If one violates a commitment to which one is subject, one has done what in some sense one was not supposed to do. One has to some extent and in some sense done something wrong—something open to criticism.

It might be questioned whether personal decisions as such really are commitments in this sense. Suppose the decision is a completely arbitrary one, such as the decision to take the left rather than the right fork on a leisurely walk in the woods, with nothing to choose between the two options. Suppose one makes this decision when the choice point comes into view, then absent-mindedly takes the right fork.[19]

Certainly, one may well not be angry with oneself, or castigate oneself, on realizing that one has acted contrary to one's decision. But, on realizing what had happened, one might well think "Oh, I meant to take the right fork!" a thought that is suggestive of an *error,* as is the reflection "I meant to take the left fork, *but* I was so distracted I turned right instead!" It seems, then, that what one has done is indeed open to criticism, and, indeed, a matter of doing something wrong in that sense—the sense at issue here.

It will be useful to elaborate on what it is to be in a position *unilaterally to create a commitment.* Consider first the possibility that Sally decides to go shopping today if and only if the sun comes out. If she is to carry out her decision she must wait to see whether the sun comes out. Still, at the time of her decision she is already committed. She is, as we might put it, committed to go-shopping-if-and-only-if-the-sun-comes-out. Again, suppose that Sally decides to go shopping today if and only if her daughter Zoe goes out with some friends. If she is to carry out her decision she must wait to see what Zoe does. Her commitment exists in advance, however, irrespective of Zoe's decisions or actions.

What, though, if what Sally decides is this: if and only if Zoe goes out with her friends, I'll decide to go shopping today? Note that the decision in question is not that if and only if Zoe goes out with her friends, Sally will decide *whether* to go shopping. Rather, the content of her possibly upcoming decision is already fixed: she will decide *to go shopping.* One can imagine circumstances in which Sally's decision to decide a certain way would make perfect sense.[20] Perhaps Sally hates to shop and the decision to go shopping is always difficult. In order to make it she has to engage in various preliminary rituals. She needs to shop soon, but Zoe's staying home would provide a good excuse not to shop today. She thus decides to make the decision to shop if and only if Zoe goes out. She will then to do whatever she needs to do in order to make that decision.

There are, then, two decisions at issue in this case. The first is a decision to decide a certain way, if and only if certain conditions hold. The second is the decision decided upon. The conditions for making the latter decision involve the action of another person. Does that mean that the second decision is not a personal one? It seems not, for Sally is surely in a position unilaterally to *make* the decision, even though she has made a prior decision to make it if and only if someone else, namely Zoe, first does a particular thing. Once having made it, she is in a position unilaterally to change her mind.

An important point with respect to *personal* commitments is this. Suppose Janice decides to lunch at the Eaterie, does not change her mind about this, but finds herself walking absentmindedly in the direction opposite to the Eaterie, thus acting contrary to her decision. Having realized what is going on, she might well chide herself for this lapse. This indicates that she is, and understands herself to be, *answerable to herself* for any failures in relation to her decision. Failing special background circumstances, she is *answerable only to herself* in relation to such a lapse.

It is now time to turn to joint commitment. To put it briefly, a joint commitment is the commitment *of two or more people*. It is not, then, constituted by a set of personal commitments such as might be created by a set of concordant personal decisions, resulting in two or more people each with a personal commitment. I shall refer to this feature of joint commitment as its *holism*.[21] To say that it has this feature is by no means to say all that can be said.

There follows a reasonably comprehensive list of central features of joint commitment. It may not be exhaustive. I do not attempt a full explanation of each point. I mostly leave aside such questions as how the features relate to each other, whether there are any redundancies in the list, and my reasons for including a given feature in the list. I should emphasize that I take myself to be articulating a fundamental everyday concept, rather than making some kind of stipulation. For mnemonic convenience I give each feature a short label.

I start with the core feature, which has already been noted:

1. *Holism.* A joint commitment is a commitment of two or more people.

The other features are numbered 1a., 1b., and so on to indicate that 1. is indeed the core feature.

1a. *Answerability, obligations, and rights.* Each party is answerable to all parties for any violation of the joint commitment. This is a function of its jointness. One can argue, further, that the language of obligations and rights is applicable here. More precisely, where there is a joint commitment the parties have ensuing rights against and obligations toward each other. These are obligations to act in accordance with the commitment, and rights to such performance.[22] These obligations and rights may or may not best be characterized as *moral* obligations and rights, depending on how these latter are defined.[23]

1b. *Creation.* The creation of a joint commitment requires the participation of all the parties. In some cases background joint commitments that are the creation of all the parties allow for some person or body to create new joint commitments for them all by acting in specified ways. This involves, in effect, the creation of a person or body with authority unilaterally to create joint commitments for the parties.[24] These may be referred to as *secondary* cases, with the other cases being the *primary* or *basic* cases of joint commitment. Note that this point does not address *the means* by which a joint commitment is created, but rather *who must be involved* in its creation. I discuss the means in the section The Genesis of Joint Commitment, below.

1c. *Rescission.* A joint commitment is not rescindable by either party unilaterally, but only by the parties together. Again, in some cases there may be special background understandings or explicit preliminaries that allow, in effect, for unilateral rescission. The situation described here is the "default" situation. The *two-person case* has some special features. For instance, if one person deliberately violates the commitment the nonviolator may have the option of "unilaterally" rescinding it. This would be because the violator has indicated concurrence with such rescinding.[25]

1di. *Dependent "individual" commitments.* When there is a joint commitment, each of the parties is committed through it. One may, therefore, speak of the associated "individual commitments" of the parties. These commitments exist through the joint commitment: they are dependent on its existence for their own. As to the content of these individual commitments, each is presumably committed to promoting the object of the joint commitment to the best of his or her ability in conjuction with the other parties. (On the object or content of a joint commitment see 1e *Content*, below.)

1dii. *Dependent commitments not personal.* Given their existence through the joint commitment, these "individual commitments" are not *personal* commitments: they are not, or not ultimately, the unilateral creation of the respective persons, they cannot be unilaterally rescinded, and one is answerable to all for their violation, which is, in effect, a violation of the commitment of all—the joint commitment.

1diii. *Interdependence of dependent commitments.* The dependent individual commitments are interdependent in the sense that there cannot be a single such commitment, pertaining to a given individual, existing in the absence of any other such commitments. Thus given a two-person joint commitment, and *ceteris paribus*, one person's dependent individual commitment cannot exist unless the other's does. These commitments must arise and fall together. Again, this is because of the dependence on each of these individual commitments on the joint commitment (see 1di *Dependent "individual" commitments*, above).

1div. *Simultaneity of dependent commitments.* The dependent individual commitments of the parties come into being simultaneously at the time of the creation of the joint commitment. Some qualifications may be necessary here, but this is at least true with respect to the dependent individual commitments of those creating an original joint commitment *de novo*. (In a two-person case, simultaneity follows from interdependence, though not conversely.)[26]

1e. *Content*. Joint commitments are always commitments to "act as a body" in a specified way, where "acting" is taken in a broad sense. Thus people may jointly commit to *deciding* as a body, to *accepting* a certain goal as a body, to *intending* as a body, to *believing* as a body a certain proposition, and so on. The force of the qualifier "as a body" is roughly this: the parties are jointly committed together to constitute, as far as is possible, a single body that acts in the way in question. For example, they are jointly committed to constitute, as far as possible, a single body that accepts goal *G* as its own.

THE GENESIS OF JOINT COMMITMENT

So far I have noted only that all of the parties must in some way be involved in the creation of such a commitment. I have not yet addressed the means by which a joint commitment is created by the parties.

A Problematic Explanation

Michael Robins (2002) wonders how "two or more people could ever *become* jointly committed if they weren't already 'joined at the hip.'" Why might the possibility of creating a joint commitment *de novo* seem problematic? It will do so if one makes the following assumption: a joint commitment is created by means of the expression of conditional personal commitments. I shall call this *the conditional personal commitments assumption, or CPC.*

More fully, the CPC may be interpreted in terms of a pair of *matching conditional personal intentions*, where each such intention has been expressed by its possessor in such a way that the existence of each member of the pair is common knowledge between the parties. One of the pair may have been formed in reaction to the other.[27]

What is a conditional personal intention? One might initially characterize such an intention as one expressible by a statement of the form "I intend to do A, if (or only if) a certain condition holds." That granted, it will be helpful to distinguish among conditional personal intentions as follows. For simplicity I shall focus on sufficient conditions.

An *internally conditional* personal intention is expressible by a statement of the form: "I intend this: to do such-and-such if a certain condition holds." An *externally conditional* personal intention is expressible, rather, by a statement of the form: "If a certain condition holds, I intend to do such-and-such."[28] In other words, the condition of an externally conditional intention is a condition of the existence of the intention as such.[29]

An externally conditional intention can at the same time be internally conditional. The condition of an externally conditional intention is, in other words, the condition for an *actual* intention as opposed to one that is *categorical in form*. The condition of an internally conditional intention is a condition for an intention categorical in form.

There is a good theoretical reason to invoke personal intentions as opposed to promises or agreements as part of the process by which joint commitments are created. It is quite plausible to see promises and agreements as themselves incorporating a joint commitment.[30] There is a related problem about invoking an *exchange*, in any substantial sense: there is reason to think of an exchange as itself involving one or more joint commitments.[31] The same goes, indeed, for standard everyday forms of communication, such as *telling, informing*, and so on.[32]

Consider now a case in which the CPC conditions hold. Suppose that in Claire's presence Phyllis remarks loudly: "I intend to do what I can to promote my going for a walk with Claire, if and only if Claire so intends [that is, if and only if Claire intends to do what she can to promote our going for a walk]." Claire then remarks, in similar fashion: "I intend likewise [that is, I intend to do what *I* can to promote my going for a walk with Phyllis, if *she* so intends]." There is one obvious problem here. If the intentions expressed are *externally* conditional, it may be hard to see how the parties can end up with *actual* personal intentions or commitments. If the intentions are *internally* conditional, it may be hard to see how the parties can end up with *categorical* commitments each to do what she can to promote their walking together.[33]

There is, however, a more crucial problem for the CPC. Suppose for the sake of argument that both Claire and Phyllis have somehow appropriately acquired actual, categorical personal intentions as a result of each one's expression of a conditional personal intention, and each of the parties now personally intends to do what she can to contribute to their going for a walk. The intention each now has is, precisely, a personal intention. In other words, the result is *a conjunction of personal commitments*.

Now a joint commitment—as I understand it—is not, nor does it entail, a conjunction of *personal* commitments to promote the object of the joint commitment. It does not, of course, rule out such a conjunction. There is no logical entailment either way. It is plausible to suppose, then, that the CPC can be ruled out a priori.

One might be inclined to make the CPC if one understands a joint commitment to be something constituted by a set of personal commitments. This might be called the PC, or personal commitments assumption. One may, indeed, think that an acceptable account of any so-called joint commitment must accord with the PC. This thought may stem from a prevalent philosophical stance toward social phenomena that I have elsewhere called "singularism."[34] That is the view that—in the human case—such phenomena are all ultimately composed of the *personal* beliefs, attitudes, actions, and so on (including commitments) of *single human beings*. Evidently, singularism rules out any kind of commitment that is not, at base, either a personal commitment or a logical function of the personal commitments of the relevant parties.[35] The singularist cannot, then, appeal to joint commitments in the sense at issue here

A More Plausible Approach

In my own discussions of joint commitment formation, I have claimed that the parties must openly express something, where these expressions must be common knowledge between the parties.[36] The something that must be expressed is one and the same thing for each expressor, *mutatis mutandis*. We have already seen that something seems not to be a conditional personal intention. What is it, then?

In *On Social Facts*, I contemplated a number of different formulations of what needs to be expressed.[37] One such formulation refers to: "a *conditional commitment of one's will*, made with the understanding that if and only if it is common knowledge that the relevant others have expressed similar commitments, the wills in question are unconditionally and jointly committed" (Gilbert 1989, p. 198, italics in original). I take this formulation to include crucial elements that any adequate account of the creation of a joint commitment should include. Insofar as certain background circumstances may change the picture, these may be considered elements of the basic case.

What is key is the incorporation of an holistic notion of joint commitment.[38] The formulation correctly implies that the parties to any joint commitment must possess this notion. Also rightly present is the idea that, as the parties understand, the existence of the relevant joint commitment and hence each one's being committed through it depends on each one's expressing the same thing, *mutatis mutandis*.

The reference to the expression of a "conditional commitment" of one's will by the parties may tend to suggest the expression of a conditional personal intention whose condition is satisfied if and only if each of the relevant parties expresses a similar intention, the end result being a set of unconditional personal intentions. Though I have been so interpreted, I do not believe that it was ever my intention to suggest this.[39] From the outset, I have contemplated and tended to prefer other formulations.[40] As we shall see, this is not to say that there is no kind of *conditionality* in the picture.

Rather than referring to the expression of a conditional commitment, I often refer to expressions of willingness *to be jointly committed* in some way. I now tend to write of *readiness* to be jointly committed, which is less liable to be taken to imply a strong form of voluntariness. As I have argued elsewhere, it is possible to enter a joint commitment in the context of strong pressure to do so.[41]

It may help to avoid confusion at this point to distinguish an expression of readiness to be jointly committed from what I referred to in *On Social Facts* as *quasi-readiness*.[42] I invoked quasi-readiness in the context of a discussion of *joint readiness* to act together in some way. I take it that joint readiness is often referred to in common parlance. Thus a gang member may say to the other members "So, we're ready to go, right?"

In connection with the creation of joint readiness, I wrote of the need for each individual's expression of quasi-readiness. I argued that concordant expressions of quasi-readiness, in conditions of common knowledge, were necessary and sufficient for joint readiness.

In terms of joint commitment and personal readiness for joint commitment, an expression of one's quasi-readiness amounts to an expression of *personal* readiness to be jointly committed with the relevant persons to being *ready as a body*, or *jointly ready*. Thus not all expressions of personal readiness to be jointly committed in some way or other are expressions of quasi-readiness in my technical sense.

I take it that, in the basic case of joint commitment, matching expressions of personal readiness *to enter a particular joint commitment* are necessary to create that joint commitment. These expressions must be made openly and it must be common knowledge between the parties that they have occurred.

Suppose that Jim is personally ready to be jointly committed in a particular way with Rose and openly expresses this personal readiness. He understands that the relevant joint commitment will come into being *only if* Rose similarly does her part, and there is common knowledge between them that this has occurred.

I propose that concordant expressions of personal readiness for a particular joint commitment are not just necessary but also sufficient—given conditions of common knowledge—to create a basic case of joint commitment. What more could be necessary? What less could be adequate? Those who express personal readiness for a particular joint commitment will understand this, since they understand what a joint commitment is.

It is easy to construe familiar types of everyday interaction in terms of this account of the genesis of joint action. Suppose that, in conditions of common knowledge between Jim and Rose, the following occurs. Jim says to Rose "Shall we dance?" Rose responds "Yes! Let's." Given a certain understanding of dancing together, the account suggests the following interpretation of the core of what transpires. In saying "Shall we dance?" Jim openly expresses his own readiness to enter a joint commitment with Rose in favor of their dancing together.[43] Rose's "Yes! Let's" openly expresses her own readiness to do so, and, as they both understand, this expression does all that remains to be done in order to create the relevant joint commitment. At this point, then, they are jointly committed. As a result, each one is answerable to the other for violation of the commitment, and all of the other features of a joint commitment are present.

It is important to note that Jim's "Shall we dance?" may play multiple roles, as can Rose's "Yes! Let's." In the scenario envisaged each, in effect, openly expresses readiness for *a number of distinct joint commitments*. As a result of one and the same pair of expressions, at a minimum a *question is asked, an agreement made, a goal jointly accepted*. The important if minute phenomenon of mutual recognition is also achieved[44]

"SOCIAL ATOMS" AND THEIR STRUCTURE

The contents of possible joint commitments are quite varied. People can not only jointly commit to intend as a body to do such-and-such, but they can jointly commit to *believe* as a body that such-and-such, to *require* as a body that such-and-such be done, and so on. I use the technical phase *plural subject* to refer to *any set of jointly committed persons*, whatever the content of the particular joint commitment in question.

I have argued at length that paradigmatic *social groups*—paradigmatic families, discussion groups, guilds, unions, armies, and so on—are plural subjects. I have argued, in addition, that all of the following, and more, can be understood as plural subject phenomena: *social rules* and *conventions, group languages, everyday agreements, collective beliefs* and *values*, and *genuinely collective emotions*.[45]

Here I would suggest that the *social atoms* are plural subjects. The structure of the social atom, then, is the structure of joint commitment. On this account, social atoms may be very small and transient or large and relatively enduring. They exist in the momentary unity of strangers who exchange pleasantries on a public road, as well as in the enduring bonds of married couples and whole societies.

As to the last point, though I have focused in this discussion on the smallest possible social unit—in sociological terms, the *dyad*—there is no reason in principle why large populations may not create joint commitments for themselves. Here the parties will express their readiness to be jointly committed with certain others described in general terms, such as "people living on this island," "women," and so on. As long as there can be common knowledge of the openness of these expressions, the conditions for the creation of a joint commitment can be fulfilled. Hence the parties to a given joint commitment need not know each other or even know of each other as individuals.

If people regularly form plural subjects the practical implications of this can hardly be overemphasized. Three significant general points are as follows.

First, the joint commitments that lie at the base of plural subjects are powerful *behavioral constraints*. This is due to the *normative force* of all commitment in conjunction with special features of joint commitment.

To expand a little, my own understanding of the situation is roughly this. Setting aside unwitting deviation, or deviation that is physically or psychologically compelled, if Jack is subject to a standing commitment that he cannot unilaterally rescind, he may *rationally* choose not to conform to that commitment in certain circumstances only.

I do not have in mind here rationality in the game-theorist's sense that relates to the maximization of one's payoff according to one's own unidimensional utility function. I have in mind, rather, rationality in the broader sense of according with the dictates of reason.[46]

I take it that it *will* sometimes be rational in this sense to deviate from an unrescinded joint commitment. For instance, it will be rational to break off from a joint walk without first obtaining one's partner's permission if one must do so in order to avert a great evil. Indeed, in such a case reason may dictate that one so break off, as opposed to simply permitting such behavior. Here I evidently envisage that, from a rational point of view, moral considerations may allow one to act against personal or joint commitments in at least some circumstances.

The case of desire, inclination, or psychological tendency is different. I take it that, all things being equal, one's commitments trump one's desires and the rest from a rational point of view. As to "all else being equal": at some point it may become immoral to frustrate a certain desire. But then the case is no longer one of desire simply. In sum, if one is not physically or psychologically blocked from doing so, rationality will dictate that one conform to a standing commitment that he or she cannot rescind if all that runs counter to it is desire, inclination, or psychological tendency.

A joint commitment, of course, is not just a commitment that one cannot unilaterally rescind. It is common knowledge among the parties that any one is answerable to the others if he or she deviates. Ideally, these others would be called in and their permission sought for what would otherwise constitute a violation of their rights, rights inherent in the joint commitment. In addition, as is common knowledge, if their permission is not obtained, they have the standing to take action in response to this violation of their rights.[47]

All things considered, then, to the extent that human beings are or aspire to be rational in the sense in question, one can expect that their behavior when subject to a joint commitment will in large measure be organized around that commitment. Not being able to rescind it, they will do what they can to conform, in the absence of countervailing moral considerations, and in spite of countervailing desires and the like.

A second important point about plural subjects is that, considered apart from any disturbing influences, plural subjects are *self-contained* dynamical systems. The underlying joint commitment alone is sufficient to rationalize behavior—there is no need for a personal decision by each of the participants in favor of fulfillment of the joint commitment. Each is committed through the joint commitment, and therefore already has a reason to act of the type that a personal decision would give.

Insofar as they are capable of forming plural subjects, then, human beings are capable of creating self-contained systems of action within which their own specific personalities—their own personal beliefs, values, and goals—are to a large extent redundant. They need play little role in the workings of the plural subject system.

Nonetheless, and this is the third point, human beings have or are capable of developing their own specific personalities, which, as has just been seen, can lead to conflicts within their jointly committed selves. Georg Simmel asserted "Society is . . . a structure which consists of beings who stand inside and outside of it at the same time."[48] This can, evidently, be said of plural subjects. I may be jointly committed with you to intend as a body to work on our paper today. I "stand inside" the plural subject being subject to the joint commitment that constitutes it. But I may not want to work on the paper today, and I may even decide that, by my own lights, morality requires that I fail to do so. Insofar as I have personal desires and values, I "stand outside" the plural subject.

Evidently, there is always a chance that—by dint of reason or temptation—I will act in ways that violate the obligations to my fellow members of a given plural subject. One can predict, therefore, that there will be pressure from both inside and outside the individual for him to repress his personality so that conformity to the joint commitment is easier to bear. One can also predict that if conformity becomes too hard to bear, the plural subject system may break down.

AN APPLICATION OF THESE IDEAS

Among other things, the theory of plural subjects can throw light on an idea that has raised concerns at both the practical and the theoretical level, that is: the idea of collective moral responsibility or—in its negative form—collective moral guilt.[49] Briefly to explain how this is so, I start by mentioning four possible concerns about attributions of collective guilt. The first two are practical: they relate not so much to the logic—or illogic—of the notion of collective guilt as to the supposed practical consequences of making use of the notion. I shall sketch two contrasting concerns of this kind.

First there is the *white-washing worry*. This is the worry that group members who bear personal guilt in some matter may improperly appeal to collective guilt in an attempt to stave off judgments against them personally.

Thus a group member might aver: "I am not guilty in this matter. The *group* acted badly and the *group* is guilty." Or, in a similar vein: "I was only a cog in a wheel."

One who speaks in this way implies, in effect, that should his or her group be guilty of some wrong, he or she would be absolved. This assumption may be referred to as the *disjunctive assumption*. One who takes seriously the white-washing worry may well accept the disjunctive assumption.[50] After all, if it is *false*, one could rebuff the envisaged appeals to collective guilt by simply pointing that out.[51]

I turn next to a quite different worry. Rather than assuming that collective guilt automatically exculpates individual group members, one may assume that it automatically taints them. More specifically, one may assume that, if a group bears guilt in some matter, then all of its members bear guilt in relation to that matter. Call this the *implication assumption*.

A practical worry associated with this—the *imputation worry*—is that those who wish to accuse or to inflict punitive damage on some or all of the members of a given group may use the notion of collective guilt so as to incriminate those members, irrespective of the actual guilt of those members. Thus accusers may say "Your group is guilty of this, so we are fully entitled to punish *you* for it."

It is clear that the contrasting practical worries noted depend on conflicting assumptions about what we might call the structure of collective guilt. The existence of both worries raises two important questions about this structure.

First, if a group *G* bears guilt for an occurrence *O*, does this mean that the individual members of *G*—as opposed to *G* itself—are guilt-free in relation to *O*? Second, if a group *G* bears guilt for an occurrence *O*, does this mean that the individual members of *G* are guilty to some degree in relation to *O*?

Evidently, the answer to both questions cannot be positive, because a positive answer to either one entails a negative answer to the other. It is possible, however, that the answer to both questions is negative. In other words, the guilt of a group *G* may not imply *anything* about the guilt or innocence of all members of *G*. Indeed, it may not imply anything about the guilt or innocence of any members of *G*, though it may suggest that there are at least some guilty parties. If that is so, then both the white-washing worry and the imputation worry will be defused. One might put things thus: the realm of collective guilt and the realm of personal guilt do not overlap.

I turn now to two contrasting theoretical worries. These question the very possibility of genuinely collective guilt. The first worry starts with the *reductionist assumption* about what collective guilt must amount to, insofar as there is such a thing. For a group *G* to bear guilt for some occurrence *O*, it says, is—simply—for all or most members of *G* to bear personal guilt in relation to *O*.

The associated worry is this: If a group G's guilt is simply the personal guilt of G's members, then there is no such thing as genuinely collective guilt. That is, there is really no such thing as the guilt of the group itself as opposed to the personal guilt of its several members. This worry may be referred to as the *reductionist worry.*

The second worry stems ultimately from skepticism about collective as opposed to individual agency. Recall Max Weber's: "There is no such thing as a collective personality which '*acts.*'" According to what I shall call the *antiholist worry,* to imagine that there is such a thing as genuinely collective guilt is to allow that there is such a thing as genuinely collective action, when there is not. It is, therefore, to involve oneself in an unacceptable holism, treating groups as "wholes" capable of action—when they are not. The idea of collective guilt is therefore at best simply unrealistic. At worst, *it makes no sense.*

I propose that the theory of plural subjects can dissolve the worries mentioned, both practical and theoretical. The argument is roughly this. First, it allows for *a viable notion of genuinely collective moral guilt.* In other words, according to plural subject theory, there can be a collective analogue of a paradigmatic case of personal moral guilt. More specifically, a population of human beings can fulfill the following conditions: it can form an intention of its own and act on that intention. It can also—as a collective—believe that what it does is wrong. And it may be subject to no external pressure from outside the group that might mitigate its guilt. In short, the theoretical worries appear to be groundless.

Second, it allows for *a radical disjunction between the guilt of a group and the guilt of any of its members.* A group, in other words, can meet the criteria for moral guilt, while it is still an open question whether all, or indeed any, of its individual members bears personal moral guilt in the matter. This clearly has important consequences for the appropriateness or otherwise of certain responses to actual cases of collective moral guilt.

Even assuming the guilt of a given group and a right to punish, individual members of the group may intelligibly be assumed innocent until they are proven guilty. At the same time, they may indeed be personally guilty in the matter of the group's action. Everything will depend on the facts of the individual case, including the degree to which the person in question participated in the group action, whether and to what degree he or she was pressured into participating, whether he or she knew that the action was taking place, and so on. In short, the practical worries are groundless also.

That is not to say that there are no important questions relating to collective moral guilt. There are. For instance, is there a morally acceptable way to punish a morally guilty group as such?[52] In this area, and in others, much has to do with the fact that the social atom is constituted by "beings that stand inside and outside of it at the same time."

ACKNOWLEDGMENTS

Thanks to Professors Paul Bloomfield and Frederick Schmitt for comments and discussions relating to material in this chapter. Responsibility for the views expressed here is mine alone. I should like to take this opportunity warmly to express my gratitude to Professor Schmitt for his long-standing support of my work, and for the significant time and labor he has put into promoting awareness of the burgeoning fields of social epistemology and metaphysics.

NOTES

1. For a lengthy critical appraisal of Weber's concept of a social action see Gilbert (1989, ch. 2). Weber introduces this concept in Weber (1987, p. 88ff).

2. Cf. Gilbert (1989, pp. 442–44).

3. Other authors, including social psychologists and cognitive scientists, have made use of the phrase *joint commitment*. See for instance, Baron, Amazeen, and Beck (1994) (social psychology), and Cohen, Levesque, and Smith (1997) (cognitive science/AI). I am not sure that any have used the phrase precisely in the sense I have in mind. It would be an interesting project carefully to compare and contrast the relevant notions with respect to their explicit or implicit structure, implications, and correspondence with an intuitive concept. In any case, what is at issue here is joint commitment as I understand it.

4. I focus on and offer an explanation of another observation in Gilbert (1989, 1990). This is the understanding among those who act together that, by virtue of their acting together, each has obligations toward and rights against the other parties. The present discussion highlights a different observation en route to the presentation of my account of joint activity, and, more generally, the foundation of human social behavior.

5. There are various ways of characterizing common knowledge, some quite complex. See Lewis (1969), Schiffer (1972), and Gilbert (1989). For present purposes one might characterize it roughly and informally as follows: the fact that p is common knowledge between persons A and B if and only if the fact that p is entirely out in the open between persons A and B. It would then be absurd, for instance, for A to try to hide the fact that p from B.

6. Bittner (2002) resists the permission point. It has also provoked resistance more than once when I have made it in public lectures.

7. Bittner (2002) explicitly avows this attitude.

8. Cf. Bratman (1993a), where each party "reserves the right" to call off the joint enterprise at any time. In Gilbert (2000, p. 35n36), I suggest that what is involved in such a "reservation of right" is essentially an agreement between the parties to treat the situation *as if* it did not have properties it does in fact have, that is, as if each party had the right unilaterally to call off the joint enterprise. *Mutatis mutandis*, this may be the best way of viewing the case in the text above: as involving an agreement to behave *as if* one party does not require the other's permission

to withdraw from the joint activity. That would amount, *in effect*, to the granting of permission in advance.

9. The distinction in the text between private and societal conventions is not intended to be overly sharp. In the examples given the cases differ at least in the following way. With the private convention the parties know each other personally and their convention develops in the course of their personal relationship. With the societal convention, a given party to the convention may well not know every other member personally. One may recognize another, however, as a fellow-member of the society in question.

10. I thank Frederick Schmitt for this observation, personal communication, May 2002.

11. Bittner (2002) makes this suggestion.

12. I do not say this latter puzzle cannot be solved. Indeed, a solution for it is to be found in the account of acting together that I propose. Both the rights in question and the permission requirement are grounded, according to that account, in the nature of joint activity. See the text that follows.

13. Frederick Schmitt suggested this likelihood of this response, personal communication, June 2002.

14. This condition is not that distant from the accounts of acting together of Michael Bratman, Seumas Miller, and Christopher Kutz. See Bratman (1993a), Miller (1992a), and Kutz (2000a).

15. Robins (1984) makes a useful related point about *preferences*, which may underpin intentions: "preferences are the kind of thing that are liable to change . . . perhaps frequent change" (p. 134). This is part of a thoughtful discussion of the "preferences and expectations" based account of social conventions in Lewis (1969). Robins also explains the "strong degree of expectation" that accompanies a *promise* as follows: "for this *is* a way that people can *assure* others that they *will* do their part" (1984, p. 133, emphases in original). In contrast, one does not provide such assurance simply by *having an intention* that is common knowledge between oneself and relevant others. Cf. Pratt (2001, pp. 152–53), who argues, somewhat more strongly, that "assurance is not inspired by *convincing* another of one's intention to perform" (p. 153, my emphasis). Bratman (1996) discusses the stability of intention. I commented on an earlier version of this paper at the Conference on Methods, New York, 1994.

16. The following issue arises in connection with this model. Going for a walk, according to this model, involves a crucial mental component: an intention. What is the content of that intention? It is natural to specify it as follows: it is an intention to *go for a walk*. To give an account of *going for a walk* in terms of an intention to *go for a walk* may seem, however, to involve a troublesome circularity. If *our* going for a walk involves *our* intention, the content of that intention would presumably be specifiable as our *going for a walk*. That, too, may seem to involve a troublesome circularity. I set aside this question here as a general question for action theory, allowing that the resolutions for the single and for the collective case may vary. I assume the propriety, at least in a rough description, of referring to an intention to "do *X*" as a way of characterizing the intention that animates one's doing *X*, where "doing *X*" is a standard everyday act description (possibly the description of a joint act) such as "going for a walk." For a thoughtful discussion on this question see Kutz (2000a, pp. 85–8).

17. For some critical discussion of alternative accounts of acting together and re-lated phenomena from Michael Bratman (1993a), John Searle (1990), and Raimo Tuomela (1984, 1995), see Gilbert (2000, ch. 9). I critique the account in Kutz (2000a) in Gilbert (2002a).

18. The discussion that follows draws in particular on Gilbert (2002b).

19. Frederick Schmitt raised this question, personal communication, June 2002.

20. Here I am indebted to Pink (1996, p. 192).

21. *Holism* is usually contrasted with *individualism*. These labels do not have a clearly defined and established meaning in the literature. See Gilbert (1989, ch. 7) for a discussion of various types of individualism. See also Gilbert (2000, ch. 9) for an as-sessment of a variety of accounts of acting together in terms of a particular under-standing of individualism and a distinction between *internal* and *external* holism in an account of a social phenomenon.

22. Cf. Gilbert (1999a, section 4). There I argue that obligations and rights inhere in joint commitment.

23. See Gilbert (1993c, 1999a, 1999b).

24. Cf. Gilbert (1989, p. 206). The text there refers to "joint acceptance that *X* is to count as *Y*," which I parse as "*joint commitment to accept as a body* that *X* is to count as *Y*."

25. Gilbert (1996) discusses the consequences of violation of joint commitments of various kinds and expresses my current inclination to understand violation in certain two-person cases as rendering the commitment *voidable* rather than *void* (pp. 14–16, 381–83). This would not materially affect the argument in Gilbert (1993a), in which I supposed the alternative.

26. As to possible qualifications, I have in mind cases where, after an initial joint commitment is made, say between two people, another person or persons "joins" the original two. See Gilbert (1989, p. 220): one can construe the phrase "pool of wills" there in terms of joint commitment.

27. Focusing on conditional personal intentions accords with the proposals of a number of authors including the carefully considered proposal in Velleman (1997b).

28. See Gilbert (1993b) for discussion of a parallel distinction between internally and externally conditional *promises* (Gilbert 1996, pp. 317–19). For present purposes the question whether there is something suspect in the idea of an externally condi-tional personal intention may be waived.

29. Velleman (1997b) appears to have externally conditional personal intentions in mind. See, for instance page 45, third full paragraph. There are various questions about the status of externally conditional intentions that I shall waive here.

30. See Gilbert 1993b (Gilbert 1996, ch. 13 pp. 333–34).

31. This connects with a worry I have about the positive proposal regarding *agree-ments* made in Bach (1995), a thoughtful and fine-grained essay that came to my at-tention only recently and that I cannot address directly here.

32. See Gilbert (1989, p. 434).

33. Robins (2002) focuses his concerns in this area.

34. Gilbert (1989). I note there that singularism is a possible version of individual-ism (pp. 428–31).

35. Some of my own early statements have undoubtedly helped to suggest the

CPC. Thus Velleman (1997b) takes off from remarks of my own. On these early statements see the text that follows.

36. Gilbert (1989, pp. 185–97). See also pages 182–84, which distinguishes and posits both an "expression" condition and an "expressed" condition. The present discussion omits various technical details.

37. Gilbert (1989, pp. 197–98, 408–10) and elsewhere.

38. That an holistic conception of joint commitment is at issue is indicated in the preceding discussion of plural subjecthood in Gilbert (1989, pp. 163–64). See also the summary discussion in the final chapter, especially pages 409–11, and elsewhere. In Gilbert (1987), I wrote: "if *all* openly express such a commitment they are then *committed as a body* in a certain way" (Gilbert 1996, p. 204, italics in original). I have subsequently clarified and consolidated points made somewhat roughly and scattered about in the initial though long-meditated discussion in Gilbert (1989). See Gilbert (1996, Introduction, section V).

39. In several places I cautiously wrote of "a *special kind of* conditional commitment" (emphasis added). See for instance Gilbert (1989, p. 198).

40. See for instance, Gilbert (1989, p. 18). See also the text that follows.

41. On the relation of joint commitment and voluntariness see Gilbert (1989, p.140), Gilbert (1993c) (joint commitment as embodied in a joint decision), and elsewhere.

42. See Gilbert (1989, pp. 185–86, 195–99).

43. More elaborately, the joint commitment is to accept as a body the goal of their dancing together. In this case Jim and Rose make an explicit agreement, so there is a concurrent and intuitively primary joint commitment to accept as a body the joint decision to dance together, that is, to accept as a body the goal of their dancing together.

44. Gilbert (1989).

45. See Gilbert (1989, 1996, 2000).

46. See Gilbert (2002c, also 1999c).

47. This last point is presumably relevant primarily to the prudential concerns of the agent considering deviation.

48. Simmel (1971b).

49. This discussion is drawn from a conference address at the University of Konstanz, April 2002. See also Gilbert (2000, ch. 8) and elsewhere. Another topic of both theoretical and practical concern to which plural subject theory is germane is that of citizens' obligations with respect to their country's political and legal institutions. See Gilbert (1999b) and elsewhere.

50. Neier (1998, p. 212) cites a discussion of Dwight McDonald's, written shortly after World War II, in which McDonald makes the following claims (the words quoted are Neier's): "The concept of collective guilt . . . embodies a Hegelian, statist approach in which individuals lack will, thought, and conscience except as these are united in the 'organic totality' of the state. This view . . . leads directly to the absolution, or self-absolution, of those who actually commit great crimes."

51. The disjunctive assumption may underlie the Anglo-American law of complicity and conspiracy, for instance. This, it has been said, "treats the acting group as conceptually prior to its individual members," which is, in effect, "to naturalize the group itself, treating it as the culpable party" (Kutz 2000a, p. 236). Kutz suggests that if one treats the group as the culpable party one may then react toward each participant

without proper discrimination. Thus, in the law in question, the individual participants may be treated equally, and equally harshly. Kutz cites an English case, *Regina
v. Hyde* (pp. 230–32). The white-washing worry envisages an alternative scenario in
which those who think a group bears guilt for its actions think it is not appropriate to
punish individual group members at all for what they did as participants in the
group's action. That judgment seems more concordant with the "naturalization" or
"reification" of groups.

52. For some remarks on this see Gilbert (2002a, p. 187).

3

Practical Intersubjectivity

Abraham Sesshu Roth

The intentions of others often enter into your practical reasoning, even when you're acting on your own. Given all the agents around you, you'll come to grief if what they're up to is never a consideration in what you decide to do and how you do it. There are occasions, however, when the intentions of another (or others) figure in your practical reasoning in a particularly intimate and decisive fashion. I speak of there being on such occasions a practical intersubjectivity of intentions holding between you and the other individual(s). I try to identify this practical intersubjectivity and to take some preliminary steps toward giving a philosophical account of it.

Occasions of practical intersubjectivity are usually those where individuals share agency, or do things jointly, such as when they walk together, kiss, or paint a house together. I do not assume that all instances of practical intersubjectivity are instances of shared agency. But the converse is true: any instance of shared agency involves a practical intersubjectivity holding between the participants. An account of shared agency (or related notions like shared activity, joint action, etc.) is inadequate if it fails to handle practical intersubjectivity.

The chapter is structured as follows. In the first section, I present an example to illustrate this idea of practical intersubjectivity, at least as it appears in the context of shared agency. Practical intersubjectivity is a normative phenomenon, and it is on this basis that in the next section, Intersubjectivity and the Coordination of Intentions, I distinguish it from the mere coordination of intentions some have recognized as essential for shared activity. The task of the third section, Why Not Intersubjectivity on the Cheap?, is to show how practical intersubjectivity cannot be adequately described in terms of ordinary intentions familiar from the study of individual agency. Such approaches fail to handle the rational dynamics of intention revision when practical intersubjectivity is in place between agents. Finally, the last section, Accessibility, lays the groundwork for the revision in our understanding of intention necessary for adequately describing practical intersubjectivity. An important challenge to understanding practical intersubjectivity in terms of intentions as I do here stems from the idea that, fundamentally, one can only intend one's own actions. I contend that this stricture should be relaxed. An advantage of so revising our understanding of intentions is that it yields a satisfying explanation of the social phenomenon of commands.[1]

PRACTICAL INTERSUBJECTIVITY

Intentions as Rational Constraints

Suppose that you and I have decided to drive to Vegas together to try our luck at blackjack. We have agreed to take your car, to set out after the morning rush hour, and to take turns driving. One of the details we haven't yet worked out is who will drive when. It turns out that you had to drive a cab all night to pay off some of your gambling debts not covered by your graduate student stipend and so could use a break from driving. So you go ahead and decide to drive the second leg of the trip, figuring that I wouldn't have any objection to this. Moreover, you're correct in your supposition. When you express your intention to me, I don't object and I go ahead and take the driver's seat to drive the first leg.

Why haven't I objected? There are two interestingly different sorts of stories we can tell to fill out our scenario to answer this question. First, upon hearing of your intention, I might consider the matter of who is to drive when and come to my own conclusion about it. Perhaps I prefer to drive the first leg—my salary as faculty member has (so far) covered my gambling debts; I haven't driven a cab all night and am well rested. Or, perhaps I don't much care when I drive, and because you want to drive the second leg, I decide to drive the first leg. There are other possibilities for this sort of story. What's important is that *I resolve the matter for myself.* Since my conclusion fits with yours, there is no reason for me to object to your intention.

On the second story, I don't object because I simply don't concern myself with trying to figure out who should drive. I consider it a matter that has already been settled—by your decision. Given that you intend to drive the second leg, I act accordingly.

In the first story, your intention, if it does figure in my practical reasoning, will only figure as a *consideration.* It is a factor in my decision, one consideration among a number that I might weigh in trying to answer the practical question of who is to drive when. On the second story, I do not face this practical question because it has already been answered by you. What is left for me to do is simply to act in accordance with how you've answered the question; that is, I act in accordance with your intention. If there is any further reasoning for me to do, it will take your practical conclusion for granted. Your intention will serve as a defeasible *rational constraint* on my subsequent practical reasoning.[2] I will only consider intending and acting in ways that are consistent with or cohere with your intention. In particular, I will intend to drive the first leg of the trip, thereby making explicit what was implicit in your intention to drive the second leg.

The way in which your intention figures in my practical reasoning in the second story—as a rational constraint rather than a mere consideration—is of particular interest for me here.[3] I want to emphasize that it is not an unusual way of reasoning. This kind of thinking is perfectly natural and happens all the time. Some may not feel that this example is a very good illustration of a common and natural way of thinking, perhaps because they feel that the issue of who will drive when is controversial and not something that can be so easily settled in the way I've described. But deciding who drives when needn't be a controversial matter. Consider a modification to our example: you decide that you're going to drive the second leg not because it's your preference to do so, but because you think that I have some preference for driving the first leg. Maybe I'm reticent and haven't expressed my preference, but you know me well enough to have reason to think that I'd like to get behind the wheel sooner rather than later. So now you've decided to drive the second leg, and I take the matter of who will drive which leg to have been settled by you. More generally, take cases where individuals are fairly confident that any decisions made by one will not run roughshod over the preferences and expectations of the others. This confidence might be due perhaps to the familiarity of the individuals with one another and the good will there is between them. One's confidence in the intentions of others might also be based on the nature of the activity engaged in, its circumstances and environment, or the institutions within which it is carried out.

So in our example, though I may have a preference about what to do, I do not get to the point of making a decision on the matter. You get there first and settle the issue. There is nothing left for me to do but to take your intention as a rational constraint and to reason and act accordingly. I think it fair to say that many deliberative or practical matters are settled in this fashion.[4]

The way in which an intention serves as a rational constraint on practical reasoning should be familiar from discussions of individual practical reasoning. When I form an intention to spend the whole day at the beach, I can take it for granted that I will not be spending the day at the library (assuming the library is not on the beach).[5] My intention to go to the beach is not a mere consideration in favor of the beach option as opposed to the library option.[6]

Rather, it serves as a constraint on my practical reasoning and the deliberative problems I take up. So long as I maintain the intention to go to the beach, going to the library is not an option for me.[7]

My suggestion is that just as one's own intentions serve as rational constraints on one's practical reasoning, it seems that there are natural forms of reasoning that allow one individual's intention to serve as a rational constraint on another's reasoning.

Conflicts between Intentions

Though your intention might have the status of a rational constraint on my practical reasoning, we should not assume that there will never be occasion for a conflict between your intention and one of mine. After all, my own intentions serve as rational constraints on my practical reasoning, and sometimes they conflict with one another. Thus, you may have gone ahead and formed an intention to drive the second leg of the trip and not the first, not realizing that I have similarly intended to drive the second leg and not the first. Our intentions conflict. Given background facts that can be taken for granted by us, these intentions cannot both be satisfied. We cannot drive the same car at once, nor can the car drive itself. We'll get nowhere at this rate.

So one problem with having conflicting intentions is that it is unlikely that we'll have the coordination in behavior necessary for driving together to Vegas. But there's something worrisome about conflicting intentions in this context, even if by chance our behavior ends up being coordinated. You and I might have conflicting intentions about who will drive which leg of the trip, but I might fail to act on mine. Lack of sleep causes me to forget to hand you the keys at the start of the trip. I absent-mindedly hop into the driver's seat, and I continue to drive for several hours until you finally announce that it's your turn to drive.[8] There is the suspicion that something is amiss here, even though there's no failure of coordination in behavior.

The idea of intentions as rational constraints helps us articulate this worry. Consider the individual case first. My own intentions serve as rational constraints on my practical reasoning. My intention to A is, in virtue of its content, intelligibly related to other intentions that I have or could possibly have. There is, for example, the intention concerning the means to A-ing. And there's the intention *not* to A. And there's the intention to B, which I can recognize would preclude A-ing, given my beliefs and background assumptions. In virtue of these intelligible relations and my intention to A, I rationally ought or ought not to have certain other intentions. Thus, coherence requires that I intend the means to A-ing.[9] And consistency requires that I refrain from adopting the intention not to A, or some other intentions the satisfaction of which would preclude my A-ing. To the extent that I fail to live up to these principles of consistency and coherence, I am liable to the charge of irrationality.[10]

I suggest that the lingering worry with the conflicting intentions in the interpersonal case is akin to the problem in the individual case. The conflict between our intentions regarding who will drive when opens each of us to the charge of irrationality. The rational tension might not be so evident if it is unclear that we're doing something together. But so long as this is kept in mind, then it is quite obvious that we have here a kind of incoherence. This is evidenced by the evident tension in the following assertion: "We (you and I) intend to drive to Vegas together, but I intend to drive the second leg, and you also intend to drive the second leg." This violates a norm of rationality, much in the way that the following does: "I intend to spend the whole day at the beach today, and I intend to stay inside this library all day."[11] So the worry with having conflicting intentions about who will drive when is that you and I have intentions that, in the context of our intention to drive to Vegas together, seem to subject us to *rational* criticism. Our conflicting intentions in the case of driving to Vegas together amount to something like the kind of inconsistency in intentions for which an individual might be criticized. The difference, however, is that the inconsistency appears to hold across two (or more) individuals.

So just as my own intentions are intelligibly related to one another in virtue of their contents, so too are the intentions of different individuals. That is, we might speak of the intention of one participant in some activity being consistent or inconsistent with the intention of another participant. (Likewise for coherence.) Moreover, I am entertaining the possibility that these intentions might rationally *engage* one another. This is to say that the intentions of one individual might be rationally relevant for another, serving as rational constraints on the latter's practical reasoning. In some circumstances, if you form an intention, principles of consistency or coherence of intentions may *require* me to take up, discard, or otherwise revise my activity-related intentions.[12] If I fail to meet these requirements, I am subject to a form of rational criticism.

So suppose that there is this sort of rational engagement between the attitudes of certain individuals, where the intentions of each serve as rational constraints for the other(s). I will speak of there being a practical intersubjectivity holding between these individuals. It is an intersubjectivity in light of the symmetry or equality of authoritative status: each individual is in a position to issue intentions that serve as rational constraints for the rest.[13] The intersubjectivity is practical because it is defined in terms of a rational engagement of *intentions*, as opposed to the epistemic or theoretical intersubjectivity of beliefs.[14]

Limitations in Scope

The practical intersubjectivity I have in mind need not be universal in scope. While everyone most likely falls under some instance of practical intersubjectivity, I don't assume that there is some single instance of practical intersubjectivity that holds between everyone.[15] I have suggested that when you and I drive to Vegas together, the activity-related intentions of each of us will serve as rational constraints for the other. Correspondingly, you and I are subject to a rational demand not to have inconsistent or conflicting intentions. The same cannot be said of other individuals who are not engaged in that same activity. Let me illustrate.

Suppose that on our drive to Vegas we come across a roadblock. It has been set up by a man on a mission to prevent access to that city, perhaps for moral or religious reasons. His intention conflicts with ours. Not all of the intentions of the three of us can be satisfied given the circumstances. In this sense, there's an inconsistency that holds across all three of us. But the charge of irrationality that might have been made against you and me (if, e.g., we had conflicting intentions about who will drive when) does not similarly hold against us and the man who seeks to block our way. My own intentions must not conflict with one another on pain of irrationality. And I take your activity-related intention as one with which my intentions should not conflict on pain of irrationality. But the intention of the blocker does not so present itself to me; I do not take his intention to be a rational constraint on my practical reasoning. A practical intersubjectivity holds between you and me; it does not hold between me and the blocker.[16]

Though the intentions of the blocker do not have the status of rational constraints for my practical reasoning, there are nevertheless ways in which his intentions can be relevant for what I do. First of all, the blocker's intention might pose an obstacle for me, much in the way that a dust storm or mudslide on the highway might. Such obstacles might force me to reconsider my intention: if I think that I cannot *A* because of some obstacle, then many philosophers hold that I cannot intend to *A* and will have to revise my intention. Even if, contrary to this view, I can maintain my intention to go to Vegas, it might no longer be worth the trouble. Given what the blocker is up to, I'll need to revise my intention and think of something else to do. But so long as I think that the blocker will fail to act as he intends, this sort of consideration will not force me to change my intention. (Even if I think that the blocker will succeed and so change my mind about going to Vegas, I am not so much seeking consistency between our intentions, but rather just modifying my own intention in light of new information regarding what I think I can accomplish or new information regarding the benefits of the project.)

Of course, the blocker is an agent acting for reasons, not a mere obstacle like a mudslide on the highway. This gives us a second way in which his intention can be relevant for my practical reasoning: his reasons might serve as reasons for me as well. For example, his reason for setting up the roadblock might be that gambling is a sin or that one should not act in a way that benefits the mob.[17] Either way, his reason to set up the roadblock might also serve as a reason for my not going to Vegas to gamble. And the blocker's actions might present me with reasons against going to Vegas, and thus be an occasion for me to reconsider what I'm doing. So the blocker's intention, in virtue of the reasons underlying it, might get me to change my intention. Now, if I do revise my intention, it was not because his intention served as a rational constraint on my practical reasoning, that is, as something with which my intentions should be consistent. Rather, if I accept his reasons as relevant for what I do, these reasons only serve as *pro tanto* considerations against going to Vegas. That's to say that I might have these reasons while also having conflicting reasons in favor of going to Vegas and gambling. If I revise my intention in accord with the blocker's, it's not because the blocker's intention settles the issue for me but because I was faced with these opposing reasons or considerations—for and against going—and decided in favor of those reasons that happen to agree with the blocker's. Had his intention served as a rational constraint for me, I would not consider whether to continue on to Vegas. I would have taken it for granted that I would not.

So, the intentions of the blocker might have an effect on my practical reasoning and get me to revise my intention, either by presenting me with mere obstacles or with reasons against what I'm doing. In neither case is the blocker's impact that of what I have defined as a rational constraint on my practical reasoning. This is in contrast with the status of the activity-related intentions of a fellow participant in shared activity. It is in this sense that the practical intersubjectivity in the Vegas example is limited between you and me and does not extend to the blocker.

Given that the blocker's intentions don't serve as rational constraints while those of a fellow participant do, we can draw the contrast between the blocker and fellow participant in the following manner: the blocker's intentions are subject to undermining or circumvention whereas those of the fellow participant are not.

Consider cases where the blocker's intention conflicts with mine.[18] Here, there doesn't seem to be any rational proscription against circumventing or undermining the blocker's intention. If his reasons are inadequate or misguided, and if he insists on his course of action, it might be rational for me to try to circumvent or undermine his intention.[19] The decision is, after all, mine to make. If I've already satisfactorily taken into consideration the relevant reasons behind his actions and he and I are still at odds, then the only way that the blocker's intention has any further relevance for me is as a fact about the world or my environment I need to face up to in pursuing my course of action. Perhaps his intention poses an insurmountable obstacle, or one not worth surmounting, and I should give up what I'm doing. But it might instead be an obstacle that can be cleared away or gotten around. The fact that it has the status of an obstacle entails that at least in principle it is subject to this sort of strategy.[20] Thus, it *might* be that the most reasonable course of action available to me in the circumstances is to circumvent or undermine the blocker's intention.

In contrast, the intention of a fellow participant is not similarly subject to circumvention or undermining by me. As a rational constraint in my practical reasoning, his intention is not presented to me as an object or state of affairs that, if it stands in the way of what I'm doing, is subject to undermining or circumvention. A rational constraint is supposed to settle what it is that I'm to do. If there is no proscription against undermining or circumventing certain intentions, then those intentions will not settle anything for me and cannot count as rational constraints in my practical reasoning. So assuming that a fellow participant's intentions do serve as rational constraints for me, they are not subject to undermining or circumvention.[21]

So, a practical intersubjectivity of intentions holds for example between participants of shared activity but does not extend to nonparticipants. The intersubjectivity consists in the rational engagement between the activity-related intentions of the participants. There is a rational demand to maintain consistency and some level of coherence between the relevant intentions. This is what it means to say that the intentions of fellow subjects of practical intersubjectivity serve as rational constraints on one's own practical reasoning. To the extent that one fails to treat his or her intentions as rational constraints, one will be subject to a form of irrationality. If a practical intersubjectivity holds among individuals, the intentions of each are not subject to circumvention or undermining by any of the others.

I don't mean to have given anything like a conclusive argument for thinking that any practical intersubjectivity actually exists. I've described a case that I take to exhibit this intersubjectivity, but others might want to try to describe the case differently. Still, the example serves to gesture at what I have in mind. A fair bit more needs to be said about practical intersubjectivity. To get a better fix on this idea, I would like to contrast it with certain forms of coordination some of which have been offered as necessary conditions for shared activity and related phenomena.

INTERSUBJECTIVITY AND THE COORDINATION OF INTENTIONS

Let me turn for the moment to shared activity.[22] This phenomenon involves coordinated behavior or action toward some common end. This sort of coordinated behavior or action can be traced to the coordination of intentions of the various participants. So it is natural to take the coordination of *intentions* as central to shared activity.[23]

Satisfying the intention-coordination condition will require each participant to fill in and otherwise modify his set of activity-related intentions in a way that maintains consistency and coherence not only with his own intentions, but also with the activity-related intentions of the others. This will not require that all participants have the same set of intentions, in the sense that each participant's set of activity-related intentions specify the same satisfaction conditions. Coordination is possible with diverging sets of intentions so long as these sets of intentions are to a sufficient extent mutually satisfiable.[24]

How is the coordination necessary for shared activity related to practical intersubjectivity which has been our concern so far? Because both are a matter of maintaining consistency and coherence between the intentions of different individuals, we might be tempted to identify one with the other. Would this be mistaken? Would it, for example, be wrong to think that the problem with our conflicting intentions about who drives when is simply that we've failed to satisfy this intention coordination condition?

To see the important distinction between intention coordination on the one hand, and practical intersubjectivity on the other, consider what happens when some conflict emerges between the intentions of different participants. What can we say about this case solely on the basis of the intention coordination condition? One thing is clear: there will be less coordination of intentions. Indeed, the conflict of intentions can be so serious that there won't be sufficient coordination of intentions for the condition to be satisfied, and we'll no longer have shared activity. But if the intention coordination condition is all we have to go on, we cannot say that there *should not* be this conflict of intentions, that the participants *ought* (at least *prima facie*) to modify their intentions in order to avoid this sort of conflict in their intentions.[25] There is, correspondingly, nothing in this condition to suggest that a lack of coordination entails the possibility of a *mistake* or failure on the part of one individual or the other (or both). The mere fact that there is a coordination of intentions between individuals does not mean that there is any normative commitment, prima facie or otherwise, to sustaining it at that level, or at any level at all. Coordination per se seems not to be normative.[26]

The emergence of any conflict between the intentions of two individuals is, in and of itself, the reduction or undermining of intention coordination.[27] Not so for intersubjectivity. Indeed, it is often in circumstances of conflict that it becomes more evident that intersubjectivity is in place, or in force. A rational or normative demand tends to be more evident when it is unmet. Practical intersubjectivity involves the normative demand for interpersonal coordination in terms of consistency and coherence of intentions. This demand goes unmet when, for example, someone makes a mistake or otherwise fails to intend in a way that is consistent with the relevant others. The notion of mistake or failure is essential to that of normative demand.[28] Given that practical intersubjectivity involves a normative demand, this intersubjectivity and normative demand in principle must be able to remain in force when less or perhaps even none of the coordination called for is in place.[29]

So, conflicts of intention point to the normative character of intersubjectivity and the non-normative character of intention coordination. When a practical intersubjectivity holds between several individuals, each is subject to interpersonal norms of consistency and coherence in their intentions. There is some rational demand for each to coordinate his intentions with the others. The intention coordination condition involves no such normative demand on the individuals.

We've distinguished practical intersubjectivity from the intention coordination condition in terms of the normativity of the former and the non-normativity of the latter. Practical intersubjectivity involves a normative demand for coordination. As a characterization of practical intersubjectivity, this is fine as far as it goes. But it is not sufficient. It is, after all, possible to bring about the coordination of intentions through mere causal manipulation, or through threats, intimidation, and coercion. This won't do as a way of satisfying the normativity of practical intersubjectivity, and rational engagement does not countenance coordination being imposed in such fashion. The core of the idea of there being a rational engagement of intention between individuals is that what each intends can serve as a rational constraint on the practical reasoning and intention formation of the other(s). This is what's missing when I coerce you into intending in a way that is consistent with me; if our intentions are coordinated only because I've coerced you, then your intentions never had the status of a rational constraint on my practical reasoning and intention formation.[30]

WHY NOT INTERSUBJECTIVITY ON THE CHEAP?

In practical intersubjectivity, the intentions of another might serve as rational constraints in my practical reasoning. We've seen that this involves a normative demand to coordinate one's intentions with those of another; in certain situations my intentions rationally *should* engage those of another, so that my practical reasoning and intention formation can be constrained by their intentions. In the example of the drive to Vegas, you intend to drive the second leg of the trip, and given the practical intersubjectivity that holds between us, there is a rational demand for me drive the first leg.

There is a way of characterizing this demand—and thereby giving an account of practical intersubjectivity—that many find compelling, but which I think is misguided. As we'll see, this approach may be described as individualistic. It is worth seeing why individualism will not work.

Individualism provides a simple answer to the question of when practical intersubjectivity is in place: whether intersubjectivity holds between some individuals is a matter of each person having the right sort of individual intention. Returning to our example, a simple version of individualism holds that the central condition for the intersubjectivity holding between me and you is that I have the intention of driving to Vegas with you and that you have the corresponding intention to drive to Vegas with me.[31]

An individualism of this sort insists that I should intend to drive the first leg simply as a matter of maintaining a consistency among my own intentions. Given the *fact* that you intend to drive the second leg, the only intention for me to form that would be consistent or coherent with my own intention to drive to Vegas with you would be the intention for me to drive the first leg. In these circumstances, no other intention of mine will allow me to realize my intention to drive to Vegas with you. This suggests a reductive strategy: interpersonal consistency and coordination of intentions is reduced to intrapersonal consistency and coordination. The demand to maintain consistency and coherence with another party to intersubjectivity just turns out to be a matter of maintaining a consistency and coherence among one's own intentions.

The problem with this sort of individualism should be fairly clear in light of the discussion in the previous sections. The individualist suggests that in general the only way to satisfy my intention of driving to Vegas with you is by intending to drive the first segment. This mistakenly assumes that your intention to drive the second segment is a fixed point, some inviolable feature of my environment. But it needn't be. My intention to drive to Vegas with you might be satisfied if I were somehow to trick or coerce you into driving the first segment. If all that is demanded of me is maintaining consistency among my own intentions, then nothing would rule out this sort of strategy.

But we've seen that this sort of circumvention or undermining of another's intention is incompatible with that intention's status as a rational constraint on your practical reasoning. In practical intersubjectivity, each agent accords the other a certain authority such that the other's intentions have a special status—that of a rational constraint. Just as one accords to one's own intention a rational and practical authority so that it, along with the norm of consistency, imposes a defeasible constraint on what further intentions one forms, so in the case of practical intersubjectivity another's intention is accorded an authority that, along with an interpersonal norm of consistency, imposes constraints on what further intentions one forms. As it stands, the individualist proposal fails to capture this idea. Each individual regards the intentions of others as rationally inert—lacking the impact on his practical reasoning that his own intentions have, and always subject to undermining or circumvention.

I should reiterate that taking another's intention as a rational constraint does not entail that there is no possibility of a conflict between his intention and yours. Conflicts in the interpersonal case can arise just as my own intentions sometimes make conflicting demands of me. In the individual case, undermining or circumventing one of one's conflicting intentions exhibits a kind of irrationality.[32] Rather, one or both of the conflicting intentions must be revised through rational decision. Correspondingly, it would be a sign of irrationality (of a social variety) were one to have to resort to strategies of circumvention—even if it is a reasonable tactic to adopt when one is acting on one's own. Such strategies involve a failure to recognize that the intention in question has some sort of rational authority over one. In recognizing some element of authority in the other's intention, one acknowledges not only the demand for coordination with the other's intention, but also the possibility that in the event of conflict, rational negotiation may require one to revise one's own intention.

The individualist account as it stands fails to capture the thought that the intentions of one individual can serve as rational constraints for another. Why not then revise the proposal so that it requires as a condition of intersubjectivity that each individual grant the requisite status or authority to the intentions of the other? The central thought of this more sophisticated individualism is that your intention has the requisite status and corresponding impact on my reasoning in virtue of a special meta-intention I form: the intention to coordinate my intentions with yours. I call this a *bridge* intention and this more sophisticated form of individualism the bridge intention proposal.[33]

The bridge intention proposal is not without its virtues. First, it affords a straightforward account of the source of the normative demand for coordination. In general, the intention to A involves a commitment to A-ing, and one is thereby subject to a (defeasible) normative demand to A. Thus, the intention to coordinate involves a normative demand to coordinate.

Second—and in an improvement over the simple individualism of the previous proposal—the bridge intention proposal has a story to tell about the status your intention has in my practical reasoning. Take your intention to drive the second leg of the trip. We saw earlier that even if I have an intention to drive together with you to Vegas, your intention cannot serve as a rational constraint for me because there is nothing to stop me from circumventing or undermining it. But now my bridge intention to coordinate with your intentions prevents me from doing this. So on the current proposal it seems that your intention to drive the second leg of the trip to Vegas can serve as a rational constraint for my practical reasoning. Let me elaborate.

My bridge intention to coordinate with your intentions effectively transfers to you some element of discretion over what I will do. Presumably this discretion will not be unlimited. I will not grant every one of your intentions this status, but only those that pertain to our trip to Vegas. And among those intentions, there are limits to what you might get me to do; some of the things you decide might be completely unacceptable for me. Within limits, there is a range of intentions or decisions you may form that I will accept as settling the matter for me. So long as the range within which I allow you to exercise discretion is not arbitrarily narrowed around what I myself would decide on any particular occasion, my bridge intention will genuinely extend to you and your intentions some authority over my practical reasoning. Thus, while I myself would have decided to *B* on some occasion, you might form an intention that in effect settles that I am to do *A* instead. My bridge intention, then, makes a difference and allows your intentions to have a substantive impact on my practical reasoning.[34]

But despite its virtues, the bridge intention proposal is unsatisfactory. Static cases, where intentions are filled out or elaborated but not significantly revised, are handled adequately. But the proposal loses its grip when we turn to ordinary dynamic cases where there is more significant intention revision in light of changed circumstances. I proceed by describing a case that poses a problem for the bridge intention proposal.

Presenting the case requires a little setup. Notice first that the practical intersubjectivity that holds between a couple of individuals is often limited in the sense that it concerns only certain sorts of intentions, usually those concerning some activity. Thus, in the example of going to Vegas together, I only take as rational constraints those of your intentions that pertain to the trip to Vegas. Unrelated intentions, such as those involved in your plans for next year, or your intention to smoke a cigarette, will not have a similar status. So practical intersubjectivity is circumscribed so that not all of any individual's intentions are taken as rational constraints by the other individual(s). Only one's intentions that in some way pertain to the activity at hand will serve as rational constraints for others. The bridge intention proposal will have to reflect this fact. Thus, my bridge intention will not be to coordinate with your intentions in general, but to coordinate with your intentions as they pertain to filling out and implementing the intention to drive to Vegas together. More generally, the bridge intention will be of the form *I intend to coordinate with your A-related intentions*, where "*A*" denotes the shared activity at hand, and *A*-related intentions are those intentions we form in filling out and executing the intention to *A*. In the case of driving to Vegas together, the bridge intention proposal would have to say that we each have the intention to drive to Vegas with the other, and moreover, we each have the bridge intention to coordinate intentions pertaining to driving to Vegas together.

A further preliminary. Whenever one has an intention, there are some ways that one would be willing to fill it out in carrying it out and other ways that one would not be willing to fill it out. And there are some circumstances that would lead one to modify the intention (revising it, or even giving it up) and other circumstances that don't prompt any modification. Moreover, how intentions are filled out, modified, or defeated can be different in different people, depending on a host of background factors, such as beliefs, concerns, and character.

Now here's the sort of case that's a problem for the bridge intention proposal. Take any two-person case (the argument can be generalized) where one participant (you) forms an intention that conflicts with some activity-related intention of another (me), and that this new, conflicting intention of yours is a result of how you've filled out, modified, or defeated the overall intention concerning the activity. Thus, whereas the original intention was to drive to Vegas with me, your new, revised intention is to *take a bus* to Vegas with me. Or maybe it's the intention to go with me to *Reno* instead. Whatever the case, let us suppose that you think that this is a perfectly reasonable way to revise the intention, in light of the circumstances. For example, the blocker has done a good job and the 15 is impassable, so you think that we should go to Reno instead, given that neither of us minds a lot of driving. Or perhaps you hear about a great deal for bus tickets, and neither of us was excited about doing the driving anyway. Your revised intention, then, is not crazy, and neither of us thinks that it is.

The bridge intention proposal will not adequately capture the normative demand for coordination that I will face in light of how you revise your intention. Recall that on this proposal, the source of the demand to coordinate with your intention, and hence the source of the status or authority your intentions have in my practical reasoning, is my bridge intention. More specifically, it's my bridge intention to coordinate with your intentions relevant for filling out and implementing the intention to drive to Vegas together. But now you do not have any such intentions for me to coordinate with. Your intention now is to take a *bus* to Vegas, or perhaps it's the intention to drive together *to Reno*. My bridge intention has nothing to say about these intentions of yours. As a result, I no longer face any demand to coordinate my intentions with you. The special status or authority your intentions previously had for me *completely evaporates*. Your intention is now like those of some nonparticipant. Conflicts between our intentions no longer demand the rational resolution they did before. It is now open to me to somehow circumvent or undermine your intention. So if the bridge intention proposal of the individualist is correct, your intentions lose the special status they're supposed to have for me. No substantive practical intersubjectivity would remain between us when you revise your intention in the manner described.

This consequence of the bridge intention proposal is seriously mistaken, and is a reason, I think, to reject it. I think that the correct and natural view to take about this case is that your intention retains its authority as a rational constraint for me. Reasonable revision of intentions does not straightforwardly undermine practical intersubjectivity in this way. Of course, your revised intention very well may conflict with my intention, for I might still be thinking of heading to Vegas rather than Reno, or I may have revised the intention in a different and incompatible manner. But we've seen that such conflicts of rational constraints do not in themselves rule out practical intersubjectivity. Rather, when a practical intersubjectivity is in place between two individuals, and there is a conflict between their intentions, then there is a rational demand for them to render their intentions consistent; and it is not open to one to circumvent or undermine the other's intention.

This is exactly what the advocate of the bridge intention strategy *cannot* say. On the bridge intention proposal, your intentions might regain their status as rational constraint for me only if I were to adopt a new bridge intention to coordinate with your intentions pertaining to the new activity. Why would I do this? Presumably, I will make a *decision* about what is expressed in your intention. And this highlights the authority your intention lacks, for my making this decision is precisely what it is for me *not* to take your intention as a rational constraint. Your intention is no longer the sort of thing that is supposed to settle what it is that I'm to do. In effect, any revision of intention of the sort described here will require that practical intersubjectivity be restarted. And this would undermine what is central to the idea of practical intersubjectivity, viz., the thought that the intentions of one individual might serve as rational constraints in the practical reasoning of another.[35]

At this point, the individualist might try to defend the bridge intention proposal along the following lines. Suppose that our reason for going to Vegas is to gamble. Thus the relevant bridge intention very likely will be not merely to coordinate intentions pertaining to going to Vegas, but to coordinate intentions pertaining to gambling. Thus, when you revise the intention to one of going to Reno, my bridge intention is broad enough to ensure that your new intention has the necessary authority and will serve as a rational constraint for me.

The individualist's reply assumes that there will be a common further goal beyond going to Vegas together. It's not clear that this need be the case; perhaps my aim in going to Vegas is not to gamble (as it is in your case), but to take in the special kitsch peculiar to Vegas—one that Reno cannot provide. But let us suppose for the sake of argument that we share the same reasons for going to Vegas: we both are going to Vegas in order to gamble. Thus we both have the intention to gamble. It doesn't mean that this intention to gamble is somehow *freestanding*. Gambling is an end that can be satisfied by going to Vegas, but there is no reason to think that it is because of this end that we've decided to go to Vegas. On the contrary, we may have adopted this end in order to make the most of going to Vegas. Or perhaps for us the end of gambling comes packaged with going to Vegas and that we would not otherwise pursue or intend gambling.[36] Either way, the end of going to Vegas is as it were an end in itself and not merely a means to gambling. If this is the case—and I stipulate that it is in our example—then my bridge intention (and yours) will be to coordinate with your intentions pertaining to going to Vegas (or going to Vegas to gamble); it will not be the broader intention to coordinate with your intentions pertaining to gambling. If this is right, then the bridge intention proposal will not have the resources to account for the authority or status retained by your revised intention to go to Reno.[37]

I turn now to another case of intention revision that spells trouble for the bridge intention proposal. Suppose I revise my bridge intention to coordinate with your intentions. This is presumably something I can do, given that the bridge intention is, by hypothesis, an individual intention. It is therefore mine to reconsider should circumstances arise that I judge to warrant reconsideration. If something does come up that gives me good reason to revise my bridge intention, I may do so—even though you don't think it's a reason to revise this intention. Once I revise the bridge intention, the intentions you have (supposing they are not geared to the revised bridge intention, assuming I even have one) will not have the status of rational constraint for me. I am free to ignore (circumvent or undermine) your intention that would have me *A*. I would be able to do some *B* instead.

But this seems to give me a way of shielding myself from any sort of rational objection to my *B*-ing rather than *A*-ing. In revising my bridge intention, I sweep away any sort of authority you may have had as a party to the intersubjectivity between us. Your intentions no longer have a status that demands my coordination. It was this authority and status that was the basis of your objection that by *B*-ing I am not maintaining the proper sort of consistency or coherence between our intentions. By revising my bridge intention, your intentions no longer can make any claim on me. This doesn't seem right. I should not be able so easily to undercut the special status your intentions have for me.

I do not mean to be suggesting that one may never rationally act against the sort of demand to coordinate that we find in practical intersubjectivity. One may sometimes be able to extricate oneself from the demands of practical intersubjectivity and even do this unilaterally.[38] What I'm objecting to here is the possibility that one can simply *dissolve* the status had by the others' intentions so that they are no longer the sort of things that can make a demand on one. The mistake here is to represent (1) a case where there is a conflict of rational demands (and one acts on one demand rather than another) as (2) a case where there is no conflict of rational demands at all. We have in (1) a case that requires a rational resolution between these differing rational constraints. I may not simply ignore (circumvent or undermine) your intention in the manner that the bridge intention strategy would seem to allow.[39]

I think that I have said enough to raise serious worries about the prospects of individualistic approaches to practical intersubjectivity. I now consider a challenge to understanding practical intersubjectivity in terms of rational constraints.[40]

ACCESSIBILITY

When your intentions serve as rational constraints in my practical reasoning, they settle practical matters for me much in the way that my own intentions do. This suggests that you are often in a position to have intentions concerning what it is that I'm to do. For example, your intention to drive the second leg of the trip to Vegas will require me to drive the first.[41] Your intention may have been explicitly formulated only in terms of what you are to do (drive the second leg), leaving implicit what I am to do (drive the first). But in cases like this where the rationally demanded coordination rules out all but one course of action for me, there is no reason to think that what I'm to do could not figure explicitly in your intention.[42] Thus, if your intention has the status of rational constraint and thereby settles what I'm to do, there is an important sense in which what I do is *accessible* to your intentions. According to the Accessibility Thesis, whether explicitly or implicitly, when practical intersubjectivity holds between you and me, you may intend my action much in the manner in which you intend your own (and vice versa).[43]

Practical intersubjectivity and the sort of accessibility it entails are at odds with the idea that, fundamentally, one can only intend one's own actions. The Own Action Stricture[44] on intending is widespread among philosophers of action and mind. Sellars, for example, says that

> Intentions pertaining to the actions of others are not "intentions to do" in the primary sense in which *I shall do A* is an intention to do. Thus, in spite of their superficial similarity, *Tom shall do A* and *I shall do A* do not have the same conceptual structure. The former has the form
>
> *(ceteris paribus) I shall do that which is necessary to make it the case that Tom does A*
>
> whereas the latter cannot, without the absurdity of an infinite regress, be supposed to have the form
>
> *(ceteris paribus) I shall do that which is necessary to make it the case that I do A.]* (1968, p. 184)[45]

Perhaps we can avoid the conflict between the Accessibility Thesis and the Own Action Stricture because the accessibility underlying practical intersubjectivity is not as strong as I may have suggested. Sellars allows that my actions can figure in the content of your intention as the intended consequence (in a causal sense) of something you do. This is not normally the way in which your own actions figure in your intentions. But perhaps this weakened form of access will do for the purposes of practical intersubjectivity.

On this proposal, what I do is related to your intention much in the way that a rock and what it does is related to me when I use it as a paperweight, that is, when I intend that it hold these papers down (where this is understood as intending to do something that causes/leads to the rock holding down these papers). But surely this is not the sort of accessibility we find in practical intersubjectivity. Notice that the rock is not in any way *responsible* for keeping the papers from blowing about. The rock is, obviously, not subject to a rational demand to behave in any way. If it does not keep the papers from blowing about, it is not itself somehow at fault. (If anything, I am at fault for not placing it properly or for failing to act on my intention at all.) Now, supposing the accessibility of my actions to your intentions is understood along these exclusively causal lines, then your intention would be to do something to cause/bring about my *A*-ing. But then I would not thereby be responsible for *A*-ing; I would not thereby be subject to any rational or normative demand to *A*. If anything, my not *A*-ing would reflect a failure on *your* part; you would have failed to do something that causes me to *A*. We have seen, however, that in practical intersubjectivity, I *am* subject to a (defeasible) rational demand to *A* when your intention serves as rational constraint for me. The sense in which my action is accessible to your intention should mark the rational demand to which I am subject when your intention serves as rational constraint for me. The purely causal sense of accessibility therefore will not do for our purposes.

We cannot accommodate the Accessibility Thesis to the Own Action Stricture by weakening accessibility in the manner suggested. Practical intersubjectivity and the accessibility it entails will force us to reject the claim that fundamentally we can only intend our own actions. In rejecting the Own Action Stricture, I am not suggesting that it's possible for your intentions to have some sort of magical access to my actions. Your intention serves as a rational constraint for me, and I act accordingly. Some process must underlie this, much in the way that some psychological process (involving in part a form of remembering) allows me to exercise my ability to act on a prior intention of my own. Moreover, the process that allows for my acting in accord with the rational constraint you set for me could very well involve certain acts on your part. For example, you might have to perform a speech act to communicate your intention to me. Surely something like this must happen, and rejecting the Own Action Stricture doesn't commit me to denying that it does.

The Own Action Stricture derives some of its appeal from being confused with a different and very plausible idea. This is the thought that typically the only way one's intentions can have the impact on the world that they're supposed to have is through one's actions. Thus, realizing my intention that I have a nice meal tonight will require me to *do* something. Similarly, realizing your intention for me to drive the second leg of the Vegas trip will require you to do something, such as communicate your intention to me. This strikes me as plausible, and it can be accepted without granting what I deny: that your intention for me to drive the second leg of the trip is to be understood as the intention to do something that will cause me to drive the second leg of the trip.

Recall that intention involves commitment. My intention to *A* involves a (defeasible) commitment to *A*. I become subject to certain norms so that I am rationally criticizable if my subsequent practical reasoning and action fail to be in accord with the intention. The Own Action Stricture entails that the only way for me to have such a commitment and to be subject to the corresponding norms is through some intention of my own. I will never be subject to this sort of commitment in virtue of another's intention. This is the idea that our inquiry into practical intersubjectivity forces us to reject.

Once we distinguish the Own Action Stricture from the more plausible point regarding what is necessary for realizing one's intentions, there is little to be said in favor of the stricture. And the existence of practical intersubjectivity gives us a reason to reject it.

There is, moreover, another reason to think that the Own Action Stricture on intending must be mistaken. A common form of interaction between individuals involves one *commanding* another to do this or that. I hold that the notion of command involves the expression[46] of one person's intention regarding what another is to do. Just as Estelle's intention to go to the store is supposed to settle what it is that she is going to do, so it is when Naomi commands Estelle to go to the store. The intention underlying Naomi's command is supposed to settle what it is that Estelle is to do—as if it were an intention Estelle herself had generated.

Notice that Naomi's intention underlying her command is not the intention to do something that will cause Estelle to go to the store. Such an intention would not capture the sense in which Estelle would be responsible for going to the store. Estelle would not face any sort of rational demand to comply; nothing speaks against her ignoring or circumventing Naomi's intention. If Naomi's intention were simply to do something to cause Estelle to go to the store, this would fail to reflect the way in which the command is supposed to settle and commit Estelle to a course of action.[47]

Insistence on the Own Action Stricture would, therefore, rule out the sort of intention familiar to us from the case of commands.[48] This gives us another reason to reject this stricture.

It is time to take stock of what has been done and to note what is yet to be done. I have characterized practical intersubjectivity in terms of certain interpersonal norms of practical reasoning. More specifically, practical intersubjectivity holds between individuals when the intentions of each serve as rational constraints for the others. Each is subject to a rational demand to coordinate her intentions with the others. This normativity distinguishes practical intersubjectivity from the coordination condition often seen as a necessary condition for shared activity. Individualistic reductions of the rational demand one faces in practical intersubjectivity do not succeed, failing in particular to capture the dynamics of intention revision. Finally, practical intersubjectivity entails that it is mistaken to think that one can only intend one's own actions. But this in any case is mistaken, as the case of commands illustrates.

A host of interesting questions remain. Two in particular are worth mentioning, if only to dispel certain confusions that may arise from assuming that somehow I have answered them. First, in practical intersubjectivity, an individual has a kind of authority so that her intentions have the status of rational constraints for others. How, in general, does one individual acquire this sort of authority over another?[49] Second, and relatedly, just when does practical intersubjectivity hold between individuals? I think it is clear that practical intersubjectivity very often does hold between individuals and that it can be sustained through some revision of intentions. (My arguments against individualism rely on this fact.) But I do not deny that often it might be difficult to discern whether practical intersubjectivity is in place, and I have not offered any formula that yields a simple answer to this question.

There are no easy answers to either of these questions. But their difficulty should not tempt us to adopt a skepticism about practical intersubjectivity. To succumb to this temptation would be to blind ourselves to the social reality that surrounds us and pervades our agency.

ACKNOWLEDGMENTS

I got a lot of help from conversations with or comments from Tyler Burge, Lisa Downing, Bill Hart, Barbara Herman, Seana Shiffrin, Fred Schmitt, David Kaplan, Hans Lottenbach, Chris McMahon, and members of a seminar I taught at UCLA during the spring of 2002. I gave a related paper as a talk at the Philosophy Department at UCSB, and benefited from discussion with the audience there, especially Matt Hanser and Kevin Falvey.

NOTES

1. The story I tell here is incomplete. While the form of intention that I identify overcomes certain important obstacles to understanding practical intersubjectivity in terms of intentions, there are other aspects of this intersubjectivity that call for further developments in the proposal and point to important ways in which the sort of intentions implicated in practical intersubjectivity and shared agency differ from the sort we find in commands. It is therefore more accurate to say that the sort of intention we find in shared activity, and the sort we find in the phenomenon of commands, are species in a common genus.

2. The constraint is defeasible for it might be revised given new information or the discovery of conflicts with other constraints (see below). The term *constraint* is meant to mark how the intention has the status of something that both structures and limits practical thought. That said, I'm not especially invested in the term. One might talk instead of rational commitment, default, or presumption.

3. Besides intentions, someone's wants or desires may also figure as rational constraints in my practical reasoning. But if wants and desires are not subject to norms of consistency and coherence the way intentions are, there is the possibility that when I take up your desire as a rational constraint, I might run afoul of your intentions (in the case where you have decided against acting on that desire).

4. I have in mind a case of relative equals; each individual has the authority or status to issue intentions that serve as rational constraints for the other. Nevertheless, there is no guarantee that each will exercise his or her authority to the same extent. It would be worrying if, between us, you were always the one settling these practical issues. I come to resent the control you exert over what we're doing, and you become irritated at how my passivity forces you to do all the planning and decision making. The possibility of such problematic relationships should not, however, put into question the very idea that one individual's intentions might serve as rational constraints for another. A similar problem exists in the case of individual intentions. Someone might have the tendency to form too many intentions too early on in the course of some activity, with a resulting loss of spontaneity and sensitivity to circumstance. That the ability to form intentions for the future might not be well exercised does not put into question the very idea of forming such individual intentions, which commit oneself to a course of action and serve as rational constraints in one's subsequent practical reasoning.

5. This is a point nicely made and developed by Harman (1976, 1986) and Bratman (1987).

6. If it were, then we'd be led to illegitimate bootstrapping. For discussion, see Broome (2001), Bratman (1987), and Velleman (1997b).

7. This is not to say that nothing will ever come up to prompt me to reconsider my intention to go to the beach. In that case, going to the library can become an option for me.

8. I am not sure whether this case where there is coordinated behavior despite conflicting intentions should count as genuinely shared activity.

9. I don't mean to suggest that the intending of means is the only way to increase coherence. Given that one intends *A,* one might form some intention *B* not because *B* is a means to or otherwise facilitates *A*-ing, but because having *B* as an end would make better sense of *A*-ing; *A*-ing would be more worthwhile in such a context. For example, suppose I had an interest in seeing the desert. Then it might be more worthwhile to go to Vegas if I were to take it as an opportunity to see the desert. Apart from its intrinsic merits, a trip to Vegas has the added benefit of being *convenient* for seeing the desert. So I adopt the intention to see the desert as a matter of coherence, though it is certainly not a means to going to Vegas. Another intention I might adopt is to dress in a rat-pack sort of way, or perhaps don my Elvis outfit, and stay not at a newer family-oriented hotel, but at a seedy old establishment. By introducing an element of kitsch into the activity, greater sense is made of it. Adopting the intention to dress in this way is not a means toward the end of going to Vegas, nor need it facilitate it—it could even make it harder. But this intention, too, is adopted as a matter of coherence.

10. That both intentions and beliefs are subject to principles of consistency and coherence has tempted some to identify intention as a kind of belief. See Harman (1976).

11. It needn't be the case that I am irrational in making these sorts of statements (or in thinking the corresponding thoughts). After all, these expressions might be thought or uttered when one realizes that one has been forgetful or has otherwise made a mistake. There is a rational tension here, and one is irrational if one doesn't see it as a problem or is otherwise complacent about resolving it. (Of course, I might see it as a problem, but there might be more urgent things to attend to, like getting out of this burning house.)

12. Why only activity-related intentions? I might have some intention that is not connected with the activity in question, and this might conflict with some nonactivity-related intention held by another participant. It doesn't seem to me that there is a rational demand for us to eliminate this conflict—at least, there is no rational demand having to do with the activity we share at the moment.

13. The idea that the intentions of one might serve as rational constraints for another is also manifest in more hierarchical situations, where not everyone has the same status to issue rational constraints for others (see below).

14. Sellars discusses the logical engagement of intentions between individuals in the course of defending a quasi-Kantian account of morality. See especially Sellars (1968), but also Sellars (1963b). Also relevant for practical intersubjectivity is the distinctive sort of commitments, identified in Gilbert (1989, 1990), between participants in shared activity. I discuss these commitments in some detail in Roth (2002).

The demand to maintain consistency and coherence with the intentions of another raises issues of authority and entitlement. For *A* to be able to form an intention that serves as rational constraint for *B*, *A* must have some sort of authority to settle what *B* is to do. Correlatively, *B* must have some sort of entitlement to the practical conclusion embodied in *A*'s intention. This issue is raised in my discussion of the idea of acting directly on another's intention, in Roth (2002).

My focus is on cases where one individual forms an intention that serves as rational constraint for another. I have not suggested how individuals may settle practical matters by *deliberating together*. No doubt we sometimes arrive at our intentions in this manner. However, it would be too impractical to settle *every* issue between us by deliberating together. When people do in fact deliberate together, they'll communicate and exchange of ideas regarding what to do until a point is reached where one or the other individual (or both) will be in a position to be confident to form an intention that will serve as a rational constraint for herself and the other. (And particularly complicated or momentous decisions might involve a period subsequent to the initial decision making during which one sees if the decision/intention will stick, so to speak.)

15. Nor do I deny it. I leave it as an open question.

16. At least, the intersubjectivity that holds between you and me does not hold between me and the blocker. There may be some other intersubjectivity that does hold between me and the blocker, one that is broader than the one that holds between you and me. But there need not be, and I will be assuming here that there is not.

17. Thanks to Seana Shiffrin for the latter consideration.

18. In one situation, the blocker's reasons might be accepted by me but outweighed by other considerations in favor of continuing to Vegas. In another situation, I might simply reject his considerations as misguided, confused, and so on.

19. Of course, there may be legal or moral proscriptions against circumventing or undermining the blocker's intention.

20. Again, I am setting aside the possibility that there is something like a moral rule or principle that disallows taking this kind of stance against the blocker. It might be that it is rationally permissible to undermine the blocker's intention but not morally permissible. Alternatively, it might turn out that some sort of practical intersubjectivity does in fact hold between me and the blocker, contrary to what I have stipulated in the setup of the example. If so, I would not be able to undermine his intention, as I presently argue is the case with respect to a fellow participant.

21. Since one's own intentions are rational constraints on one's own practical reasoning, a similar line of thought explains why it would be problematic and a sign of irrationality if one were to try to circumvent or undermine one's own intentions.

Bratman (1992) includes a no-coercion condition on shared cooperative activity. He is moved by the intuition that coercion is not a part of cooperative activity. But we can see now that there is a further consideration behind such a principle, one that might explain Bratman's intuition. To the extent that shared cooperative activity involves a practical intersubjectivity, it seems that the no-coercion condition might be based on the idea that coercion is not compatible with the thought that each individual takes the intentions of the others as rational constraints.

22. Recall that my focus has been on practical intersubjectivity, which I take to be necessary for but perhaps not limited to shared activity. Though the example of driving to Vegas is an instance of shared activity, my purpose in describing it is to illustrate points about practical intersubjectivity. I am not trying to give an account of shared activity or agency, and I am simply assuming that this case of going to Vegas is an example thereof.

Practical intersubjectivity (or something very close to it) might be in place between individuals who are not engaged in shared activity when for example they are engaged in the pursuit of individual goals under the restriction that they not interfere with one another. In accommodating one another, each will take intentions of the other as rational constraints (at least insofar as they respect the consistency condition, if not the coherence condition). But there is no explicit shared intention, such as to build a house together, or to go to Vegas together, and the like. (I find it strained to insist that there is an activity that they are doing together, viz., together accommodating one another. But not much hinges on this.)

23. Some theorists resist distinguishing intention as some psychological attitude distinct from intentional action and so would resist any fundamental distinction between the coordination of intention and the coordination of action. On such a view, then, the coordination of action pretty much just is the coordination of intention. To the extent that the former is central to shared activity, so is the latter.

24. To make use of a term from Bratman (1992), the intentions must *mesh*. For example, I might intend that we stop at a cheap place for lunch and not care about the decor, and you might intend that we stop at a tacky place for lunch and not care about the price. Our intentions are not the same; they specify different satisfaction conditions. But it seems that their coordination is possible, given the background beliefs or assumptions that there is a cheap and tacky restaurant somewhere along our route.

A proper formulation of the coordination condition is rather difficult. While some level of coordination of intentions is necessary for shared activity, it would be mistaken to require complete satisfaction of all activity-related intentions. Shared activity might be had even while some important though nonessential activity-related intentions go unsatisfied and some conflicts between participants go unresolved. I would go so far as to say that this is the norm. We need therefore to allow that two sets of activity-related intentions *mesh* to the extent that their intentions are mutually satisfiable (this is to revise Bratman's usage, which makes mesh to be incompatible with *any* conflict or mutual unsatisfiability of intentions [Bratman 1992, p. 332]. Two sets of activity-related intentions *clash* to the extent that their intentions conflict. Thus, my intentions relevant for our ride to Vegas mesh with yours to the extent that we agree on when to drive, what car to use, what route to take, and so on. But our respective sets of activity-related intentions clash to the extent that we have a conflict over who will drive which leg of the trip. Then, the level of coordination between our activity-related intentions is determined by two factors: the level of mesh and agreement between the two sets of intentions and the extent to which they clash. The coordination condition for shared activity will require some sufficient level of coordination so understood in terms of mesh and clash. I think that the boundaries between what counts as shared activity and what does not are vague, and so the vagueness of the coordination condition seems appropriate. However, I don't pretend that the proposal is not in need of refinement. (Another source of complexity: How many participants in shared activity can fail to have sufficiently coordinated intentions before there is no shared activity? And to what extent can one's intentions fail to coordinate with the rest before one will no longer count as a participant?)

25. There can, of course, be a hypothetical ought: if there is to be shared activity, there should not be this conflict of intentions.

26. I do not deny that the concept of intention is normative. I reject the idea that it is a purely causal/functional concept. The point is that the *coordination* of intentions is not normative—at least the coordination of individual intentions of different individuals is not.

27. Reducing the level of coordination will not necessarily lead to a failure to satisfy the intention coordination condition on shared activity; whether it does will depend on how stringently the condition is formulated. If it is formulated so as not to allow *any* conflict, then the condition would go unsatisfied. But I think most would agree that, so formulated, the condition is too severe as a condition for shared activity.

28. One is tempted to say that normativity entails the possibility of error. But that would be too strong, for it would seem to render incoherent the notion of infallibility, and that doesn't seem right. Rather, we want to say, roughly, that were someone not to conform to the normative demand, then they would be making a mistake.

29. One might think that *some* coordination of intention is a condition for intersubjectivity. Because it is normative, the very idea of intersubjectivity goes with that of mistake or failure—in this case miscoordination. So we can't require *perfect* coordination of intentions as a condition for intersubjectivity. For as soon as there was miscoordination, intersubjectivity and its normative demand would not be in place. The normative demand of intersubjectivity would become empty: holding only for those for whom it is otiose, and not applying to those for whom it would be substantive.

We will need to address at some point the nature and extent of coordination that would be a condition for intersubjectivity. It might be that coordination plays a part of a genetic condition for intersubjectivity, and that it is possible for the coordination to disappear even while the intersubjectivity and the normative demand remains.

30. See the remarks on Bratman in note 21 above.

31. The inspiration for this position can be found in Tuomela and Miller (1988), who claim that in what they call joint activity, each participant has a "we-intention," where this is analyzed in terms of individual intentions of the form *I intend to do my part in our A-ing*. It should be noted that Tuomela are Miller are not there defending a view meant to provide an account of practical intersubjectivity.

32. This is not to say that it can't be a rational strategy. But if one needs to resort to this sort of strategy, then one suffers from some form of irrationality. For example, it might be rational for me to try to undermine some compulsive intention. Another case where it might make sense to adopt a strategy of undermining an intention is when I lack a sort of rational unity over time (e.g., my day self doesn't want to eat M&M's, but my night self does—and not because it's a compulsion; at bedtime, I decide in a deliberate and cool-headed fashion that eating M&M's now is a fine thing to do, whereas six hours earlier, and the next morning as well, I think that I really should not eat the M&M's).

33. Bratman (1992, pp. 332–34) defends a view like this, although it is not formulated as an account of practical intersubjectivity. He attributes to each participant in shared activity an intention to mesh subplans.

34. The nature of the sort of reduction being attempted by the sophisticated individualist will depend upon how the content of the bridge intention is formulated. If my bridge intention is to accord to your intentions the authority requisite for their serving as rational constraints for me, then the individualist might be appealing to concepts that can no longer be considered purely individualistic in content. In that case, the individualist is not offering a conceptual reduction of practical intersubjectivity; but the account is individualistic in that nothing besides intentions of individuals is appealed to. On the other hand, the individualist might attempt a more ambitious and controversial semantic reduction and try to specify the content of the bridge intention in arguably individualistic terms. On this view, my bridge intention might be something like the intention to form intentions that are consistent and coherent with the intentions you form. Both sorts of proposals will be susceptible to the criticism I give below.

35. Think of how the very notion of one's own intentions serving as a rational constraint is undermined if every time I were to act on a prior intention, I could not take the previous decision for granted, and would have to decide the matter anew.

I don't deny that there are ways in which an individual might revise an intention that would lead to the dissolution of the practical intersubjectivity holding between them. But the bridge intention proposal has the implausible consequence that the intersubjectivity is dissolved *every time* that someone revises an intention in a way that is not anticipated by the bridge intention.

36. Though gambling may be higher in the order of justification, this does not mean that it is higher in the order of what it is that we're settled on doing, let alone what it is that we're settled on doing together.

37. Another suggestion on behalf of the individualist is to relax the bridge intention in our example to something like the intention to coordinate with your intentions pertaining to our going to Vegas, *or to any similar activity*. But what would count as

sufficiently similar activity? Similarity is notoriously vague and there are many different dimensions along which activities might resemble one another. What activities
count as similar to going to Vegas? Would spending the weekend playing blackjack
on the home computer count as sufficiently similar? Would going sightseeing in the
desert count as sufficiently similar? Or going gambling in Reno? Or going to Grace-
land (supposing you had in mind kitsch when heading to Vegas in the first place)?
Even if we set aside this worry and grant that we can make sense of similarity here,
there is the further worry that it's not at all clear that the rational revision of intentions
must lead from the intention to perform one activity to the intention to perform an
activity similar to that originally intended. For example, on our way to Vegas, we're
held up by a traffic jam (no doubt because of the blocker). So we decide to head
home and get ahead of schedule doing research for a paper we're planning to jointly
author. Given the circumstances, it could make a lot of sense to revise the intention
in this fashion. But this activity really doesn't seem to be similar to that of going to Vegas to hang out in the casinos.

38. *Pace* Gilbert, who characterizes her central notion of joint commitment in
terms of the claim that no one party to such a commitment can withdraw from it unilaterally. See Gilbert (1999). That said, I should add that Gilbert's work has been influential in my thought.

39. It is useful to compare this with an analogous proposal regarding the status
one's own intentions or decisions have on what one will do. Suppose that at time t1,
I decide/intend to send a paper to an editor at some later time t2. My decision/inten-
tion should settle the matter of what I will do at t2. It is now t2. Given my decision,
and the fact that nothing has since come up that gives me reason not act on it, I
should be sending the paper now. Why? Is it because at t2 I have what amounts to a
diachronic bridge intention to act on the prior intention I formed at t1? That couldn't
be it. For nothing would stop me from discarding the intention to act on the prior intention, in which case the prior intention would lose its status to demand any sort of
behavior on my part. But, in fact, the intention does retain its status for me. My prior
intention *persists*, and isn't merely *represented* in my subsequent practical reasoning
and action by the intention to act on that prior intention.

40. The arguments presented against individualism—of both the simple form and
the more sophisticated bridge intention proposal—rely on the thought that they fail
to reflect what is evident: that practical intersubjectivity persists through some revision of intention. Of course, there is some revision in intention that *would* bring practical intersubjectivity to a halt. The issue of when it is that a practical intersubjectivity
holds between individuals is a difficult and interesting one that needs further explo-
ration. Its difficulty is obscured by individualism, which gives an overly simplistic
(and as we've seen, mistaken) answer in terms of the special individual intentions ascribed to each party to intersubjectivity.

41. This isn't always the case. Often the intentions of yours with which I'm supposed to coordinate may be such as to leave me significant latitude in deciding what
to do. Nevertheless, in principle, and often in practice, your intention can narrow
things down so much as to specify just what action I am to take.

42. Once we admit this, there is nothing to stop us from allowing for the possibility that your intention might have explicit content that exclusively concerns what *I*
am to do. For example, your intention might have been for me to do *all* the driving.

43. Accessibility in its purest (and perhaps most controversial) form is manifested when your intentions specifically concern what I'm to do. But accessibility more generally is manifest whenever your intentions serve as rational constraints for me.

44. To adapt Michael Bratman's term for the view.

45. Other proponents include Baier (1970), and more recently Stoutland (1997), who holds

> an agent can intend only to do something *herself*. She cannot intend anyone else to do some act, but at best intend to do something herself that gets someone else to do the act. I cannot intend *you* to buy *me* a dinner; I can only intend to do something which might result in that. (55–56)

See also Velleman (1997b) for important discussion of another related thesis that might also raise worries for what I say about practical intersubjectivity here. I hope to discuss that article on a different occasion.

46. Anscombe (1963, p. 5) rightly points out that commands are expressions; there is no such thing as an unexpressed command. Intentions, however, are not themselves expressions, though they may be expressed. Talk of expressions of commands is redundant. The current thesis is that a command is an expression of one individual's intention regarding what some other individual is to do.

47. Often we utter things that sound like commands in contexts where no relations of authority are in place. These are not genuine or substantive commands and do not carry with them the sort of status that induce a commitment in the individual to whom they're issued.

48. One way in which the situation of commands differs from that of practical intersubjectivity lies with the nature of the relations between the relevant parties. In the case of commands, there tends to be an asymmetry: only one individual usually has the authority to settle practical issues for the other. In the case of practical intersubjectivity, authority is symmetrical: each individual has some authority with respect to the other so that each can issue intentions that serve as rational constraints for the other.

49. Corresponding to this question of authority is the question of how it is that one individual is *entitled* to the practical or deliberative conclusions of another. These issues receive some discussion in Roth (2002).

4

The We-Mode and the I-Mode

Raimo Tuomela

INTRODUCING COLLECTIVITY

The social world, especially its macro aspects, cannot adequately be studied without making use of the distinction between the notions of having an attitude or acting as a *group member* versus as a *private person*. These intuitive notions are the core of my distinction between the *we-mode* and the *I-mode*. In this chapter I present detailed analyses of these two notions and show that the we-mode is not reducible to the I-mode. I also consider the problem whether in some contexts thinking and acting in the we-mode is required or is in some sense better than thinking and acting in the I-mode. There is, however, much involved here, as will be seen. I start by discussing some relevant matters in general terms and give my analyses in the sections Functioning as a Group Member and The Varieties of the We-Mode and the I-Mode.

Let me illustrate the distinction between the I-mode and the we-mode in the case of the attitude of having a goal. A person can have as his goal to ventilate the room, to achieve a Ph.D., or to have an ice cream. These are normally "private" or "merely personal" goals; and, when regarded as nonindexical types of goals, they can be shared. On the other hand, some people might have as their shared goal to reduce the ozone hole or to build a house together. These latter kinds of goals are collective goals. Collective goals are in the first place attributed to collectives (of agents) or to several agents collectively or jointly. In a derivative, distributed sense also single agents can be said to have collective goals, and this presupposes that the agents in question believe that also some others have or will have the goal in question. If it is our goal to reduce the ozone hole, this goal can, for this reason, also be attributed to you and me.

93

When concerned with goals, I discuss only *intended* goals—that is, goals that the goal holders intend to achieve. Goals can here be regarded as intention contents, which the agents can have either in the I-mode or in the we-mode sense. There are two features about goals that I wish to emphasize here (see Tuomela 2000a, ch. 2). First, an intended goal in the I-mode is a goal that a rational goal-holder must believe that he can achieve (or can probably achieve) by means of his own actions. Second, an I-mode goal is something the achievement of which is prima facie "for" (that is, "for the use of") the goal-holder. In contrast, when an agent has a collective we-mode goal, he is not required to believe that he alone can achieve it. Instead, rational holders of a collective we-mode goal are assumed to mutually believe that they by their collective activities can (or probably can) suitably achieve their goal. A collective we-mode goal is in the first place "for" (that is, for the use of) the collective (social group) in question and, in this context equivalently, is one held in the we-mode. The "use" aspect of a goal here relates to the use of appropriate goal expressions such as "We will achieve p" as premises in inferential group contexts, to extralinguistic activities related to the achievement of the goal in question, as well as, in principle, to the employment of the goal state for the group's purposes once it has been achieved. (As to the notion of a social group or collective, we need only assume that the members believe that they belong to the group in question, but need not here enter a deeper and more informative analysis.)

Whatever a full-blown collective we-mode goal is taken to be in detail, it will have to satisfy a certain collectivity condition, which an I-mode goal (or a private goal) does not satisfy. Before discussing this condition, let me characterize social attitudes, or more specifically (weak) "we-attitudes," from another perspective (cf. Tuomela 1995, ch. 1, 2000a, 2002). We-attitudes are attitudes involving social beliefs. We consider a person's we-attitude related to a "plain" attitude, say ATT, which has a certain content p. Here ATT can be a plain want, goal, intention, belief, wish, or the like. A we-attitude in its *core* sense is defined as follows relative to a social group g: The person (1) has $ATT(p)$ and (2) believes that the others in g also have $ATT(p)$ and also (3) believes (or at least is disposed to believe) that it is mutually believed (or in a weaker case, plainly believed) that the members have $ATT(p)$. If the we-attitude (which we can denote by $WATT(p)$) so defined expresses a goal, it can be either the person's I-mode goal or his we-mode collective goal.

Consider the example in which some people have as their goal to visit Naples. This goal can be expressed by the sentence "Our goal is to visit Naples." If visiting Naples were only the private goal of each person in question, which possibility is linguistically allowed by the mentioned goal-expressing sentence, then each person's goal would be satisfied when he has visited Naples. However, in the we-mode or properly collective case that does not suffice. In the latter case the persons must collectively accept the goal for their group in the sense that each of them is to visit Naples. Accordingly, this collective acceptance must show up in action in that the group members are collectively committed to seeing to it that every one of them visits Naples. In the I-mode case, on the contrary, every person individually sees to it that he gets to Naples, thus satisfying his private goal.

A we-mode collective goal that can be distributed among the participants will accordingly have to satisfy the following Collectivity Condition (CC):

(CC) It is true on "quasi-conceptual" grounds and hence necessarily that a goal content p is satisfied for (that is, in the case of) a member of a collective g and, indeed, for g if and only if it is satisfied for every member of g.

Here the qualification "on quasi-conceptual grounds" is taken to entail that the collective goal-content p is collective due to the collective acceptance (not necessarily joint, plan-based acceptance) by the members of g as their collective goal. The collective acceptance concerns the conative proposition "Our goal is p" (or, equivalently, "We will achieve p") and is assumed to be necessarily truth-equivalent to the correct assertability for them of the aforementioned proposition. In (CC) the notion of satisfaction for a goal holder involves that the goal state or event comes about due to the collective effort by the group members (see note 4). Collective acceptance here entails that each participant has accepted the goal and thus aims at contributing to the satisfaction of p. The participants are assumed to be collectively committed to what they have accepted, and there must also be at least shared belief about the participants' acceptances. In all, the members can be said to construct collective goals by their conceptual activities, by their collective acceptances and allowances.[1]

We can also say that a full-blown collective goal is a common goal that by its conceptual nature is simultaneously fulfilled for the participants, and the simultaneous satisfactions of the individuals' corresponding personalized collective intentions to act together are necessary connected due to the mentioned collective acceptance. Collective acceptance can vary in strength, so to speak, and range from joint, plan-based acceptance to shared acceptance-belief (cf. Tuomela and Balzer 1999; Tuomela 2002a). The stronger the kind of collective acceptance that is involved, the stronger the necessity. In general, the content of (CC) must be assumed to be mutually known to the participants. However, the agents need not have beliefs directly about (CC)— the connection can be generated in a roundabout way due to their *de re* beliefs that they are engaged in the same project. An I-mode attitude does not satisfy (CC), even if due to some reason the members' goal would happen to be simultaneously satisfied (respectively unsatisfied) for all the members of g.[2]

(*CC*) trivially generalizes to any attitude, say want, wish, belief, or the like. Let us call such an arbitrary attitude ATT and assume that its content is something *p*:

(*CC**)   It is true on "quasi-conceptual" grounds and hence necessarily that ATT-content *p* is satisfied for a member of a collective *g* and for *g* if and only if it is satisfied for every member of *g*.

Generally speaking, in our present context the collectively accepted attitude-expressing sentence can concern a shared we-attitude WATT(*p*). In the case of intended collective goals (and intentions) the surface form of the attitude-expressing sentence, say *s*, could be "We will achieve *p*," where "will" expresses intending and *p* represents a goal state. In the case of collective beliefs (which strictly speaking will be acceptances and may be called acceptance beliefs), the formula *s* may take the form "We believe that *p*" or "It is our view that *p*." In the case of wishes, *s* may be "We wish that *p*," and so on. Also normative statements can be involved. Thus *s* may be "Everyone in *g* ought to do *X* when in *C*." Actually I propose that *s* be understood in a more general sense as a dot-quoted sentence *.s.*, in Sellars's terms, and thus also allowed to be a "mental sentence" or a thought in "Mentalese."[3] A dot-quoted sentence *.s.* is one that plays the same role in a given language or representational system as *s* plays in our base language, here English.

It can be shown that the idea that collective acceptance for the group is necessarily truth-equivalent to the correct assertability of the accepted proposition in the case of collective attitudes (that is, the CAT formula of note 1) together with the assumption that the collective acceptance of *s* involves collective commitment to the use of *s* entails the truth of the (generalized) collectivity condition (see Tuomela 2000a). The assumption of collective acceptance for the group involving collective commitment also makes WATT(*p*) a we-mode attitude in the core sense (see criterion a1. in the section The Varieties of the We-Mode and the I-Mode).

I concentrate on the case of structured groups and regard unstructured ones as special cases of them—that is, special cases with "empty" or "nil" structure. I am here speaking especially of structuration (social position structure) in terms of social norms, either rule-norms or proper social norms in the sense of Tuomela (1995, ch. 1). In the case of both kinds of social norms, we must be dealing with a normative codification of them that I have earlier explicated in terms of (normative) *task-right systems* attributable to group positions.

While it ought to be the case that a position-holder acts in the we-mode, he can in an instrumental sense perform his tasks without being committed to the group's constitutive goals. He can—can as a matter of social fact—

instrumentally function (or, better, quasi-function) as a group member just by doing his "work," that is, just by taking care of his specific duties without purporting to act *for* the group and without aiming at furthering the group's basic goals and values. He would then, so to speak, be exhibiting the right bodily actions, but his reason for performing a group-task *T* would be, roughly, "I perform *T* because it is conducive to my personal interests" and not "I perform *T* at least in part because it is my duty and furthers, or at least does not contradict, the group's interests." We can accordingly say that, when acting for the group, "forgroupness" will be the agent's partial reason for action. This is what is needed of institutional action, at least to some extent. Arguably, unless there is some amount of we-mode institutional acting, the institution cannot be maintained and does not even properly exist as an institution, precisely because an institution is constituted as a group phenomenon requiring acting for the group (cf. Tuomela 2002a, ch. 6). As to the functional "maintenance" aspect, it is to be understood in the functional terms of how well the group succeeds in its attempts to satisfy its constitutive goals. Thus functioning on the basis of private reasons must be assumed not to be dysfunctional for the group.

The consequence of my assumptions is that, while genuine and full-blown group activities require we-mode thinking and acting, still some position holders or, more generally, some group members acting qua group members may act as group members in the weak, I-mode sense, as long as some suitable degree of overall functionality is upheld in the group. Such personal reasons can concern the basic interests of the group but are still adopted for the group member's own sake (e.g., the agent may derive personal satisfaction from group success). My present point about the exceptional possibility of I-mode acting also applies to norm following in general and even to fulfilling an agreement, as long there is some amount of we-mode acting in the group. Considering the latter example, one may take an instrumental attitude toward agreements and only contribute to their fulfillment as long as such activity is not too costly or has more overall utility than not obeying the agreement.

What is lacking in the I-mode cases is acting with the group perspective—that is, forgroupness—and collective commitment to the fulfillment of the agreement. Such collective commitment involves not only commitment to satisfying one's part of the agreement but also commitment to participation in a broader sense (possibly involving helping, persuading, coercion, etc.) in the context in which the participants try to see to it that the agreement is fulfilled and thus indeed fulfilled for the group in question. Each participant accordingly accepts that he or she is responsible to the others for performing his or her part and is normatively (at least in both an instrumental and a social sense of normativity) entitled to expect that the other participants perform theirs.

For the purposes of this chapter, we need only have available a weak no-tion of we-mode collective commitment. It can be exemplified as follows in the case of two persons, you and me. If we are collectively committed to a proposition *s* (or, to be more precise, .*s*.) expressing our joint action or proj-ect (or other joint content), the following must be true: I take myself to be committed to *s* and will act accordingly, in part because I believe that I ought to use *s* as a premise in my inferences related to group contexts and act on its truth in the context of acting as a member of the group ("us"); and I be-lieve that you are also similarly committed to *s* and will act accordingly in part because of your similar personal normative thoughts. Furthermore, we both believe that all this is mutually believed by us. Here *s* could be "We will do *X* together" and we are talking about your and my commitment to em-ploying it for the use of the group. In the present weak sense of collective commitment, my account goes in terms of shared we-belief only and collec-tive commitment is thus analyzed in terms of attitudes concerned with bind-ing oneself normatively to an item. Hence direct communication is not re-quired and even less is explicit agreement making at stake. (Note that I-mode collective acceptance does not involve collective commitment even in this weak sense.) What we have here is already a weak version of we-mode collective commitment—to be clearly distinguished from aggregated private (that is, I-mode) commitment.

We may speak both of a collection of persons being collectively commit-ted to using a sentence and, derivatively, of each of those persons being so collectively committed.

FUNCTIONING AS A GROUP MEMBER

In this next section I analyze the notions of the we-mode and the I-mode in detail. These notions depend on the notion of functioning (that is, thinking and acting) qua a group member. We recall that one can act as a group mem-ber also in the I-mode, although both on constitutive and functional grounds not all group members can (always) act in the I-mode, but some must have a group reason ("forgroupness") for their action. The present section gives an analysis of the notion of functioning (acting) as a group member.

In any group it is possible to perform freely chosen actions qua a group member provided that these actions—or, more broadly, activities, including mental ones—are within the realm of "concern" of the group, that is, pro-vided they belong to topics that are of concern or are of significance for the group in a group context (as opposed to a private context). Such actions are to be (rationally) collectively accepted by the group (basically either through normative, group-binding group acceptance or through the we-acceptances by the group members or their majority—cf. Tuomela 1995, ch. 7 and 2002a, ch. 5). The non-normative acceptance or belief here could be of the form of a we-acceptance within the group, g: ideally, everyone accepts a topic T, to be a topic of concern for g, and believes that everyone so accepts and also believes that this is mutually believed in g. So we get a notion of group concern: topic T is within the realm of group g's concern if and only if T is we-accepted to be in the group g's realm of concern. Group g's realm of concern C consists of a set of topics $\{T_1, \ldots, T_m\}$. A topic T_i which is within the realm of g's concern, consists of a set of contents involving, but not reducible to, content-satisfying or content-maintaining actions or activities (types) X_j; let us call their set $\mathbf{X}_i$. Considering the union of the set of actions $\mathbf{X}_i$, that is, $\cup_i \mathbf{X}_i$, we can classify those actions as follows from the point of view of acting qua a group member.

The general case is that of a structured group with positions (the unstructured case can be regarded as its special case with no specific positions over and above group membership). I first classify the types of actions within the realm of a (structured) group's concern, that is, actions falling within the realm $\cup_i \mathbf{X}_i$ that are assumed to be conducive to the group's basic goals, beliefs, and standards:

1. positional actions (related to a group position or role), which include a) actions (tasks) that the position holder in question *ought to* perform, perhaps in a special way, in certain circumstances and b) actions that he or she *may* (is permitted to) perform in some circumstances;
2. actions that other group norms (e.g., norms that are not position specific) as well as group standards require or allow;
3. actions and joint actions that do not, or at least need not, belong to classes 1. or 2. and that are based on situational intention formation or agreement making that has not been codified in the task-right system of g or the group norms of g, but that still are consistent with actions in 1. and 2.;
4. freely chosen actions or activities (and possibly joint actions), which include actions and activities not within classes 1.–3., which, although not incompatible with them, still are actions within the realm of concern of g and rationally (understood broadly to amount to *reasonably*) collectively accepted by, or acceptable to, the members of g as such actions.

The notion of functioning qua group member in the present sense would require much discussion, but to avoid that I make some simplifying assumptions. One thing that must be said immediately here is, however, that the previous classes are classes of actions. Attitudes can be dealt with similarly. Thus, we may speak of attitude contents and actions within the realm of concern of group g, and in the above classification we may speak also of attitudes in addition to actions. The important thing to notice here is that those attitudes are based on acceptances and thus something that one can acquire by means of one's intentional action.

Basically, to function as a group member is to act intentionally within the group's realm of concern. Such action can be either successful or unsuccessful. What is required is that the group member in question will intentionally attempt to act in a way related to what he or she takes to be the group's realm of concern such that he or she does not violate the group's central, constitutive goals, beliefs, standards, and norms (briefly, its "ethos"). The ethos is at least a kind of underlying or "presupposition" reason for the member's action in this context. (Let me note that we can understand the notion of ethos in a wide sense in which every group can be taken to have an ethos—some basic ends or beliefs or something closely analogous.)

As said, full success in action will not be required. There may thus be failures due to false beliefs about the group's norms and standards, due to lack of skill, or due to environmental obstacles. *Functioning as a group member* (relative to group g) in the positional case, that is, in a structured group, is equivalent to acting intentionally, with the purpose to satisfy or at least not to contradict the ethos of g, in one of the senses 1.–4., or attempting so to act. I later use this notion when speaking of functioning (thinking and acting) qua group member. In contrast to functioning as a group member, one can be a group member without *always* acting as a group member and one can act within the realm of the group's concern but fail to obey the ethos of the group (e.g., one can even perform treasonable acts against the group and its ethos). As noted, although on the level of the group, so to speak, functioning as a group member is constituted as a we-mode notion with the inbuilt forgroupness reason, a group member can still function as a single group member (relative to g) in the weak, I-mode sense of the section Introducing Collectivity.

Actions in 1. are of course typical positional actions that accordingly qualify as acting qua a member of g in one's position. Subclass b) of 1. thus consists of actions that the holder of a position may choose from. (The task-right system specifying a) and b) may contain rule norms and/or proper social norms in the sense of Tuomela 1995, ch. 1.) However, classes 2.–4. can occur also in the positional case and in other cases. Note that in the case of unstructured groups, class 1. is empty. The notion of rational collective acceptance in 4. is assumed to take into account what is generally presupposed of action in the community in question. Thus it will respect the standards and generally accepted criteria of classifying actions within that community. (I mention in the section The Pros and Cons of the We-Mode cases of mental activities falling within 4., and related to this category my approach can also accept unintentional actions, viz., actions based on false beliefs, as a group member; but in general I concentrate on intentional actions—see Tuomela 2002a, chs 3–4, for relevant collective "pattern-governed" behaviors.)

THE VARIETIES OF THE WE-MODE AND THE I-MODE

I next present precise analyses of the notions of the we-mode and the I-mode. These analyses improve and complement my earlier treatments (cf. Tuomela 1984, 1995, 2000a, 2002a).

My most central variables of classification in this context are: (1) unstructured versus structured group (with the additional simplifying assumption that in a normatively structured group every member is a position holder, which assumption excludes mixed groups); (2) functioning as a group member versus not functioning (fully) as a group member; (3) acting for the group (for the use of the group, contributing toward the satisfaction of the group ethos, thus group goals or purposes) versus acting for himself or herself (for his or her use, contributing toward the satisfaction of his or her own private goals or purposes); and (4) a group member's being only privately committed versus his her being collectively committed qua a group member.

I assume that the person A, about whose attitudes we are speaking, is a member of the group g in question, and I regard the collective acceptance of an attitude as a *we-attitude* (see Tuomela and Balzer 1999; Tuomela 2002a, ch. 5, for this latter assumption). Group membership here need not involve more than that A regards himself or herself as a member of g and typically also that the other members of g tend to regard him or her as a member of g.

In the case of structured groups with positions we could have a case where p is "A ought to perform X in C" for a certain position holder A. Thus, suppose ATT = (acceptance) belief, "Group g accepts as its view that A ought to perform X in C." On the jointness level and using an "internal" perspective we get correspondingly: "We, the members of g, collectively accept that our, that is, g's, belief (view) is that A ought to perform X in C." Group g thus has bound itself to the view that p. It can accordingly be said that g is "view committed" (committed in the way an agent is committed to beliefs) to p. We, the members of g, accordingly are collectively view-committed to p. Thus collective acceptance in the present we-mode case does involve collective commitment to the collectively accepted item in the sense that the members have collectively committed themselves to using content p in their relevant inferences (via the proposition s in which p occurs as an element) and to acting on the basis of its truth when acting as group members. We may also say—equivalently, upon analysis—that the group members are in this case collectively committed to the appropriate employment of the Sellarsian dot-quoted sentence $.s.$, which has the logical form B(we, $.p.$), where

B represents acceptance belief (here B is assumed to apply both to collective agents such as "we" and to single agents such as group members). In the general case the group members would analogously be collectively committed to using the we-attitude-expressing sentence ATT(we, p), or, basically equivalently, they would be collectively ATT-committed to the content p, where ATT commitment involves their being committed in the specific manner that ATT involves in terms of its direction of fit in the context of collective acceptance for the group. In the case of intentions and related attitudes, the direction of fit is world-to-mind; in the case of beliefs and related attitudes it is (typically) mind-to-world; whereas in the case of emotions (except for the possible beliefs entailed by them) the direction of fit is empty (the "null" direction of fit); cf. Searle (2001).

The talk about the commitment to the sentence s concerns the appropriate inferential uses of $.s.$, while the talk about being ATT-committed to p is a more nonlinguistically flavored way of speaking of the commitment at hand.

The group members are collectively committed to using s (or rather $.s.$) not only in their overt theoretical and practical inferences and overt actions appropriately based on such inferences but also in their covert thinking (assuming that some version of the analogy theory of thinking is true so that we can employ either $.s.$ or its counterpart in "Mentalese" in the present context or indeed take $.s.$ also to cover the mental uses). The contexts in which commitment becomes manifested in action are—in my quasi-Sellarsian system—in part based on various world-mind, mind-mind, mind-world rules of thinking (conceptual activities) in the covert case and on world-language, language-language, language-world rules of languaging (conceptual activities) in the overt case. (From here on I do not explicitly use dot-quoted sentences, although they represent my "official" way of presenting the matter—with the reminder that in the most general case we should speak of "thought representations" or something like that instead of using the linguistic term "sentence.")

The group case is in general more "intellectually loaded" than the private case, and the group (that is, "we") is not relevantly comparable with "I." While a single agent can have beliefs in terms of direct confrontation with reality such as rendered by "This is a brown table," in the group case the concept of "we" must enter the picture when conceptualized thinking is involved. Thus in the full-blown group case (where the group functions as a unit) the corresponding formulation in the case of direct confrontation is "We believe that this is a brown table" (or "It is our view that this is a brown table" or something analogous). The idea here is that the subject of the belief must be committed to the content and that this needs grammatical expression as well. At least in all "conative" (action-related) cases such as planning and executing collective action, such reflection of the attitude (e.g., belief) is required (but cf. note 4 for a special, nonreflective and nonconative case).

To elaborate, if a group collectively accepts something as its view, it binds itself to this view and this involves a kind of group pressure—for example, (potential) correction by other members. This gives social normative content to the collective commitment as there then will be normative social expectations concerning what to do. Here the group members are socially committed to each other to do what is required or appropriate. Full-blown collective commitment thus includes social commitment. We also get an argument for a stronger commitment than there is in the case of private beliefs, because the group is involved both in the conceptual content of the attitude and—so to speak—in the holding of the attitude. In the case of private commitment the social normative aspect need not be present: the agent need only bind himself or herself in a descriptive sense—so that he or she, at least if relevantly rational, to some extent persists in holding the attitude.

I now go on to define a number of central notions. My account gives criteria for "modeness" from a third person point of view. However, the actors are assumed in general to act intentionally and thus to know what they are doing under about the right descriptions (that is, the descriptions used in my formulations). In my definitions I will use the phrase "ATT-commitment" to mean the action dispositions relevant to satisfying or upholding ATT, as the case may be. For instance, in the case of ATT = intention, ATT-commitment requires the appropriate use of the accepted proposition s and especially it requires that the members are disposed to try to make true the content of s, here of "We will do X" (where "will" is conatively used). In the case of acceptance belief it entails the disposition to act on the truth of "Our view is p." In all cases the members are committed to using the sentence s in appropriate theoretical and practical inferences. ATT-commitment to p thus means acting in the way required by and appropriate to ATT in order to satisfy p or act on its truth, and so on, as the case may be. Note that s is assumed to express the attitude ATT with content p, thus s will contain ATT and p as its elements, so to speak. For instance, we might have s = ATT(we, p), and here we may say that the primary commitment, related to the direction of fit (as determined by ATT), concerns p. However, there is also the accompanying commitment to use s in appropriate contexts (e.g., in the intention case to assert or to "premise" the sentence "We will do X," when asked about what the participants will do together). Let us recall that when ATT(we, p) has been collectively accepted, the participants have the shared we-attitude WATT toward p (below taken to belong to the realm of concern of the group).

In my analyses the notion of group can be taken to be a weak one that does not entail that it can act (either in an objective or in an intersubjective sense of "can"). However, the members of the group must believe (either in a *de dicto* sense, that is, under a certain description, or in a *de re* sense, that is, in the sense of direct acquaintance with if not all at least some typical members) that they are its members. The group is "we" for them, but this need not be a "conative" we, one leading to collective activities; it can be a "nonconative" we, one relating to commonly experiencing things of common concern. The notion of functioning as a group member is, of course, to be understood in the previously analyzed sense. The group *g* in question can be either a structured or an unstructured one. Here are the basic analyses, to be discussed later:

a1. Agent *A*, a member of group *g*, has a certain attitude ATT with content *p* in the *we-mode* relative to group *g* in a certain situation *C* if and only if *A* has ATT with content *p* and this attitude (and accordingly the sentence *s* expressing it) has been collectively accepted (and is mutually believed) in *g* as *g*'s attitude, and *A* is functioning (that is, experiencing, thinking, and/or acting) qua group member of *g* and is collectively ATT committed to content *p* at least in part for *g* (that is, for the use of *g*) in *C*.

a2. Agent *A*, a member of group *g*, has a certain attitude ATT with content *p* in the *weak we-mode* relative to group *g* in a certain situation *C* if and only if *A* has ATT with content *p* and is functioning qua group member and is also collectively ATT committed to content *p* at least in part for *g* (that is, for the use of *g*) in *C*.

b1. Agent *A*, a member of group *g*, has a certain attitude ATT with content *p* in the (plain) *I-mode* relative to *g* in a certain situation *C* if and only if *A* has ATT with content *p* and, relative to *g*, is privately ATT committed to content *p* and privately functioning as a group member at least in part for himself or herself in *C*.

b2. Agent *A*, a member of group *g*, has a certain attitude ATT with content *p* in the *progroup I-mode* relative to group *g* in a certain situation *C* if and only if *A* has ATT with content *p* and, relative to *g*, is privately ATT-committed to content *p* in part for himself or herself and in part for *g* in *C*.

b3. Agent *A*, a member of group *g*, has a certain attitude ATT with content *p* in the *instrumental I-mode* relative to group *g* in a certain situation *C* if and only if *A* has ATT with content *p* and, relative to *g*, is privately ATT-committed to content *p* at least in part for himself or herself in *C*.

c. Agent *A* has a certain attitude ATT with content *p* in the *private mode* in a certain situation *C* if and only if *A* has ATT and, relative to all groups, is privately ATT committed to content *p* only for himself or herself in *C*.

Action modes can now be accounted for by means of attitude modes and the because-of relation ("because" in general expressing both reason and cause): An action is performed in a certain kind of mode (in the above sense) if and only if it is performed because of an attitude had in that same mode. Furthermore, we can take the psychologically effective reasons for action to be contents of attitudes or, in some special cases, the attitudes themselves (cf. Tuomela 2000a and Searle 2001 for such a view). Then the present account of an action performed because of an attitude in a certain mode amounts to saying that this action is performed for the reason expressed by the content of that attitude or, in some cases, that attitude itself such that the reason is in the mode that the attitude is. In this sense we can speak of, for example, we-mode and I-mode reasons for action.

Let me now motivate the above definitions of the various modes. In all of the above cases, the group member in question may function as a group member—even in cases involving only private commitment. In a1., a2., and b3., he or she is indeed required to function as a group member. In the we-mode cases a1. and a2., it is rather obvious why A is required to function as a group member—otherwise there would not be any point in requiring him or her to act for the group reason assumed to respect the ethos of the group. In the case of b3., the whole point of the notion is to explicate the sense in which one can, so to speak, mimic true, we-mode group activity without really engaging in it from an inner point of view, that is, in terms of one's motivation. Generally speaking, one can overtly act in the right way and even act for the right reason (e.g., group reason) without being truly motivated to the activity in question. The "modes" that I am analyzing here do not as such require that one full-heartedly motivationally adopts the reasons and actions in question. I comment later on the motivational situation after a more detailed discussion of the analyses.

The first of them, a1., gives the most central idea of we-modeness based on collective acceptance with collective commitment. This account makes p satisfy the (*CC*) (as shown in Tuomela 2000a, ch. 2). Paradigm cases of we-mode attitudes are we-intentions involving collective commitment (as in the analysis I have given, e.g., in Tuomela 1995, ch. 3), joint actions based on shared we-intentions, as well as normative, group-binding group attitudes and actions. Agent A may here be committed to functioning as a group member either because he takes the group to be of intrinsic value or because it has instrumental value for him. The former case gives the fullest sense in which he can identify himself with the group.

Criterion a2. is also central, but it does not by itself satisfy the Collectivity Condition. Thus if the attitude in question is to be a properly collective we-mode attitude, (*CC*) must also be taken to be fulfilled. Criterion a2. basically requires in the case of unstructured groups that a member A, when acting as a group member, is disposed to satisfy or, in the case of a collective content such as joint action, to participate in the satisfaction of the goal content and to be collectively committed ("we-committed" might be a better phrase) to it. Collective commitment or we-commitment here means minimally that he is committed and takes the other participants also to be similarly committed and, furthermore, takes this to be mutually believed in the group. In other words, *A* is we-committed to the joint action, say *X*. If *A* is personally committed to *X*, he will be disposed to perform *X* or to participate in its performance, as the case may be. The requirement of collective commitment strengthens the disposition by adding a social aspect, that is, social commitment to others, to it.

The group members' having an attitude, and acting toward its satisfaction in the present kind of case, give unity to the group in terms of the process related to the appropriate use of *s* and of being committed to its content (to *p* in the ATT-related sense, if *s* = ATT(we, *p*)). So the basic argument for a2. goes in terms of functionality, we can say. In the weakest case the participants are not required, for example, to help or pressure each other in this satisfaction process, although that is the case if the participants' having the attitude in question is based on their agreement (and thus strong collective acceptance) to have it. Still, even in the simplest case, agent *A* is assumed to act at least in part for the group, that is, in a way conducive to the relevant group goals and purposes, so that the group is at least in part meant by the agent to be the beneficiary of the satisfaction of ATT.

What the notion of a strong we-modeness, as defined by a1., adds to this is the cognitively more demanding requirement of the collective acceptance of the attitude *as the group's attitude*. Then the CAT formula of note 1 will be satisfied and, by entailment, the Collectivity Condition for ATT will be satisfied. Thus, given that ATT is shared in the group, we are clearly dealing with a shared collective attitude in the we-mode. If there is a conflict with individual motivation and group motivation the latter wins. Thus, when acting as a group member in the we-mode—in sense a1. or in sense a2.—a member will perform the right positional action. When an agent is assumed to act in part for her group, this normally (and unless otherwise specified) means that her motivation for her group is larger than her motivation for herself, and analogously for acting in part for herself.

We note of our analysantia that a1. entails a2.

I wish to allow that a2. be understood also to cover a very weak case of we-modeness. This is the sense in which two or more people experience (e.g., perceive) the same thing together (say a hare jumping in front of them), while nonreflectively and rudimentarily believing or we-believing that, but without necessarily being prompted to act together because of this experience. In this context, the group members must be assumed to "function" in the special sense of experientially focusing on the content *p* in the ATT way (e.g., to visual perceptually focus on there being a hare over there or their focusing on thinking of Vienna, and so on) and also on the others being similarly focused. We can say that an active or occurrent ATT is required instead of a merely dispositional one.[4] However, upon reflection (e.g., when asked about the matter), they are assumed to be disposed to say things like "We shared ATT(p)" (e.g., "We were watching a hare together"), where the sharing amounts to their having the same we-attitude toward p, that is, by their sharing WATT(p). Thus they are in this weak conditional permissibility sense collectively committed to the sentence p and also to "We share WATT(p)." Planning joint action and acting jointly require this much reflective cognition.

Case b1. of the (plain) I-mode is simple, as it contains no group considerations except that A is taken to be a group member, but here is "off duty" and has the attitude and acts as a private person (although technically his or her action may—or may not—satisfy my definition of acting as a group member). There is group-relativity with respect to group g, as acting in the g-context is required and A is allowed to have his or her attitude in the we-mode concerning some other group. Note that definition c. of the private mode makes A absolutely "group free" in that there is no relativity to a group, that is, any group, at all: A is not intentionally functioning as a member of any group. We note the triviality that c. entails b1.

As to b2., A is here, so to speak, trying to satisfy the attitude largely privately for the group or at least in part for the benefit of the group. So even if he is not acting as a group member his attitude involves progroup thinking (no matter how reflective or unreflective it is). When a quantitative measure of motivation is available we may require that in b2. at least half of A's motivation concerns acting so as to serve the group's basic goals and purposes. What happens if there is a conflict between individual and group motivation? Suppose the group goal requires A to perform X while his individual goals would lead him to perform $-X$. Then we have two possibilities: (1) group motivation wins in the case of conflict (qualitative case), or when the utility for A from performing the group-motivated action X is not smaller than the utility accruing from $-X$ (utility-based quantitative case), A will perform X, (2) individual motivation wins in the case of conflict (qualitative case), or when the utility of X is not strictly greater than that accruing from $-X$, A will perform $-X$.

Obviously, (1) is the more group-oriented case. It can be emphasized that even in case (1) we-mode action wins over progroup I-mode action in the sense that, while both modes lead to the performance of X, there is collective commitment in the we-mode case but only private commitment in the I-mode case. As collective commitment adds a social dimension (a participant's commitment to others to perform X, accompanied by their normative expectations that he will perform it), A is disposed more easily to give up (the consummation of) X in the I-mode case than in the we-mode case. We note about our analysantia that b2 is compatible with b1.

The notion of instrumental I-mode b3. is also a simple and obvious one. The person A here takes a strictly instrumental attitude and thinks of her and perhaps only of her own personal goals and purposes. The central idea is that she in a way uses the group as her instrument for her own goals (which as such may be egoistic or altruistic). In order to be able to do that, she acts as a group member although only weakly and not with the right ultimate reason, even if her actions and sayings may be the right ones. What she will do in the kind of situation of conflicting motivation considered above is left open by definition b3., the matter being heavily dependent on context.

Here are some obvious small points:

- Collective ATT commitment to p here entails the commitment to act (at least in part) for the group.
- Acting as a group member in the fullest sense entails acting (at least in part) for the group, forgroupness thus being at least an underlying reason for the action. (However, one may act as a group member in a weaker sense not requiring wholehearted motivational acceptance of forgroupness.)

The following observations indicate that the we-mode is not reducible to the I-mode, nor vice versa. While the we-mode represents group-level thinking and acting and as a concept is an holistic one, ontically it pertains to individuals and does not postulate supraindividual entitics.

Consider next the following claims:

- The I-mode (in any of the senses b1., b2., or b3) does not entail the we-mode (either in the sense a1. or a2.) or its absence.
- The we-mode (in sense a1. or a2.) does not entail the I-mode (in sense b1., b2., or b3.) or the private mode.

Let me briefly discuss these theses in terms of a simple example. Consider an intentional token of an attitude or action X, that qualifies as acting as a group member. Such an action can be identified either broadly or narrowly. The narrow identification involves the reason that serves to make it intentional. This reason will here be either the we-mode reason or the I-mode reason in the sense discussed in the section Introducing Collectivity, that is, it is a reason that the agent intentionally has either as a group member or as private person. Suppose X is waving one's hand and indicates the wide identification of its tokens. Also suppose there are two different narrow identifications of a certain token of X making it both a personal greeting (I-mode reason) and a token of voting (we-mode reason). If a token is a greeting, it is *not* a voting, and conversely. Thus, the above theses should not be understood in this sense.

However, if the present token of hand waving is a token of an I-mode action (greeting), this does not entail that it is also a token of a we-mode action (voting), or vice versa, although there happens to be a coincidence in this particular case. This is the sense in which I mean the above theses to be understood.

Next, there can be mixed cases. For instance, people working in an organization accept to act in the we-mode concerning the basic rules of the organization serving its ethos. In the same context they may act in the I-mode and, for example, compete with each other (cf. competing salesmen in the same business company). Let us jot this down as: Social activities such as group actions and social practices may involve mixtures of we-mode and I-mode actions.

THE PROS AND CONS OF THE WE-MODE

Let me now present some arguments for the need to employ we-mode notions in one's theorizing and for acting on the basis of we-mode attitudes in ordinary social life. The reasons favoring we-mode thinking and acting can be *conceptual* and/or *constitutive* in the sense of showing how the we-mode can serve to constitute new, emergent things, or they can be *rational* in the sense that instrumental or end rationality favors the we-mode over the I-mode, or they can be *factual* in some looser sense than strict rationality involves.

I will concentrate on the we-mode in the senses a1. and a2. In these notions the requirements of *functioning as a group member* and the presence of *forgroupness* and *collective commitment* are central. We may understand functioning as a group member in a strong sense entailing forgroupness and collective commitment (cf. above). In my discussion below I contrast we-mode activities with I-mode activities and, concerning the latter, be mainly concerned with b2. and b3., that is, progroup I-mode and instrumental I-mode, because they come closest to the we-mode and thus are the hardest to defeat.

As demonstrated, forgroupness involves acting so as to involve or produce something for the use of the group, and it thus concerns what is thought by the group members (or in the case of some nondemocratic groups, the group) to be in the interest of the group in the sense of serving at least to some extent the group's and its members' constitutive goals or interests (rational or objective ends) to the extent they are compatible (which is not always the case, for here also the I-mode goals of the members must count). We recall that full-blown acting as a group member requires that the ethos of the group not be violated. This is a kind of cooperation-generating feature. Furthermore, this central feature tends—at least to some extent—to lead to harmonious social relations between group members. The group—regarded as some kind of unity—becomes central in people's activities. This typically (because of the cooperative design of organizations and institutions) requires of the members that their resulting we-mode action, governed by the group's goals and interests, not be *strategic* action vis-à-vis the internal affairs taking place in the group (although it of course may be strategic concerning other groups). However, group goals may of course require coordination and other kinds of strategic action, but that is not my present concern.

In the we-mode case things are being put in the public domain (or rather the group domain) precisely in the sense forgroupness does it: forgroupness licenses the use of collectively accepted ideas in practical inference and action related to the group domain. In other words, we get *shareware* for the group members. In principle, everybody is assumed to contribute to the group good, to do his fair share, but is also allowed to have his piece of the shared group cake (products of the joint enterprise), so to speak. However, this should not based on strategic exchange calculation (or that's the idea anyhow), even if in actual practice also such calculation might be the basis of one's action. In all, the I-mode relates to strategic thinking and to optimizing a person's utilities whereas the we-mode relates to her group's good (goals and interests) and to its prospering, at least typically.

Note, however, that my we-mode explicates are somewhat idealized and that in actual practice they often are mixed with strategic I-mode thinking and acting also in group contexts. Thus, in realistic cases of the performance of a joint action, say *X*, people might do all that *X* requires but they might still harm others and try to satisfy their own private interests perhaps by strategic means (cf. a member secretly plotting against some other members to achieve leadership while still performing his "official" tasks satisfactorily). This is something relating to the *way* or *manner* of doing *X* but not to the achievement of *X* itself. My account (cf. a1. and a2.) really requires acting for the benefit of the group and this does not allow people to harm each other, at least not to any substantial degree. The requirement of acting as a group member for the group guarantees that. One may of course relax the idealized notions a1. and a2. of the we-mode and require harmonious and cooperative thinking and acting only with respect to *X* but not with respect to all the manner aspects related to *X*. However, my current concern is not so much "realism" but finding central conceptual notions required for describing social life.

What about negative consequences that we-mode thinking and acting can have? Without entering this topic properly, let me just remind the reader of various "crowding" effects (cf. "too many cooks spoil the broth"). Of course morally bad things may be involved, too. They are often normatively blocked and sanctioned in actual practice. But here again real life may turn out to be different, if the group does not function morally appropriately concerning its members and concerning other groups.[5]

Given the above prelude, I now try to find some concrete examples that show that in some contexts we-mode thinking and acting is required for successful action.

1. My perhaps strongest case is given by the important class of *normative group properties* such as *normative group beliefs*. Such normative, group-binding properties require we-modeness (see Tuomela 1995, chs. 5–7, for a discussion of normative group attitudes versus non-normative attitudes based on shared "we-attitudes").[6] Normative group beliefs and goals, and the like, are based on some operative members (e.g., a governing board in a corporation) acting for the group and creating its views and goals, and the like. The operative members act as members of the group and for the group, being collectively committed to what they accept for the group. Thus, what they do is in the we-mode. (Also the nonoperative members are similarly collectively committed in cases where they have authorized the operative members to form views for the group, or at least they ought to be so committed.) We-mode attitudes are causally real, and they obviously may affect the persons' actions in ways differing from the causal impact of their relevant I-mode attitudes. The social world abounds with cases like this. Normative group properties are accordingly needed for the correct description and for the explanation of social life, and this gives a necessity argument of the constitutive kind for the need of we-mode thinking and acting in many central contexts.

I wish to emphasize that totally new things emerge or may emerge especially in the present kind of a group context. For instance, there will be we-mode beliefs, which, first, are acceptances and often not genuine psychological beliefs and, second, may involve group standards and norms deriving from the group's basic goals and interests (cf. a group's belief that a supernatural god exists or that the earth is flat). Thus new kinds of beliefs (acceptances) arise and give the people new ways of "seeing the world." There will also be compromise beliefs, which possibly no single member finds privately acceptable (cf., for instance, a case of voting in which no one's first choice is elected). In this kind of case, acting against one's private belief (goal, etc.) in group contexts becomes possible. (Note that one can of course belong to several groups and have different acceptance beliefs relative to those different groups, although this may cause "schizophrenic" difficulties in some cases involving inconsistency.)[7]

To illustrate the difference between we-mode group beliefs and I-mode group beliefs, here understood in terms of the we-attitude analysis as we-beliefs, we discuss the following simple example involving a conflict. Consider a dyad *g* consisting of *a* and *b* and assume both for the case of normative (we-mode) and non-normative (viz., I-mode) group belief (I use "B" for belief): (1) $B_a(p)$ and (2) $-B_b(p)$ (or possibly even $B_b(-p)$).

Beliefs (1) and (2) are I-mode beliefs or, possibly, acceptances. Now, we may, in addition, have in the normative case (but not in the non-normative case, except when we are dealing with the peculiar and problematic case where (1) and (2) really represent beliefs): (3) a and b jointly accept p.

Let me emphasize that in the normative case (3) must be a we-mode joint acceptance belief (and in the mentioned peculiar non-normative case it might also be one). Assuming that the group's "authority system" (roughly: decision-making system) is at work, we then have for the normative case: (4) $B_g(p)$, which says that the group has the normative, group-binding belief that p.

But in the non-normative case construed here as an aggregative, shared we-belief account, which involves only I-mode beliefs, we, on the contrary, get: (5) $-B_g(p)$. Thus we can conclude that we-mode group beliefs and other normative group attitudes exist and can be significantly different from I-mode group beliefs.

Nevertheless, it is possible (at least when (3) happens to hold for both the normative and the non-normative case) that within both approaches: (6) B_g (both a and b jointly accept p as the belief of g).

2. Leaving group beliefs and the feature of forgroupness, let us next consider collective commitment, the other central element in we-modeness. It contains the idea of commitment to the group's projects and joint activities and, more generally, to the group's central institutions and organizations. So, for any such *collective project* as we may call it using this umbrella term, the group members (or at least the operative members in the case of structured groups) are collectively committed to the project, say X. In addition every member (well, at least operative member) is committed to performing his share of the project, and, finally, in the fullest case the members are obligated to their fellow members to perform their parts and are analogously entitled to the others' performances of their parts. Collective commitment in this full sense also entails that the group members ought to help each other in their part performances in the case of unexpected difficulties, given that such helping does not seriously interfere and impede their own part performances. Even coercion can perhaps sometimes be required—in the case of stubborn or lazy group members. (Cf. the practical inference schemas that I have discussed, e.g., in Tuomela 1995, 2000a.) There is also the persistence aspect to collective commitment. The people should keep on performing their tasks also in the face of difficulties and should not give up their commitment at least without consulting others

and getting their permission. Collective commitment also helps to create smoother performance of activities and practices, especially in the long run (cf. iterated collective action dilemma situations with an incentive for free riding).

To show in terms of a concrete example how collective commitment will in some cases lead to success when aggregated personal commitment does not, consider the following example. Suppose some people are in a situation of distress in the Alps after a heavy snowstorm. They need help from outsiders to be able to survive. They might just think of themselves in the I-mode, and being keen on saving their own skins, they could possibly leave one injured person lying on the ground, possibly not even knowing about his situation, when the rescue helicopter arrives. On the other hand, they could act in the we-mode as a group and collectively see to it that everyone gets rescued. In general, collective commitment can yield a better result here than private altruism, supposing that the persons would be altruistic. This contingent assumption may be false, whereas collective commitment can be formed in all cases in principle.

This example indicates what collective commitment, involved in the we-mode, can yield over and above what mere aggregated private commitment (related to the I-mode) gives. Here we-mode thinking and acting is needed to save the lives of all people in distress. The contents of the people's intentions or aims are different (to save one's own life versus to save every group member's life), but the situation still is physically the same in the two cases. (A standard way of comparison is to compare the performance of a task X either as an aggregated I-mode activity or as a we-mode joint action; cf. below.)

3. There are cases of we-mode joint action in which the joint action—a we-mode action—is strictly required and aggregated I-mode action is not sufficient. Thus there are cases of *necessarily* many-person actions such as certain games (e.g., tennis) or rituals (e.g., conferral of doctoral degrees) where we-mode action is required on conceptual grounds; and there are cases of joint activity in which we-mode joint action is required on factual grounds (cf. carrying a heavy table upstairs). There are also institutional cases requiring we-mode action—see 5.) below.

4. Furthermore, even when we-mode acting is not strictly required, there are often specific instrumental gains that we-mode thinking and action can bring forth. As I have elsewhere discussed the matter in length in terms of the gains due to joint action and cooperation, I will be brief here (see Tuomela 1995, ch. 4, and especially the long discussion in chs. 11–13 of Tuomela 2000a). These instrumental or "economy" gains include many kinds of things, most of which are familiar practically to

everyone. In terms of joint action, here assumed to be we-mode action, the participants can often achieve better results as compared with I-mode action. Here we should think not only of the "easy" case of people acting separately but also the case in which they act "jointly" (with the kind of coordination that a task requires) either in the progroup or in the instrumental I-mode sense. One can hypothesize that there are cases in which various economy gains are still to be achieved, for example, in terms of saving energy, resources, and time and in terms of achieving better quality of products and better reliability of performance and higher likelihood of success. We-mode action, with its cooperative atmosphere, can also be more pleasant (in a social sense) than I-mode action. In general, using terminology from game theory, one can argue that in many cases we-mode joint action is both *individually and collectively more rational* than I-mode coordinative interaction and "joint action." (Recall from the first section that in the instrumental I-mode case there can even be a "quasi-agreement" and/or a "quasi-joint" plan that the participants are carrying out in a coordinated fashion—but even in such cases the we-mode may give more "utility.")

5. Social institutions in their intuitive core sense can be regarded as social practices where group members act qua group members in a committed way. This entails that social institutions are basically constituted by we-mode acting. Thus even such economic activities as selling and buying constitutively require some amount of we-mode exchange, even if the institution can tolerate a considerable amount of relevant I-mode activity. More generally, the notion of we-mode thinking and acting is a central building block in the conceptual construction of the social world. (I cannot here use space to argue for this view but refer the reader to Tuomela 2002a.)

6. My account of we-mode cooperation is also relevant to moral and social philosophy, for it can be argued that we-mode cooperation typically must play a big role when accounting for moral and just behavior. While extreme liberalism in social philosophy deals only (or at least primarily) with individual actions and private goals, other forms of liberalism (such as Rawls's) employ collective goal notions, here analyzed as we-mode notions (cf. the notion of a political good or egalitarian liberty). Accordingly, Rawls's (1993) political liberalism regards justice as fairness, as a society-wide collective goal to be achieved by means of cooperative collective action. Arguably, what Rawls means by cooperation is basically full-blown cooperation in the we-mode sense. We-mode cooperation and we-mode attitudes in general are relevant also to other political philosophies relying on collective goals such as common goods—cf. communitarianism, republicanism, and socialism.[8]

Resembling remarks can be made concerning moral theories emphasizing the role of cooperation: in general these theories require each person to do her part, perhaps conditionally on others doing their parts, concerning actions leading to the common good or actions which are good for all. My account of we-mode cooperation is clearly relevant to this kind of moral theory. The distinction between I-mode and we-mode action (especially cooperation) also can be used to clarify the distinction between situations in which each person is treated as a means to the others' ends (I-mode case) and situations where others (or their successes) are, so to speak, part of one's end (typically a we-mode case). A related point is that we-mode cooperation incorporates the idea of being helpful to others, a suitable version of this idea being a generally accepted moral principle. In relation to Rawls's theory of justice, such a principle would say that people are morally obliged to cooperate as long as the cooperation leads to just results. (One can also plausibly argue that no just results can be had if people do not cooperate.)

Furthermore, collective responsibility involves we-mode considerations. As argued in Mäkelä and Tuomela (2002), a group's responsibility for its actions and their consequences entails that the members must be acting in the we-mode to have a share in collective responsibility (at least in the case of responsibility understood as blameworthiness). The group is responsible for a group member's acting as a group member in the we-mode (see Mäkelä and Tuomela 2002). When a group member acts as a group member in the we-mode the group in a sense acts via the member in question. This need not, however, be the full kind of normative, group-binding group action that is involved when the group is taken to act as a group or as a team (see Tuomela 1995, ch. 5, for this stronger notion).

THE WE-MODE AND THE CENTIPEDE

I argue below more tightly for the centrality of the we-mode by means of a problematic example frequently considered in the literature on rational action. I thus concentrate on the kind of collective action dilemma illustrated by the Centipede (a sequential Prisoner's Dilemma). Let me start by a brief consideration of a thesis of motivation concerning in part collective (including we-mode) reasons (I draw on Tuomela 2000a, ch. 11, below):

Motivation Thesis: One may cooperate for one's I-mode reasons, which are allowed to be selfish or other-regarding as well as short-term or long-term, or for one's collective (e.g., we-mode) reasons; these reasons may be in conflict with each other, serving to create collective action dilemmas. There are situations of social interaction in which acting for a collective reason rationally furthers also the I-mode interests (preferences, goals) of the participants. In some such situations I-mode interests cannot be satisfied to a maximal or optimal degree (relative to the possibilities inherent in the situation) or cannot even be satisfied to any degree at all without acting for a collective reason. These situations (also the latter kind of situations) include (1) cases with no conflict between the different participants' I-mode interests or between a participant's I-mode interests and collective interests (cf. for example jointly carrying a table and instances of pure coordination) and (2) collective action dilemmas, that is, instances involving a conflict between I-mode and collective interests (preferences, goals).

Case (1) does not here need discussion, as there is no conflict-inducing competition between I-mode and collective (e.g., we-mode) reasons here. I thus concentrate on subthesis (2) and have chosen to discuss the case of the Centipede. I argue below that in some circumstances it is rational for the participants to form and act on we-mode goals (and for we-mode reasons) and that indeed sometimes it is necessary for an individually and/or collectively optimal result.

Let us now consider the Centipede. Let me start by presenting Hume's often-cited example illustrating the difficulties in cooperation:

> Your corn is ripe today; mine will be so tomorrow. 'Tis profitable for us both that I shou'd labour with you today, and that you shou'd aid me tomorrow. I have no kindness for you, and know that you have as little for me. I will not, therefore, take any pains on your account; and should I labour with you on my account, I know I shou'd be disappointed, and that I shou'd in vain depend upon your gratitude. Here then I leave you to labour alone: You treat me in the same manner. The seasons change; and both of us lose our harvests for want of mutual confidence and security. (1965 III.II.v)

We can ask whether it is rational for "you" and "me" to cooperate. Since a "collective action dilemma" is involved here, it is far from clear that it is. This situation actually has the preference structure of a Centipede, viz. a sequential Prisoner's Dilemma. That is, the following preference ranking applies antecedently for the "me" of the joint outcomes: (1) I do not help you but you help me; (2) I help you and you help me; (3) I do not help you and you do not help me; (4) I help you but you do not help me. "You" has an analogous ranking. (The Centipede has been widely discussed in the literature; see e.g., Bicchieri 1993; Hollis 1998; and Tuomela 2000a, ch. 11.)

It is rather obvious that in this kind of situation the players, you and I, can make an agreement to help each other and, in the general case, to split the result in a fair way. If we indeed succeed in acting on such a plan (which is far from being self-enforcing), we are dealing with cooperative agreement-based joint action. If indeed the players sincerely and with collective commitment obey the agreement in question, they act in a we-mode sense, and then the considerations presented in our discussion of the I-mode notions b1. and b2. in the section Functioning as a Group Member are pertinent. It was argued there that the we-mode "wins" over both the progroup I-mode and the instrumental I-mode.

The Centipede has a wide range of applications. For one thing, it can be taken to represent cases of conditional promising—for example, in case one of the farmers has promised to help the other one provided the latter first helps him. Furthermore, it seems that repeated Centipede cases can represent conflicts resembling those in the mid-East between Jews and Palestin-ians and with repeated, but failing attempts (which may on some occasions lead far to the right in the Centipede tree; cf. below) to achieve lasting peace. From a formal point of view, the Centipede is basically a Prisoner's Dilemma structure with several ordered choices and, game-theoretically speaking, with perfect information. It can still be regarded as a single rather than a repeated game, although it strategically and psychologically bears some resemblance to the latter. I argue below that there are different and, indeed, incompatible rational solutions to it (see Tuomela 2000a, ch. 11, for a detailed discussion). Basically, if one is rational in a short-term sense, which is the sense of rationality used in standard game theory, it is rational to defect immediately. This can be shown by means of the "backward induction" argument, for instance (cf. the works cited above) or by other arguments (cf. below).

To keep things technically simple, I now discuss a small Centipede that has only three choice points (the discussion below connects to the treatment in Bicchieri 1993):

$$
\begin{array}{ccc}
s_1 & S & s_2 \\
a \to & b \to & c \to (2, 3) \\
|d_1 & |D & |d_2 \\
(2, 0) & (1, 2) & (3, 1)
\end{array}
$$

The "straight on" choices are labeled s_1, S, and s_2 (from left to right). The "down" choices are labeled d_1, D, and d_2.

We assume that the players have a correct mutual belief about the structure of the game (available choices, information sets, and payoffs or given utilities). Each player is assumed to be rational in the (formal) sense of maximizing his expected utilities. Going beyond this, I distinguish between two substantially different ways of being rational, involving a distinction between a short-term and a long-term, trust-involving way of being rational. I argue that collective reasons for action can not only matter but also that they can rationally justify a change from defection (going down) to cooperation (going straight). Thus, short-term rational and long-term rational players will play in an opposite way.

Suppose I am a "distrustful" rational agent (player 1) at node a. By this I mean just that, for one reason or other, I do not have a strong expectation that the other player will go straight if I decided to start by going straight. How should I reason? Suppose I take player 2 to be similarly rational. Then I gather that I should go down at a. Why? This would give me a better payoff than going straight, since I believe that 2 is rational and believe he thinks that I am too. Thus, if 2 were now at node b he would move down, thinking that I would go down at c in any case were I to find myself there. Analogously, player 2, were he at node b, would think that it is rational for him to move down because he thinks that player 1, qua a rational person, would move down at c. (See Tuomela 2000a, ch. 11, for a detailed technical argument using this idea for proving the short-term rationality of moving down.)

Thus, a merely short-term rational person will always play down. This is based on his judgment that playing down gives a higher expected utility than playing straight. That this is so depends on his view that the other player is also acting short-term rationally. Things would be different if he could trust the other person and believe that he is acting long-term rationally and is going to go straight in the next round. However, the kind of solution in which the players reach the very end of the game is reasonable and collectively rational. It is also individually rational if the final outcome is fairly divided. Of course, if the players were disposed to bind themselves to cooperation, they could make an agreement always to continue the game until its very end. Here we do not, however, go to this extreme, but investigate other possibilities, which do not rely on binding agreements.

More specifically, the central underlying idea here is that players acting rationally in the long-term sense act as if they had as their shared goal to reach at least the last decision point in the Centipede (node c in our example). They need not be assumed to have agreed upon the goal or have promised to cooperate. They need not even properly be said to have that goal, but from a behavioral or overt point of view they would be acting in the right way, that is, both choosing straight, up to that point. (I later discuss the last move in the game.)

How can such trust-based long-term rational acting be given a theoretical justification? The players are still assumed to maximize their expected utility, with the (private) utilities as given in the game description. For long-term rationality to lead to where it is supposed to lead, each player must expect that the other one will cooperate (will choose straight), given that one cooperates (chooses straight). The expectation may be a flat-out belief or it may just be a probabilistic estimate high enough to make the expected utility of moving straight exceed the expected utility of moving down. We can correspondingly assume that each player intends to go straight, given that (he expects that) the other one will (or is likely to) go straight, this being shared knowledge among them. This is a kind of trust aspect concerning the cooperativeness of the other player. As is demonstrated, such mutual expectation will serve to make reciprocal cooperation (choosing straight) profitable for both.

The motives underlying cooperation (going straight) here may, in the case of both players, be based on selfish considerations, because both players will gain the more the farther to the right in the game tree they arrive. We can speak of "trust-rationality" or long-term rationality in the present long-term case concerning a sequence of moves. It is rationality in the sense of long-term maximization of expected utility (EU) related to a longer sequence of moves (as opposed to the local maximization involved in short-term rationality) and it also involves that a long-term rational player takes the other player to cooperate (move straight) with sufficiently high probability. Note that the experimentation with the straight choice here is of course possible if a player can assume that the other player responds similarly (that is, to a straight choice with a straight choice) at least with some suitable probability (cf. below). Thus, long-term rationality will have a practical effect only in this case—if a rational player thought that the other would definitely go down at the next node he himself would have to go down at the present node.

We again face the problem of explaining how a rationally (here: long-term rationally) acting person can choose straight. First, if the agents strive to achieve at least the last decision point, each gets an individually clearly better result than if the game ended at the first node (recall also the money game, for instance). This long-term result can be taken to make it justified and rational to try out risky means (e.g., choosing s_1), which in other conditions may be irrational in our example. The main problem here is to justify the rationality of the first straight move, and the basic justificatory idea accordingly is this: the first player is here assumed at least tentatively to give up the assumption that the other player is acting short-term rationally and instead to test whether the other player in the present situation is, or can be induced to be, a conditional cooperator like himself. This he does by choosing s_1—signaling thereby his cooperative attitude—and by continuing to go straight if the other player responds similarly. By choosing straight, the first player intends to indicate to the other player that he is disposed to continue the game to achieve a better result, that is, is using the strategy to cooperate if the other one cooperates. If the other player accepts this "offer" of mutual continuation, the players start to trust each other as cooperators, and the game gets going in the desired direction. Note that the players need not be cooperators in any intrinsic sense, for the game of Centipede itself contains the incentive for the players to try to go on with the game—the farther in the game they get, the more they can gain.

Consider our example game. Here we can have, with two different p-values, for a long-term rational player 1:

i) $EU(s) = p(S/s_1) \, u(C) = 0.9 \times 3 = 2.7$ (> 2 while $EU(d) = 2$).
ii) $EU(s) = p(S/s_1) \, u(C) = 0.6 \times 3 = 1.8$ (< 2).

It is assumed here that at the last decision point c a long-term rational player chooses to go down (the case where she continues to go straight will be commented on below). Case i) clearly makes it rational to go straight. In contrast, case ii) does not warrant continuing the game but recommends down choice. To recall, player 1 is justified in making the probability high enough for making the choice of s_1 rational for the following reason. He thinks that the possible gain compared to the loss (from going down) is sufficiently great to warrant trying to get to point c (or the last decision point, more generally) and believes that the other player also thinks similarly. Thus he experimentally tries to confirm his belief about the other player and chooses s_1. If the other player responds by also going straight, his belief has been confirmed. In the first step, however, the only justification available is the shared relative gain idea. (The case where our agent reasons in terms net utilities is discussed in Tuomela 2000a, ch. 11, where also other more technical issues are treated.)

Let us now consider the end of the game. Up to the last decision point mere trust-involving long-term rationality of the players suffices for a rational solution (that is, for arriving to that decision point), without changing the structure of the game. At that point we arguably need either collective or altruistic considerations that at least make going straight subjectively as attractive as going down. The basic collective source of utility that may be operating here is that the players may value their group getting a higher utility, even at the penalty of a decrease in their own private utility. This collective source may be either (1) an I-mode preference with a collective content (a progroup I-mode reason) or (2) a we-mode preference (a we-mode reason in sense a1. or a2. of the section Functioning as a Group Member). Altruism (regarded as an I-mode reason concerned with the other player's welfare) may also be operating here; and if something resembling promises concerning the continuation of the game have been made, moral or quasi-moral reasons come into play.

The central reason for the need of a collective or social factor here is that a player at the last node (node c in our example) cannot move right merely on the basis of long-term rationality, as long-term considerations and trust cannot play a role in this choice. Our player must think other-regardingly or collectively. We suppose that the game has been defined either directly in terms of given utilities or in terms of objective payoffs (e.g., money), such that the given utilities directly reflect these objective payoffs. An other-regarding (e.g., altruistic) choice at the last choice point would mean going straight (and it would mean a change of the game). For instance, the player's other-regarding, broadly altruistic reason here could be expressed in the form "I move straight because I want you, being poorer than I, to benefit." We can even include I-mode goals with some impersonal collective content ("My straight choice would benefit our group") in our first type of collective and social reasons as long as they do not amount to the adoption of the we-mode—cf. the progroup I-mode sense b2.—of the The Varieties of the We-Mode and the I-Mode.

The second type of collective-social reason would be reason based on we-mode attitudes, especially we-mode goals. In this case a player can value group utility and try to act together with the other(s) so that the group's preferences are optimally satisfied. For instance he could act on a shared group goal as expressed by the following rationale: "I move straight because that gives 2 + 3 (=5) 'utiles' to our group, whereas the down choice would give only 3 + 1 (= 4). Regrettably, I lose one utile myself, but I can tolerate this in view of our collective gain."

We recall from our definitions of the various modes from the section The Varieties of the We-Mode and the I-Mode that group considerations related to the social expectations involved in collective commitment may well tilt the balance in favor of the collectively valued action (here going straight), even if it goes against an agent's given utilities—assumed here not to contain the commitment factor. The given utilities were formed prior to the rise of the social obligations and expectations that the participants' agreement or shared plan situationally created. One might even suggest that in the *we-mode* case (a1. or a2.) there need be no change when going from given to final utilities, but only a change in the strength of commitments due to collective and social factors (social expectations and perhaps obligations). The other way to go is to include the impact of commitments on one's utilities and say that there is a change in utilities due to the mentioned social and collective factors.

The *progroup* I-mode may also lead to cooperation at the last node, but remember that as our agent is lacking social motivation and, *ceteris paribus*, that may alternatively lead him on balance to choose down. A player acting in the *instrumental* I-mode is likely to defect at the last node.[9]

In real life, genuine acting for altruistic reasons clearly seems to occur (see, e.g., the anecdotal and experimental evidence given in Sober and Wilson 1998). There seems to be also acting for we-mode or group reasons (cf., e.g., van Vugt, Snyder, Tyler, and Biel 2000). Each of these kinds of unselfish reasons can occur in the context of cooperation and each of them may be required for rational cooperation on some occasions. Recent experimental evidence for the actual occurrence of reasons of both kind (1) and kind (2) is to be found in Kollock's (1998) experiments concerning PD; this evidence supports also the Centipede situation, which is an extended PD.

Long-term rationality may solve the alleged conflict between rationality and the s_1 choice mentioned above. There is a conflict when rationality is taken to be short-term rationality, but that need not be the case if long-term rationality is involved. There are thus different rationality contents involved here. One may think that players have or may have different rationality-related personality features. One person is more trustful of others than another and can thus afford to be more long-term rational than the other. This dispositional difference of degree may be exhibited as a qualitative difference in choices: the straight choice will be made instead of going down.

Let me finally point out that highly similar results can be obtained for the game of Chicken as well, keeping in mind the roles of commitment and threat in this game. Considering the extended form of a simple two-person example of Chicken, long-term rational players acting for a collective reason can rationally achieve the collective outcome (C, C) in it, whereas short-term rational players will settle for the only equilibrium (C, D) of this game.[10]

CONCLUSION

In this chapter I have tried to clarify the ideas of thinking and acting as a group member (the intuitive idea of the we-mode) versus as a private person (the intuitive idea of the I-mode). Various analytic notions of the we-mode and the I-mode were developed in the chapter and argued for. In the latter half of the chapter, the function of the we-mode was investigated in various contexts. As basically all group contexts typically involve we-mode thinking and acting and often are constituted by the we-mode, the topic is very rich. Several cases where the we-mode is required or is (or can be) instrumentally useful were presented. The case of group attitudes such as normatively group-binding group attitudes (e.g., beliefs) was argued to be one of the cases basically constituted by we-mode thinking and acting; and the same goes for typical cases of joint action. Cooperation in dilemma situations can be brought about in terms of we-mode action in typical cases, although that may not be needed on instrumental grounds. Various institutional cases also offer examples of we-mode thinking and acting, which not only is instrumentally and functionally useful but "constitutively" required. The very notion of a social institution is a case in point.[11]

ACKNOWLEDGMENTS

I wish to thank Kaarlo Miller, Pekka Mäkelä, Raul Hakli, Maj Tuomela, and the audiences at the colloquium "Action Theory and Social Ontology" (University of Miami, January 2002) and at the workshop on action theory held at the Swedish Collegium for Advanced Study in the Social Sciences (Uppsala, May 2002) for comments.

NOTES

1. Collective acceptance must be assumed to satisfy the following "CAT formula" (discussed, e.g., in Tuomela and Balzer 1999, p. 181):

> *Collective Acceptance Thesis (CAT)*: A sentence *s* is *collective* (or *collective-social*) in a primary "constructivist" sense in a group *g* if and only if the following is true for *g*: a) the members of *g* collectively accept *s*, and b) they collectively accept *s* if and only if *s* is correctly assertable.

In the analysans a) is the assumption of the categorical collective acceptance of *s* while clause b) is a partial characterization of the kind of collective acceptance that is needed here.

In logical terms using Forgroup for forgroupness and CA for collective acceptance,

> (*CAT**) Sentence *s* is *collective* (or *collective-social*) in a primary constructivist sense in *g* if and only if Forgroup(CA(g, s) & (CA(g, s) $\leftrightarrow$ s)).

Here we are dealing with the we-mode case provided the group is also taken to be collectively committed (CoCom) to the accepted sentence (proposition). So, from a theoretician's point of view we have the description Forgroup(CA(g, s)) & CoCom(g, s), where *s* may be ATT(we, *p*), with "we" being the participants' pronoun for *g*. Then *s* expresses a we-attitude. Collective acceptance amounts to coming to hold and holding an appropriate we-attitude (belonging either to the intention family or to the belief family of attitudes) and to acting on that attitude (see Tuomela and Balzer 1999 and Tuomela 2002a, ch. 5, for discussion).

2. However, one may also take broader view of the notion of collective content. Thus, Miller and Tuomela (2001, p. 6) define collective content as follows:

> Goal *P* of an agent *X* has *collective content* if and only if (*X* believes that there is a mutual belief that) *P* is satisfied for *X* if and only if it has to be satisfied for a plurality of *X*'s group members sharing *P*.

In the sense of this definition, the satisfaction of a collective attitude (here goal) necessarily involves collective content. However, it is to be kept in mind that the very action bringing about the satisfaction of the attitude can be a singular action or state rather than an action involving (in the sense of acting together) several persons. The latter is also part and parcel of we-mode collective attitudes in the following sense, recalling that we-mode collective attitudes involve at least some degree of collective commitment to the content by the group. We can now distinguish between collective action realizing the collective commitment in question, viz., an action by which the participants try to see to it that the goal comes about (or is maintained, as the case may be). Let us call this a c-action, and distinguish it clearly from the actual concrete means-action (m-action) that serves (normally causally) to bring about the goal-state. My suggestion is to treat c-action as belonging to underlying presuppositions rather than to content. Nevertheless, c-action, which is we-mode acting together understood in a broad sense, is needed in the case of full-blown we-mode collective attitudes.

We have noticed that if the correct satisfaction belief for a goal requires that it is to be achieved together by many persons, then it is a collective goal. But as seen, if this means the m-action, the present criterion gives a sufficient but not a necessary condition for collectivity. The satisfaction of the aforementioned CAT formula of note 1, nevertheless, gives both a necessary and sufficient condition for collectivity, as shown in Tuomela (2000a) and Tuomela and Balzer (2002). The CAT formula is more successful basically because it (implicitly) deals with c-actions rather than m-actions in the above sense.

3. Sellars developed his philosophy of language and philosophy of mind in numerous papers since the late 1940s. For the purposes of this chapter, Sellars (1963a), (1969), and (1981) are especially central.

4. The present idea of weak, experiential we-modeness can also be formulated as follows by explicitly relating the group members, in the simple dyadic case below A and B, to each other:

> A and B function in a we-mode relation and form a "we" (however temporarily) if and only if there is an ATT and a content p such that they actively share ATT toward the same content p and are collectively ATT committed to p, and they are in addition disposed to express their attitudes in effect by "We share WATT(p)" —for example, when asked about the matter.

Here active sharing of WATT(p) entails that both agents have ATT(p) and focus attentively to their having it and believe in an active, occurrent way that the other one has ATT(p) and also that they both mutually believe that. (This kind of weak we-modeness seems pertinent to a face-to-face relationship.)

I would like to refer the reader to Schutz's view of the we-relation, which bears intuitive similarity to what has just been said. According to him, "[t]he face-to-face relationship in which the partners are aware of each other and sympathetically participate in each other's lives for however short a time we shall call the 'pure We-relationship'" (Schutz 1967, p. 164). The pure we-relationship is to be distinguished from "living in the We-relationship": "Moreover, while I am living in the We-relationship, I am really living in our common stream of consciousness" (p. 167). "The pure We-relationship involves our awareness of each other's presence and also the knowledge of each that the other is aware of him" (p. 168). In his later work he gives an example:

> Among those objects which we experience in the vivid present are other people's behavior and thoughts. In listening to a lecturer, for instance, we seem to participate immediately in the development of his stream of thought. But—and this point is obviously a decisive one— our attitude in doing so is quite different from that we adopt in turning to our stream of thought by reflection. We catch the Other's thought in its vivid presence and not *modo praeterito;* that is, we catch it as a "Now" and not as a "Just Now." (Schutz 1962, p. 173)

In colloquial terms, reflection is always "one step" behind vividly present experience. There is not space here to properly comment on Schutz's view. Let me just say that his otherwise interesting account is marred by a lack of a proper account of (propositional) mental states and their conditions of satisfaction. For a modern reader terms like "stream of consciousness" cry out for analysis.

5. Collective thinking and the emphasis on group life when discussing social issues seem to be somewhat of an emotional issue even in academic discussion. That kind of aversion of course should not count when discussing philosophical and theoretical problems. Of course, holists and individualists alike should not forget, for example, the danger of totalitarianism on the national level. It is a cliché to say that the names Hitler, Mussolini, and Stalin in our recent history give us sad examples of group thinking, various religions with a totalitarian "ambition" or "aim" may also qualify, and the same goes for football hooliganism and other similar phenomena on the level of smaller groups. The light and the dark sides of group thinking are all available, and it is up to the people to raise their children in such a way that totalitarian disasters in the future will be avoided.

6. Let me here state the analysis of normative group beliefs that I have given in Tuomela (1992a) and (1995), without here giving an analysis of the involved notions in this context:

Group g *accepts* ("believes") that p in a normative, group-binding sense in the social and normative circumstances C if and only if in C there are operative members $x_1, \ldots, x_m$ of g in respective positions $P_1, \ldots, P_m$ such that

a) the agents x_1, b. . . , x_m, when they are performing their (we-mode) tasks in their positions $P_1, \ldots, P_m$ and due to their exercising the relevant authority system of g (intentionally) jointly accept p and because of this exercise of the authority system they ought to continue to accept and positionally believe it;

(b) there is a mutual knowledge among the operative members $x_1, \ldots, x_m$ to the effect that (a);

(c) because of (a), the (full-fledged and adequately informed) nonoperative members of g tend to tacitly accept—or at least ought to accept—p, as members of g;

(d) there is a mutual knowledge in g to the effect that (c).

Here the authority system means the group's system of joint intention formation, which also authorizes the operative members to act for the group. Joint acceptance in this context requires explicit or implicit agreement making, which entails a group-binding obligation. For instance, the members of a board may vote or otherwise jointly decide or agree on a certain view p for g.

In general, joint acceptance—a special case of collective acceptance—amounts to coming to hold and holding a relevant we-attitude. It can be a we-mode we-intention or a we-mode we-belief or both. The present kind of "positional" account applies also to group action and group attitudes. (See Tuomela 1995, chs. 5–7, and, for belief versus acceptance, Tuomela 2000c; cf. Gilbert 1987, 1989 for a somewhat similar account of group beliefs concerned with unstructured groups.)

Groups can have beliefs also in weaker group-binding senses that, however, all require collective commitment to the accepted item. Thus there are group beliefs based on the participants leading each other to have normative participation expectations. These normative expectations are personal expectations having the objective justification coming from the others' promising-like behavior (language use is not required here, though). There can also be group-binding group beliefs that are not based on agreements or promises or other such normative devices, but even in those cases, the collective commitment involved in collective or joint acceptance will be the binding force (see Tuomela 2003 for a discussion of such group beliefs).

7. The discrepancy between group beliefs and private or personal beliefs and other attitudes is a well-known phenomenon, which I have here formulated as a kind of discrepancy between the we-mode and the I-mode. In addition to my work reported in Tuomela (1992a) and (1995), the analyses by Gilbert (1987, 1989), which I have commented on in the aforementioned places, Pettit's (2001) recent discussion is worth mentioning. Pettit concentrates on simple voting type of situation, where the group's view is determined in terms of a simple rule such as the majority principle. He shows that in such cases the group members' reasons for a conclusion (view) may lead them, for instance, to collectively accept a view the (deductively sufficient) reasons for which they collectively reject (see, e.g., Pettit 2001, p. 112). He argues that an organized group should be consistent and "collectivize" its reasons. This is quite acceptable. However, one wonders why Pettit has chosen to deal mainly with voting types of cases in which no genuine group processes (such as group discussion, negotiating, and bargaining) occur. In normal cases it is very easy to show that group discussion often leads to compromises that do not represent any member's first choice. Furthermore, there are problems with Pettit's discussion. His first two major examples do not work as they should, assuming that all relevant information has to be taken into account by the agents in their reasoning. They deal with deductive reasoning, where, first, the group members are assumed to infer, if they find the premises true, in terms of the same deductively sufficient reasons for a conclusion. His argument forgets, however, that in this kind of restricted case obviously all the premises (which are sufficient for the conclusion only jointly) must be simultaneously true. However, Pettit incorrectly applies the majority vote principle to the single premises to get his discrepancy result. When correctly applied to the conjunction of the premises the majority principle does not give the claimed discrepancy result. (This note owes to comments by Kaarlo Miller.)

8. In Tuomela (2000a) I discuss Rawls's (1971, 1993) theory of political liberalism and argue that it involves we-mode collective goals and we-mode cooperation.

9. It can be noted here that corresponding to our calculations for a (merely) long-term rational player we can also calculate EU values for a collectively long-term rational player. To make our numerical example work properly, let us change the values (2, 3) for the end node to (2½, 3). Then, using our first way of calculating expected utilities, it becomes rational for player 1 to choose straight until the very end of the game—as compared with the strategy of going down at the first choice point. I would like to emphasize that a consideration of a collective reason in a sense is embedded here, for player 1 would otherwise (that is, when acting selfishly) have chosen the strategy to go straight up to c and then go down, that strategy having a higher expected utility than the one requiring her to go straight at c. (Analogous considerations can be presented for the general case and for player 2.)

10. The social psychological "Social Identity Theory" (or the "Self-Categorization Theory," as its later version is called) contains ideas somewhat similar to those expressed in this chapter, although my emphasis has not been on the social identity of persons, the main concern of Social Identity Theory (cf. Turner, Hogg, Oakes, Reicher, and Wetherell 1987). This theory defines "social identity" as those aspects of an individual's self-concept that are based upon social group or category membership together with emotional, evaluative and other psychological correlates—for example, the self defined as male, European, Londoner, and so on. The most distinctive theo-

retical feature of the self-categorization analysis of group formation and group cohesion is the idea that these depend upon the perception of self and others as a cognitive unit (in contrast to nonmembers) within the psychological frame of reference, and not upon mutual interpersonal attraction and need satisfaction (Turner et al. 1987, p. 64).

The basic—and recently empirically debated—hypotheses of this theory (according to Turner et al. 1987, p. 36) are, first, that people are motivated to establish a positively valued distinctiveness for groups with which they identify in contrast to relevant out-groups, and, second, that when social identity in terms of some group membership is unsatisfactory, members will attempt to leave that group (psychologically or in reality) to join some more positively distinct group and/or make their existing group more positively distinct. According to the self-categorization theory, the group has psychological reality in the sense that there is a specific psychological process, that is, self-categorization or self-grouping, which corresponds to and underlies the distinctive features of group behavior (p. 66). This suggests that acting and functioning as a group member is closely related to taking oneself to have a certain kind of group identity in the sense of the self-categorization theory (which sense is somewhat too vague to allow a more precise comparison).

11. After finishing the present chapter, I have investigated in more detail some of the topics dealt with above in Tuomela and Tuomela (2003). In that paper several kinds of acting as a group member are distinguished (the notion used in the present chapter is called acting as a group member in the standard sense) and the kind of social commitment that full-blown collective commitment contains is investigated in depth. As a consequence, some minor changes in the explications of the I-mode notions b1., b2., and b3. presented in this chapter are called for. Readers interested in such refinement should consult the new joint paper.

5

Joint Action: From Individualism to Supraindividualism

Frederick F. Schmitt

In everyday life we casually say that people act jointly. Mary and Jill, we say, have taken a walk together. In giving an illuminating paraphrase of such an attribution of joint action, we wish to make the attribution come out literally true. This wish is one motor driving almost all recent analyses of joint action. It seems to exclude a *supraindividualist* account of joint action. That is, it seems to exclude an account on which Mary and Jill act jointly just in case the pair, Mary and Jill, is a single agent that acts, in a sense closely analogous to that in which an individual agent acts. For it does not seem that there is any supraindividual agent, the pair, Mary and Jill. I too doubt that there is a supraindividual agent, and so I feel the need for an analysis that avoids treating Mary and Jill's joint action as the action of a single agent, the pair. My problem is that I have been unable to find such an analysis. The failures of attempts at such analysis seem to force us to a supraindividualist account. My burden in this chapter is to make a partial case along these lines for a supraindividualist account.[1] One upshot will be that attributions of joint action are not literally true.

To preserve the literal truth of joint action talk, we naturally start with *strict individualism*: a joint action attribution simply conjoins a number of attributions of singular actions and admissible attitudes to individuals, together with attributions of admissible relations between these attitudes and actions (e.g., S. Miller 2001a).[2] "Singular" here is a contrary (though perhaps not the contradictory) of "joint": a *singular* action is a nonjoint action of an individual. (I add the qualification "perhaps not a contradictory" because there may be nonsingular individual actions that are not joint but rather *participant* actions—actions participating in a joint action. I say "perhaps" to avoid begging the question against strict individualism:

129

whether participant actions are nonsingular is one point at issue between strict individualism and opposing views—a strict individualist will maintain that a joint action is made of singular participant actions.) An *admissible* attitude or relation is one that can be fully characterized without employing collectivity concepts like "joint" or "group." On strict individualism, individuals *A* and *B* perform a certain joint action just in case each performs certain singular actions, has certain singular attitudes (beliefs, ends, intentions), and these actions and attitudes are related by approved relations. "Mary and Jill take a walk together" says no more than that Mary walks (singularly), and Jill walks, and each does so in the presence of, or as a consequence of, admissible mental attitudes.

Alternatives to strict individualism may deviate from it in any of several ways. According to strict individualism, a joint action attribution is a conjunction of attributions of singular actions and admissible attitudes to individuals, together with attributions of admissible relations between these attitudes and actions. One alternative to strict individualism would deviate from it by referring to actions without the qualification "singular." A second alternative would refer to attitudes or relations without the qualification "admissible." A third alternative would refer in a special way—"plurally"—to singular actions and admissible attitudes.[3] (If we used "singular" in contrast with "plural" in "plural reference," then the word would mean something different from "singular" as we have so far used it.) Let me describe these alternatives in a bit more detail, starting with views quite close to strict individualism.

As far as *actions* are concerned, one may say that a joint action attribution is a conjunction of attributions of actions without the restriction that they are *singular* individual actions. This remains close to strict individualism if at the same time one avoids referring to action types that entail joint action (Bratman 1992, 1993a). Call this *all-but-action individualism*.

As far as *attitudes* and *relations* are concerned, one may say that a joint action attribution is a conjunction of attributions, retaining the strict individualist limitation to singular actions of individuals but dropping the "admissible" qualification on attitudes and relations. This view remains close to strict individualism if it allows only those inadmissible attitudes that are so because their content *mentions* collectivities. The view makes a more substantial departure from strict individualism if it allows as well *nonsingular attitudes*—attitudes that are not recognized by traditional individual motivation theory. For example, the account may refer to nonsingular reasons possessed by individuals—*participant* reasons individuals have in virtue of membership in a group or other collectivity (Gilbert 1989). Or the account might refer to "we"-attitudes (or irreducibly collective attitudes) of individuals, and not just "I"-attitudes (Tuomela 1995 and Searle 1995). Roughly, a "we"-attitude is an attitude of an individual that, in the presence of like attitudes of other individuals, amounts to a joint attitude. These individual attitudes are nonsingular but individualist in the sense that an individual can possess one even if no one else possesses any related attitude. These alternative accounts fit under the heading: *all-but-attitude individualism*.

For a greater departure from strict individualism than the foregoing views, one may characterize joint action in terms, not of nonsingular attitudes of individuals that together add up to joint attitudes, but directly in terms of *nonindividual*—that is, *joint*—attitudes, together with their relations to some action or other, where it is left unspecified whether the action is singular or joint, or the agent of the action is an individual or nonindividual. For example, one might characterize joint action as an action that is done from a joint commitment to act (Gilbert 1996, 2000). This account leaves it unspecified whether the relevant action is singular or joint and leaves it to the relation of the action to the joint commitment to make the action joint. This *nonindividual attitude* account, as we may call it, entails supraindividualism *if* the nonindividual attitudes, relations, and actions to which it refers suffice for supraindividual agency and action. But a nonindividual attitude account need not entail supraindividualism.

I doubt whether an account of joint action short of supraindividualism can succeed. To substantiate this doubt would require covering all of the alternative accounts—an endeavor beyond my means here. Instead, I sample a strict individualist account, Seumas Miller's, and an all-but-action individualist account, Michael Bratman's. I give these a thorough review. The troubles with these accounts will suggest a supraindividualist view.

STRICT INDIVIDUALISM: DOES JOINT ACTION ENTAIL INTERDEPENDENT SINGULAR ACTIONS?

On a strict individualist account, an attribution of joint action is a conjunction of attributions of singular actions and admissible attitudes to individuals, together with admissible relations between attitudes and actions. It is natural to think of a joint action as a conjunction of *interdependent interpersonal actions*: individual participants A and B act jointly just in case A performs some singular action x and B performs some singular action y, and x and y are interdependent. Here we may think of interdependence as *counterfactual* interdependence: if A didn't perform x, B wouldn't perform y, and conversely.[4]

As natural as this idea may be, interdependence is neither necessary nor sufficient for joint action. The objection to sufficiency in particular forces a retreat from strict individualism to all-but-action individualism. There is a very long story to tell about this, and it is worth telling in detail, because it reveals the poverty of strict individualism. I work here with the most richly developed strict individualist account, Seumas Miller's (2001a). According to

Miller's account, a joint action consists of interdependent actions with little or no conflict. Miller reads "little or no conflict" as "under a collective end."

> *A*'s individual action *x* and *B*'s individual action *y* in situation *s* constitute a joint action if and only if:
>
>   (1) *A* intentionally performs *x* in *s* (and *B* intentionally performs *y* in *s*);
>   (2) *A* *x*s in *s* if and only if (he believes) *B* has *y*ed, is *y*-ing or will *y* in *s* (and *B* *y*s in *s* if and only if (he believes) *A* has *x*ed, is *x*-ing or will *x* in *s*);
>   (3) *A* has end, *e*, and *A* *x*s in *s* in order to realize *e* (and *B* has *e*, and *B* *y*s in *s* in order to realize *e*);
>   (4) *A* and *B* each mutually truly believes that *A* has performed, is performing or will perform *x* in *s* and that *B* has performed, is performing or will perform *y* in *s*;
>   (5) each agent mutually truly believes that (2) and (3). (p. 57)

Condition (2) requires that actions *x* and *y* be interdependent, while (3) requires what Miller calls a "collective" end. (Conditions (4) and (5) are mutual true belief conditions that will play only a minor role in our discussion.) As I read (2), it requires that *A* *x*s in the belief that *B* *y*s. (I follow Miller in using "*x*" as a variable for both a particular action and an action type expressed by a verb. This is a convenience that can be avoided only at a cost to the exposition.) Condition (2) is also understood to impose two pairs of counterfactual conditionals: *A* would *x* in the belief that *B* *y*s, if *A* believed that *B* *y*s; and *A* would not *x*, if *A* did not believe that *B* *y*s (and similarly for *B*). In addition, (2) is understood as imposing interdependence only relative to end *e*. That is, it is required only that *A* would *x* if *B* *y*ed as long as *A* has end *e*; it is not required that *A* would *x* if *B* *y*ed, if *A* were to abandon *e*.

Condition (3) requires a collective end, in Miller's strictly individualist sense of "collective" (rather than in the ordinary English sense of "collective" I earlier employed):

> *A* and *B* have a collective end *e* (of bringing about a single state of affairs *t*) just in case each has an end *e*, and *e* is necessarily shared by *A* and *B*.

> End *e* is necessarily shared by *A* and *B* just in case *A* and *B* each independently has as an end bringing about *t*; and *A* and *B* must each act in order to realize *t*. (paraphrase, p. 58)

The notion of a collective end is thus definable as a conjunction of admissible individual ends without reference to jointness or collectivities (in the ordinary sense). Accordingly, it counts as strictly individualist for our purposes. What does Miller mean when, defining "necessarily shared," he says "*A* and *B* must each act in order to realize *t*"? Does he mean the *strong*, entailment requirement that satisfying the end *e*, or realizing the state *t*, *entails* that *A* and *B* each acts for the end *e* (or for the end of realizing *t*)? Or does he mean the *weak*, feasibility requirement that it is *feasible* for *A* and *B* (or for anyone?) to bring about *t* only by *A* and *B* (or some two individuals?) each acting in order to realize *t*? I will not choose between the weak and strong interpretations here, but consider Miller's account on each of them when the difference is relevant.

Let me begin by arguing that interdependence (condition (2)) is not necessary for joint action. As I have mentioned, I read (2) as having three components:

(2a) *A* wouldn't *x* if *A* didn't believe that *B* *y*s (as long as *A* maintains collective end *e*) (and similarly for *B*);

(2b) *A* would *x* in the belief that *B* *y*s, if *A* believed *B* *y*s (and similarly for *B*);

(2c) *A* *x*s in the belief that *B* *y*s (and similarly for *B*).

None of these conditions is necessary for joint action. I focus here on (2a).

(2a) is too strong. Let us limit our attention to a simple joint action of lifting an object, say, a sofa. Alan and Betty agree to lift a sofa jointly by each lifting one side of the sofa. Alan is moving furniture in his apartment, and he asks his neighbor Betty for help. They agree to lift the sofa jointly. As a result of this agreement, Alan and Betty each has an end of lifting the whole sofa (a collective end in the weak, feasibility sense) and also an end of doing so jointly (a collective end in both the weak and the strong senses). Alan grabs one side and Betty the other. Each then proceeds to lift his or her side of the sofa. We may suppose that each acts in order to fulfill their agreement and thus in order to satisfy the aforementioned ends (as instrumental to fulfilling the agreement). This case therefore meets the collective end condition (3). In these circumstances, Alan and Betty's action of lifting the sofa would normally be a joint action. Even so, (2a) need not be satisfied. Suppose that Alan could still manage his action *x* of lifting his side of the sofa, even if Betty didn't *y*. We may imagine that this is a two-piece sofa, either side of which can be lifted without the other. Suppose that Alan lifts his side even though he does not believe that Betty will lift her side. Alan believes that Betty is unreliable in fulfilling her agreements, and he does not expect Betty to do as she has agreed. Alan nevertheless needs to have the sofa lifted, and he proceeds to lift his side on the off chance that Betty will fulfill her part of the bargain. Moreover, Alan is scrupulous and prefers strongly to do what would fulfill his part of the agreement should Betty do her part. Thus, Alan acts in order to satisfy the ends of lifting the whole sofa and of jointly lifting the sofa, even though he does not expect these ends to be satisfied. And he intends to lift his side no matter what Betty does. As it happens, Betty does follow through for the same ends, and the two of them lift the sofa jointly. Thus, (2a) is too strong for joint action.[5] The same example straightforwardly tells against the necessity of (2c).

Thus, joint action does not require interdependent singular actions. It is worth noting that a similar point tells against a requirement that is, in some respects, the opposite of the interdependence requirement—a (counterfactual) *mutual responsiveness* requirement. That is, it tells against the requirement that if *B* were to perform differently from the way he does, *A* would also perform differently, in ways intended by *A* to further the collective end *e*. The requirement of mutual responsiveness may be suggested by an observation about individual action. One sign that a person is engaged in the action of baking a cake, say, is that he would attempt to compensate for errors or accidents in a way that furthers the end of baking a cake. For example, if *A* put too much milk in the batter, *A* would compensate for this by adding more flour to the batter. To the extent that a person would not so compensate, we would have reason to doubt that he is baking a cake. Similarly, it might be suggested that two people walking through a field count as walking jointly only if their actions not only fit together in such a way as to satisfy the collective end of walking jointly, but would do so even if one of them were to behave differently.

But joint action does not require mutual responsiveness. Suppose Elmo and Flip agree to bake a cake, and they do so jointly. Elmo mixes the batter while Flip greases the pan, and so on. Suppose they do so with the common end of jointly baking the cake. Suppose, however, that Elmo, a well-known pastry chef, is fussy about how the cake is baked and would refuse to contribute to baking it if Flip were to act even slightly differently from the way he does. This joint action does not meet the requirement of mutual responsiveness under the collective end of jointly baking the cake.[6]

It is not surprising that mutual responsiveness is not necessary for joint action. For its analogue is not necessary for individual action. Pastry chef Elmo may be so fussy that he would not continue baking a cake if he were to make even a slight mistake. His action is not (counterfactually) sequentially responsive, but it is still an action, even a perfect one.

These reflections lead to the conclusion that interdependence and mutual responsiveness are too strong for joint action. Indeed, the case of Alan and Betty shows as well that joint action does not even entail interpersonal singular actions, if that means actions in which an agent takes account, in reasoning about the action, of what others do or intend to do. Alan and Betty can lift the sofa jointly even if neither takes any account of what the other does or intends to do. They take account only of what the other has agreed to do.

STRICT INDIVIDUALISM: DOES JOINT ACTION ENTAIL A COLLECTIVE END?

Continuing with our long story about strict individualism, let us turn now to the other central component of Miller's interdependence account—his plausible collective end requirement (3). Is a collective end necessary for joint action? No.

To see the problem with (3), the first thing to appreciate is that it is a very strong condition on an end. A collective end (in either the strong or the weak sense), recall, is one that can be satisfied only if A and B each acts in order to realize the state t at which the end aims. But even the end of *jointly* lifting the sofa need not meet this condition. Suppose, to revisit our earlier case, Alan and Betty agree to lift the sofa jointly. The end of jointly lifting the sofa need not be a collective end, as Miller defines "collective end." This end is satisfied by the state of affairs of jointly lifting the sofa. This state of affairs requires each individual to participate in the joint action of lifting the sofa. But satisfying the end of jointly lifting the sofa does not by itself require that each individual acts *in order to* realize this state of affairs, as required for a collective end. It requires only that each individual acts *in such a way that* the state of affairs is realized. Each individual must act so that a joint action is performed, but the performance of a joint action does not by itself require that each individual acts in order that the joint action be performed. So the end of jointly lifting the sofa need not be a collective end.

This example so far shows that the requirement of a collective end is a very strong one, not that it is too strong for joint action. But we can revise the example to tell against necessity. Alan and Betty can act jointly even if there is no collective end. Suppose they agree to lift the sofa, but they do not explicitly agree to lift it *jointly*. Suppose each lifts his or her side in order to fulfill this agreement. Instrumental to fulfilling the agreement is lifting the sofa. Each acts in order to lift the sofa. But lifting the sofa need not be a collective end in either the weak or strong sense. For it need not be that lifting the sofa is feasible only if each lifts. Perhaps Alan can lift the sofa by himself. Suppose, in addition, that neither acts in order to lift the sofa jointly; neither cares about whether they perform a joint action. Then they act for the noncollective end of lifting the sofa, not for the end of jointly lifting it (which would be collective if they acted for it). Then there is no collective end in this case, and neither acts for such an end. But Alan and Betty do act jointly. So joint action does not entail a collective end (in either the weak or the strong sense).

One might defend the requirement of a collective end by saying that the example shows only that Miller has placed too strong a requirement on a collective end. Perhaps the requirement should be not that A and B must both act *in order to* realize the state of affairs t, but rather that A and B must both act *if* the state of affairs is to be realized. The end of joint action does satisfy this easier requirement.[7] Even so, the same example tells against this easier requirement. Alan and Betty, in the revised example just described, do not have the easier collective end of jointly lifting. (Nor do they act *for* that end, as required by (3).) They have only the noncollective end of lifting the sofa. There is no end meeting the easier requirement in this case.

Could a strict individualist get around these objections to the collective end requirement (3) by weakening the requirement from a collective end to a mere *common* end? Could one require only that *A* and *B* have the *same* end, though not necessarily an end that can be satisfied only by each acting in order to realize the state of affairs *f*? I am not sure that even a common end is necessary.

The most likely argument for a common end requirement is that individuals can perform a joint action only if each has as an end that the joint action be performed. If each must have the end of joint action, then they must have a common end. But it does not seem that this end is necessary for joint action, even for joint action from agreement. It is plausible enough that if two individuals *agree* to act jointly, then they act jointly if each acts in fulfillment of the agreement. And acting in fulfillment of the agreement often involves having the end of fulfilling the agreement. Having this end in turn requires that each has as an end instrumental to fulfilling the agreement the end of acting jointly. But it is not true that acting in fulfillment of the agreement always requires having the end of fulfilling the agreement. Alan does not expect Betty to carry through with her part of the agreement. In this case, he need not have the end of fulfilling the agreement. He might nevertheless do his part on the off chance that Betty will follow through with hers. If Betty does follow through, the action is joint. At most, what is required for acting in fulfillment of the agreement is that Alan has the end of fulfilling his part of the agreement, or the conditional end of doing his part in fulfilling it, if it is fulfilled. This is a case in which a joint action is performed, but the partners do not have the end of acting jointly. At most, what is necessary for a joint action is that each has the end of doing his or her part if there is a joint action. This does not require a common end, though it does require that each has a *singular* conditional end of doing his or her part if there is a joint action. Thus, I concede that a joint action may require certain singular conditional ends—an important concession. But I see no case that it requires a *common* end.[8]

STRICT INDIVIDUALISM: DOES INTERDEPENDENCE UNDER A COLLECTIVE END SUFFICE FOR JOINT ACTION?

So far, we have a case that interdependence and a collective end are not necessary for joint action. Let us continue further with our long story about strict individualism and turn to the question whether interdependent action under a collective end (Miller's conditions (1)–(5)) is enough for joint action. I will argue that the conditions are too weak.

First, we can describe cases in which the conditions are met but there is no joint action. Suppose Sim and Tim are hermits living in the wild, unconnected to each other. Each believes that he should pay tribute to the same god, Chocolatae, by placing food in the forest. Each accordingly places food in the forest. After a time, however, Sim runs low on food and has so little that the amount he can spare would by itself be inadequate for tribute. Sim believes that offering less than an adequate amount would offend the god. The same is true of Tim. Yet Sim and Tim continue to place food in the forest in tribute. For each believes that his placing an amount of food that would by itself be inadequate for tribute is nevertheless adequate if there is enough other food in the forest nearby. Sim recognizes that Tim places food in such an amount that Sim's food is adequate in the presence of Tim's; and Tim likewise. Sim would not continue to place food in tribute if Tim did not do so, and Tim likewise. So their actions are interdependent. (We may suppose that each knows that the other pays tribute and that their actions are interdependent, and each knows that the other knows this.) But intuitively, there is no joint action, at least as far as we have described the case. Sim and Tim are not acting together to pay tribute. Each pays tribute separately. It's just that neither would do so if the other did not. So far, we have interdependent actions but not joint action.

Can we also conclude that interdependent action under a collective end is not sufficient for joint action? In the case as described, Sim and Tim do have a collective end in the weaker sense of "collective end." For they have the common end of (someone's) paying tribute to the god, and this is an end that it is feasible to satisfy only if each acts (for the end). As matters stand, no one would pay tribute to the god if each did not act for the end of paying tribute. Sim would not act for the end of paying tribute to the god if Tim did not leave food in the forest, and Tim would not leave food in the forest if he did not leave food for the end of paying tribute to the god. So the end of paying tribute to the god is satisfied only if each acts in order to realize the state of affairs. Thus, interdependent action under a collective end in the weaker sense is not sufficient for joint action.

However, we do not yet have a case in which Sim and Tim have a collective end in the strong, entailment sense. For satisfying their common end of paying tribute to the god does not *entail* that each acts (for that end). But we can amend the case so that they have a common end that is collective in the stronger sense. We can stipulate the meaning of "paying communal tribute" so that it conforms to this constraint: any individual *A* pays communal tribute only if everyone pays tribute in the ordinary sense (for the end of paying communal tribute), and at least two people pay tribute in the ordinary sense (for this end). We can now revise the case so that Sim and Tim each pays communal tribute. Sim's paying communal tribute entails his placing food in the forest for the end of paying tribute while someone else places food in tribute to the god. Thus, satisfying the common end of paying communal tribute entails that each acts (for that end). So Sim and Tim have the collective end of paying communal tribute in the strong, entailment sense of "collective end." But amending the case in this way does not seem to change it into a case of joint action. Each performs the singular action of paying communal tribute to the god, but there is no joint action, even though singular paying communal tribute requires one to pay tribute while another pays communal tribute. Tim's paying communal tribute is no more than a logical condition on Sim's action. It does not pool with Sim's actions to form a joint action, any more than Sim's action of paying "tree blossom tribute" is joint with the behavior of trees, in a stipulated sense of paying tree blossom tribute on which a tribute requires that an individual pays tribute only if the trees blossom. So interdependent action under a collective end, in either the weak or the strong sense of "collective end," is not sufficient for joint action.

The lesson seems to be that interdependent action under a collective end is insufficient for joint action because it leaves open that B's action is merely a logical condition on A's satisfying the collective end. It does not ensure that B's action pools with A's to make a joint action.

Now, I do not expect a strict individualist like Miller to agree straight away with my intuition that Sim and Tim do not perform a joint action. Miller offers as an example of a joint action a case in which two individuals, A and B, walking in opposite directions on a path, each take an end of a tree blocking the path and lift the tree out of the way. I agree that this *could* be a joint action, but I do not think it *must* be. I concede that it may be a joint action if, for instance, in A's and B's society, it is a convention to join together to move a tree from one's path, and in moving the tree, A and B are following this convention. I would also concede that it may be a joint action if A would undertake to aid B in his part of the effort should B stumble (and vice versa), or if A would pause to discuss with B how to proceed (and vice versa). But apart from conventions, agreements, and counterfactual mutual responsiveness, I do not see that this must be a joint action.

I would like to avoid resting my case here merely on intuitions that may clash with Miller's own. So let me inquire in a stepwise fashion into what is needed to make a joint action.

Suppose Gus and Heather, strangers to one another, sit beside each other on a bench in Central Park. Each falls asleep. When they awake, they discover to their amazement that someone has placed a board across their laps. We may suppose that Gus's bearing the weight of the board and Heather's bearing the weight of the board are interdependent in the sense that the board would simply fall to the ground if each did not bear his or her share of the weight. Now, while they were sleeping, Gus and Heather could be correctly described as jointly bearing the weight of the board. This is a joint condition in some sense of "joint" (though not of course a joint action, since bearing the weight of the board is not an action). But clearly, this is not a joint condition in anything like the sense of "joint" in which we are trying to define joint action. It is a noncollective joint condition, not a collective joint condition. Gus and Heather jointly bear the weight of the board in the same sense in which the joists in a wall jointly bear the weight of the header.

Let us consider what happens when we turn this into a case of *action*. Suppose Gus is standing not far from Heather, each unaware of the presence of the other. Ignatz comes along and, unknown to Heather, asks Gus to hold one end of a board, and Gus obliges. Unknown to Gus, Ignatz asks Heather to hold the other end of the board. (We may suppose that Gus and Heather are both very nearsighted and hard of hearing.) Gus performs the action of holding one end of the board. Heather performs the action of holding the other end of the board. We may again suppose interdependence of the actions. We can correctly say that Gus and Heather jointly hold the board, and thus act jointly. But this is clearly the noncollective sense of "jointly" in which Gus and Heather jointly bear the weight of the board in the earlier case. They do not act jointly in the collective sense of "jointly." (Nor is there a single action of Gus and Heather that can be called joint. Evidently, a requirement of a collectively joint action is that there is a *single* action of *A* and *B* that is joint.)

Now, in the case as I have described it, Gus is unaware of Heather's action, and vice versa, and one might wonder whether this lack of knowledge is what is responsible for the lack of collectively joint action. So let us alter the case. Suppose Ignatz lets Gus know that Heather is holding the other end of the board, and Ignatz lets Heather know that Gus is holding the other end. And, to ensure mutual knowledge, suppose Ignatz lets Gus know that Heather knows this, and conversely. (Suppose, too, that Gus and Heather are aware of the interdependence of their actions.) Does adding mutual knowledge make it the case that Gus and Heather act jointly in the collective sense? I think not. To see that it does not, consider that adding such knowledge, in the preceding case of bearing the weight of the board, does not secure a collectively joint condition. Gus and Heather, aroused from sleep by the placing of the board, might each become aware that the other is involved, but this does not make it the case that they jointly bear the weight of the board in the collective sense.

It remains to consider whether adding a collective end (in Miller's strict individualist sense of "collective end") can make Gus and Heather's (noncollective, in the ordinary sense) acting in holding the board a collectively joint action. Let us back up a bit and suppose that Gus thinks Heather is merely *unknowingly* holding the board—thinks that Heather's holding the board is not an action. Gus embraces the end of acting to hold the board while (as a nonaction) another is holding it. Gus holds the board for that end. And mutatis mutandis for Heather. This clearly does not give us a collectively joint action. Suppose next that Gus thinks Heather is *acting* to hold the board. Gus embraces the end of someone's acting to hold the board while another acts to hold it, and Gus acts for this end. Heather embraces the same end and acts for it. This is a collective end in the stronger (and also the weaker) sense of "collective end," because satisfying the end entails that each acts to hold the board. Thus, we have interdependent actions under a collective end. But intuitively this does not advance us to a collectively joint action, any more than we would get a joint condition if Gus and Heather each embraced the end of (someone's) bearing the weight of the board while another also bears its weight, and acted for that end.

Do we finally reach a collectively joint action if we add to these suppositions that Gus and Heather *mutually know* that Heather embraces this collective end and acts for the end? I cannot see how adding mutual knowledge can give us a collectively joint action here, any more than we would get a collectively joint condition if Gus and Heather mutually knew that there is a collective end in the case of bearing the weight of the board.

What is missing in these cases of interdependent action that makes them fall short of collectively joint action? The dependency of *A*'s action on *B*'s action does not pool *A*'s and *B*'s actions into a joint action. These cases are like the one in which *A* depends on an inanimate event that occurs to *B*. In the case in which Gus and Heather both act to hold the board, the dependency of Gus's action of holding the board on Heather's action of holding it is no different from the dependency of Gus's action on Heather's nonaction of holding the board in the earlier case. It matters for joint action that *B* is engaged in an action, rather than merely a bodily motion—or perhaps more accurately, that B goes through a bodily motion that is part of a bodily motion corresponding to an action. This means that it matters that *B*'s bodily motion results (in a certain way) from some intention. And it must result from an intention in a way that relates it to *A*'s bodily motion and to the way *A*'s motion results from an intention. The actions of *A* and *B* need not be interdependent. However, *A*'s bodily motion corresponding to action *x* must be pooled with *B*'s bodily motion corresponding to *y* to form a bodily motion corresponding to a joint action of *A* and *B*. Typically, *A*'s bodily motion corresponding to *x* would not be part of a bodily motion corresponding to a joint action if *B*'s bodily motion corresponding to *y* did not occur. So there is typically an interdependence between these bodily motions. This interdependence is a consequence of the pooling of actions *x* and *y*, but it does not by itself give an account of such a pooling. What is clear is that *A*'s bodily motion corresponding to *x* cannot merely relate to *B*'s bodily motion corresponding to *y* in the manner of a dependency that might as well be a dependency on background conditions that make *A*'s action possible. *A*'s and *B*'s bodily motions must be treated equally by *A* and *B* in such a way as to form parts of a single action of *A* and *B*. It is hard to see how this could happen unless attitudes in which *A* and *B* are involved are directed toward *A*'s bodily motion and *B*'s bodily motion in such a way as to make them parts of

From Individualism to Supraindividualism 141

a bodily motion corresponding to one action. Some attitude must do the work instead of interdependence.

Evidently, a collective end is not the right attitude to make the bodily motions parts of a bodily motion corresponding to a joint action. The required attitude must be directed only toward bodily motions that are parts of the joint action and not toward conditions that are mere background conditions of the singular actions. The mere requirement of a collective end for which A and B act cannot ensure that there is an action corresponding to a bodily motion that has as parts only bodily motions corresponding to individual actions, rather than background conditions. Nor does specifying that the relevant end be the end of performing a joint action do the job. The specification of this end does not entail that the bodily motion corresponding to y is not a mere background condition for x. What is true is that if A's and B's having the end of a joint action, and performing x and y for this end, entailed that A and B perform a joint action, then specifying the end of a joint action would rule out a mere background condition. But in fact having the end of a joint action (and performing x and y for this end) does not entail that A and B perform a joint action. An end differs from an intention in a respect relevant to this point. If an agent has the end of doing x, and performs an action for that end, it does not follow that the agent does x. But if an agent intends to do a basic action x, and performs an action from that intention, it follows that the agent does x.[9] Requiring that A and B intend to perform a joint action and that they act from this intention would therefore seem more likely to rule out a mere background condition than requiring that A and B act for the end of a joint action.

The strict individualist must locate singular attitudes of the participants that bind the actions x and y into a joint action. The task is roughly analogous to finding attitudes of an individual agent that bind the parts of that agent's complex singular action—for example, baking a cake—into a single action of that agent. We cannot say that your actions of mixing the batter, pouring it into the mold, and so on constitute an action of baking a cake just in case you have an end of your baking a cake and perform these actions for that end. For it does not follow from the fact that you perform the actions for the end of baking a cake that these actions are more than mere instruments to the end of baking the cake. You might be doing them as a warm-up exercise. What is needed is an attitude that puts all of these actions on a par as constituting a single action of baking the cake. A better idea is that these actions constitute an action of baking a cake just in case you have the *intention* of baking a cake and perform these actions *from* that intention. This seems to entail that each action is a constituent of the single action of baking a cake and not a mere instrument for that action. Now, we could attempt an analogous account of joint action (though, as I will argue, an incomplete one) along these lines: A's action x and B's action y constitute a joint action just in case A and B have the joint intention of performing *j*, *A* and *B* perform *j* from the intention to perform *j*, and *j* corresponds to a bodily motion of *A* and *B* of which bodily motions corresponding to *x* and *y* are parts. But this is a *supraindividualist* account of joint action. We must ask whether there is an individualist account along these lines. I will take this up in the section All-But-Action Individualism: Do Individual Intentions Suffice?.

STRICT INDIVIDUALISM: ARE JOINT
ACTIONS CONSTITUTED BY INDIVIDUAL ACTIONS?

I have so far been concerned with a specific strict individualist account according to which an attribution of joint action attributes interdependent interpersonal actions under a collective end. I have argued that this condition is neither necessary nor sufficient for joint action. In this section, I would like to raise an objection that applies to all versions of strict individualism, not just the interdependent interpersonal action account. I do so by criticizing the assumption, explicit in Miller's account, that a joint action is wholly constituted by singular actions. His definiendum is "*A*'s individual action *x* and *B*'s individual action *y* in situation *s* constitute a joint action." This presupposes that *x* and *y* wholly constitute the joint action. Any version of strict individualism must presuppose something like this. The presupposition is clearly not that *x* and *y* each *is identical with* the joint action. Rather, "constitute" must somehow fuse *x* and *y* into a single action. I wish to argue that no joint actions are wholly constituted by singular actions.[10] It will follow that strict individualism does not give sufficient conditions for joint action.

The first point against the presupposition that joint actions are wholly constituted by singular actions is that, in many joint actions, the bodily motions of *A* and *B* that correspond to the joint action are not exhausted by bodily motions that correspond to singular actions of *A* or of *B*. Suppose that, as the result of an agreement, Jane and Kate simultaneously grab the handle of a very heavy sledgehammer, lift it together, and smash a rock. Suppose neither could lift the hammer alone. Neither Jane nor Kate performs an action of lifting the hammer or smashing the rock. Each does perform various singular actions in the course of the joint lifting and smashing, but these actions are not actions of lifting or smashing. Each performs such singular actions as lifting the arm in a certain way while the hand is on the hammer or turning the wrist in a certain direction. But these singular actions do not by themselves exhaust the joint lifting or the joint smashing. The bodily motions of Jane and Kate that correspond to the singular actions do not exhaust the bodily motions of Jane and Kate that correspond to the joint action. In many joint physical actions of this sort, *A* and *B* will go through bodily motions that contribute to the joint action but do not themselves correspond to singular actions. These motions may be bodily motions of a sort that would under other circumstances count as part of the bodily motion that corresponds to an individual action. For example, A turns her arm in a certain way that would be a part of the bodily motion corresponding to A's swinging the hammer were A acting alone. Such bodily motions do not themselves correspond to singular actions or perhaps even to action-parts of singular actions.

In the case of many (if not all) joint actions, A and B go through bodily motions that do not correspond to any singular action because they lack complete control over their contribution to the joint action. But these unintended motions may nevertheless be part of the bodily motion that corresponds to the joint action. Jane might force the hammer in a certain direction and cause Kate to move her hand in such a way as to reinforce this direction, though Kate does not intend any such motion. The motion of Kate's hand does not correspond to a singular action of Kate.

In some joint actions, quite a few of the bodily motions of A and B that compose the bodily motion corresponding to the joint action fail to correspond to any singular action of A or of B, or even to any parts of singular actions. This is true, for example, when two people walk arm-in-arm in a drunken stupor. They jointly walk, and their motions compose the walk, but quite a few of their motions do not correspond to singular actions on their part. They twist and careen and inadvertently prop one another up—all part of the joint walk but not of any singular actions.

None of this is surprising. Something analogous is true of singular actions. In many singular actions, the agent goes through bodily motions that do not correspond to any singular action, or even any part of a singular action other than the whole overall action, because he lacks control over the overall action. These bodily motions may, however, compose the bodily motion corresponding to the overall action. Suppose Abe pumps water from a well by cranking the pump handle. Rust in the fulcrum might cause Abe's hand to slip in an unintended way. The slippage is part of the overall action of cranking the handle, but it does not correspond to any action of Abe. It follows that we cannot understand Abe's action as constituted merely by subactions of Abe. The same point holds for joint action. We cannot understand a joint action of A and B as constituted by singular actions of A and B.

These points show that strict individualism does not say what it is for an *arbitrary* action to be joint, only what it is for an action wholly constituted by two singular actions to be joint. So strict individualism does not give sufficient conditions for joint action. A joint action is not always constituted by singular actions. No account that presupposes that all joint actions are wholly constituted by singular actions can be sufficient. This presupposition is further undermined by the following points. For these points, I assume a mereological sum view of constitution: x and y constitute a joint action j just in case j is the mereological sum of x and y. However, I believe that the points I make go through on any natural reading of "constitution."

First, on the mereological sum view of constitution, the proposal that a joint action is always wholly constituted by singular actions runs afoul of the plausible principle that a joint action is necessarily joint. Suppose Elmo does most of the work of baking a cake, but Flip helps by holding the mixing bowl, opening the oven door, and such. Presumably, the mereological sum of these actions can occur when Elmo does *all* of the work and Flip does not participate. For the sum can occur if a substantial portion of the actions in the sum occur. But the joint action performed by Elmo and Flip cannot occur without *both* agents participating.[11] For, plausibly, a joint action is necessarily joint. Thus, on the mereological sum view of constitution, the claim that such a joint action is wholly constituted by singular actions conflicts with the plausible principle that a joint action is necessarily joint.

Second, the claim that a joint action is always wholly constituted by singular actions runs afoul of the plausible idea that a joint action can occur without the particular individual partners involved in it. The numerically same annual free-for-all marathon race could be run in a given year even if a large proportion of the runners were different. But a mereological sum of actions necessarily involves a significant portion of the original partners, because it involves a significant portion of the numerically same singular actions, and the individual agents of those actions are essential to the actions. So, on the mereological sum view, the marathon race could not have a large proportion of different runners. Thus, in this sort of case, the mereological sum of singular actions is tied counterfactually to the individual agents in a way that a joint action is not. Because the two have different counterfactual identity conditions, they cannot be identical.

A third point parallels the second. A joint action can occur without the mereological sum of the singular actions involved in it occurring. For a joint action can occur without very many of the singular actions occurring. Suppose a relay race involves a hundred runners. We can imagine the same race occurring, but curtailed on account of rain after forty runners. The mereological sum does not occur, but the joint action does. Thus, not all joint actions have the same counterfactual occurrence conditions as their associated mereological sums. So these joint actions are not the mereological sums of singular actions.

Fourth, a joint action essentially belongs to some action type, so there being a joint action entails that some action distinct from the singular actions x and y involved in the joint action essentially belongs to an action type. Elmo and Flip's baking a cake may belong essentially to the type baking a cake. But does the mereological sum of Elmo and Flip's singular actions belong essentially to the type baking a cake? Perhaps most of the steps taken by Elmo and Flip can occur in an action that terminates in cupcakes, rather than a cake. This might well be the same mereological sum as the mereological sum of the singular actions that go into baking the cake. But it would not be the same joint action, because it is not of the type: baking a cake.

This last point is fully general across joint actions. It shows that *no* joint action is a mereological sum of singular actions. For all joint actions belong essentially to action types, and no mereological sums of singular actions do.

In short, no joint action is wholly constituted by the singular actions it involves on the mereological sum view of constitution. Similar points cast doubt on whether a joint action can be wholly constituted by singular actions in any sense of "constitution" available to the strict individualist.[12] Note that these points do not depend on the details of Miller's account of joint actions. They show that no account of joint action, strict individualist or otherwise, can identify a joint action with a mereological sum of singular actions. No account can presuppose that singular actions constitute a joint action. Because strict individualist accounts presuppose this, they must be mistaken.

However, even if these points succeed against strict individualist accounts, an individualist thesis could survive. It might be claimed that the occurrence of singular actions x of A and y of B (meeting, say, conditions (1)–(5)) *entails* the occurrence of *some* joint action. Even if x and y do not constitute a joint action in the sense that their mereological sum is *identical* with some joint action, the *entailment* might still go through. However, the points against constitution also argue against the sufficiency of singular actions for some joint action (under (1)–(5)). For the occurrence of singular actions meeting these conditions entails the occurrence of the mereological sum of those actions. But it does not entail the occurrence of any action that is *necessarily* joint, as all joint actions are. Nor does it entail the occurrence of an action that can occur without the particular partners involved in it. It does not entail the occurrence of an action that can occur without the singular actions involved in it occurring. Nor does it entail the occurrence of something that essentially belongs to an action type. So our objections to constitution also show that interdependence under a collective end is not sufficient for the occurrence of some joint action.

Can we generalize this point against the sufficiency of Miller's (1)–(5) to all versions of strict individualism? I think so. I see no way that strict individualist conditions could impose on singular actions what is required to entail an action that is necessarily joint, that can occur without being done by the agents of the singular actions and without these actions themselves occurring, and that essentially belongs to an action type. Properties of the singular actions, even modal and relational properties, do not determine in which counterfactual conditions the joint action occurs, which nonactual individuals can be partners in the action, which nonactual singular actions can be involved in the action, and what the essential action type of the joint action is. Regarding the essential action type of the joint action, the types of the singular actions do not determine any particular type of joint action. And adding modal properties and relations between them does not do so either. Clearly, we must add attitudes. Yet nothing short of an attitude toward a joint action type will determine a joint action type. (I return momentarily to what kind of attitude is needed.) Strict individualism cannot carry the burden of an account of joint action. It cannot specify the essential agent of the action, the possible partners and singular actions involved, or the essential action type.[13]

There is nothing surprising in this. Joint actions are no different from singular actions in this regard. Singular actions cannot be identified with mereological sums of singular actions that are their parts, for reasons related to the third and fourth points against constitution. For one point, suppose I bake a cake. The mereological sum of my actions could occur without my baking the cake. For example, the mereological sum could occur if I left off after putting the cake in the oven and Flip finished the action of baking the cake. Then the action of baking the cake would be joint, hence not an action of mine, hence not the same action as the one I performed, because it has a different, joint agent. So my baking the cake isn't identical with this mereological sum. For another point, suppose again that I bake a cake. Now suppose, counterfactually, that I perform most of the actions involved in baking a cake but in the end make cupcakes. My counterfactual action is not numerically the same as my action of baking a cake, even though it involves the same mereological sum. So singular actions are not mereological sums of subactions that are their parts.

Properties of subactions, even modal and relational properties, do not determine in which counterfactual circumstances the overall action occurs, which subactions can be parts of the overall action, and what the (essential) type of the overall action is. The types of the subactions do not determine the type of the overall action, nor do their modal and relational properties. Nothing short of an attitude toward the overall action can determine the overall type. In the case of a singular action composed of subactions, the intention of the agent from which the overall action is performed determines its type (on the assumption that the intention is successful). Which subactions can compose it are in turn determined (in part) by its type.

Note that intentions, rather than ends, determine the action type. If I mix the batter, pour it into the mould, put the mould in the oven, and remove it later, my merely acting *for the end* of baking a cake is not enough to make all of this an action of baking a cake, even on the assumption that I succeed in this end and bake a cake. It might be that each of my steps was merely part of a warm-up exercise for my end of baking a cake. I did not take these steps as part of a single composite action. If, however, I perform each step *from the intention* to bake a cake, then the steps are subactions that are parts of my baking a cake. Performing an action x for an end of performing an action z does not entail that x is part of z even assuming success in the end.

But performing an action x from the intention to perform z entails that x is part of z, assuming success in the intention.[14] So intentions, unlike ends, can do the job of determining action types.

This suggests an account of joint action. The action type is determined by the intention of the agent from which the action is performed (assuming success in this intention), and which singular actions a joint action can involve are determined by the agent and the action type. Referring to acting for the end of a joint action, even a collective end, does not specify the type of a joint action (even assuming success in the end) because acting for this end can be instrumental to the joint action, rather than composing it. An action performed from an intention to perform a joint action composes the joint action (assuming that the intention is successful).

What is suggested by all this is an account of joint action by analogy with singular action. In singular action, several actions do not constitute an overall action. Rather, they compose an overall action when they are performed from the intention to perform the overall action. The agent and action types of the overall action are determined by this intention. To develop such an account, we must move away from Miller's account along two dimensions. We must dispense with referring to singular actions x and y. A joint action is never wholly constituted by singular actions x and y, and x and y do not determine joint agency or joint action type. Evidently, we must specify the joint action type by referring to the type mentioned in the content of the attitude. We must also move from reference to singular ends to reference to singular intentions, because ends do not determine agency or action type. I consider an individualist effort along these lines in the section All-But-Action Individualism: Do Individual Intentions Suffice?, below.

STRICT INDIVIDUALISM: ARE INDIVIDUALS THE AGENTS IN JOINT AGENCY?

There is another difficulty with the strict individualist account related to the difficulties with constitution we have just discussed. The format of the strict individualist account is "A's individual action x and B's individual action y constitute a joint action just in case A, B, x, and y have certain properties." But this presupposes that individuals A and B perform a joint action *tout court*—as individuals. This presupposition is incorrect. In at least some cases, individuals perform a joint action only *as members of a collectivity*. In particular, when A and B perform a joint action, and this joint action is the joint action of a group to which A and B belong, we cannot say that A and B perform the action *tout court*, but only as members of the group. In such a case, the group's performing a joint action does not even entail that members A and B perform the action *tout court*. But I wish also to make a stronger claim. In at least some, and perhaps all cases of joint action, we should deny that individuals perform a joint action *tout court*, whether or not we assume that they perform it as members of a group.

It is natural to assume that:

(G) A group of which *A*, *B*, and *C* happen to be the sole members performs a joint action *j* just in case *A*, *B*, and *C* jointly perform *j*.

Natural as this condition may be, it does not survive close inspection. This is because distinct groups can have the same individuals as members, and distinct groups with the same members can differ in the joint actions they perform.

Let me adapt an example of Gilbert's (1989). Suppose *A*, *B*, and *C* are the sole members of the Library Committee and also of the Food Committee of the College. Suppose the Library Committee pays for a book. According to the biconditional (G) above, the members *A*, *B*, and *C* jointly pay for the book. But then, applying (G) again, it follows that the Food Committee pays for the book, because its members are *A*, *B*, and *C*. Yet this need not be so. The Food Committee need not pay for the book. So we should reject (G). (G) must be revised to say:

(G') A group of which *A*, *B*, and *C* happen to be the sole members performs a joint action *j* just in case *A*, *B*, and *C* perform *j as members of the group.*

This revised biconditional (G') correctly distinguishes the joint actions of the Library Committee from those of the Food Committee, even though these committees have the same members. As far as it goes, the revised biconditional seems fine.

But is (G') available to a strict individualist? The expression "jointly perform *j* as members of the group" is obscure and begs explication. Might an individualist understand it by saying that members of the group perform *j* as members of the group just in case they perform *j* jointly *tout court* and they meet some additional condition? In the above case, *A*, *B*, and *C* jointly pay for the book *tout court*. The Library Committee pays for the book because this is so and the additional condition is met. But the Food Committee does not pay for the book because, although *A*, *B*, and *C* jointly pay for it *tout court*, the additional condition is not met.

This proposal faces the task of saying what additional condition must be met for a group's joint action. But apart from whatever difficulties may be involved in this task, the proposal seems implausible. It is implausible that members of a group jointly perform the action *tout court* in cases of group action. First, it is not obvious why, in the above case, we should say that *A*, *B*, and *C* perform the joint action of paying *tout court*, rather than saying that they do not. What it seems natural to say is that *A*, *B*, and *C* do (in one way) and do not (in another way) jointly pay. As members of the Library Committee, they jointly pay, but as members of the Food Committee, they do not. The best sense we can make of this would seem to be that it expresses the claim that the Library Committee performs the joint action of paying, while the Food Committee does not.

Second, it seems possible for there to be conflicting actions across groups with the same members. Yet saying that members perform a joint action *tout court* rules out the possibility of such conflicts. The following case of conflicting recommendation seems possible, even if farfetched. The Library Committee decides to recommend purchasing a book. The Food Committee decides to recommend not purchasing the book. Each committee has its own agenda and makes decisions in line with these agenda. When *A*, *B*, and *C* meet as members of the Library Committee, they judge, from the vantage of the Committee, that purchasing is the right thing to do, and they recommend accordingly. They reach the opposite conclusion when they meet as members of the Food Committee. Conflicting recommendations come out of the two committees. Perhaps this falls under abnormal psychology, but it seems possible. On the proposal that a joint group action entails that the members act jointly *tout court*, the fact that the Library Committee recommends purchase entails that *A*, *B*, and *C* jointly recommend purchasing *tout court*, while the fact that the Food Committee recommends not purchasing entails that *A*, *B*, and *C* recommend not purchasing *tout court*. But in this case, *A*, *B*, and *C* both recommend purchasing *tout court* and recommend not purchasing *tout court*. Yet it seems impossible for the same agent(s) both to recommend to a party to do *x* *tout court* and also to recommend to a party not to do *x* *tout court*. One reason that this seems impossible is that recommending to someone not to do *x* *tout court* seems to entail not recommending to them to do *x* *tout court*. Another reason it seems impossible is that the agent's (or agents') joint recommendation to do *x* *tout court* would be undermined by its (their) contemporaneous joint recommendation not to do *x* *tout court*. We have here an argument that a group's joint action of recommending cannot be construed as the members' jointly recommending *tout court*.

So far, this shows that there are some action types *J* for which there are possible instances of group joint action that are not joint actions *tout court*. But I take it that we can infer from this that *no* instances of these action types *J* are instances of joint action *tout court*. For instances of these action types in which there are conflicts are not fundamentally different with respect to jointness from instances of these action types in which there are no conflicts. There is nothing about the *jointness* of the actions in the case of conflicting joint recommendations above that differs from the jointness in joint recommendations that do not conflict. So we can conclude that for all instances of these action types, the joint actions are not *tout court*. But now we can generalize further to instances of *other* action types for which conflict is impossible. For it does not seem that other action types are fundamentally different with respect to jointness than action types for which conflict is possible. For example, it may be that lifting their fingers is an action type for which conflict in joint action is impossible. It may be that it is impossible for *A* and *B* both to lift their fingers jointly and not to lift their fingers jointly as members of different groups. But the nature of jointness for the action type of lifting their fingers does not seem different from the nature of jointness for the action type of recommending. This leads to the conclusion that joint action is not *tout court* for any group joint action types.

I have argued that a *group* joint action is not *tout court*. This is an objection to strict individualism. Could the strict individualist respond by retrenching, restricting the account of joint actions to cases in which *A* and *B* perform a joint action, but no *group* performs the joint action? The claim would be that for all joint actions that are not group actions, *A* and *B* perform the joint action *tout court*. This is not an option if, as I think, all joint actions are group actions (or the actions of a collectivity of some kind). But I can offer no argument for this assumption here. However, I doubt that any joint action is *tout court*, whether it is a group action or not. In support of this doubt, I would make the following point. It is doubtful that the *jointness* of arbitrary joint actions differs fundamentally from the *jointness* of group joint actions. Suppose that in a one-time event, Mary and Jill agree to go for a walk together and subsequently go for the walk. This would be a nongroup joint action if there ever are any such actions. But I see no reason to think that this action differs in the nature of its jointness from the jointness involved in a walk that Mary and Jill take as members of the newly formed Walking Club, a group of which they are the sole members. If these joint actions do not differ in the nature of their jointness, then arbitrary joint actions are no more *tout court* than the joint actions of groups. So we have seen enough to undermine a general strict individualism and raise a serious doubt about whether joint action is ever *tout court*.

ALL-BUT-ACTION INDIVIDUALISM: DO INDIVIDUAL INTENTIONS SUFFICE?

These criticisms of strict individualism suggest the following alternative individualist account of joint action. To avoid the objection that joint actions are not wholly constituted by singular actions, we simply replace the reference to singular actions *x* and *y* with the expression "we *J*" without specifying that "*J*" expresses a joint action type. To address the criticism that attitudes toward singular actions are not enough to determine joint agency, we must refer to attitudes that determine joint agency—determine in particular what agent performs the joint action, in which counterfactual conditions the joint action occurs, which nonactual individuals can be partners, which nonactual singular actions can be involved in the action, and what the essential type of the action is. For this purpose, we refer to attitudes toward our *J*ing. We also move from Miller's choice of collective end as an attitude to intentions.

Michael Bratman (1992, 1993a) has proposed an account along just these lines. To be precise, he has proposed an account of shared cooperative activity, rather than joint action. Shared cooperative activity, I take it, is joint activity in which the partners are mutually responsive. If so we can adapt Bratman's account to joint action by subtracting mutual responsiveness from his conditions. His account, so adapted, imposes these conditions on joint action:

Our *J*-ing is a joint action of *A* and *B* only if
   (A) we *J*;
   (B) *A* intends that we *J*, and *B* intends that we *J*;
   (C) we *J* because *A* intends that we *J* and *B* intends that we *J*.[15]

Here I am *A* and you are *B*.

Unfortunately, this individual intentions account fares little better than the interdependent actions under a collective end account. There are two difficulties. First, it does not work to employ "we *J*" rather than Miller's "*A* *x*s and *B* *y*s." Doing so introduces a circularity. If the account is to cover all action types, it must cover action types the instantiation of which entails a joint action. For example, it must cover essentially joint action types (e.g., playing tennis or walking together). But then "*J*" must express not only action types that do not entail a joint action, but also action types that entail a joint action. Of course, the account does not explicitly employ the description "action types that entail a joint action," but it does quantify over such types, and this is inconsistent with individualism. Bratman responds to this circularity objection by stipulating that "we *J*" not be "cooperatively loaded"—that is, not entail that there is a joint action. But this response avoids the circularity problem at the cost of incompleteness. The account does not then cover action types *J* that entail a joint action.

Could Bratman get around the incompleteness by extending his account in this way? Could he say that conditions (A), (B), and (C) are sufficient for a joint action, and in addition to this, any action that entails an action of type *J'* meeting these conditions is also a joint action? This would work only if for every action *j* of an essentially joint action type, there is a merely accidentally joint type *J'* meeting conditions (A), (B), and (C), and the instantiation of this type *J'* is entailed by the joint action *j*. If this does indeed hold, the extended version of Bratman's account would cover all instances of essentially joint action. But does it hold? I don't know; but even if it does, the extended account leaves another problem. The account now says that an action of an essentially joint type is joint because it entails an action meeting conditions (A), (B), and (C). But those conditions specify only intentions toward the action of our *J*ing, for an accidentally joint *J*. They do not specify any intentions toward the essentially joint action itself. And it is hard to see how the latter action could be joint merely because the partners have intentions toward a distinct (accidentally) joint action, our *J*ing. It would seem that if any intention makes an action *j* joint, it would have to be an intention toward the action *j* itself, and not toward some other action. So the proposed extension of Bratman's conditions (A), (B), and (C) misidentifies the conditions that make an action joint. Moreover, because, to avoid circularity, the account must leave "we" neutral between a distributive reference to individuals and a reference to a joint agent, it does not specify the joint *agent* of the joint action, even one of a cooperatively neutral type *J*. I am inclined, then, to say that the account must either lapse into circularity or fall short of identifying the conditions in virtue of which arbitrary joint actions are joint.

A second and equally serious difficulty for Bratman's account is this. The account makes two moves away from Miller, moves that, I argued, are forced on an individualist. One move is to employ "we *J*," rather than referring to individual actions; the other is to refer to intentions rather than ends. But these moves turn out to be *incompatible*. To see this, we may begin by noting that Bratman's account has been attacked on the ground that (B) is not a necessary condition of joint action (Velleman 1997b). For in a joint action, *A* cannot intend that we *J*. The difficulty is not that an agent cannot intend that another agent perform an action. It is rather that *A* cannot intend that *p* unless *A* thinks that this intention settles that *p*. In this regard, an intention differs from an end: *A* can have as an end that *p* even if *A* does not think that this end settles that *p*. Applying this point about intention to Bratman's account, *A* cannot intend that we *J* unless *A* thinks that his intention that we *J* settles that we *J*. But in a joint action, *A* does not think that his intention that we *J* settles that we *J*. It is, in part, up to *B* whether we *J* because it is (in part) up to *B* whether *B* does his part in our *J*ing. So condition (B) is not a necessary condition of joint action. I think this is a grave objection to Bratman's account. It shows that an individualist cannot avoid the objections to Miller's account by *both* employing "we *J*" rather than "*A* *x*s and *B* *y*s" *and* at the same time referring to intentions rather than ends. These moves pull in opposite directions, the former move toward individual control and the latter away from it. They are incompatible moves.

Bratman has responded to this objection by arguing that it is possible for *A* to think (correctly) that his intention settles that we *J*, while at the same time thinking (correctly) that it is in part up to *B* whether we *J* (and whether *B* does his part in our *J*ing) (Bratman 1997). Abe intends to pump water into the house and moves the pump handle to do so. However, Abe's success depends on another agent, Bill, who must turn a valve to increase the water pressure if Abe's pumping is to succeed. Suppose, in addition, that, as Abe knows, Bill monitors Abe's activity and turns the valve when and only when Abe begins to move the pump handle. This sets up a nonaccidental regularity between Abe's intention to pump and Abe's action of pumping, on the one hand, and Bill's intention to turn the valve and Bill's turning the valve, on the other. This regularity entails the counterfactual dependency: if Bill did not intend to turn the valve, Abe would not pump water into the house. This dependency of Abe's pumping on Bill's intention does not prevent Abe from intending to pump water into the house, any more than would be so if Bill were replaced with an automatic detector of Abe's activity together with a motor to turn the valve. The fact that Abe's success in pumping water into the house depends on Bill's intentions does not prevent Abe from intending to pump water into the house. Abe thinks (correctly) that his intention to pump water into the house settles that he pumps water into the house, while also thinking (correctly) that it is up to Bill whether he turns the valve and thus whether Abe pumps water into the house. There is no conflict between these.

All this is correct, but it does not show that in a case of joint action, there is no conflict between: *A* thinks that *A*'s intention settles that we *J*, and *A* thinks that our *J*ing is in part up to *B*. In the example of Abe, there is no conflict between the thought that Abe's intention to pump settles that he pumps, and his thought that his pumping is in part up to Bill, because his intention to pump is sufficient for Bill's intending to pump and hence for Bill's pumping. Abe's intention settles that he pumps by settling that Bill intends to pump. It is in part up to Bill whether Abe pumps in the sense that Bill's intention is necessary and sufficient for Abe's pumping—a necessary and sufficient link in the chain from Abe's intention to pump to the water's pumping. But in the case of joint action, *A*'s intention that we *J*, if such there be, is not sufficient for *B*'s intention to do his part in our *J*ing and for *B*'s doing his part in our *J*ing, and thus it does not settle that we *J*. If any intention that we *J* were involved at all, *B*'s intention that we *J*, as well as *A*'s intention that we *J*, would have to be necessary for *B*'s doing his part in our *J*ing and thus necessary for our *J*ing. And *B*'s intention to do his part would not depend solely on *A*'s intention that we *J*; it would depend as well on *B*'s intention that we *J*. Since *A*'s intention that we *J* is not sufficient for *B*'s doing his part, it does not settle that we *J*. It cannot both be that *A*'s intention that we *J* settles that we *J* and also that it is up to *B* that we *J*, in the sense in which, in a joint action, it is up to *B* that we *J*. For *A*'s intention that we *J* settles that we *J* only if it *suffices* for our *J*ing, while it is up to *B* that we *J* only if *A*'s intention that we *J* does *not* suffice for our *J*ing but our *J*ing requires *B*'s intention that we *J* as well. Since a joint action requires that it is up to *B* that we *J* in a sense different from the sense in which it is up to

Bill whether Abe pumps the water, and since *A*'s intention cannot settle that we *J* if it is up to *B* whether we *J* in this sense, it follows that *A*'s intention cannot settle that we *J* in a joint action. And if *A*'s intention cannot settle that we *J*, then *A* cannot intend that we *J*.

These reflections support the conclusion that (B) is not necessary for a joint action. We cannot require that *A* intends that we *J* (and so does *B*), for reasons specific to intention, reasons that do not apply to ends. So "we *J*" and individual intentions are incompatible. We cannot save all-but-action individualism by moving to Bratman's account.[16]

Let it also be noted that the intention account faces a difficulty parallel to one that afflicts the end account: individual intentions do not seem to be necessary for joint action, any more than individual ends are necessary.[17] *A* and *B* can agree to perform a joint action without either of them intending to do his or her part in the action. Still, if they do fulfill the agreement, the result is a joint action. Fulfilling the agreement seems to require at most that each individual has the conditional intention to do his or her part if there is a joint action, rather than the unconditional intention to do his or her part in the agreed joint action. In our earlier case of Alan and Betty, Alan has no reason to expect that Betty will follow through, and without such an expectation, he cannot intend to fulfill his part in the agreed joint action; he can only intend to do so conditional on Betty's doing her part.

These reflections lead to the conclusion that we cannot salvage an individualist account by moving from individual actions *x* and *y* to "we *J*," and we cannot do so by moving from individual ends to intentions. These two moves are incompatible with one another, and neither solves the problems facing strict individualism.

SUPRAINDIVIDUALISM

Joint actions, according to our everyday casual attributions, occur in a variety of circumstances. They occur when individuals agree to perform a joint action and each acts in fulfillment of the agreement, and they also occur when individuals act habitually in a coordinated fashion.[18] It is not necessary for a partner *A* in a joint action to act from the intention that his or her action contributes to a joint action, as just noted. But it may be necessary that *A* acts from *A*'s *conditional* intention that: his or her action contributes to a joint action if there is a joint action. This is a conditional intention to contribute to a particular joint action *j* of a type *J*.

A's acting and *B*'s acting from this conditional intention is clearly not sufficient for a joint action. *A* and *B* might each act from the intention to contribute to *j*, but fail to do so. One way in which they might fail to do so is by failing to satisfy their conditional intentions. Perhaps *A* and *B* think they're wielding the same sledgehammer, when in fact they grab different sledge-hammers. In this case, there is no joint action of wielding the sledgehammer. But even in cases in which *A* and *B* do satisfy their conditional intentions, they need not act jointly. For their actions need not constitute a single joint action. Compare with individual action. Suppose *A* mixes the batter from the conditional intention of contributing to baking the cake, if *A* bakes the cake. Suppose *A* pours the batter in the mold from the same conditional intention, and so on. These actions need not add up to a single action of baking the cake. What is missing is acting from the *unconditional* intention of baking the cake. Similarly, *A*'s and *B*'s actions from their conditional intentions need not add up to a single joint action. What is missing is acting from an *unconditional* intention of joint action. This cannot in general, however, be *A*'s unconditional intention and *B*'s unconditional intention, because individual unconditional intentions are not necessary for joint action.

All this points to an account of joint action that makes joint action analogous to singular action:

An action *j* is a joint action only if
 (1) there is an agent *C* who performs *j* from *C*'s intention of performing *j*; and
 (2) *C* is not an individual

The intention here is a joint intention, since it is an intention from which the agent performs the action, and thus an intention of the agent. Such an intention involves jointly taking the intention to settle that the action will be done. It also involves a joint commitment to jointly reason practically on the assumption that the action will be done. A good bit of the account of joint action will consist of spelling out just what joint intention involves along these lines. This is work for another occasion.

Conditions (1) and (2) are necessary but not sufficient for joint action. Consider an organization of individuals like the one described in Searle's Chinese Room Argument (Searle 1984a, ch. 2). I side with most parties to the debate over the Chinese Room in thinking that it is possible for such an organization to be an agent, have intentions, and perform actions from those intentions. (Of course, Searle emphatically denies this.). Such an organization may be an agent, but even in a case in which diverse individuals process information in the Room, the organization is clearly not a *joint* agent, and its actions are not joint actions, despite satisfying (1) and (2).[19] The individuals involved in such an organization are not partners in the organization in the sense in which the members of a social group are partners in the group. When the organization acts, the individuals involved in the organization do not act jointly. They are merely cogs in mechanisms in the organization that realize the intentional states or actions of the organization, as mechanisms in the body realize singular actions. This shows the need for an additional condition in the account of joint action.

One condition that may be extensionally adequate (for joint *bodily* actions) is:

(3) The bodily motion corresponding to *j* is a mereological sum of bodily motions corresponding to singular actions of at least two individual agents, each performed from the conditional intention of contributing to *j* if *j* occurs.

This condition might well hold in all cases of joint bodily action if, as I have suggested may be true, joint action requires that the partners act from the conditional intention of contributing to the joint action if it occurs. Condition (3) avoids specifying that the individual agents involved are the partners of joint action, and this is just as well, because at this point we have no account of what it is to be a partner in the joint action. Plausibly, the partners of a joint action include those whose actions correspond to bodily motions that are parts of the bodily motion corresponding to the joint action, when those actions are performed from the conditional intention to contribute to the joint action if the joint action occurs. Condition (3) rules out the actions of organizations like the Chinese Room because their actions do not correspond to bodily motions that are mereological sums of bodily motions corresponding to singular actions from conditional intentions. Of course there is a question *why* we should treat the class of actions in which (3) is satisfied—joint actions—as a distinguished class apart from actions of organizations like the Chinese Room. But this is a question I have to set aside here.[20]

ELIMINATIVISM

Perhaps the most troubling consequence of our supraindividualist account of joint action is its eliminativism about joint action. Supraindividualism is of course a thesis about what we're attributing when we make our everyday casual attributions of joint actions. It is a thesis about what joint actions, as we ordinarily conceive them, would involve if they existed. But the account has ontological consequences: in the presence of innocuous claims about the nature of mentality, it entails *eliminativism* about joint actions: there aren't any. There *could be* joint agents and actions as conceived on supraindividualism, but in fact there are none.

The case against supraindividual agents is this. We can comprehend some episode of bodily motion involving several individuals "from the intentional stance."[21] That is, we can treat the bodily motions of the individuals as parts of a single bodily motion corresponding to an action of a nonindividual agent. We can attribute an intention to *J* to this hypothesized supraindividual agent, along with background mental states, dispositions, and capacities needed to support this intention. And we can predict the agent's action and bodily motion from these attributions.

The difficulty arises when we begin to list the supporting mental states, dispositions, and capacities required for an agent to have an intention to *J*, for an agent to act from an intention, and for someone to be an agent. First, an intention to *J* entails certain beliefs and ends. For example, if you intend to *x*, you must believe that you have not already *x*ed and that it is within your power to *x*. To have the relevant beliefs, you must have the concept of *x*ing and the concept of the power to *x*. Again, if you intend to *x*, you must have as ends doing things that it is necessary to do in order to *x*. In addition to beliefs and ends, an intention to *J* entails a disposition to reason practically under the constraint that the agent *J*s. This disposition entails a rich enough cognitive competence to reason under constraints—to make assumptions and to choose ends and means that conform to those assumptions. It also entails having any concepts involved in the assumption that the agent *J*s. Moreover, in typical cases of intention, this disposition is manifested in some actual practical reasoning. An intention to *J*, finally, entails a disposition to endeavor to *J* (i.e., to attempt to *J* under appropriate or designated circumstances, and to attempt to bring about circumstances appropriate to *J*ing).[22] An attempt to *J* under appropriate or designated circumstances entails being able to recognize which circumstances are appropriate or designated. If you attempt to talk under appropriate circumstances—for example, when others are listening—you must be able to recognize when others are listening. Thus, an intention to *J* entails a broad array of cognitive states, dispositions, and capacities.

Second, much is required for action. An agent acts only if he or she believes certain things and has certain ends. You lift a finger only if you believe that you lift a finger (or believe that you attempt to do so). Presumably, this requires you to have a diversity of beliefs about related topics. You could hardly have a belief about raising your finger without having beliefs about fingers, and more generally body parts, and about acts like raising and lowering. You could not have the belief that you have the power to raise your finger without having beliefs about other powers to do things. It is hard to see how you could have these beliefs without a great many other beliefs about the world.

Third, much is required for agency. To be an agent you must have cognitive, motivational, and conative faculties. To have a cognitive faculty, it is presumably not enough merely to have a few beliefs on a restricted range of topics. You must have beliefs on diverse topics. Similar remarks apply to a motivational and a conative faculty.

These rich requirements for intention, action, and agency cast doubt on whether there are joint agents with intentions to act who act from those intentions. Suppose a joint agent intends to lift a sofa and acts from that intention. This requires the joint agent to believe such things as that there is a sofa, that this agent has not already lifted the sofa, that it is within the agent's power to lift the sofa, that the agent does lift the sofa or endeavors to do so, that this is a sofa not some other kind of furniture, that what is wanted is lifting not lowering or turning or heaving, and the like. The agent must have a diverse set of beliefs and ends. The agent must also have a disposition to reason practically under the constraint that a sofa is to be lifted and a disposition to attempt to lift the sofa.

How plausible is it that there is such an agent? When *A* and *B* do what we describe as jointly lifting the sofa, do they also jointly believe that this is a sofa, not a chair or a table or a tree? If you believe that this is a sofa, and not some other kind of furniture, then, I take it, you believe that it is used for sitting and accommodates more than one sitter at a time. You believe that it is not *F*, for some sufficiently broad selection of types of furniture *F*, though there may not be any particular types you need to distinguish from sofas. So you believe that it isn't a chair or bench. If the difference between a sofa and a bench is that a sofa is upholstered and a bench is not, then you must believe that this is upholstered. The question, then, is whether *A* and *B* jointly believe that this is used for sitting, that it is upholstered, and so on. Plausibly, you believe *p* only if you are disposed to reason theoretically from the premise that *p*. Is it true that *A* and *B* are disposed to (theoretically) reason jointly from the premise that this is upholstered, and so on? We do casually ascribe joint actions in cases in which *A* and *B* are not so disposed. Perhaps *A* and *B* are longstanding rivals who wish to agree on as little as possible and accordingly refuse to engage in (what we would call) joint theoretical reasoning from any premise to any conclusion. Then *A* and *B* do not jointly believe that this is upholstered. This does not stop us from saying that *A* and *B* act jointly. But *A* and *B* lack the features needed to qualify as acting jointly on the supraindividualist account. Could someone reply that *A* and *B* do act jointly here: they do not jointly lift the *sofa*, but they jointly lift *something*? But I do not find this persuasive. For the same point goes for *lifting* as for *sofa*. What if *A* and *B* are unwilling to (theoretically) reason jointly from the premise that they are lifting *something*? This does not prevent us from casually saying that they jointly lift a sofa. Yet on the supraindividualist account, this casual attribution is mistaken. Similar remarks apply in answer to the question whether *A* and *B* really have a disposition to reason jointly under the constraint that a sofa is to be lifted, or a disposition to attempt jointly to lift the sofa.

It is worth adding to these points that in paradigmatic casual attributions of joint action, the conditions that are supposed to set up the joint action—for example, an agreement to act jointly—do not entail the relevant joint beliefs or ends, or the relevant dispositions to reason jointly or to attempt to engage in the action. For example, agreeing to lift the sofa does not entail a disposition to theoretically reason jointly from the premise that it is upholstered, and so on. What is true is that in a typical case of agreement to act jointly, once *A* and *B* agree, the probability that they will engage in activities that look outwardly like joint theoretical reasoning from certain premises, and like joint practical reasoning under the relevant constraints, increases. *A* and *B* will tend each to accept the obvious consequences of the fact that this is a sofa. So once they have agreed to lift it, they will tend each to reason in the same way about how to treat the sofa—for example, as upholstered furniture. This will lead to overt agreements about means for accomplishing the end of lifting the sofa. The two will tend to perform some coordinated singular actions that would accompany genuine joint action. But this only shows that in cases of agreement, people will have a greater tendency to perform some singular actions that would accompany genuine joint action when they agree, not that an agreement entails such a tendency—still less that it entails the relevant joint beliefs or dispositions to reason jointly. This pertains to cases of agreement. A similar point applies to habitual coordinated action.

If these thoughts are on the right track, the supraindividualist account leads to the conclusion that joint actions are rare or nonexistent. Why, then, do we so naturally think that an agreement between *A* and *B* to *J* sets up a joint agent and joint action, or that a habitual coordinated action does? Here is one explanation. When we think this, we indulge in an imaginative construction based on some facts. In the case of agreement, the facts are that *A*'s and *B*'s agreement to lift the sofa sets up commitments and obligations on their part. To speak more cautiously, in the case of *apparent* agreement, there are *apparent* commitments and obligations. An agreement is already a joint action; so on the supraindividualist account, there aren't really any agreements. Moreover, there aren't any real joint commitments. But appearances are sufficient for our purposes here. The apparent commitments and obligations tend to set up individual dispositions to perform singular actions that would accompany the fulfillment of these obligations. People like to do what they can to fulfill their apparent obligations. The relevant apparent obligations include: to follow through unless it is agreed not to, to jointly treat the sofa in a manner consistent with lifting it, to jointly accept that it is a sofa. *A* and *B* cannot really fulfill these obligations, because there are no such obligations, and their fulfillment would require joint action in any case. But *A* and *B* will tend to approximate in their singular actions what would be involved in fulfilling such obligations.

There is a question how people could be motivated to do what they can to fulfill merely apparent obligations. But I take it that it requires philosophical argument to establish that these obligations are merely apparent; it isn't obvious that they are. And even one fully persuaded by these arguments might not be able to overcome lifelong tendencies to treat them as real. A similar answer should be given to the question how we could attribute joint

actions if there are none: it takes philosophical argument to establish that
that there are no joint actions.

A habit of coordination does not directly establish a commitment to behave, as an agreement does. But it does set up mutual and third-party expectations for behavior, which in turn create obligations on the part of the
coordinated individuals, which in turn pressure these individuals to fulfill expectations. If people have a habit of coordinating their lifting activities, this
will lead to the expectation that they will jointly accept that something is a
sofa, which will in turn cause behavior that approximates the singular actions that would accompany jointly accepting that it is a sofa. In this way, a
habit of coordination will lead to an approximation of the actions, attitudes,
and dispositions required for joint action. This could pass for genuine joint
action.

Thus, (apparent) agreement and a habit of coordination, in their different
ways, typically do bring about an approximation of the dispositions required
for joint action and agency.

This, then, is one idea about why we so naturally think that agreement and
habitual coordinated behavior bring about joint actions and agency. Here is
a different idea. We casually attribute a wide range of beliefs and ends, dispositions, and capacities to corporations, governments, and other organizations with a stable structure of apparent agreements and habits of coordination. We say that the Ford Corporation slashes prices to compete with
General Motors. The Ford Corporation believes that General Motors is a
threat to its business, desires to reduce that threat, believes that by slashing
prices it can do so, forms the intention of doing so, and acts from that intention. It is natural to say that the Ford Corporation has a competence in the
economics of sales, pricing, and market competition, can discriminate
threats from nonthreats, understands what reduces threats, has a variety of
beliefs about General Motors and other rival corporations, employs business
and engineering concepts relevant to the automobile industry, and so on. We
comfortably say that the Ford Corporation has the sorts of background beliefs and desires attendant upon an intention to slash prices and upon the
end of competing with General Motors. We are comfortable saying these
things because the Ford Corporation has so much structure that we expect
to observe behavior compatible with, and naturally explained by, the attribution of such beliefs, intentions, dispositions, and capacities. In the Ford
Corporation, there are roles governed by regularities that routinely cause individual behavior that can be explained by attributing joint agency. The Ford
Corporation is not so very far from a genuine agent.

The proposal is that we casually take organizations like the Ford Corporation as paradigmatic joint agents, and in doing so we approximate the literal
truth to some substantial degree. Once we have gotten comfortable thinking
of corporations as joint agents, we are primed to extend attributions of joint

agency to cases that fit less well. We recognize that apparent partners in agreements and habits of coordination bear some resemblance to organizations. Agreements and habits of coordination set up some relevant dispositions. So we fall into speaking of these as instances of joint action and agency.

Thus, we have two alternative stories of why we casually speak of action and agency in all of these cases. There may be truth in each of these stories. I will not try to decide between them here. Whatever the correct story, a supraindividualist is faced with the question what point there might be to talking this way when such talk is literally false. Does such talk facilitate the prediction or explanation of behavior? In the case of organizations, attributing action and agency to the organization does allow prediction and explanation of behavior, in a way that bypasses attributing action and agency to the individuals. We don't need to know what individuals' dispositions are to be able to predict what the Ford Corporation will do. The Corporation will act to further its interests, given its beliefs. Of course, this requires that individuals in the Corporation act in certain ways, but we do not need to consider what those ways might be, or the causes of those actions, to predict what the Corporation will do. There is considerable utility in being able to predict behavior in ignorance of individual motivation. But is something analogous true of instances of ad hoc agreements and habits of coordination? Here too we can predict behavior without worrying about individual motivation. If two people (apparently) agree to do something, they will generally do it (to an approximation). We don't need to know whether each intends to do it. So talk of joint action has the same predictive-explanatory utility in these cases as in the case of organizations, albeit for a more modest range of behavior.[23]

If what I have been saying is right, the supraindividualist account has some extraordinary, even preposterous consequences. It denies that two people ever take a walk, eat dinner together, converse, promise, argue, or contract—do most of the things that seem to distinguish human beings from nonhuman animals, and perhaps some of the things that seem not to distinguish us. One can respond to this by rejecting supraindividualism and insisting that there must be an adequate individualist account of joint action. I have claimed that we do not currently have any idea what such an account might be. Alternatively, one may seek a partial reconciliation between supraindividualism and common sense by observing that human beings engage in many activities that approximate joint action to one degree or another. I believe that this is the more promising approach at the present time.

I have claimed that a supraindividualist account of joint action is suggested by the troubles with individualist accounts. I have argued that on a supraindividualist account, there are few if any genuine joint actions or agents. However, organizations approximate genuine agents to a substantial degree, and even in the case of joint actions from ad hoc agreements or habitual coordination, there is a predictive point to speaking of joint agency. To develop a supraindividualist account, we will need to examine more closely just how a joint agent differs from Searle's Chinese Room. We will need to consider further the extent to which genuine joint agents are realized. And we will need to look more intently at the point of talk of joint agency.

NOTES

1. My account is closest to Brooks (1981, 1986), French (1984), Clark (1994), and Rovane (1997).
2. Strict individualism has also been called *singularism* (Gilbert 1989).
3. See Yi (2002, forthcoming) for discussion of plural reference, or reference to many things as such. One difficulty with the plural reference approach is that it does not distinguish between joint conditions of inanimate things and joint actions of agents. It gives the same plural reference analysis of "The two pillars jointly bear the weight of the ceiling" and "Hercules and Atlas jointly held up the sky for a moment." Yet the relevant senses of "jointly" seem to be different, although the latter sense may entail the former. So the account offers at best one ingredient in an account of joint action.

Another difficulty with the plural reference approach is that it offers no account of the counterfactual conditions of agenthood. Under what conditions could a joint action *j* of *A* and *B* be performed by *A*, *B*, and *C*? The account seems constitutionally unable to say, because it analyzes "*A* and *B* perform a joint action of walking" as "*A* and *B* walk jointly," and it says no more about the latter than that "*A* and *B*" refers plurally. The account does not seem to recognize, or may indeed be inconsistent with, the claim that there is a joint action performed by *A* and *B*.

4. Some remarks on action: For convenience, I assume a narrow (Kim-Goldman) individuation of action by action types: *A*'s pumping water is distinct from *A*'s cranking the pump handle. I believe that what I say can be translated to conform to a broad (Davidsonian) individuation. What relation between action and intention do I assume? I will allow that nonbasic actions can be unintentional. You can perform an action of pumping water into the house without intending to do so. For example, you might not foresee the consequences of cranking the handle. But in this case, there must be some other action *y*—cranking the handle—you intend to perform such that you pump water by doing *y*. On another point, it is possible to perform a nonbasic action and have an intention to perform that action, but not perform the action *from* that intention. In the case of basic action, an intention to perform the action is plausibly necessary, and it seems necessary to perform the action from the intention to perform it. For simplicity, I overlook here any distinction there may be between *A*'s intending to do *x* and *A*'s intending that *A* does *x*. What is the relation between an intention and an end? I assume that if an agent intends to run, then she has as an end her running. An intention to do *x* settles that one will do *x* for purposes of practical reasoning. An end of doing *x* requires only that one will endeavor to bring it about that one does *x* under the right circumstances.

5. Could Miller respond that (2a) really does hold relative to the end of *jointly lifting the sofa?* For Alan would not lift his side if Betty didn't lift her side, given only the end of *jointly* lifting the sofa. (2a) does fail relative to Alan's total system of ends, which makes Alan's lifting his part of the sofa an overriding end, but (2a) is satisfied relative to the end of jointly lifting the sofa. In reply, (2a) need not hold even relative to the end of jointly lifting the sofa. Even relative to this end, Alan might go ahead and lift his side even if he does not believe that Betty lifts her side. Alan might still *hope* that Betty will lift her side, and he might accordingly regard his lifting his side as his best instrument for bringing about the joint action.

6. Actual mutual responsiveness may be necessary for some joint actions, but only because they are of a type that (whether individual or joint) requires it. For example, Elmo and Flip can't jointly bake the cake if Elmo does all the work up until the point where the cake is removed from the oven, but Flip refuses to remove the cake from the oven. Performing the action of baking a cake, whether individual or joint, requires removing the cake from the oven at the end. This has to do with the type of action, not with the nature of joint action.

7. Note that this requirement is weaker than Miller's collective end requirement on either the strong or the weak reading. That is why I am calling it the "easier" requirement.

8. At this point, we can see that the mutual true belief conditions (4) and (5) of Miller's account of joint action are too strong. Condition (4) is too strong because, as the case of Alan and Betty shows, A need not believe that B will y and need not even discover later that B has *y*ed. Condition (5) is too strong because in the cases of joint action we have described, conditions (2) and (3) are not even satisfied, so A and B cannot truly believe that (2) and (3), as (5) requires. Moreover, A may believe (correctly) that his *x*ing does not depend on B's *y*ing.

9. Of course, I could have the intention of raising my finger, attempt to do so, and fail to perform that action, but rather cause my wrist to turn. But I take it the latter would not be an action or at least not one performed *from* the intention to lift my finger.

10. On a supraindividualist view, a joint action is not even *partly* constituted by singular actions. Nevertheless, it seems right to say that the bodily motion corresponding to a joint action is constituted by the bodily motions corresponding to singular actions x and y, in a mereological sum sense of "constitution." Moreover, it is not out of the question to think of a joint action of baking a cake as constituted by singular actions in something like the sense in which an individual's action of baking a cake is constituted by the individual's actions of mixing the batter, pouring it into the mold, and so on. In the latter case, the individual's action is constituted by these actions in the sense that it is performed *by* the individual's performing these actions. In the case of a joint action of baking a cake, one might say that it is performed (by A and B) by A's mixing the batter, B's pouring the batter into the mold, and so on. I am skeptical about this because it runs afoul of the plausible principle that when an agent C performs an action x by performing an action y, it must be C who performs y. Perhaps one might attempt to reconcile these by saying that A's mixing the batter just is a joint action of A and B of mixing the batter. But this in turn runs afoul of the plausible principle that actions are individuated by their agents.

11. A supraindividualist is perhaps more likely to find this claim attractive than a strict individualist is. The supraindividualist could argue for it on the ground that an

action necessarily has the agent it in fact has, and a joint agent is necessarily joint. A strict individualist would of course deny that a joint action has one agent, but a strict individualist who rejects a mereological view of constitution, in favor of an aggregate sum view (see the following endnote) could still accept that a joint action necessarily has the individual agents it in fact has. However, that claim is implausible, because Elmo and Flip's joint action of baking the cake could, it seems, be performed by Elmo, Flip, and Gus instead of Elmo and Flip.

12. The second and third objections to the mereological sum view of constitution also apply to the aggregate view.

13. These points also tell against the following two alternative formulations of Miller's account:

There is a joint action *j* just in case there are individuals *A* and *B*, and singular actions *x* of *A* and *y* of *B*, such that *j* is wholly constituted by *x* and *y*, and *x* and *y* meet conditions (1)–(5).

A and *B* act jointly just in case there are singular actions *x* of *A* and *y* of *B*, and there is a *j* such that *j* is wholly constituted by *x* and *y*, and *x* and *y* meet conditions (1)–(5).

In arguing that joint actions are never wholly constituted by singular actions, we have also established that the requirement that *j* is wholly constituted by *x* and *y* is too strong.

14. It seems possible to act from an intention without satisfying it. I could crank the handle from my intention to pump water but fail to pump water because none comes forth.

15. (B) and (C) are shown to be too strong by our examples of joint action resulting from agreement. If *A* intends that we *J*, then *A* expects that we *J*. But Alice and Bob perform a joint action of lifting the sofa even though Alice does not expect that they will lift the sofa.

16. One might have another worry about Bratman's account. Condition (C), properly understood, requires that we *J* from *A*'s intention that we *J* and from *B*'s intention that we *J*. But is it possible for an agent to act from another's intention? Perhaps it is. Abe Roth argues persuasively that another's intention can rationally constrain my reasoning ("Practical Intersubjectivity," this volume). This is not far from the idea that another's intention can be mine, and that I can act from another's intention.

17. See Gilbert (2000, ch. 2) for arguments in favor of this conclusion.

18. I take it that in the latter case, it is possible for individuals to act without any agreement or expression of willingness to act jointly. Indeed, we can conceive of individuals who have habitually acted in coordination from time immemorial. Suppose two such immortal beings have, every day from eternity, met at noon at a quarry and together wielded a sledgehammer to crush a rock. I take it that each wielding could be a joint action, even if these individuals never agreed or expressed willingness to wield the hammer jointly.

19. For a discussion of organizations that are not collectivities, see Gilbert (1989, pp. 230–32).

20. I have one reservation about (3): it rules out the apparent possibility that in a joint action no partner performs an action. The case of two people walking arm-in-

arm in a drunken stupor verges on a case in which all actions are joint, none singular. One way to make room for such a case would be to weaken (3) to say that the bodily motion corresponding to *j* is composed only of bodily motions that diverse individual agents cause to occur with the intention of contributing to *j* if *j* occurs. But this is not quite right, because an agent who is not a partner could cause such an event.

21. See Dennett (1987) for the intentional stance. See Clark (1994) for a discussion of the relation of the intentional stance to collective agency. Clark is concerned to debunk the scientific explanatory utility of applying the intentional stance to a corporation. This is consistent with my point that applying the intentional stance to a corporation may suffice for the sort of explanations of actions we seek in common life. See Philip Pettit, this volume, for a defense of the claim that social integrates are genuine agents.

22. Here I follow roughly some elements of Bratman's (1999a, 1999b) account of intention.

23. Of course, this story must be complicated when we add condition (3) to joint action, because it introduces conditional individual intentions. However, we do not need to know all relevant intentions of this sort to ascribe a joint action—only enough to satisfy (3).

6

Groups with Minds of Their Own

Philip Pettit

There is a type of organization found in certain collectivities that makes them into subjects in their own right, giving them a way of being minded that is starkly discontinuous with the mentality of their members. This claim in social ontology is strong enough to ground talk of such collectivities as entities that are psychologically autonomous and that constitute institutional persons. Yet unlike some traditional doctrines (Runciman 1997), it does not spring from a rejection of common sense. This chapter shows that the claim is supported by the implications of a distinctive social paradox—the discursive dilemma—and is consistent with a denial that our minds are subsumed in a higher form of *Geist* or in any variety of collective consciousness. Although the chapter generates a rich, metaphysical brew, the ingredients it deploys all come from austere and sober analysis.

The chapter is in six sections. In the first, I introduce the doctrinal paradox, a predicament recently identified in jurisprudence, and in the second, I explain how it generalizes to constitute the discursive dilemma. In the third section, I show that that dilemma is going to arise for any group or grouping—henceforth I shall just say, group—that espouses or avows purposes, and that such purposive collectivities are bound to resolve it by imposing the discipline of reason at the collective rather than the individual level. In the fourth and fifth sections, I argue that groups of this kind—social integrates, as I call them—will constitute intentional and personal subjects. And then in the sixth section, I look briefly at how we should think of the relationship between institutional persons of this kind and the natural persons who sustain them.

THE DOCTRINAL PARADOX

The discursive dilemma is a generalized version of the doctrinal paradox that has recently been identified in jurisprudence by Lewis Kornhauser and Lawrence Sager (Kornhauser and Sager 1993; Kornhauser 1996). This paradox arises when a multimember court has to make a decision on the basis of received doctrine as to the considerations that ought to determine the resolution of a case: that is, on the basis of a conceptual sequencing of the matters to be decided (Chapman 1998). It consists in the fact that the standard practice whereby judges make their individual decisions on the case, and then aggregate their votes, can lead to a different result from that which would have ensued had they voted instead on whether the relevant considerations obtained and let those votes dictate how the case should be resolved.

A good example of the doctrinal paradox is provided by this simple case where a three-judge court has to decide on a tort case. Under relevant legal doctrine let us suppose that the court has to judge the defendant liable if and only if it finds, first, that the defendant's negligence was causally responsible for the injury to the plaintiff and, second, that the defendant had a duty of care toward the plaintiff. Now imagine that the three judges, A, B, and C, vote as follows on those issues and on the doctrinally related matter of whether the defendant is indeed liable.

	Cause of harm?	Duty of care?	Liable?
A.	Yes	No	No
B.	No	Yes	No
C.	Yes	Yes	Yes

Matrix 1

There are two salient ways in which the court might in principle make its decision in a case like this. Let us suppose that each judge votes on each premise and on the conclusion and does so in a perfectly rational manner. The judges might aggregate their votes in respect of the conclusion—the liability issue—and let the majority view on that issue determine their collective finding. Call this the conclusion-centered procedure. Under such a procedure, the defendant would go free, because there are two votes against liability. Or the judges might aggregate their votes on the individual premises—the causation and duty issues; let the majority view on each premise determine whether or not it is collectively endorsed; and let the conclusion be accepted—that the defendant is liable—if and only if both premises are collectively endorsed. Call this the premise-centered procedure. Since each premise commands majority support, the defendant would be found liable under this procedure. The doctrinal paradox, as presented in the jurisprudential literature, consists in the fact that the two procedures described yield different outcomes.

Another simple example from the jurisprudential area is provided by a case where a three-judge court has to decide on whether a defendant is liable under a charge of breach of contract (Kornhauser and Sager 1993, p. 11). According to legal doctrine, the court should find against the defendant if and only if it finds, first that a valid contract was in place, and second that the defendant's behavior was such as to breach the sort of contract that was allegedly in place. Now imagine that the three judges, A, B, and C, vote as follows on those issues and on the doctrinally related matter of whether the defendant is indeed liable.

	Contract?	Breach?	Liable?
A.	Yes	No	No
B.	No	Yes	No
C.	Yes	Yes	Yes

Matrix 2

In this case, as in the previous example, the judges might each conduct their own reasoning and then decide the case in a conclusion-centered way, by reference to the votes in the final column. Or they might decide the case in a premise-centered way by looking to the majority opinions in each of the first two columns and then letting those opinions decide the issue of liability. If they adopted the conclusion-centered approach, they would find for the defendant; if they took the premise-centered approach, then they would find against.

The paradox illustrated will arise wherever a majority in the group supports each of the premises, different majorities support different premises, and the intersection or overlap of those majorities is not itself a majority in the group. The fact that those in that overlap are not themselves a majority—in the cases considered there is only one judge, C, in the intersection—explains why there is only a minority in favor of the conclusion.[1]

The doctrinal paradox is not confined to cases where a court has to make a decision by reference to a conjunction of premises. It can also arise in cases where the court has to make its decision by reference to a disjunction of considerations; that is, in cases where the support required for a positive conclusion is only that one or more of the premises be endorsed. This is unsurprising, of course, given that a disjunction of premises, p or q, is equivalent to the negation of a conjunction: not-(not-p and not-q). Still, it may be worth illustrating the possibility.

Imagine that three judges have to make a decision on whether or not someone should be given a retrial; that a retrial is required either in the event of inadmissible evidence having been used previously or in the event of the appellant's having been forced to confess; and that the voting goes as follows among the judges (Kornhauser and Sager 1993, p. 40):

	Inadmissible evidence?	Forced confession?	Retrial?
A.	Yes	No	Yes
B.	No	Yes	Yes
C.	No	No	No

Matrix 3

This case also illustrates a doctrinal paradox, because the conclusion-centered procedure will lead to giving the defendant a retrial and a premise-centered procedure will not: at least not, so long as majority voting is all that is required for the group to reject one of the premises (see Pettit 2001).

THE DISCURSIVE DILEMMA

It should be clear that the doctrinal paradox will generalize in a number of dimensions, representing a possibility that may materialize with any number of decision makers greater than two and with any number of premises greater than one, whether those premises be conjunctively or disjunctively organized. But there are other, perhaps less obvious ways in which it can be generalized also and I now look at three of these. These give us reason, as we shall see later, to speak of a discursive dilemma. I describe them respectively as the social generalization, the diachronic generalization, and the *modus tollens* generalization.

The Social Generalization

A paradox of the sort illustrated will arise not just when legal doctrine dictates that certain considerations are conceptually or epistemically prior to a certain issue—an issue on which a conclusion has to be reached—and that judgments on those considerations ought to dictate the judgment on the conclusion. It will arise whenever a group of people discourse together with a view to forming an opinion on a certain matter that rationally connects, by the lights of all concerned, with other issues.

Consider an issue that might arise in a workplace, among the employees of a company: for simplicity, as we may assume, a company owned by the employees. The issue is whether to forgo a pay-raise in order to spend the money thereby saved on introducing a set of workplace safety measures: say, measures to guard against electrocution. Let us suppose for convenience that the employees are to make the decision—perhaps because of prior resolution—on the basis of considering three separable issues: first, how serious the danger is; second, how effective the safety measure that a pay-sacrifice would buy is likely to be; and third, whether the pay-sacrifice is bearable for members individually. If an employee thinks that the danger is sufficiently serious, the safety measure sufficiently effective, and the pay-sacrifice sufficiently bearable, he or she will vote for the sacrifice; otherwise he or she will vote against. And so each will have to consider the three issues and then look to what should be concluded about the pay-sacrifice.

Imagine now that after appropriate dialogue and deliberation the employees are disposed to vote on the relevant premises and conclusion in the pattern illustrated by the following matrix for a group of three workers. The letters *A*, *B*, and *C* represent the three employees and the "Yes" or "No" on any row represents the disposition of the relevant employee to admit or reject the corresponding premise or conclusion.

	Serious danger?	Effective measure?	Bearable loss?	Pay-sacrifice?
A.	Yes	No	Yes	No
B.	No	Yes	Yes	No
C.	Yes	Yes	No	No

Matrix 4

If this is the pattern in which the employees vote, then a different decision will be made, depending on whether the group judgment is driven by how members judge on the premises or by how they judge on the conclusion. Looking at the matrix, we can see that though everyone individually rejects the pay-sacrifice, a majority supports each of the premises. If we think that the views of the employees on the conclusion should determine the group decision, then we will say that the group-conclusion should be to reject the pay-sacrifice: there are only "No"s in the final column. But if we think that the views of the employees on the premises should determine the group-decision, then we will say that the group conclusion should be to accept the pay-sacrifice: there are more "Yes"s than "No"s in each of the premise columns.

There are familiar practices of group deliberation and decision making corresponding to the conclusion-centered and premise-centered options. Thus the group would go the conclusion-centered way if members entered into deliberation and dialogue and then each cast their personal vote on whether to endorse the pay-sacrifice or not; in that case the decision would be against the pay-sacrifice. The group would go the premise-centered way, on the other hand, if there was a chairperson who took a vote on each of the premises—say, a show of hands—and then let logic decide the outcome; in this case the decision would be in favor of the pay-sacrifice.

This example is stylized but should serve to indicate that the paradox is not confined to the domain in which legal doctrine dictates that certain judgments are to be made by reference to certain considerations. There are many social groups that have to make judgments on various issues and that routinely do so by reference to considerations that are privileged within the group.

One set of examples will be provided by the groups that are charged by an external authority with making certain decisions on the basis of designated considerations, and on that basis only. Instances of the category will be appointment and promotions committees; committees charged with deciding who is to win a certain prize or contract; trusts that have to make judgments on the basis of prior instructions; associations or the executives of associations that have to justify their actions by reference to the group's charter; corporations that have to comply with policies endorsed by their shareholders; public bodies, be they bureaucratic committees or appointed boards, that have to discharge specific briefs; and governments that are more or less bound to party programs and principles. With all such groups there is likely to be a problem as to whether the group should make its judgment on a certain issue in a premise-centered or conclusion-centered way; it will always be possible that those procedures will lead in different directions.

For a second set of examples consider those groups where it is a matter of internal aspiration that members find common grounds by which to justify whatever line they collectively take. Think of the political movement that has to work out a policy program; or the association that has to decide on the terms of its constitution; or the church that has to give an account of itself in the public forum; or the learned academy that seeks a voice in the larger world of politics and journalism. In such cases members of the group may not have access to an antecedently agreed set of considerations on the basis of which to justify particular judgments. But their identification with one another will support a wish to reach agreement on such a set of reasons. To the extent that that wish gets to be satisfied, they will have to face the issue, sooner or later, as to whether they should make their decisions in a premise-centered or conclusion-centered way.

The Diachronic Generalization

For all that has been said, however, the paradox may still seem unlikely to figure much in ordinary social life. The reason is that whereas the judges in a courtroom routinely have to make their judgments by reference to shared considerations, people in other social groups will often reach collective decisions on an incompletely theorized basis (Sunstein 1999). There will be a majority, perhaps even a consensus, in favor of a certain line on some issue but there will be no agreement among the parties to that majority or consensus on the reasons that support the line. The parties will each vote that line for reasons of their own—reasons related to their own interests or their own judgments of the common interest—and there will only be a partial overlap between the different considerations they each take into account. Thus there will be no possibility of their resorting to a premise-centered procedure, let alone any prospect of that procedure yielding a different result from the conclusion-centered alternative.

But sound as this consideration is, social groups will still have to deal routinely with the choice between these two procedures. In all of the examples so far considered, the premises and the conclusion are up for synchronic determination, whether at the individual or the collective level. Under the conclusion-centered procedure, each person has to make up their own mind on the reasons they are considering in premise position—assuming they do judge by reasons—and at the same time on the conclusion that those reasons support. Under the premise-centered procedure, the group has to make up its mind on the reasons that are relevant by everyone's lights and at the same time on the conclusion that is to be derived from those premise-judgments. But the problem of choosing between such procedures may arise for a group in a diachronic as distinct from a synchronic way and is likely to arise much more generally on this basis.

Suppose that over a period of time a group makes a judgment on each of a set of issues, deciding them all by majority vote and perhaps deciding them on incompletely theorized grounds: different members of the group are moved by different considerations. Sooner or later such a group is bound to face an issue such that how it should judge on that issue is determined by the judgments it previously endorsed on other issues. And in such an event the group will face the old choice between adopting a conclusion-centered procedure and adopting a premise-centered one. The members may take a majority vote on the new issue facing them, running the risk of adopting a view that is inconsistent with the views that they previously espoused as a collectivity. Or they may allow the previously espoused views to dictate the view that they should take on this new issue.

The courts will often face diachronic examples of the problem illustrated as well as the synchronic examples that we considered; this will happen when previous judgments of the court dictate the judgment that it ought to make on an issue currently before it. But, more important for our purposes, even social groups that differ from the courts in routinely securing only incompletely theorized agreements will have to confront diachronic examples of the problem. They may escape the synchronic problem through not being capable of agreeing on common considerations by which different issues are to be judged. But that is no guarantee that they will be able to escape the problem as it arises in diachronic form.

The *Modus Tollens* Generalization

The third and last point to note in generalization of the doctrinal paradox is that the options that we have been describing as the conclusion-centered procedure and the premise-centered procedure are not exhaustive of the alternatives available. The problem involved in the doctrinal paradox, even as it arises in legal and synchronic contexts, has a more general cast than the jurisprudential literature suggests.

The best way to see that the options are not exhaustive is to consider what a group may do if it finds that, relying on majority vote, it endorses each of a given set of premises while rejecting a conclusion that they support: say, deductively support. One grand option is for the collectivity to let the majority vote stand on each issue, thereby reflecting the views of its members on the different issues, while allowing the collective views to be inconsistent with one another. This approach, in effect, would vindicate the conclusion-centered procedure. But what now are the alternatives?

One possibility is for the group to ignore the majority vote on the conclusion, as in the premise-centered procedure, and to let the majority votes on the premises dictate the collective view on the conclusion. But another equally salient possibility, neglected as irrelevant in the legal context, is to ignore the majority vote on one of the premises, letting the majority votes on the other premises together with the majority vote on the conclusion dictate the collective view to be taken on that premise. The first possibility involves the collectivity practicing *modus ponens*, the second has it practice *modus tollens* instead. These two options can be seen as different forms of a single grand option that stands exhaustively opposed to the first alternative described above. Where that alternative would have the collectivity reflect the individual views of its members on each issue, this second option would have the group ensure that the views collectively espoused across those issues are mutually consistent.

It should now be clear why I speak of a discursive dilemma rather than a doctrinal paradox. The problem arises because of the requirements of discourse as such, not just because of the demands of legal doctrine. And the problem represents a hard choice or dilemma, not anything that strictly deserves to be called a paradox. The hard choice that a group in this dilemma faces is whether to let the views of the collectivity on any issue be fully responsive to the individual views of members, thereby running the risk of collective inconsistency; or whether to ensure that the views of the group are collectively rational, even where that means compromising responsiveness to the views of individual members on one or another issue. You can have individual responsiveness or collective rationality but you cannot have both—or at least you cannot have both for sure.

In arguing that the discursive dilemma presents groups with a hard choice, of course, I am assuming that they will not be happy to avoid that choice by insisting on voting by unanimity rather than majority, for example, since that would make them unable to come to agreement on many pressing questions. And equally I am assuming that collectivities will not simply refuse to draw out the implications of their views, avoiding inconsistency by avoiding deductive closure. But I say no more here on the general possibilities that arise in this area. Christian List and I have argued elsewhere for a relevant impossibility theorem (List and Pettit 2002a, 2002b).[2]

RESOLVING THE DILEMMA BY COLLECTIVIZING REASON

Any groups that seek to make deliberative, reasoned judgments, then, face a dilemma. They may maximize responsiveness to individual views, running the risk of collectively endorsing inconsistent sets of propositions. Or they may impose the discipline of reason at the collective level, running the risk of collectively endorsing a conclusion that a majority of them—perhaps even all of them—individually reject. I show in this section that many groups respond to the dilemma by adopting the second alternative—by collectivizing reason—and I go on to argue in the following two sections that groups that collectivize reason deserve ontological recognition as intentional and personal subjects.

Groups come in many different shapes and sizes (French 1984). Some are just unorganized collocations like the set of pedestrians on a given street or the people who live in the same postal area. Some are sets related in other arbitrary ways, like those who have even telephone numbers or those who are first born to their mothers. And some are classes of people who share a common feature—say, accent or mannerism—that affects how others treat them but not necessarily how they behave themselves. Yet other groups are united by a commonality, due to nature or artifice, that does affect how they behave themselves. It may affect how they behave toward one another, without leading them to do anything in common, as with linguistic groups, Internet chat groups, and other enduring or episodic networks. Or it may also affect how they behave, as we say, to a shared purpose.

Purposive groups come themselves in a number of varieties (Stoljar 1973). They include organizations that have a specific function to discharge, such as museums, libraries, trusts, and states, as well as more episodic entities like the appointments committee or the jury or the commission of inquiry. And they also include groups that do not have any one specific function but that are associated with a characteristic goal, involving the outside world or the group's own members or perhaps a mix of both. Examples would include the political party, the trade union, and the business corporation, as well as the small group of colleagues involved in collaborative research and the set of friends arranging a joint holiday.

I argue in this section that purposive groups will almost inevitably confront examples of the discursive dilemma and that, short of resorting to deception, they will be under enormous pressure to collectivize reason: usually, though not inevitably, to collectivize reason by practicing *modus ponens*—as in the premise-centered procedure—rather than *modus tollens*. In mounting this argument I shall speak as if every member of a purposive group participates equally with others in voting on what the group should do. I return to that assumption in the last section, where I try to show that the argument can survive variations in such detail.

My argument is in three parts. I argue first that a purposive collectivity will inevitably confront discursive dilemmas; second, that it will be under enormous pressure to collectivize reason in those dilemmas; and third, that in the general run of cases it will collectivize reason by following the premise-centered procedure.

The first part of the argument can be formulated in these steps.

1. Any collection of individuals who coordinate their actions around the pursuit of a common purpose—more on what this involves in the next section—will have to endorse judgments that dictate how they are to act; these will bear on the opportunities available for action, the best available means of furthering their purpose, and so on.

2. The pursuit of such a common purpose will usually require explicit discussion and deliberation about the judgments the collectivity ought to endorse—it will not be like the activity of a tug-of-war team—so that over time the group will generate a history of judgments that it is on record as making.

3. Those past judgments will inevitably constrain the judgment that the group ought to make in various new cases; only one particular judgment in this or that case will be consistent—or coherent in some looser way—with the past judgments.

4. And so the group will find itself confronted with discursive dilemmas; it will be faced across time with sets of rationally connected issues such that it will have to choose between maximizing responsiveness to the views of individual members and ensuring collective rationality.

This argument shows that discursive dilemmas of a diachronic sort are going to be more or less unavoidable for purposive groups but it is consistent, of course, with such groups also having to face synchronic dilemmas; I abstract from that possibility here. The second part of the argument goes on to show that any group of the kind envisaged will be pressured to impose the discipline of reason at the collective level. It involves a further three steps.

5. The group will not be an effective or credible promoter of its assumed purpose if it tolerates inconsistency or incoherence in its judgments across time; not all the actions shaped by those discordant judgments can advance, or be represented as advancing, one and the same purpose.
6. Every such group will need to be an effective promoter of its assumed purpose and will need to be able to present itself as an effective promoter of that purpose; it will lose any hold on members, or any respect among outsiders, if cannot do this.
7. And so every purposive group is bound to try to collectivize reason, achieving and acting on collective judgments that pass reason-related tests like consistency.

How will a purposive group be disposed to collectivize reason? We do not need to answer this question for purposes of the present argument. But it is worth noting that two plausible, further steps argue that such a group will generally, though not of course inevitably, have to follow something like the premise-driven procedure illustrated in our earlier examples.

8. The group will be unable to present itself as an effective promoter of its purpose if it invariably seeks to establish consistency and coherence in the cases envisaged by renouncing one or other of its past commitments: if it never allows its present judgment to be dictated by past judgments; there will be no possibility of taking such a routinely inconstant entity seriously.
9. Thus, any such purposive collectivity must avoid automatic recourse to the revision of past commitments; it must show that those commitments are sufficiently robust for us to be able to expect that the group will frequently be guided by them in its future judgments.

The force of this three-part line of argument can be readily illustrated. Suppose that a political party announces in March, say on the basis of majority vote among its members, that it will not increase taxes if it gets into government. Suppose that it announces in June, again on the basis of majority vote, that it will increase defense spending. And now imagine that it faces the issue in September as to whether it will increase government spending in other areas of policy or organization. Should it allow a majority vote on that issue too?

If the party does allow a majority vote, then we know that even in the event of individual members being perfectly consistent across time, the vote may favor increasing government spending in other areas. Thus the party will face the hard choice between being responsive to the views of its individual members and ensuring the collective rationality of the views it endorses. The members may vote in the pattern of members A to C in the following matrix.

	Increase taxes?	Increase defense spending?	Increase other spending?
A.	No	Yes	No (reduce)
B.	No	No (reduce)	Yes
C.	Yes	Yes	Yes

Matrix 5

But the party cannot tolerate collective inconsistency, because that would make it a laughing-stock among its followers and in the electorate at large; it could no longer claim to be seriously committed to its alleged purpose. And so it must not allow its judgments to be made in such a way that the discipline of reason is imposed only at the individual level; it has to ensure that that discipline is imposed at the collective level. In the ordinary run of things, the party will make its judgments after a premise-driven pattern, using a *modus ponens* type of procedure. It may occasionally revoke earlier judgments in order to be able in consistency to sustain a judgment that is supported by a majority. But it cannot make a general practice of this, on pain of again becoming a laughing-stock. It must frequently allow past judgments to serve as endorsed premises that dictate later commitments.

This argument with the political party is going to apply, quite obviously, to a large range of enduring and episodic collectivities. The argument does not rule out the possibility that those groups will occasionally adopt another course. They may choose to reject an earlier commitment in this or that case, for example, rather than revise their spontaneous judgment on the issue currently before them. Or they may even choose to live, overtly or covertly, with an inconsistency. But it is hard to see how they could generally fail in these regards and constitute effective or credible agents.

Instead of speaking of groups that collectivize reason in the manner of these collectivities I shall talk from now on of integrations of people, of integrated collectivities, and of social integrates. This way of speaking sounds a contrast with those groups that do not reason at all or that do not impose the discipline of reason at the collective level. These we naturally describe as aggregations of people, as aggregated collectivities or just as aggregates. I go on in the next two sections to argue that in an intuitive and important sense social integrates are going to be intentional and personal subjects. I continue to assume in this argument that members of social integrates all take an equal part in voting on what those collectivities should do; I come back to that assumption in the final section of the paper.

SOCIAL INTEGRATES ARE INTENTIONAL SUBJECTS

Are integrations of people likely to constitute intentional subjects, displaying intentional states like beliefs and desires, judgments and intentions, and performing the actions that such states rationalize? In particular, are integrations of people likely to constitute intentional subjects in their own right? Are we going to have to itemize them, side by side with their members—if you like, over and beyond their members—in any serious inventory of intentional subjects?

In a well-known discussion, Anthony Quinton (1975–76) maintains not. He argues that to ascribe judgments, intentions, and the like to social groups is just a way of ascribing them, in a summative way, to individuals in those groups.

We do, of course, speak freely of the mental properties and acts of a group in the way we do of individual people. Groups are said to have beliefs, emotions, and attitudes and to take decisions and make promises. But these ways of speaking are plainly metaphorical. To ascribe mental predicates to a group is always an indirect way of ascribing such predicates to its members. With such mental states as beliefs and attitudes, the ascriptions are of what I have called a summative kind. To say that the industrial working class is determined to resist anti-trade union laws is to say that all or most industrial workers are so minded. (p. 17)

The position adopted here by Quinton amounts to a straightforward eliminativism about collective intentional subjects. It suggests that only singular entities can constitute intentional subjects—for this reason it might also be called "singularism" (Gilbert 1989, p. 12)—and that collectivities can be described as subjects "only by figment, and for the sake of brevity of discussion" (Austin 1875, p. 364).

One reason why the position described amounts to eliminativism is this. If a collectivity can be said to form a certain belief or desire, a certain judgment or intention, so far as all or most of its members do, then it would be misleading to say that it constituted an intentional subject over and beyond its members. Asked to say how many such subjects were present in a certain domain it would be quite arbitrary to count the individuals there, and then to count the collectivity also. We might as well count as subjects, not just the total set of people there, but also every subset in which majority or unanimous attitudes give us a basis on which to ascribe corresponding attitudes to that collection of people.

This criticism suggests that Quinton tells too simple a story about the attitudes that we expect to find on the part of individuals of whom we say that they collectively judge or intend something. More recent work on the conditions that might lead us to ascribe such joint attitudes, and to posit collective subjects, has stressed the fact that we usually expect a complex web of mutual awareness on the part of individuals involved (Gilbert 1989; Searle 1995; Tuomela 1995; Bratman 1999a). Thus, Michael Bratman (1999a) argues that you and I will have a shared intention to do something just in case (1) you intend that we do it and I intend that we do it; (2) we each intend that we do it because (1) holds; and (3) those clauses are matters of which we are each aware, each aware that we are each aware, and so on in the usual hierarchy of mutual knowledge.

Suppose we complicate the Quinton story in some such pattern, adopting one of these mutual-awareness analyses. Will that undercut his eliminativism, giving us reason to think that apart from singular subjects there are also collective ones? It will certainly evade the criticism just made, for it will make it much harder than Quinton does for a collection of individuals to deserve to be described as having certain mental properties. But it will not avoid another problem. It will not ensure that a collectivity displays the sort of rationality that we expect in the performance of any system we would describe as an intentional subject. So at any rate I shall argue.

What sort of rationality do we expect in an intentional subject? By a line of argument that has been widely endorsed in recent philosophical thought, a system will count as an intentional subject only if it preserves intentional attitudes over time and forms, unforms, and acts on those attitudes—at least within intuitively feasible limits and under intuitively favorable conditions—in a rationally permissible manner: in a phrase, only if it displays a certain rational unity (Pettit 1992, ch.1). If the system believes that p and comes across evidence that not-p, it must tend to unform that belief. If the system believes that p and learns that if p then q, it must come to form the belief that q or to unform one of the other beliefs. If the system desires that p, believes that by X-ing it can bring it about that p, and believes that other things are equal, then it must tend to X. And so on.

Even if we introduce the sort of complexity postulated in mutual-awareness stories about collective subjects, that will not guarantee that those subjects have the rational unity associated with intentionality. Those stories are all consistent with the collectivity's acting by conventions that allow rational disunity. The convention established in the mutual awareness of members may ordain, for example, that the collectivity shall be deemed to judge or intend whatever a majority of members vote for its judging or intending at that time. And we know from discussion of the discursive dilemma that if such a convention obtains—if the attitudes of the collectivity are required to be continuous in that majoritarian way with the current votes of members—then the collectivity may be guilty of grievous irrationality over time. It may be as wayward in the postures it assumes as the most casual aggregate of individuals; it may fail to materialize as anything that deserves to be taken as an intentional subject in its own right.

In order for a collectivity to count as an intentional subject, not only must there be a basis in the behavior of participating members for ascribing judgments and intentions and such attitudes to the collective; that is the point on which the mutual-awareness literature rightly insists. There must also be a basis for thinking of the collectivity as a subject that is rationally unified in such a way that, within feasible limits and under favorable conditions, we can expect it to live up to the constraints of rationality; we can expect it to enter and exit states of belief and desire, judgment and intention, in a way that makes rational sense and we can expect it to perform in action as those states require. Indeed, were there a basis for ascribing such states to a collectivity, and a basis for expecting this sort of rational unity, then it is hard to see any reason why we should deny that the collectivity was an intentional subject in its own right.

How to secure the dual basis that is necessary for a collectivity to be an intentional subject? The argument of the last section suggests a salient recipe. By ensuring that the collectivity represents an integration of individuals, not just a casual aggregate. Specifically, by ensuring, first, that the collectivity has a shared purpose and forms the judgments and intentions associated with pursuit of that purpose; and second, that it collectivizes reason in forming those judgments and intentions.

I said and say nothing on what it is for a collectivity to form and have a shared purpose, or to form and have certain judgments and intentions. Presumably that can be analyzed on something like the lines explored in the mutual-awareness approach; it has to do, plausibly, with the conventions, and the associated structures of common knowledge, that prevail in the collectivity. Assuming that there is an established, conventional sense in which a collectivity has a shared purpose, and forms associated judgments and intentions, the fact that it collectivizes reason in the course of that enterprise— the fact that it is a social integrate—means that it will display precisely the sort of rational unity required of an intentional subject. Let the collectivity have made certain judgments and formed certain intentions in the past. And now imagine that it faces a theoretical or practical issue where those judgments and intentions rationally require a particular response. We can rely on the integrated collectivity to respond as those intentional states rationally require, or to make rationally permissible adjustments that undercut the requirements. Or at least we can rely on it to do this under intuitively favorable conditions and within intuitively feasible limits.

The integrated collectivity has common purposes and forms associated judgments and intentions, unlike the collections envisaged in Quinton's account. And the integrated collectivity can be relied upon to achieve a rational unity in the judgments and intentions endorsed, unlike the group that meets only the mutual-awareness conditions for forming collective attitudes. It satisfies the dual basis that is necessary for a collectivity to count as an intentional subject. But is the satisfaction of these two conditions sufficient as well as necessary for the integrated collectivity to count as an intentional subject, in particular an intentional subject that is distinct from the individual subjects who make it up?

If we are to recognize the integrated collectivity as an intentional subject, then we must admit of course that it is a subject of an unusual kind. It does not have its own faculties of perception or memory, for example, though it may be able to register and endorse facts perceived or remembered by others: in particular, by its own members. Under our characterization it is incapable of forming degrees of belief and desire in the ordinary fashion of animal subjects; its beliefs are recorded as on-off judgments, its desires as on-off intentions. And the judgments and intentions that it forms are typically restricted to the narrow domain engaged by the particular purposes that its members share. Notwithstanding these features, however, I think that it is reasonable, even compulsory, to think of the integrated collectivity as an intentional subject.

The basis for this claim is that the integrated collectivity, as characterized, is going to display all the functional marks of an intentional subject and that there is no reason to discount those marks as mere appearances. Within relevant domains it will generally act in a manner that is rationalized by independently discernible representations and goals; and within relevant domains it will generally form and unform those representations in a manner that is rationalized by the evidence that we take to be at its disposal. In particular, it will manifest this sort of functional organization, not just at a time, but over time; it will display the degree of constancy as well as the degree of coherence that we expect in any intentional subject. But given that the integrated collectivity functions in these ways like an intentional subject, the question is whether that functional appearance is proof that it really is an intentional subject.

Why might someone deny that an entity that displays the functional marks of an intentional subject, as the integrated collectivity does, is not really an intentional subject? One ground might be that intentionality requires not just a certain form of organization, but also the realization of that form in inherently mental material, whatever that is thought to be. Few would endorse this consideration among contemporary thinkers, however, because there appears to be nothing inherently mental about the biological material out of which our individual minds are fashioned (but see Searle 1983). Another ground for the denial might be that the functional marks of intentional subjectivity have to come about as a result of the subject's internal organization, and not in virtue of some form of remote control or advance rigging (Jackson 1992). But this is hardly relevant to the integrated collectivity, because its judgments and intentions are clearly formed in the required, internal fashion. Still another sort of ground for denying that functional organization is sufficient for being an intentional subject is that something more is required— say, natural selection or individual training (Millikan 1984; Papineau 1987; Dretske 1988)—for the attitudes of the subject to have determinate contents. This is not relevant in the case of the integrated collectivity, however, because the contents of its judgments and intentions will inherit determinacy from the presumptively determinate words that are used by its members to express those contents.

The usual grounds for driving a wedge between functionally behaving like an intentional subject and actually being an intentional subject are unlikely, as this quick survey shows, to cause a problem with the integrated collectivity. If further grounds for making such a separation between appearance and reality are lacking, therefore, we have every reason to treat the integrated collectivity as an intentional subject. And such grounds, so far as I can see, are indeed lacking. I can think of only one other consideration that might be invoked against counting integrated collectivities as intentional subjects and it does not raise a serious problem.

The consideration is that if we treat integrated collectivities as intentional subjects, then we may be involved in a sort of double-counting. We will be counting the individual members of the collectivity as intentional subjects. And then we will be going on to say that apart from those members, there is a further subject present too: the collectivity that they compose. But I do not think that this makes for an objection. The integrated collectivity will not be distinct from its individual members, in the sense that it will not be capable of existing in the absence of such members. But it will be distinct in the sense of being a centre for the formation of attitudes that are capable of being quite discontinuous from the attitudes of the members. This is one of the lessons of the discursive dilemma.

Consider the case of the worker-owners who have to decide on whether to forgo a pay-raise in order to purchase a device for guarding against the danger of electrocution. Imagine that they cast their votes after the pattern illustrated in Matrix 4 and that they follow the premise-centered procedure in determining what to think about the issue. In such a case the group will form a judgment on the question of the pay-sacrifice that is directly in conflict with the unanimous vote of its members. It will form a judgment that is in the starkest possible discontinuity with the corresponding judgments of its members.

As the point applies to judgment, so it naturally extends to intention. The collectivity of workers that makes a judgment in favor of the pay-sacrifice will be firmly disposed to act accordingly, under the procedure it adopts, and in that sense it will form a corresponding intention. Thus the chairperson will be entitled by the premise-driven procedure to announce on the basis of the premise-votes: "Colleagues, our intention is fixed: we will forego the pay-raise." But at the moment where the intention of the integrated group is thereby fixed, no one member will intend that the group act in that way, or that he or she play their part in the group's acting in that way. Such individual intentions will follow on the formation of the group intention, of course, since the group can only act through the actions of its members. But they are not the stuff out of which the group intention is constructed; on the contrary, they are effects that the formation of the group intention plays a role in bringing about.

These discontinuities between collective judgments and intentions, on the one hand, and the judgments and intentions of members, on the other, make vivid the sense in which a social integrate is an intentional subject that is distinct from its members. They represent the cost that must be paid if a collectivity is to achieve the rational unity that we expect in any intentional subject. Rational unity is a constraint that binds the attitudes of the collectivity at any time and across different times, and the satisfaction of that constraint means that those attitudes cannot be smoothly continuous with the corresponding attitudes of members.

In arguing that a social integrate is an intentional subject that is distinct from its members—that exists over and beyond its members—I hasten to add that I am not postulating any ontological mystery. The argument is consistent with the supervenience claim that if we replicate how things are with and between individuals in a collectivity—in particular, replicate their individual judgments and their individual dispositions to accept a certain procedure—then we will replicate all the collective judgments and intentions that the group makes. Collective judgments and intentions may be discontinuous with what happens at the individual level but they cannot vary independently of what happens there; they do not constitute an ontologically emergent realm.[3]

SOCIAL INTEGRATES ARE INSTITUTIONAL PERSONS

This discontinuity between an integrated collectivity and its members, and the fact that such a collectivity can constitute a distinct intentional subject, is quite surprising. But there is more to come. For it turns out that the way in which the judgments and intentions of social integrates are formed and policed forces us to think of those collectivities as institutional persons. It leads us to see that like individual human beings, and unlike nonhuman animals, they display everything that is strictly necessary in personal as distinct from just intentional subjects.

What distinguishes personal from merely intentional subjects? As I assumed in the previous discussion that intentional subjects have to display a certain rational unity, so I make a parallel assumption in discussing this question. I assume that whereas intentional subjects must have intentional states and perform associated actions in a way that satisfies rational unity—whether or not they are aware of doing so—persons must be capable of being held to that ideal; they must be such that they can be held responsible for failures to unify their intentional states and actions in a rational way

(Rovane 1997; Pettit 2001, ch. 4). Rational unity is a constraint that intentional systems must be designed to fulfill, if only at subpersonal, unconscious levels. Rational unification is a project for which persons must be taken to assume responsibility, at least on a case-by-case basis.

The commitment that persons make to rational unification, according to this account, means that persons don't just possess intentional states and perform corresponding actions. They also avow those states and actions, acknowledging them as their own. And, avowing them, they hold themselves open to criticism in the event of not proving to live up to them: not proving to satisfy rational unity in their regard. Let a person avow a belief that p and a belief that if p then q, for example, and we can expect them to form and avow the belief that q. Or if they fail to do so, then we can expect them to have a justification or an excuse to offer. The justification may be that they had a change of mind in respect of "p" or "if p then q," the excuse that the conditions under which they were operating made it difficult to think straight.

The assumption that persons are marked off from ordinary intentional subjects—say, nonhuman animals—by the commitment to rational unification makes for a rich conception of personhood. But for that very reason it will hardly be contested in the present context, for the richness of the account should make it harder rather than easier to argue that integrations of people count as persons. In any case I say nothing more in its defense here. I shall take as persons those intentional agents who can avow their intentional states and the actions they perform in words—or in signs of some other sort—and who can then be held to the associated expectations. We may describe as persons those human beings who do not yet have this capacity, who no longer have it, or who do not have it at all. But that usage is readily seen as an extension based on the fact that they are of a kind—that is, of a species—with creatures who are persons in that strict sense.

Assuming that persons are intentional agents who make and can be held to avowals, what are we to say of integrated groups? I have no hesitation in arguing that this means that they are institutional persons, not just institutional subjects or agents (Rovane 1997 argues a similar line). Integrated collectivities bind themselves to the discipline of reason at the collective level, and that means that they are open to criticism in the event of not achieving rational unity in relevant regards. They avow judgments, intentions, and actions and prove able to be held responsible for failures to achieve consistency and other such ideals in their associated performance. They are subjects that can be treated as properly conversable interlocutors (Pettit and Smith 1996).

Social integrates contrast in this respect with any groups that do not impose the discipline of reason at the collective level. Collectivities of this aggregate kind will not be answerable in the same way to words previously authorized or deeds previously performed. And that will be so, no matter how tight we make the mutual-awareness constraints on when they can be said to authorize words or perform deeds. It will always be possible for such an aggregate to vote in favor of a judgment or an intention or an action that is out of kilter with earlier commitments, and to do so without being exposed to legitimate criticism. Opinion poll research may tell us that the populace as a whole supports cutting taxes, increasing defense expenditure, and also increasing other expenditure. Since all the individuals involved may hold consistent views, that finding that will not give us reason to criticize the populace for holding such opinions, as we might criticize a political party for doing so. For even if it is taken as an intentional subject, the populace cannot be expected to police itself for the rational unity of the things it believes and then be held to that expectation. It does not constitute a person in the relevant sense and it contrasts in that regard with the political party.

Whenever we speak of persons, we think it is appropriate to speak of selves. We expect that persons will think of themselves in the first person and be able to self-ascribe beliefs and desires and actions by the use of an indexical expression like "I" or "my," "me" or "mine." This association between being a person and thinking in self-ascriptive terms is borne out under the characterization of persons adopted here. If a person is to avow certain states and actions, and assume responsibility for achieving rational unity in their regard, then those states and actions are bound to have a distinctive salience in their experience. Individual subjects are bound to see them—by contrast with the states and actions of others—as matters of what I believe, what I desire, what I do, and so on (Pettit 2001, ch. 4).

Why must the personal point of view have this indexical, first-personal character? Why must I as a conversable subject be aware of myself in this indexical way, rather than just under a name, say as PP? A well-known line of argument provides the answer (Perry 1979; Burge 1998). Were I to conceive of myself under a name, as PP, then there would always be a deliberative gap between my thinking that PP believes both that p and that "p" entails "q" and my actually adjusting beliefs—say, in response to conversational challenge—by coming to believe that q or by giving up one of the other beliefs. For why should my beliefs about PP's beliefs have any reason-mediated effect on what I believe and assert, short of my believing that I am PP? And if I can think that I am PP, of course, then I do think of myself in the first person, not just under a name.

So far as integrated collectivities operate on the same lines as individual persons, they will also have this capacity to think in first-person terms. From the standpoint of those in an integrated collectivity the words defended in the past, for example, will stand out from any words emanating from elsewhere as words that bind and commit them. Specifically, they will stand out for those of us in the collectivity as words that "we" as a plural subject maintain. The argument in the singular case for why I as a person must conceive of my attitudes as matters of what *I* think applies in the plural case too, showing that we, the members of an integrated collectivity, must think of the group's attitudes as matters of what *we* think.

The members of a social integrate, *S*, will face the same deliberative gap as that which appeared in the singular case, if they conceive of the existing commitments of the group just as those that *S* holds. Suppose that we in that group recognize that *S* judges both that *p* and that the truth of "*p*" entails the truth of "*q*." That will not lead us as a group to judge that *q*, unless we make the extra judgment that we are *S*. And if we do make that judgment then of course we do think of ourselves in the first person plural. As members of the integrated group, we are possessed of a personal point of view and it is marked out by this indexical usage.

The emphasis on the importance of "we" connects with the insistence by writers like Margaret Gilbert (1989), John Searle (1995), and Annette Baier (1997a) that there is no possibility of analyzing we-talk in I-talk, or indeed in impersonal talk of what named individuals do (see too Tuomela 1995, p. 183). The obstacle to reducing talk of "we" to talk of "I" will be just the obstacle that stands in the way of reducing indexical talk of what I think and do to nonindexical talk of what PP thinks and does. As there is a personal perspective that is available only with talk of "I," so there is a personal perspective that becomes available only with talk of "we."

The autonomy of "we" talk that has to obtain under our account of what it is for a collectivity to be integrated nicely emphasizes the significance of the claim that such collectivities are personal as well as intentional agents. Not only do social integrates have a rational unity that constrains their performance over time and that makes them distinct from their own members. The rational unity they display is one that they themselves police and implement in the fashion of creatures whom we can hold responsible: creatures who count as persons (McGeer and Pettit 2001). They are rationally unifying as well as rationally unified subjects and the enterprise of unification in which they are involved forces them to think in the manner of a self. It makes it natural and indispensable for members to resort to a distinctively proprietary use of "we," "us," and "ours."

Once again, I should say, there is no ontological mystery in any of this: no suggestion of reality sundering into distinct realms, for example, indexical and non-indexical. If we fix the way the world is in impersonal, nonindexical terms, then we will have fixed all the indexical truths—in particular all the I-truths and all the we-truths—as well. Indexical truths supervene on nonindexical, because the same indexical sentences will be true at the same locations of utterance in impersonally indiscernible worlds (Jackson 1998; Pettit 2000). But this sort of fixing—this ontological reducibility—is quite consistent with the perspective of non-indexical talk failing to register things in the way required for singular conversability and indeed with the perspective of I-talk failing to register things in the way required for plural conversability. Such idioms may fail to be intertranslatable, and yet not direct us to independent realms of reality.

NATURAL AND INSTITUTIONAL PERSONS

The claim just defended is that social integrates have to be regarded as persons, on a par with individual human beings. But it is consistent, of course, with acknowledging that such institutional persons differ from natural persons in as many ways as they resemble them. As we saw earlier, institutional persons are not centers of perception or memory or sentience, or even of degrees of belief and desire. Institutional persons form their collective minds only on a restricted range of matters, to do with whatever purpose they are organized to advance. And institutional persons are artificial creatures whose responses may be governed by reason, not in the spontaneous manner that is characteristic of individual human beings, but only in a painstaking fashion. Their reasoning may be as tortuous as that of the impaired human being who has to work out reflectively, case by case, that in virtue of believing that p and that if p then q, he or she ought also believe that q. Integrated collectivities are persons in virtue of being conversable and responsible centers of judgment, intention, and action. But they are persons of a bloodless, bounded, and crudely robotic variety.

Even granted this, however, there are still important questions as to how institutional and natural persons relate to one another; in particular, how institutional persons and the members who constitute them relate to one another. I address two such questions in this section.

First Question

The first is a more or less straightforward question as to the institutional profiles that members have to assume so far as they constitute a single collective person. Throughout this chapter I have been assuming that even if just one individual has to act on behalf of a collective, the members are all equal participants in the formation of the collective's judgments and intentions, having equal voting power with others. But this is unrealistic as an assumption about most real-world collectives, and the first question is how far membership is consistent with the absence of such voting power.

There are two ways in which individuals may be said to endorse a collective procedure or outcome. First, by actively voting in its favor; and second, by having a capacity for exit or contestation or something of the kind—this, as a matter of common awareness—but not exercising that power. Although active voting is the most obvious mode of endorsement, it must also be possible for people to endorse a collective pattern in the second, virtual mode. The members of a collectivity cannot vote on every procedure that they are to follow, on pain of infinite regress; the problem is akin to that which would be involved in trying to endorse as an explicit premise every principle of inference deployed in an argument (Carroll 1895). If regress is to be avoided, therefore, then some of the procedures followed by the members of a collectivity must be followed without the endorsement of an explicit vote and just on the basis that that is how things are done among members, and done without contestation.

But if all the members of a group must endorse some procedures in a virtual way—that is, by not exercising a power of exit or contestation or whatever—then it is clearly possible that on many matters of procedure, and on many outcomes, some members will play an active voting part—they may even serve as plenipotentiaries for resolving various irrationalities (List and Pettit 2002a)—while others are involved only in that virtual manner. And this is how it is, obviously, with most integrated collectivities. Such collectivities sometimes involve all of their members in deliberation on every decision. But more often they stage their decisions so that the full assembly only votes on general matters, delegating others to smaller bodies and to officers of the group. Or they may involve a membership that is largely passive, with most being involved in official decisions only to the extent of needing to be pacified. Or they may be articulated into subunits that are each passive in relation to one another. And so on: the details need not concern us.

Second Question

The second question raised by our discussion bears on how natural and institutional persons relate to one another within the psychology of a given member. Suppose that someone is faced with a decision on which they as a natural person tend to go one way, while an institutional person of which they are a member—perhaps the relevant, executive member—would tend to go another. What is to happen in such a case? For all that we have said, it might be that the psychology of the individual is taken over, willy nilly, either by the natural person associated with it or by the institutional person. Or it might be that which person is to be present in that psychology is determined, at least ideally, by considerations that the two persons can debate—debate within the same head, as it were—and reach agreement on. Or it might be that the natural person is always primary and has the task of deciding whether to act in their own name—in their own interests, perhaps, or according to their own values—or in the name of the collective. The first model is clearly crazy, suggesting that persons take over psychologies in the way demons are said to assume possession of souls. But which of the other two models is the more plausible?

My own inclination is to go for the last alternative, giving priority to natural persons. I reject the picture according to which persons, natural and institutional, are of more or less the same standing and have equal presumptive claims in the sort of case envisaged on the resources of the member's psychology (Rovane 1997 supports this image). I hold that natural persons have an inescapable priority and that in this kind of case it will be up to the natural person to decide whether or not to cede place to the institutional, acting in furtherance of the collective goal and in neglect of his or her own priorities.

There are a couple of reasons why I hold by this image rather than the other. One is that it fits well with the intentional manner in which, as it seems, natural persons go about constituting and enacting institutional agents. Natural persons are in intentional control of whether they enter or exit most of the collectives to which they belong. And when they act on behalf of a collective, they are reinforced in their identity as natural persons, and the intentional control they have as natural persons, by the way others relate to them; others call on Jones to do what the collective requires of them, others congratulate Jones for doing his or her bit, and so on.

Another reason for preferring my model is that there are cases where it is going to be quite misleading to think of two persons, one natural and the other institutional, debating within a single head as to who should be the one to prevail. That model may apply when the reasons that they take into account are agent-neutral considerations to do with what is for the best overall but it will be unrealistic where each person has an agent-relative reason—say, one to do with personal prospects or commitments or allegiances—for wanting to go their preferred way. When ordinary people diverge in that way, then reason runs out and they may have to compete in some nondeliberative manner—or toss a coin—to determine who wins. We cannot envisage a natural and an institutional person competing in that way within the same head.[4]

It is sometimes said that before we know what it is rational for a human being to do, we need to be told which identity that agent is enacting; in particular we need to be told whether they are acting in their own name or the name of a collectivity (Hurley 1989). Thus Elizabeth Anderson (2001, p. 30) defends "The Priority of Identity to Rational Principle: what principle of choice it is rational to act on depends on a prior determination of personal identity, of who one is." The line just taken suggests that this is not so. The natural person is the ultimate center of action and if it is rational for a human being to act in the name of a collectivity—that is, rational in the sense of maximizing relevant preferences—then it is rational in terms of the natural person's preferences.

CONCLUSION

In maintaining points of the kind defended in this chapter, we make contact with the tradition that the nineteenth-century German historian Otto von Gierke sought to track and to revitalize: the tradition of emphasizing the institutional personality of many groups and the significance of such personality for legal, political and social theory (Hager 1989; Runciman 1997; McLean 1999). This tradition is deeply organicist in its imagery and led adherents to speak for example of "the pulsation of a common purpose which surges, as it were, from above, into the mind and behaviour of members of any true group" (Gierke, Troeltsch, and Barker 1950, p. 61). But the organic, often overblown metaphors should not be allowed to discredit the tradition. The points they were designed to emphasize are perfectly sensible observations of the kind that our analysis of integrated groups supports.

I have argued elsewhere that consistently with being individualistic about the relation between human beings and the social regularities under which they operate—consistently with thinking that social regularities do not compromise individual agency—we may oppose the atomism that insists on the coherence of the solitary thinker; we may argue that individuals depend noncausally on one another for having the capacity to think (Pettit 1993). What we have seen in this chapter is that consistently with being individualistic we may also oppose the singularism that insists on the primacy of the isolated agent and claims that we can describe collectivities as persons only in a secondary sense.

Individualism insists on the supervenience claim that if we replicate how things are with and between individuals, then we will replicate all the social realities that obtain in their midst: there are no social properties or powers that will be left out (Macdonald and Pettit 1981; Currie 1984; Pettit 1993). But this insistence on the supervenience of the social in relation to the individual is quite consistent with emphasizing that the entities that individuals compose can assume a life of their own, deserving the attribution of discontinuous judgments and intentions and displaying all the qualities expected in personal agents.

The world of living organisms did not cease to be interesting when scientists dismissed the conceit of a *vis vitalis*. And neither should the world of social groups cease to be interesting just because we choose to exorcise the specter of a *vis socialis*. On the contrary, the recognition that the realm of collectivities is an artifact of human hands should excite the sociological, the political, and the historical imagination. The sociological, because we badly need general models of how collectivities can be created and sustained (Coleman 1974). The political, because we need to develop criteria for assessing the performance of collectivities and proposals for containing their power (Hager 1989). And the historical, because we have only the sketchiest understanding of how the most important collectivities in our lives emerged and stabilized as integrated agents (Skinner 1989).

ACKNOWLEDGMENTS

I was greatly helped in developing this chapter by conversations with John Ferejohn, Chandran Kukathas, Christian List, and Victoria McGeer. I am indebted to the discussion it received at a number of venues: the Summer Institute on "Social Ontology after *The Common Mind*," held in Erasmus University, Rotterdam, July 2000, where my commentators were Ron Mallon and Rafal Wierzschoslawski; and during seminars at Columbia and Yale. I am also grateful for a useful set of comments from Elizabeth Anderson and for discussions of the priority of identity principle with Akeel Bilgrami and Carol Rovane.

NOTES

1. The structure involved is this:
   1. there is a conclusion to be decided among the judges by reference to a conjunction of independent or separable premises—the conclusion will be endorsed if relevant premises are endorsed, and otherwise it will be rejected;
   2. each judge forms a judgment on each of the premises and a corresponding judgment on the conclusion;
   3. each of the premises is supported by a majority of judges but those majorities do not coincide with one another;
   4. the intersection of those majorities will support the conclusion, and the others reject it, in view of 1.; and
   5. the intersection of the majorities is not itself a majority; in our examples only one judge out of the three is in that intersection.
2. Let the views of certain individuals on a rationally connected set of issues be rationally satisfactory in the sense of being consistent, complete, and deductively closed. The impossibility theorem shows that any procedure whereby an equally satisfactory set of views may be derived from the individual views must fail in one of the following regards. It must be incapable of working with some profiles of individual view. Or it must fail to treat some individual or some issue even-handedly: roughly, it must let some individual or individuals be treated as less important than another— at the limit, the other may be given the status of a dictator—or it must downgrade some issue in the sense of letting the collective view on that issue be determined, not by majority vote, but by the collective views on other issues.
3. There are other ontological questions that I do not address here. One is the issue of whether a group at any time is constituted in some sense by the individuals involved or is identical with the fusion of those individuals. This parallels the familiar

sort of question raised about whether a statue is constituted by the body of clay used in its manufacture or whether it is identical with that body of clay. Different positions may be taken on this question, consistently with the claims made in the text.

4. This line of thought might be blocked by a consequentialist argument to the effect that all such divergences have to be judged ultimately by reference to agent-neutral considerations. But it would be strange to tie one's view of the relationship between natural and institutional persons to a consequentialist commitment. And in any case it is possible for consequentialists to argue that it is often best for people—best in agent-neutral terms—to think and even compete in agent-relative ways.

7

Social Ontology and Political Power

John R. Searle

The Western philosophical tradition has an especially influential component of political philosophy. The classics in the field, from Plato's *Republic* through Rawls's *Theory of Justice*, have an importance in our general culture that exceeds even most other philosophical classics. The subjects discussed in these works include descriptions of the ideal society, the nature of justice, the sources of sovereignty, the origins of political obligation, and the requirements for effective political leadership. One could even argue that the most influential single strand in the Western philosophical tradition is its political philosophy. This branch of philosophy has an extra interest because it has had at various times an influence on actual political events. The Constitution of the United States, to take a spectacular example, is the expression of the philosophical views of a number of Enlightenment thinkers, some of whom were among the framers of the Constitution itself.

In spite of its impressive achievements, I have always found our tradition of political philosophy in various ways unsatisfying. I do not think it is the best expression of Western philosophy. But my general problem with the tradition is not that it gives wrong answers to the questions it asks, but rather it seems to me it does not always ask the questions that need to be asked in the first place. Prior to answering such questions as "What is a just society?" and "What is the proper exercise of political power?" it seems to me we should answer the more fundamental questions: "What is a society in the first place?" and "What sort of power is political power anyhow?"

In this chapter I do not attempt to make a contribution to the continuing discussion in the Western philosophical tradition, but rather I shall attempt to answer a different set of questions. My aim is to explore some of the relations between the general ontology of social reality and the specific form of social reality that is political power.

SOCIAL ONTOLOGY

I want to begin the discussion by summarizing some of the elements of a theory I expounded in *The Construction of Social Reality* (Searle 1995). I say almost nothing about politics in that book, but I believe that if we take that book together with my later book, *Rationality in Action* (Searle 2001), there is an implicit political theory contained in these analyses, and in this chapter I want to make that theory explicit, if only in an abbreviated form. I also want to do it in a way that will make fully explicit the role of language and collective intentionality in the constitution of social reality and correspondingly in the constitution of political power.

This project is a part of a much larger project in contemporary philosophy. The most important question in contemporary philosophy is this: how, and to what extent, can we reconcile a certain conception that we have of ourselves as conscious, mindful, free, social and political agents in a world that consists entirely of mindless, meaningless particles in fields of force? How, and to what extent, can we get a coherent account of the totality of the world that will reconcile what we believe about ourselves with what we know for a fact from physics, chemistry, and biology. The question I tried to answer in *The Construction of Social Reality* was a question about how there can be a social and institutional reality in a world consisting of physical particles. This chapter extends that question to the question "How can there be *political* reality in a world consisting of physical particles?"

To begin, we need to make clear a distinction on which the whole analysis rests, that between those features of reality that are observer (or intentionality) independent and those that are observer (or intentionality) dependent. A feature is observer dependent if its very existence depends on the attitudes, thoughts, and intentionality of observers, users, creators, designers, buyers, sellers, and conscious intentional agents generally. Otherwise it is observer or intentionality independent. Examples of observer-dependent features include money, property, marriage, and language. Examples of observer-independent features of the world include force, mass, gravitational attraction, the chemical bond, and photosynthesis. A rough test for whether a feature is observer-independent is whether it could have existed if there had never been any conscious agents in the world. Without conscious agents there would still be force, mass, and the chemical bond, but there would not be money, property, marriage, or language. This test is only rough, because, of course, consciousness and intentionality themselves are observer-independent even though they are the source of all observer-dependent features of the world.

To say that a feature is observer-dependent does not necessarily imply that we cannot have objective knowledge of that feature. For example the piece of paper in my hand is American money and as such is observer-dependent: It is only money because we think it is money. But it is an objective fact that this is a ten dollar bill. It is not, for example, just a matter of my subjective opinion that it is money.

This example shows that in addition to the distinction between observer-dependent and observer-independent features of the world we need a distinction between epistemic objectivity and subjectivity, on the one hand, and ontological objectivity and subjectivity, on the other. *Epistemic* objectivity and subjectivity are features of *claims*. A claim is epistemically objective if its truth or falsity can be established independently of the feeling, attitudes and preferences, and so on of the makers and interpreters of the claim. Thus the claim that van Gogh was born in Holland is epistemically objective. The claim that van Gogh was a better painter than Manet is, as they say, a matter of opinion. It is epistemically subjective. On the other hand, *ontological* subjectivity and objectivity are features of *reality*. Pains, tickles, and itches are ontologically subjective because their existence depends on being experienced by a human or animal subject. Mountains, planets, and molecules are ontologically objective because their existence is not dependent on subjective experiences.

The point of these distinctions for the present discussion is this: almost all of political reality is observer-relative. For example something is an election, a parliament, a president, or a revolution only if people have certain attitudes toward the phenomenon in question. And all such phenomena thereby have an element of ontological subjectivity. The subjective attitudes of the people involved are constitutive elements of the observer-dependent phenomena. But ontological subjectivity does not by itself imply epistemic subjectivity. One can have a domain such as politics or economics whose entities are ontologically subjective, but one can still make epistemically objective claims about elements in that domain. For example, the United States presidency is an observer-relative phenomenon, hence ontologically subjective. But it is an epistemically objective fact that George W. Bush is now President.

With these distinctions in mind, let us turn to social and political reality. Aristotle famously said that man is a social animal. But the same expression in the *Politics*, "Zoon politikon" is sometimes translated as "political animal": "Man is a political animal." Quite apart from Aristotelian scholarship, that ambiguity should be interesting to us. There are lots of social animals, but man is the only political animal. So one way to put our question is to ask: "What has to be added to the fact that we are *social* animals to get the fact that we are *political* animals. And more generally, what has to be added to social reality to get to the special case of political reality?" Let us start with social facts.

The capacity for social cooperation is a biologically based capacity shared by humans and many other species. It is the capacity for collective intentionality, and collective intentionality is just the phenomenon of shared forms of intentionality in human or animal cooperation. So, for example, collective intentionality exists when a group of animals cooperates in hunting their prey, or two people are having a conversation, or a group of people are trying to organize a revolution. Collective intentionality exists both in the form of cooperative behavior and in consciously shared attitudes such as shared desires, beliefs, and intentions. Whenever two or more agents share a belief, desire, intention, or other intentional state, and where they are aware of so sharing, the agents in question have collective intentionality. It is a familiar point, often made by sociological theorists, that collective intentionality is the foundation of society. This point is made in different ways by Durkheim, Simmel, and Weber. Though they did not have the jargon I am using, and did not have a theory of intentionality, I think they were making this point, using the nineteenth-century vocabulary that was available to them. The question that—as far as I know—they did not address, and that I am addressing now, is: How do you get from social facts to institutional facts?

Collective intentionality is all that is necessary for the creation of simple forms of social reality and social facts. Indeed, I define a social fact as any fact involving the collective intentionality of two or more human or animal agents. But it is a long way from simple collective intentionality to money, property, marriage, or government, and consequently it is a long way from being a social animal to being an institutional or a political animal. What specifically has to be added to collective intentionality to get the forms of institutional reality that are characteristic of human beings, and in particular characteristic of human political reality? It seems to me that exactly two further elements are necessary: First, the imposition of function and, second, certain sorts of rules that I call "constitutive rules." It is this combination, in addition to collective intentionality, that is the foundation of what we think of as specifically *human* society.

Let us go through these features in order. Human beings use all sorts of objects to perform functions that can be performed by virtue of the physical features of the objects. At the most primitive level, we use sticks for levers and stumps to sit on. At a more advanced level we create objects so that they can perform particular functions. So early humans have chiseled stones to use them to cut with. At a more advanced level we manufacture knives to use for cutting, and chairs to sit on. Some animals are capable of very simple forms of the imposition of function. Famously, Köhler's apes were able to use a stick and a box in order to bring down bananas that were otherwise out of reach. And the famous Japanese macaque monkey Imo learned how to use seawater to wash sweet potatoes and thus improve their flavor by removing dirt and adding salt. But, in general, the use of objects with imposed functions is very limited among animals. Once animals have the capacity for collective intentionality and for the imposition of function, it is an easy step to combine the two. If one of us can use a stump to sit on, several of us can use a log as a bench or a big stick as a lever operated by us together. When we consider human capacities specifically we discover a truly remarkable phenomenon. Human beings have the capacity to impose functions on objects, which, unlike sticks, levers, boxes, and salt water, cannot perform the function solely in virtue of their physical structure, but only in virtue of a certain form of the collective acceptance of the objects as having a certain sort of status. With that status comes a function that can only be performed in virtue of the collective acceptance by the community that the object has that status, and that the status carries the function with it. Perhaps the simplest and the most obvious example of this is money. The bits of paper are able to perform their function not in virtue of their physical structure but in virtue of the fact that we have a certain set of attitudes toward them. We acknowledge that they have a certain status, we count them as money, and consequently they are able to perform their function in virtue of our acceptance of them as having that status. I propose to call such functions "status functions."

How is it possible that there can be such things as status functions? In order to explain this possibility, I have to introduce a third notion, in addition to the already explained notions of collective intentionality and the assignment of function. The third notion is that of the constitutive rule. In order to explain it, I need to note the distinction between what I call brute facts and institutional facts. Brute facts can exist without human institutions; institutional facts require human institutions for their very existence. An example of a brute fact is that this stone is larger than that stone or that the Earth is 93 million miles from the sun. An example of institutional facts is that I am a citizen of the United States or that this is a twenty dollar bill. And how are institutional facts possible? Institutional facts require human institutions. To explain such institutions we need to make a distinction between two kinds of rules, which, years ago, I baptized as "regulative rules" and "constitutive rules." Regulative rules regulate antecedently existing forms of behavior. A rule such as "drive on the right hand side of the road" regulates driving, for example. But constitutive rules not only regulate, they also create the very possibility, or define, new forms of behavior. An obvious example is the rules of chess. Chess rules do not just regulate the playing of chess, but rather, playing chess is constituted by acting according to the rules in a certain sort of way. Constitutive rules typically have the form: "*X* counts as *Y*," or "*X* counts as *Y* in context *C*." Such and such counts as a legal move of a knight in chess, such and such a position counts as check-mate, such and such a person that meets certain qualifications counts as president of the United States, and so on.

The key element in the move from the brute to the institutional, and correspondingly the move from assigned physical functions to status functions, is the move expressed in the constitutive rule. It is the move whereby we count something as having a certain status, and with that status, a certain function. So the key element that gets us from the sheer animal imposition of function and collective intentionality to the imposition of status functions is our ability to follow a set of rules, procedures, or practices, whereby we count certain things as having a certain status. Such and such a person who satisfies certain conditions counts as our president, such and such a type of object counts as money in our society, and, most important of all, as we shall see, such and such a sequence of sounds or marks counts as a sentence, and, indeed, counts as a speech act in our language. It is this feature, the distinctly human feature, to count certain things as having a status that they do not have intrinsically, and then to grant, with that status, a set of functions, which can only be performed in virtue of the collective acceptance of the status and the corresponding function, that creates the very possibility of institutional facts. Institutional facts are constituted by the existence of status functions.

At this point in the analysis a philosophical paradox arises. It has the form of a traditional paradox concerning the origin of obligations. Here is how it goes. If the existence of institutional facts requires constitutive rules, then where do the constitutive rules come from? It looks like their existence might itself be an institutional fact, and if so we would plunge into an infinite regress or circularity. Either way the analysis would collapse. The traditional form in which this paradox arises has to do with the obligation to keep promises. If the origin of the obligation to keep a promise comes from the fact that everybody has made a promise to the effect that they will keep their promises, then the analysis is obviously circular. If, on the other hand, that is not the origin of the obligation to keep a promise, then it looks like we have no analysis of where the obligation to keep a promise comes from. I hope it is clear that the form of the paradox for constitutive rules has the same logical form as the traditional puzzle about the nature of promises. For promises the puzzle is: How can the obligation of promises come into existence without a prior promise to abide by promises? For institutional facts the puzzle is: How can the constitutive rules that underlie institutional facts exist without some institution consisting of constitutive rules within which we can create constitutive rules?

In the case of the logical form of constitutive rules the problem can be stated without putting it in the form of a paradox. Even if the existence of the constitutive rule is not itself an institutional fact, at least it is an observer-relative fact. And that already makes it dependent on the consciousness and intentionality of agents, and one wants to know, what exactly is the structure of that consciousness and intentionality? How rich an apparatus is necessary in order to have the appropriate mental contents?

Here, I believe, is the solution to the paradox. Human beings have the capacity to impose status functions on objects. The imposition of those status functions can be represented in the form, "X counts as Y in C." In primitive cases you do not require an established procedure or rule in order to do this, consequently for the simplest kind of cases of the imposition of status functions, a general procedure in the form of a constitutive rule is not yet required. Consider the following sort of example. Let us suppose that a primitive tribe just regards a certain person as their chief or leader. We may suppose that they do this without being fully conscious of what they are doing, and even without having the vocabulary of "chief" or "leader." For example, suppose they do not make decisions without first consulting him, his voice carries a special weight in the decision-making process, people look to him to adjudicate conflict situations, members of the tribe obey his orders, he leads the tribe in battle, and so on. All of those features constitute his being a leader, and leadership is a case of an imposed status function on an entity that does not have that function solely in virtue of its physical structure. They accord to him a status, and with that status a function. He now *counts as* their leader.

When the practice of imposing a status function becomes regularized and established, then it becomes a constitutive rule. If the tribe makes it a matter of policy that he is the leader because he has such and such features and that any successor as leader must have these features, then they have established a constitutive rule of leadership. It is especially important that there should be publicly available constitutive rules, because the nature of status functions requires that they be collectively recognized in order to do their work, and the collective recognition requires that there be some antecedently accepted procedure in accordance with which the institutional facts can be acknowledged. Language is the obvious case of this. That is, we have procedures by which we make statements, ask questions, and give promises. And these are made possible in a way that is communicable to other people, only because of publicly recognized constitutive rules. But constitutive rules do not require other constitutive rules for their existence, at least not to the point of an infinite regress. So the solution to our initial puzzle is to grant that a regularized practice can become a constitutive rule, but there does not always have to be a constitutive rule in order that a status function be imposed in the simplest sorts of cases.

Two things to notice about status functions. First, they are always matters of positive and negative powers. The person who possesses money or property or is married has powers, rights, and obligations that he or she would not otherwise have. Notice that these powers are of a peculiar kind because they are not like, for example, electrical power or the power that one person might have over another because of brute physical force. Indeed it seems to me a kind of pun to call both the power of my car engine and the power of George W. Bush as president "powers" because they are totally different. The power of my car engine is brute power. But the powers that are constitutive of institutional facts are always matters of rights, duties, obligations, commitments, authorizations, requirements, permissions, and privileges. Notice that such powers only exist as long as they are acknowledged, recognized, or otherwise accepted. I propose to call all such powers *deontic powers*. Institutional facts are always matters of deontic powers.

The second feature to notice is that where status functions are concerned, language and symbolism have not only the function to describe the phenomena but are partly constitutive of the very phenomena described. How can that be? After all, when I say that George W. Bush is president that is a simple statement of fact, like the statement that it is raining. Why is language more constitutive of the fact in the case where the fact is that George W. Bush is president, than it is in the fact that it is raining? In order to understand this we have to understand the nature of the move from X to Y whereby we count something as having a certain status that it does not have intrinsically, but has it only relative to our attitudes. The reason that language is constitutive of institutional facts, in a way that it is not constitutive of brute facts, or other sorts of social facts, or intentional facts in general, is that the move from X to Y in the formula X counts as Y in C can only exist insofar as it is represented as existing. There is no physical feature present in the Y term that was not present in the X term. Rather the Y term just is the X term *represented* in a certain way. The ten dollar bill is a piece of paper, the president is a man. Their new statuses exist only insofar as they are represented as existing. But in order that they should be represented as existing there must be some device for representing them. And that device is some system of representation, or at the minimum some symbolic device, whereby we represent the X phenomenon as having the Y status. In order that Bush can be president, people must be able to think that he is president, but in order that they be able to think that he is president, they have to have some means for thinking that, and that means has to be linguistic or symbolic.

But what about language itself? Isn't language itself an institutional fact, and would it not thereby require some means of representing its institutional status? Language is the basic social institution, not only in the sense that language is required for the existence of other social institutions, but also that linguistic elements are, so to speak, self-identifying as linguistic. The child has an innate capacity to acquire the language to which it is exposed in infancy. The linguistic elements are self-identifying as linguistic precisely because we are brought up in a culture where we treat them as linguistic, and we have an innate capacity so to treat them. But in that way, money, property, marriage, government, and presidents of the United States are not self-identifying as such. We have to have some device for identifying them and that device is symbolic or linguistic.

It is often said, and indeed I have said it myself, that the primary function of language is to communicate, that we use language to communicate with other people, and in a limiting case, to communicate with ourselves in our thinking. But language plays an extra role, which I did not see when I wrote *Speech Acts* (Searle 1969), and that is that language is partly constitutive of all institutional reality. In order that something can be money, property, marriage, or government, people have to have appropriate thoughts about it. But in order that they have these appropriate thoughts, they have to have the devices for thinking those thoughts, and those are essentially symbolic or linguistic devices.

So far I have gone, rather rapidly, through a summary of the basic ideas that I need in order to explore the nature of political power in its relation to language. In a sense our enterprise is Aristotelian, in that we are seeking progressively more refined *differentia*, to get from the *genus* of social facts to progressively more refined specifications that will give us the *species* of political reality. We are now on the verge of being able to do that, though, of course, we need to remind ourselves that we are not following the essentialism that characterized Aristotle's approach.

THE PARADOX OF POLITICAL POWER: GOVERNMENT AND VIOLENCE

So far the account is fairly neutral about the distinctions between different sorts of institutional structures, and it might seem from such an account that there is nothing special about government, that it is just one institutional structure among others, along with families, marriages, churches, universities, and so forth. But there is a sense in which in most organized societies, the government is the ultimate institutional structure. Of course the power of governments varies enormously from liberal democracies to totalitarian states; but, all the same, governments have the power to regulate other institutional structures such as family, education, money, the economy generally, private property, and even the church. Again, governments tend to be the most highly accepted system of status functions, rivaled by the family and the church. Indeed, one of the most stunning cultural developments of the past few centuries was the rise of the nation state as the ultimate focus of collective loyalty in a society. People have, for example, been willing to fight and die for the United States, or Germany, or France, or Japan, in a way that they would not be willing to fight and die for Kansas City or Vitry-le-François.

How do governments, so to speak, get away with it? That is, how does the government manage as a system of status function superior to other status functions? One of the keys, perhaps the most important key is that typically governments have a monopoly on organized violence. Furthermore, because they have a monopoly on the police and the armed forces, they in effect have control of a territory in a way that corporations, churches, and ski clubs do not control a territory. The combination of control of the land plus a monopoly on organized violence, guarantees government the ultimate power role within competing systems of status functions. The paradox of government could be put as follows: governmental power is a system of status functions and thus rests on collective acceptance, but the collective acceptance, though not itself based on violence, can continue to function only if there is a permanent threat of violence in the form of the military and the police. Though military and police power are different from political power there is no such thing as government, no such thing as political power without police power and military power (more about this later).

The sense in which the government is the ultimate system of status functions is the sense that old time political philosophers were trying to get at when they talked about sovereignty. I think the notion of sovereignty is a relatively confused notion because it implies transitivity. But most systems of sovereignty, at least in democratic societies, are not transitive. In a dictatorship, if *A* has power over *B* and *B* has power over *C*, then *A* has power over *C*, but that is not really true in a democracy. In the United States, there is a complex series of interlocking constitutional arrangements between the three branches of government and between them and the citizenry. So the traditional notion of sovereignty may not be as useful as the traditional political philosophers hoped. Nonetheless, I think we will need a notion of the ultimate status function power in order to explain government.

Because I do not have a lot of space I am going to summarize some of the essential points about political power as a set of numbered propositions.

1. *All political power is a matter of status functions, and for that reason all political power is deontic power.*

   Deontic powers are rights, duties, obligations, authorizations, permissions, privileges, authority and the like. The power of the local party bosses and the village council as much as the power of such grander figures as presidents, prime ministers, Congress, and the Supreme Court are all derived from the possession by these entities of recognized status functions. And these status functions assign deontic powers. Political power thus differs from military power, police power or the brute physical power that the strong have over the weak. An army that occupies a foreign country has power over its citizens but such power is based on brute physical force. Among the invaders there is a recognized system of status functions, and thus there can be political relations within the army, but the relation of the occupiers to the occupied is not political unless the occupied come to accept and recognize the validity of the status functions. To the extent that the victims accept the orders of the occupiers without accepting the validity of the status functions, they act from fear and prudence. They act on reasons that are desire dependent.

I realize, of course, that all of these different forms of power—political, military, police, economic, and so on—interact and overlap in all sorts of ways. I do not suppose for a moment that there is a sharp dividing line, and I am not much concerned with the ordinary use of the word "political" as it is distinct from "economic" or "military." The point I am making, however, is that there is a different logical structure to the ontology where the power is deontic from the cases where it is, for example, based on brute force or self-interest.

The form of motivation that goes with a system of accepted status functions is essential to our concept of the political, and I will say more about it shortly. Historically, the awareness of its centrality was the underlying intuition that motivated the old Social Contract theorists. They thought that there is no way that we could have a system of political obligations, and indeed, no way we could have a political society, without something like a promise, an original promise, that would create the deontic system necessary to maintain political reality.

2. *Because all political power is a matter of status functions, all political power, though, exercised from above, comes from below.*

Because the system of status functions requires collective acceptance, all genuine political power comes from the bottom up. This is as much true in dictatorships as it is in democracies. Hitler and Stalin, for example, were both constantly obsessed by the need for security. They could never take the system of status functions as having been accepted, as a given part of reality. It had to be constantly maintained by a system of rewards and punishments and by terror.

The single most stunning political event of the second half of the twentieth century was the collapse of communism. It collapsed when the structure of collective intentionality was no longer able to maintain the system of status functions. On a smaller scale, a similar collapse of status functions occurred with the abandonment of Apartheid in South Africa. In both cases, as far as I can tell, the key element in the collapse of the system of status functions was the withdrawal of acceptance on the part of large numbers of the people involved.

3. *Even though the individual is the source of all political power, by his or her ability to engage in collective intentionality, all the same, the individual, typically, feels powerless.*

The individual typically feels that the powers that be are not in any way dependent on him or her. This is why it is so important for revolutionaries to introduce some kind of collective intentionality: class consciousness, identification with the proletariat, student solidarity, consciousness-raising among women, or some such. Because the entire structure rests on collective intentionality its destruction can be attained by creating an alternative and inconsistent form of collective intentionality

I have so far been emphasizing the role of status functions and consequently of deontic powers in the constitution of social and political reality. But that naturally forces a question on us: How does it work? How does all this stuff about status functions and deontic powers work when it comes to voting in an election or paying my income taxes? How does it work in such a way as to provide motivations for actual human behavior? It is a unique characteristic of human beings that they can create and act on desire-independent reasons for action. As far as we know, not even the higher primates have this ability. This I believe is one of the keys to understanding political ontology. Human beings have the capacity to be motivated by desire-independent reasons for action. And this leads to point number 4.

4. *The system of political status functions works at least in part because recognized deontic powers provide desire-independent reasons for action.*

Typically we think of desire-independent reasons for action as intentionally created by the agent, and promising is simply the most famous case of this. But one of the keys to understanding political ontology and political power is to see that the entire system of status functions is a system of providing desire-independent reasons for action. The recognition by the agent, that is to say by the citizen of a political community, of a status function, as valid, gives the agent a desire-independent reason for doing something. Without this there is no such thing as organized political and institutional reality.

What we are trying to explain is the difference between humans and other social animals. The first step in explaining the difference is to identify institutional reality. Institutional reality is a system of status functions, and those status functions always involve deontic powers. For example, the person who occupies an office near mine in Berkeley is the chair of the philosophy department. But the status function of being chair of the department imposes rights and obligations that the occupant did not otherwise have. In such ways there is an essential connection between status function and deontic power. But, and this is the next key step, the recognition of a status function by a conscious agent such as me can give me reasons for acting, which are independent of my immediate desires. If my chairman asks me to serve on a committee then, if I recognize his position as chairman, I have a reason for doing so, even if committees are boring and there are no penalties for my refusal.

More generally, if I have an obligation, for example, to meet someone by 9:00 A.M., I have a reason to do so, even if in the morning I do not feel like it, and the fact that the obligation requires it gives me a reason to want to do it. Thus, in the case of human society, unlike animal societies, reasons can motivate desires, instead of all reasons having to start with desires. The most obvious example of this is promising. I promise something to you and thus create a desire-independent reason for doing it. But it is important to see that where political reality is concerned, we do not need to make or create desire-independent reasons for action explicitly, as when we make promises or undertake various other commitments. The simple recognition of a set of institutional facts as valid, as binding on us, creates desire-independent reasons for action. To take an important contemporary example, many Americans do not want George W. Bush as president, and some of them even think he got the status function in an illegitimate fashion. But the important thing for the structure of deontic power in the United States is that with very few exceptions they continue to recognize his deontic powers and thus they will recognize that they have reasons for doing things that they would not otherwise have a desire to do.

It is a consequence of what I am saying that, if I am right, not all political motivation is self-interested or prudential. You can see this by contrasting political and economic motivation. The logical relations between political and economic power are extremely complex: both the economic and the political systems are systems of status functions. The political system consists of the machinery of government, together with the attendant apparatus of political parties, interest groups, and the like. The economic system consists of the economic apparatus for creating, distributing, and sustaining the distribution of wealth. Though the logical structures are similar, the systems of rational motivations are interestingly different. Economic power is mostly a matter of being able to offer economic awards incentives and penalties. The rich have more power than the poor because the poor want what the rich can pay them and thus will give the rich what they want. Political power is often like that, but not always. It is like that when the political leaders can exercise power only as long as they offer greater rewards. This has led to any number of confused theories that try to treat political relations as having the same logical structure as economic relations. But such desire-based reasons for action, even when they are in a deontic system, are not deontological. The important point to emphasize is that the essence of political power is deontic power.

5. *It is a consequence of the analysis so far that there is a distinction be-tween political power and political leadership.*

Roughly speaking, power is the ability to make people do something whether they want to do it or not. Leadership is the ability to make them want to do something they would not otherwise have wanted to do. Thus different people occupying the same position of political power with the same official status functions may differ in their effec-tiveness because one is an effective leader and the other is not. They have the same *official* position of deontic power, but different *effective* positions of deontic power. Thus both Roosevelt and Carter had the same official deontic powers—both were presidents of the United States and leaders of the Democratic Party—but Roosevelt was far more effective because he maintained deontic powers in excess of his con-stitutionally assigned powers. The ability to do that is part of what con-stitutes political leadership. Furthermore, the effective leader can con-tinue to exercise power and to maintain an informal status function even when he or she is out office.

6. *Because political powers are matters of status functions they are, in large part, linguistically constituted.*

I have said that political power is in general deontic power. It is a matter of rights, duties, obligations, authorizations, permissions, and the like. Such powers have a special ontology. The fact that George W. Bush is president has a different logical structure altogether from the fact that it is raining. The fact that it is raining consists of water drops falling out of the sky, together with facts about their meteorological his-tory, but the fact that George W. Bush is president is not in that way a natural phenomenon. That fact is constituted by an extremely complex set of explicitly verbal phenomena. There is no way that fact can exist without language. The essential component in that fact is that people regard him and accept him as president, and consequently accept a whole system of deontic powers that goes with that original accept-ance. Status functions can only exist as long as they are represented as existing, and for them to be represented as existing, there needs to be some means of representation, and that means is typically linguistic. Where political status functions are concerned it is almost invariably lin-guistic. It is important to emphasize that the content of the representa-tion need not match the actual content of the logical structure of the deontic power. For example, in order for Bush to be president people do not have to think "We have imposed on him a status function ac-cording to the formula X counts as Y in C," even though that is exactly what they have done. But they do have to be able to think something. For example, they typically think "He is president" and such thoughts are sufficient to maintain the status function.

7. *In order for a society to have a political reality it needs several other distinguishing features: first a distinction between the public and the private sphere with the political as part of the public sphere; second, the existence of nonviolent group conflicts; and third, the group conflicts must be over social goods within a structure of deontology.*

I said I would suggest some of the differentia that distinguish political facts from other sorts of social and institutional facts. But, with the important exception of the point about violence, the ontology I have given so far might fit nonpolitical structures such as religions or organized sports. They too involve collective forms of status function and consequently collective forms of deontic powers. What is special about the concept of *the political* within these sorts of systems of deontic powers?

I am not endorsing any kind of essentialism, and the concept of the political is clearly a family resemblance concept. There is no set of necessary and sufficient conditions that define the essence of the political. But there are, I believe, a number of typical distinguishing features. First, our concept of the political requires, I believe, a distinction between the public and private spheres, with politics as the paradigm public activity. Second, the concept of the political requires a concept of group conflict. But not just any group conflict is political. Organized sports involve group conflict, but they are not typically political. The essence of political conflict is that it is a conflict over social goods, and many of these social goods include deontic powers. So, for example, the right to abortion is a political issue because it involves a deontic power, the legal right of women to have their fetuses killed.

8. *A monopoly on armed violence is an essential presupposition of government.*

As I suggested earlier, the paradox of the political is this: in order that the political system can function there has to be an acceptance of a set of status functions by a sufficient number of members of the group sharing collective intentionality. But, in general, in the political system that set of status functions can only work if it is backed by the threat of armed violence. This feature distinguishes governments from churches, universities, ski clubs, and marching bands. The reason that the government can sustain itself as the ultimate system of status functions is that it maintains a constant threat of physical force. The miracle, so to speak, of democratic societies is that the system of status functions that constitutes the government has been able to exercise a control through deontic powers over the systems of status functions that constitute the military and the police. In societies where that collective acceptance ceases to work, as for example in the German Democratic Republic in 1989, the government, as they say, collapses.

CONCLUSION

One way to get at the aim of this chapter is to say that it is an attempt to describe those features of human political reality that distinguish it from other sorts of collective animal behavior. The answer that I have proposed to this question proceeds by a number of steps. Humans are distinct from other animals in that they have a capacity to create not merely a social but an institutional reality. This institutional reality is, above all, a system of deontic powers. These deontic powers provide human agents with the fundamental key for organized human society: the capacity to create and act on desire independent reasons for action.

Some of the distinguishing features of the political, within the system of desire independent reasons for action, are that the concept of the political requires that a distinction between the public and the private spheres, with the political as the preeminent public sphere; it requires the existence of group conflicts settled by nonviolent means, and it requires that the group conflict be over social goods. And the whole system has to be backed by a credible threat of armed violence. Governmental power is not the same as police power and military power, but with few exceptions, if no police and no army, then no government.

ACKNOWLEDGMENTS

I am grateful to Bruce Cain, Felix Oppenheim, and Dagmar Searle for comments on earlier versions of this chapter.

8

Conventions and Forms of Life

Edward Witherspoon

Descartes famously attempts to reconstruct scientific knowledge on an indubitable basis. In the course of rejecting all of his beliefs that can be doubted the Meditator casts off the belief that other human beings exist and even the belief that he himself is a human being. He is to consider himself an isolated thinker, and as such he is to employ standards of rational belief acceptance to evaluate candidates for belief and, if possible, to acquire knowledge. This procedure presupposes what we may call an individualist conception of reason and language: a thinker isolated from all others (as the Meditator imagines himself to be) can employ language to frame meaningful propositions, can rationally assess them, and can accept or reject them depending on his assessment. In other words, according to this conception, a thinking thing could be the lone inhabitant of the space of reasons.

The individualist conception of reason and language has an appeal that outruns that of the Cartesian epistemology in which it appears: we can find it operative in philosophers who have no truck with the quest for certainty or the reconstruction of knowledge on rationalist lines. While individualism has not gone unchallenged,[1] it has provided philosophy's dominant orientation for reflection on the relation of thinker to language. In Wittgenstein's later work, however, individualism comes under sustained criticism. Wittgenstein portrays not an isolated speaker, but tribes (our own and imagined others) engaged in language-games; for Wittgenstein, it appears that the meaning of an utterance is to be traced not to the individual who uses it, but to its socially established use. He seems to assert that language must be shared, that a language that is meaningful to just one individual is logically impossible. Wittgenstein's arguments, if cogent, call for a reorientation of the way philosophers think about the respective roles of individual and society in sustaining the meaningfulness of human speech and behavior.

That Wittgenstein's work offers a major critique of individualism and suggests a fundamental reorientation in this area of philosophy cannot be disputed. But when we try to say more precisely what Wittgenstein is criticizing, how his criticism proceeds, and how we are to think about individuals and language in lieu of individualism, we enter controversial exegetical and philosophical terrain. I argue that there is a prevalent way of interpreting Wittgenstein, which I call "conventionalism," that misses the true character of his thought. "Conventionalism" holds that, for Wittgenstein, the meaningfulness of language and of action is to be traced to systems of agreements called "forms of life." Conventionalism maintains that the nature of these agreements entails that an isolated individual cannot be party to them, and that consequently, *pace* Descartes, an isolated individual cannot belong within the space of reasons.

In this chapter, I develop an alternative reading of Wittgenstein by first laying out and then criticizing the view I label "conventionalism" or "the conventionalist interpretation of Wittgenstein." The criticism involves discussing the concept *form of life* as it appears in the *Philosophical Investigations*, so that we can see how far removed Wittgenstein's concept is from the notion of agreement that is central to the conventionalist interpretation. I then examine the private language argument, to show how it provides a critique of individualism much deeper than conventionalism's.

CONVENTIONALISM IN WINCH AND OTHERS

The interpretation of Wittgenstein that I criticize has its roots in Peter Winch's *The Idea of a Social Science* (1990). I think, on the best construal of it, Winch's book is not full-blown conventionalism, but it is easy to read it as advancing what I call conventionalism and many of its readers have done so.[2] In this chapter I don't linger over the question of the proper interpretation of Winch's book; I simply use it as a convenient and historically significant source for conventionalism.

In his book, Winch uses Wittgenstein's *Philosophical Investigations* to argue that there are essential connections between meaningful action, language, rules, and social groups. His principal concern is to determine what kind of explanations the social sciences are capable of providing. He argues that, because the object of study of the social sciences is human action, and because the distinguishing characteristic of human action is that it is meaningful, the social sciences ought to concern themselves with providing an understanding of the significance of human action. But providing such an understanding is the proper domain of philosophy, so according to Winch the social sciences ought to be conceived as branches of philosophy. Insofar as social researchers model their work on the sciences and eschew philosophical reflection on meaning, their work will be, Winch thinks, confused and fruitless.

For our purposes, the important element in Winch's book is not his assessment of the status of the social sciences, but the views about meaning that he develops from his reading of Wittgenstein. His principal thesis is that the notion of having a language, and the accompanying notions of meaning, intelligibility, and so on, "are *logically* dependent for their sense on social interaction between men" (Winch 1990, p. 44). Winch's strategy, in discussing the meaning of human action, is to develop an account of the meaningfulness of language and then to extend that account to action.

There is some unclarity regarding how Winch conceives of the meaningful action that is the proper topic of the social sciences. He writes, "The forms of activity in question are, naturally, those . . . of which we can sensibly say that they have a *meaning*, a *symbolic* character" (Winch 1990, p. 45). But behavior that has a meaning or, as Winch often puts it, that has a sense, is a broader category than behavior that is symbolic. At one point Winch appears to use "meaningful behavior" as that which contrasts with "purely reactive" behavior (Winch 1990, p. 48); he appears to think of it as behavior that means something to the agent, or is, as I would call it, intentional. Symbolic behavior would appear to be intentional action that signifies something, say, exchanging wedding rings or (in Winch's example) casting a vote. My brewing a mug of tea is intentional action, but unless I'm employing a special code (according to which I drink Lipton, say, if the police are eavesdropping) it is not symbolic.

Thus we have to revise the following passage:

Action with a sense is symbolic: it goes together with certain other actions in the sense that it *commits* the agent to behaving in one way rather than another in the future. This notion of "being committed" is most obviously appropriate where we are dealing with actions which have an immediate social significance, like economic exchange or promise-keeping. But it applies also to meaningful behaviour of a more "private" nature. (Winch 1990, p. 50)

First of all, not all action with a sense (intentional action) is symbolic. Second, for intentional but nonsymbolic action, the notion of commitment regarding future behavior is too strong for the normative relationships to which my actions belong. If I brew myself a cup of tea and then fail to drink it, I haven't violated any commitments. (What is true, as Winch notes about a related case, is that my failure to drink the tea I've made will typically call for special explanation, such as that I got distracted from my tea-drinking project, decided against drinking tea, found the cup I brewed too strong, etc.)

The truth that Winch is driving at is that being meaningful (in action and in language) is a matter of standing in normative relationships. Sayings and actions are significant because of the commitments they follow from and the commitments they entail. An agent who is saying something is acting within normative constraints involving truth-telling, relevance, appropriateness, and the like; the content of his sayings and doings is inseparable from the multifaceted rational relationships they sustain to other sayings and doings. The distinctive feature of intentional action is not that it entails commitments, but that it is capable of being the conclusion of a practical syllogism, that it is normatively connected to reasons and other actions.

Winch construes all varieties of normative evaluability, all forms of normative connection, as being governed by rules.[3] Hence his account of meaningfulness hinges on the question: what is it to follow a rule? Winch's answer derives from the observation that if we are following a rule, then there is a right and a wrong way of proceeding. And what is necessary for there to be right and wrong ways of proceeding? He addresses this via the concept of going wrong, or making a *mistake*:

> A mistake is a contravention of what is *established* as correct; as such, it must be *recognisable* as such a contravention. That is, if I make a mistake in, say, my use of a word, other people must be able to point it out to me. If this is not so, I can do what I like and there is no external check on what I do; that is, nothing is established. Establishing a standard is not an activity which it makes sense to ascribe to any individual in complete isolation from other individuals. For it is contact with other individuals which alone makes possible the external check on one's actions which is inseparable from an established standard. (Winch 1990, p. 32)

So in order for the notions of right and wrong to apply to my doings, there must be an established standard, external to me and my doings. And that requires that I be in contact with other people who recognize and can enforce the standard. Other individuals provide the external check on my behavior that gives the notions of right and wrong their grip on it.

The claim that Winch (and many other commentators) attribute to Wittgenstein, viz., that others are necessary in order for an individual to engage in meaningful activity, represents a radical break with what I have called the individualist conception of reason and language:

> [T]he philosophical elucidation of human intelligence, and the notions associated with this, requires that these notions be placed in the context of the relations between men in society. In so far as there has been a genuine revolution in philosophy in recent years, perhaps it lies in the emphasis on that fact and in the profound working out of its consequences, which we find in Wittgenstein's work. "What has to be accepted, the given, is—so one could say—forms of life." (Winch 1990, p. 40; quoting *PI*, p. 226e)

Winch here uses Wittgenstein's term "forms of life" as a name for the meaning-giving relations between individuals in society. And he subsequently asserts that these relations are the principal topic of philosophical investigation: he says that epistemology, which he regards as the central enterprise of philosophy, "will try to elucidate what is involved in the notion of a form of life as such" (Winch 1990, p. 41).

What is a form of life? Despite (or perhaps because of) his conviction that this is the central question of philosophy, Winch's answer to this is not as clear as one might wish, and this unclarity has fostered what I regard as misinterpretations of Wittgenstein. Since, according to Winch, what it is for speech or action to be meaningful is for it to be rule-governed, and since a form of life provides the necessary context for applying the notion of meaning, we may infer that for Winch a form of life is a body of meaning-conferring rules. Where do these normative principles come from? Winch writes, "the 'law-like proposition' in terms of which *N*'s reasons must be understood concerns not *N*'s dispositions but the accepted standards of reasonable behaviour current in his society" (Winch 1990, p. 81). Thus, for example:

> The behaviour of Chaucer's Troilus towards Cressida is intelligible only in the context of the conventions of courtly love. Understanding Troilus presupposes understanding those conventions, for it is from them that his acts derive their meaning. (Winch 1990, p. 82)

The meaning-giving conventions of courtly love are arbitrary in two dimensions, regarding both what is expressed and the means for expressing it. There is something highly contingent and artificial about the peculiar sorts of devotion associated with courtly love. And those relationships are expressed through symbolic actions whose meaning is achieved through a kind of societal fiat and so is arbitrary. If we assume (as Winch appears to) that the conventions of courtly love are a paradigm of what it is for there to be "accepted standards of behaviour current in [one's] society," and that these standards imbue our doings with meaning, then we must conclude, first, that what is available for individuals to express is a product of their social environment and, second, that social conventions determine what actions express what content. A form of life, on this view, will be the source of both what we express and how we express it.

More support for this understanding of the concept *form of life* emerges from Winch's remarks about the immunity of a mode of social life to criticism from outside it.

> A large part of [Pareto's] trouble here arises from the fact that he has not seen the point around which the main argument of this monograph revolves: that criteria of logic are not a direct gift of God, but arise out of, and are only intelligible in the context of, ways of living or modes of social life. It follows that

one cannot apply criteria of logic to modes of social life as such. For instance, science is one such mode and religion is another; and each has criteria of intelligibility peculiar to itself. So within science or religion actions can be logical or illogical: in science, for example, it would be illogical to refuse to be bound by the results of a properly performed experiment; in religion it would be illogical to suppose that one could pit one's own strength against God's; and so on. But we cannot sensibly say that either the practice of science itself or that of religion is either illogical or logical; both are non-logical. (Winch 1990, p. 100–01)

These passages have led many readers of Winch to interpret him as thinking of a form of life as a body of conventional rules, acceptance of which defines a social group and which is immune to criticism from outside that group.[4] The reason for this immunity seems to be that the normative standards of reasonableness are internal to forms of life ("ways of living or modes of social life"). This introduces a third element of arbitrariness. Not only does a form of life yield both what is available to be expressed and the means by which to express it, but also there can be no genuine reason for adopting one form of life rather than another. So the adoption of a form of life appears to be an arbitrary "choice" (if we can make sense of this notion where there can be no reasons) that confers meaning on the agent's doings.

In this chapter, I focus on the Winchian (or pseudo-Winchian) account of the origin of meaningfulness in social conventions. This account, which I dub "conventionalism," may be summarized in the following theses:

1. A form of life is a body of interrelated conventional rules assigning meaning to vocables or behaviors that would otherwise be meaningless. These conventional rules are arbitrary in that any expressive vehicle could be used for any content.

2. A form of life is accepted by the individuals whose form of life it is. This acceptance is arbitrary in that it is not based on reasons. It is a "nonlogical" choice.

3. The acceptance of a form of life provides the basis for the bindingness of the norms of language. What makes it the case that I ought to answer "red" when the Department of Motor Vehicles asks me the color of my car is the fact that I have accepted a rule to use that vocable for that color.

4. A necessary condition for there being rules that make my utterances and actions meaningful is the presence of others.

5. Other persons make meaningful speech and action possible by enforcing the rules that govern an agent's words and deeds (and so render them meaningful). Enforcement by others makes it the case that the rule determines a difference between correct and incorrect behavior. As enforcers of the norms that I accept, these other persons must be ca-

pable of witnessing my doings, determining whether they conform to the relevant norms, and imposing sanctions for violations.

6. Consequently, there can be no such thing as a language understood by just one person, and an isolated individual can neither use words meaningfully nor perform meaningful action.

Perhaps no actual philosopher (except Winch, on the reading of Winch [1990] I am sketching[5]) accepts these theses in just this form. But many commentators on Wittgenstein, and many other writers on language who do not have Wittgenstein explicitly in view, subscribe to some combination of them. To give some indication of the reach of these views, I'll briefly mention three particularly salient examples of philosophers who embrace at least some of them.

Saul Kripke's interpretation of Wittgenstein on rule-following (Kripke 1982) comes close to embracing all of these theses. The arithmetical operation that he labels "quus"[6] (and according to which "67 quus 58" yields "5") is something that I could have meant by "plus," and, as far as the facts about my mind and behavior can show, it *is* what I mean by "plus." But I belong to a community that enforces our familiar plus rule. Kripke's Wittgenstein argues that, considered on its own, the quus rule is just as viable a formal system as the plus rule; the convention of the community to use the plus rule makes it "correct" within that community; an individual's acceptance of the community's rule makes it binding on her, and being monitored and accepted by the community enables her in turn to use the vocable "plus" meaningfully. Kripke notes that in the absence of community enforcers, an individual cannot genuinely be said to be following rules:

> All we can say, if we consider a single person in isolation, is that our ordinary practice licenses him to apply the rule in the way it strikes him.
>
> But of course this is *not* our usual concept of following a rule. . . .
>
> [I]f one person is considered in isolation, the notion of a rule as guiding the person who adopts it can have *no* substantive content. (Kripke 1982, pp. 88–9)

Rudolf Carnap, in "Empiricism, Semantics, and Ontology" (1956), lays out a theory of meaningfulness based on linguistic frameworks. In this work he does not mention Wittgenstein, but his notion of a linguistic framework could serve as a lucid exposition of what many readers of Wittgenstein take "language-games" to be. For Carnap, a linguistic framework is a system that specifies a vocabulary, rules for constructing sentences (for framing claims) using that vocabulary, and methods by which to evaluate rival sentences (claims) so as to determine which we should accept. To be a meaningful sentence is to occupy a position within a linguistic framework. A linguistic framework is essentially arbitrary, in the senses articulated above: the structure of a linguistic framework is given by stipulation; there is no restriction (beyond internal consistency) on what concepts one is allowed to include within one's linguistic framework, and the meaning of words within the framework is arbitrarily stipulated. Moreover, the acceptance of a linguistic framework is an action for which no reason can be given (since being a reason is a relationship that obtains only between statements within a single framework). There may be *pragmatic* considerations in favor of adopting one framework over another. But for Carnap your adoption or nonadoption of a framework cannot be criticized as rational or irrational. Thus Carnap embraces versions of theses (1)–(3).

Carnap's position with respect to theses (4)–(6). is less obvious. As he sees it, the way for speakers to communicate and resolve disputes is precisely by adopting a common linguistic framework. But it appears to be possible for a single individual to adopt and adhere to a linguistic framework. (Indeed, perhaps some scientific advances can be construed as the adoption of a new linguistic framework by a lone intellectual pioneer.) So it appears that Carnap accepts (1)–(3). and rejects (4)–(6).

Margaret Gilbert occupies a similar position. In her account of the conventions of language in *On Social Facts* (Gilbert 1989), she embraces theses (1)–(3). Indeed, she provides a helpful expression of an aspect of thesis (2):

> We do not think of the rules involved in language as interpretable in terms of morality, prudence, or any sort of natural necessity. . . . On the contrary, we think of this rule as having the form of a simple fiat, "This word is to go with this sense." . . . [I]t is uncontroversial that any possible expressive vehicle could in principle express any expressible notion. There is nothing in the nature of things, morality, or whatever, which precludes a particular sound from being linked to a particular sense, and thus *to have that sense*. (Gilbert 1989, p. 386)

At the point in her book at which she most plainly embraces (1)–(3), Gilbert does not have Wittgenstein explicitly in view. But I think she would find it plausible to attribute them to him. She does explicitly attribute theses (4)–(6). to Winch and suggests that they should be attributed to Wittgenstein as well (Gilbert 1989, pp. 91–3). She herself *rejects* theses (4)–(6), and in fact explicitly embraces the possibility of a private language (as we will see in the last section of this chapter). Thus she offers a conventionalist reading of Wittgenstein (via her interpretation of Winch), even though she herself embraces only part of what I am calling conventionalism.

In this brief survey of three philosophers, we can see that the theses of what I call conventionalism divide into two groups. Theses (1)–(3). express the idea that our language is conventional—an idea which all three philosophers accept. Theses (4)–(6) express the idea that those conventions must be social—an idea on which these philosophers disagree. Yet, despite the many differences among Kripke, Carnap, and Gilbert, they agree in regarding Wittgenstein (whenever they have him in view) as a full-blown conventionalist.

I think that the attribution of any of theses (1)–(6) to Wittgenstein is a serious distortion of his thought. A notion of acceptance of a form of life is central in the *Philosophical Investigations*, but Wittgenstein's notion has nothing to do, I argue, with the adoption of conventions. The idea of a private language is under criticism in the *Investigations*, but that criticism does not take the form of *asserting* that language must necessarily be shared or shareable. Instead, Wittgenstein's aim is to bring the advocates of privacy to see that they fail to mean what they think they do, that they are not imagining what they claim to imagine. As I develop an alternative way of reading Wittgenstein, and with that an alternative way to think about our life with language, I will attempt to clarify my interpretation by contrasting it with theses (1)–(6).

RECONCEIVING "FORMS OF LIFE": FROM CONVENTION TO NATURE

While it designates a notion that is plainly central to Wittgenstein's endeavors in the *Investigations*, the term "form of life" appears only a handful of times. In these occurrences of the term, conventionalists can find a plausible basis for their reading. But I will suggest an alternative interpretation of these passages—one that meshes more smoothly with the overarching themes of the book and that is philosophically more satisfying as well. I will argue that we should think of a "form of life" not as a system of conventions, but instead as a shorthand way of referring to what is natural to human beings, where "what is natural" is to be understood in a way far removed from the notion of "nature" operative in what is called philosophical naturalism. (Although I do not purport to be giving an exposition of his views, my thinking about forms of life is greatly indebted to the work of Stanley Cavell.[7])

One of the most well-known invocations of the term "form of life" occurs in a passage that appears to sound a conventionalist note:

§241. "So you are saying that human agreement decides what is true and what is false?"—It is what human beings *say* that is true and false; and they agree in the *language* they use. That is not agreement in opinions but in form of life.

§242. If language is to be a means of communication there must be agreement not only in definitions but also (queer as this may sound) in judgments. This seems to abolish logic, but does not do so.—It is one thing to describe methods of measurement, and another to obtain and state results of measurement. But what we call "measuring" is partly determined by a certain constancy in results of measurement. (*PI*)

In §241 Wittgenstein says that human beings agree in the language they use, and he calls this "agreement in form of life." For the conventionalist, §242 indicates the character of this agreement in language *cum* agreement in form of life: we agree on a set of definitions, and we agree on whatever other methods of applying words we need in order to yield agreed-upon judgments. That these definitions and judgments are conventional is suggested by the analogy with measurement. Just as an explicit convention lies behind our use of either the metric or English system of weights and measures, so (on this reading) an implicit convention lies behind the assignment of meanings to linguistic expressions and to actions. The analogy also helps to illustrate why adopting definitions and methods for applying words is logically fundamental: a question about the size of an object is answered by employing the system of measurement we have adopted; the system of measurement itself cannot come into question in the same way.

It is a corollary of this interpretation that the concept *form of life* distinguishes groups of human beings from one another along a social or cultural dimension. A form of life represents one way of giving meaning to vocables and doings, but there are alternative ways, which yield different language-games. Moreover, any one set of connections between vocables and doings and meanings may be partial, leaving other arenas of meaningfulness to be established by other sets of connections; thus, on this interpretation, a form of life can designate a relatively self-contained cultural domain. Winch, for example, writes that "the philosophies of science, of art, of history, etc., will have the task of elucidating the peculiar natures of those forms of life called 'science', 'art', etc." (Winch 1990, p. 41). This employment of the notion of a form of life belongs to what Cavell calls the concept's "ethnological sense" (Cavell 1989, p. 41). I will be suggesting that, while our form of life has a cultural component, an exclusive stress on the concept's ethnological dimension gives a misleading picture of its role in Wittgenstein's thought.

The assumption that *form of life* is an ethnological concept is aligned with a tendency to identify forms of life with language-games. This is the tendency to suppose that to every language-game there belongs a particular form of life in which speakers of that language-game ipso facto participate. (An example of this tendency is Winch's characterization of science and art not just as different language-games, but as different forms of life.) The attribution to Wittgenstein of a one-to-one relationship between form of life and language-game finds apparent textual support not only in the statement that human beings' agreement in the language they use is agreement in form of life, but also in Wittgenstein's statement, after describing some language-games that are "easy to imagine," that "[t]o imagine a language-game means to imagine a form of life" (*PI*, §19). Many readers assume that this means there is a one-to-one correspondence between language-games and forms of life. But this isn't implied by Wittgenstein's remarks. It could be instead that whenever I imagine a language I imagine some form of life or other, but that one form of life goes along with many distinguishable language-games. Likewise, as we will see below, when Wittgenstein talks of human beings' agreement in form of life, this agreement does not have to involve speaking the same language. The conflation of the concepts form of life and language-game fosters the idea that a form of life is something I can slip into or out of, just as someone who has mastered several language-games can easily move from one of them to another.

Once a reader of Wittgenstein lights on the conventionalist approach to the concept *form of life*, related passages of the *Investigations* seem to fit right in with it. Consider this:

§240. Disputes do not break out (among mathematicians, say) over the question whether a rule has been obeyed or not. People don't come to blows over it, for example. That is part of the framework on which the working of our language is based (for example, in giving descriptions). (*PI*)

Here it looks as if Wittgenstein is referring to an area of culture we could call "mathematics," or "using mathematical calculation in giving descriptions." When Wittgenstein talks about "the framework on which the working of our language is based," the conventionalist will hear a reference to the definitions, rules, and standards employed in mathematical calculation; he will assume that Wittgenstein is noting that a convention belonging to this "framework" is that we accept the results of mathematical calculation that others arrive at.[8]

But this conventionalist interpretation of Wittgenstein's remark puts our agreement about arithmetical calculations in the wrong light. To say that it is one of our linguistic rules that we do not dispute the results of a straightforward calculation surely gets things the wrong way round. If we don't come to blows over arithmetic, that isn't because we have agreed not to, but because there is no room for a dispute. Solving arithmetical problems is a particularly pellucid process; we have universally recognized algorithms which competent speakers are capable of following, such that anyone who is in doubt about a mathematical calculation can be led through algorithmic steps to accept the correct result. This agreement in the result is not a function of a convention to accept the result others (the majority? one's elders?) arrive at; it is a function of the exercise of abilities acquired through training. As I read the passage, "the framework on which the working of our language is based" should be understood as that set of arithmetical abilities that ensures unanimity. If human beings lacked these skills, we would possess neither mathematics nor our concept of mathematical certainty. The agreement about whether a rule has been followed, or the agreement about whether a calculation is correct, that Wittgenstein is talking about is a result of shared abilities to follow arithmetical rules and to recognize when others are doing so. The uniformity that results from these abilities belongs to what Wittgenstein

would call the grammar of the concept of calculation. What it is to be a calculation is (in part) to elicit this kind of agreement: agreement not only in results, but also in how we arrive at the results.[9] That this is what calculation is
has nothing to do with conventions we either may or may not have adopted;
it is a feature of the grammar of calculation.

The contrast between Wittgenstein's view and the conventionalist interpretation may be brought out by imagining someone who does not conform to
the rules of arithmetic. For the conventionalist, someone who gives a wrong
answer to an arithmetical problem is either (1) following our rule, but making
a mistake (which further instruction ought to correct), (2) incompetent, not capable of doing arithmetic, or (3) following a different rule, which is, considered as a rule, no more correct or incorrect than ours. For examples of such
rules, we may consider Kripke's "quus" function and Wittgenstein's example
in the *Remarks on the Foundations of Mathematics* of a tribe that buys and
sells quantities of wood according to the area of ground the wood occupies,
regardless of how high the wood is piled (Wittgenstein 1978, p. 94). Are the
wood sellers "measuring wood"? Is the person who uses quaddition "calculating"? The conventionalist would reformulate these questions as: "Have these
individuals adopted the (perhaps implicit) convention in question? Do the
members of their community observe and enforce these rules?" For Wittgenstein, affirmative answers to these questions do not yet entitle us to say they
are employing an alternative rule of calculation or an alternative system of
measurement. Suppose we try to imagine a tribe using quaddition where we
use addition. Our affairs would immediately fall into confusion if we started
using quus rather than plus. Why wouldn't theirs? Well, perhaps they never
have to deal with more than 56 objects; but then we must wonder what basis
there will be for saying that they are using quaddition. Or perhaps they rarely
deal with more than 56 things, and when they do they don't seem troubled by
the (to us) anomalous results. But fleshing out this imagined scenario will be
harder than at first appears. Cavell provides an analogous imaginative fleshing
out of the wood sellers example: as one step in this elaboration he imagines
that, given the way this tribe fells trees and stacks and transports logs, wood
"naturally" comes in standard piles, "so that logs are more trouble, i.e., more
costly, to store and to load if they are strewn around" (Cavell 1979, p. 116). The
exact way we make sense of these imagined tribes need not concern us here.
But however we do it, our explanation will be an instance of the sort of explanation Cavell describes thus:

> It seems safe to suppose that if you can describe any behavior which I can recog-
> nize as that of human beings, I can give you an explanation which will make that
> behavior coherent, i.e., show it to be imaginable in terms of natural responses and
> practicalities. Though *those* natural responses may not be mine, and those practices
> not practical for me, in my environment, as I interpret it. (1979, p. 118)

And what is imaginable in terms of natural responses and practicalities is not arbitrary and is not a function of convention.

In other words, for quaddition and the wood sellers' behavior to be kinds of calculating and measuring, we cannot simply find some rule that the imagined tribe members are in accord with. The behavior that goes with the supposed rule has to be part of an intelligible life for a human being. The term "form of life" is Wittgenstein's way of referring to an intelligible human life. In asking whether the tribe-members' behavior is an intelligible life for human beings, I am not—as conventionalists would have it—merely asking pragmatic questions as to whether a given rule is advisable or not. I am pointing to the grammar of the concepts *calculating* and *measuring*. This grammar is tied to the place of calculation and measuring in our lives, and their place is not arbitrary in the conventionalist sense.

We can make a similar point with regard to the conventional notation of mathematics. The numerals we use in doing arithmetic are, let us agree, conventional; that these and not other figures have come down to us is a historical contingency. We could make an arbitrary stipulation to use a different set of figures; so we may regard our using "0," "1," and so on, as arbitrary. But what about the fact that we use a base-10 number system? Any other number system would be able to express the same content as ours. Shall we say the base-10 system is arbitrary? Our use of the base-10 system is no doubt connected with the fact that we have 10 fingers. Yet suppose we didn't use our thumbs for counting: then a base-8 system would be more convenient. (We could even use each thumb to indicate an 8, so our ten fingers could easily represent any number up to 24.) So it looks as if there is something arbitrary about whether we use a base-8 or a base-10 system. But is it arbitrary that we do not use a base-23 number system? That we use a base-10 number system is a function of how we use our bodies and of what our physical capacities are. These are not the products of convention, even if there is not exactly one way in which these capacities might be developed. It is not the case that any logically possible expressive vehicle is a possible expressive vehicle for us, because we cannot simply discard the ways we use our hands, bodies, voices.

While conventionalism has prima facie plausibility as a reading of §§240–242 of the *Investigations*, it doesn't fit well with another important appearance of the term "form of life." Wittgenstein writes:

> One can imagine an animal angry, frightened, unhappy, happy, startled. But hopeful? And why not?
> A dog believes his master is at the door. But can he also believe his master will come the day after to-morrow?—And *what* can he not do here? . . .
> Can only those hope who can talk? Only those who have mastered the use of a language. That is to say, the phenomena of hope are modes of this complicated

form of life. (If a concept refers to a character of human handwriting, it has no application to beings that do not write.) (*PI*, p. 174)

Here Wittgenstein seems to identify mastering the use of a language with
possessing a "complicated form of life."[10] Conventionalists will have to understand Wittgenstein as saying that the phenomena of hope are instituted
by agreements, which a given culture, or group with a common language,
may or may not possess. But this interpretation misses the context of the passage. Wittgenstein is not pointing to contrasts between different cultures' expressions of hope; the complicated form of life of which the phenomena of
hope and expectation are modes is not something belonging to one culture
as opposed to others. Instead, Wittgenstein is contrasting human beings—
creatures capable of hope—with other species of animals. "Form of life" here
means something like "type of organism"; we are to think of the differences
between forms of life in biological terms. Cavell calls this the "biological . . .
sense" (as opposed to the ethnological sense) of the concept *form of life*
(Cavell 1989, pp. 41–2).

The biological dimension of the concept form of life is connected with this
characterization of Wittgenstein's philosophical project:

> What we are supplying are really remarks on the natural history of human be-
> ings; we are not contributing curiosities however, but observations which no
> one has doubted, but which have escaped remark only because they are always
> before our eyes. (*PI*, §415)

Wittgenstein uses the concept *form of life* in the course of his observations
about the human animal in its life as a talker. The point of these observations
is to address philosophical perplexity. It is a bold and perhaps surprising
claim that "observations which no one has doubted" could remove philosophical problems. But as Wittgenstein sees it, philosophical reflection quite
naturally leads us away from the obvious and the everyday; it often leads us
into an inappropriately conceived quest for general theories where none are
actually needed. I will suggest that this is the case with conventionalism.

The possession of language is obviously crucial to what it is to be a human
as opposed to non-human animal. But Wittgenstein does not simply want to
stress that our linguistic ability sets us apart from other animals. He also
wants to register the biological basis for our power of speech, the innate abilities that allow human infants to learn language. I won't pretend to provide
an exhaustive list of these abilities, but I will mention a few that Wittgenstein
highlights. Human infants are equipped with a range of naturally communicative cries and behaviors: they emit different calls when hungry, when
wet, when tired, and so on. For their part, caregivers respond differentially
to these different cries and other behavioral cues. This kind of natural communication between offspring and parent marks all animals that care for

their young. What distinguishes human beings from other animals, at first, is perhaps just the range of naturally expressive behaviors that human infants are capable of. But then a child's caregivers, through their responses, initiate him into some simple uses of language. They give words to the child's states ("Oh, you're hungry aren't you?"), and at a subsequent stage they will supply words to substitute for the child's natural outbursts. Parents teach their children to call "I'm hungry" instead of fussing, "I want that" instead of grabbing at a toy, "Milk please" instead of throwing the empty cup on the floor. Wittgenstein describes one example of this kind of substitution when he answers the question "How does a human being learn the meaning of the names of sensations?—of the word 'pain' for example?":

> Here is one possibility: words are connected with the primitive, the natural, expressions of the sensation and used in their place. A child has hurt himself and he cries; and then adults talk to him and teach him exclamations and later, sentences. They teach the child new pain behaviour. (*PI*, §244)

How do caregivers effect this teaching? They must employ the abilities of the child herself—for example, her mimetic power, her spontaneous generation of behavior, an instinct we could call a desire for parental approval (although this label makes the instinct sound more intentional than it is). The caregivers direct the child's behavior by providing encouragement, approval, disapproval. How does the infant recognize encouragement, approval, disapproval? Well, she responds in different ways to the smiles, frowns, headshakes, laughter of her parents. It would overintellectualize this to say that the infant recognizes a smile as a sign of approval, but we can say that she naturally welcomes parental smiles and naturally smiles back, and this gives a behavioral toe-hold for the training Wittgenstein mentions.

Wittgenstein is also interested in the innate abilities and reactions that underlie other kinds of language use. Consider some of what enables a child to write out the sequence "0, 2, 4, 6, . . ." at the order "add 2." She must first of all have the motor skills to control the movement of her pencil, or to call out the answer, or to otherwise express the sequence. Then she must have the ability to count, to recognize patterns, to visually and aurally distinguish numerals and words, and, at another level, powers of memory and mimesis and something we could call (perhaps misleadingly) a desire to conform. There is another natural response that Wittgenstein mentions in connection with learning to follow a rule: following another's pointing by looking in the direction from wrist to fingertip, rather than from fingertip to wrist (*PI*, §185). To which we might add: following another's eyes, tracking what others are noticing, and generally being aware of what's going on around you.

These native abilities and responses are characteristics of our form of life, and our remarks about them might be considered contributions to a natural history of the obvious. But the concept *form of life* also involves features of our lives as talkers that cannot be regarded as natural in the same sense. As an example of the contrast between animal and human life Wittgenstein mentions hope; immediately afterward he mentions "grief" as a "pattern which recurs, with different variations, in the weave of our life" (*PI*, p. 174). Wittgenstein cites hope and grief as phenomena that distinguish humans from other animals. This does not mean that Wittgenstein would deny that animals are capable of something properly called "hope" (as when a dog hopes that the footfall on the stairs is that of its owner) and "grief" (as when a bird is downcast at the death of its mate). But while hope and grief are natural to us, they are not natural in the way a dog's experience of hope is; nor are they natural in the way that an infant's chortling with delight or an injured man's groaning in pain are. The phenomena of human hope and grief require conceptual resources that infants and non-linguistic animals lack: for example, an awareness of temporal duration, articulable expectations and memories, the ability to think of (imagine, remember) situations different from the actual one. While I can hope that our neighbors will return safely from a long absence, my dog cannot hope for the return of our neighbor's dog.[11] Moreover, the fact that human experience is conceptualized means that, even in those instances in which what we hope or grieve for can be described in terms that could also fit animal experience, our experiences are still radically different from those of animals. We may wail, animal-style, when a loved one dies, but we will also remember him, memorialize him, and reflect on his qualities and the course of his life. The fact that our loss is conceptualized and not just viscerally felt is an indication of the difference in kind between human grief and animal grief, and it suggests the different way in which grief and hope are natural to us. The human responses that we call "grief" and "hope" are not innate, but innate responses are the substratum out of which grief and hope develop in the normal course of human maturation. The result of such maturation is that the learned responses characteristic of grief and hope become natural to us, and so come to belong to our form of life.

The fact that human expressions of grief and hope have to be learned points to the necessity of connecting the biological dimension of the concept *form of life* with the ethnological. While grief and hope are natural to the human animal, the way they are expressed will vary from culture to culture, and even from person to person within a culture. Some people will express grief by wearing black, some by pouring ashes on their heads, some by maintaining a prayer vigil, and so on. But despite the variety in human beings' expressions of grief, the concept *grief* has a grammar, and not just anything can count as falling under it. Grief is a response to the loss of someone or something important to you; expressions of grief must be intelligible as an expression of that loss, and they normally allow for some expression of the emotions typically associated with it. (Persons who do not feel those emotions at someone's death can in some sense mourn and grieve for him; but this will be a nonstandard case that is linked with others by outward similarities.) The divergent manifestations of grief that different cultures make available to their members all count as *grief* because of some such "pattern in the weave" of the lives of these differently enculturated persons.

In learning to grieve as those in your culture do, you are learning complicated forms of response to what is typically a traumatic event. Learning how to grieve is also learning what grief is. It is not just an upwelling of brute feeling, but a pattern of feeling and action and thought that can be extended in time, that can recur, that is subject to evaluation (as, for example, appropriate or excessive). Grief is a particularly rich phenomenon, but acquiring any concept requires a similar education. In gaining concepts, a child is gaining complicated patterns of response to her environment, especially her human environment. Part of what she gains is responsiveness to the norms that structure the language and activity that surrounds her. Her acquisition of concepts transforms the quality of her experience: what begins as the brute responsiveness of crying when hungry and whimpering when cold becomes conceptualized as the experience of hunger and cold. Here we should return to Wittgenstein's idea that a part of language learning is that the child learns to substitute, say, "My stomach hurts" for the primitive cry of pain: what replaces the innate cry is not simply another cry but a bit of articulate speech, which is (as the child comes to learn) logically connected to other units of sense. The acquisition of language is not the acquisition of communicative calls different from but logically equivalent to the primitive ones. It is the provision of conceptual capacities to the child, her initiation into the going concern of language. An infant's caregivers are not simply providing words to label the experience she natively has; they are giving her the capacity to enjoy human experience. (This is a lesson of Wittgenstein's critique of Augustine's description of language acquisition.)

When a child acquires conceptualized experience, she gains a new range of natural reactions. She may, for example, naturally react to a stomachache by complaining about it (in more or less articulate speech), not just moaning; she may react to unfairness with indignation. The fact that these reactions are conceptualized means that they come within the ambit of the agent's reflection and that she can exercise freedom about them. I may react with revulsion at the physical appearance of beggars; but upon reflection I can decide that that reaction is inappropriate, and I can perhaps alter my reaction to one of, say, friendly engagement. Thus what we might call my acquired natural reactions are not hard-wired. My nature is something that can come in for critical reflection and, in some cases, alteration.[12] (For some purposes it may be useful to distinguish two levels of "natural reactions": those that are and those that are not subject to modification by the agent. But it will not be easy to draw the line. How do we regard such primitive natural reactions as eating when hungry, flinching before a threatened blow, crying out after receiving a blow? Can't all of these reactions be altered through the agent's exercise of her conceptual powers? And if such seemingly basic natural reactions are not 'hard-wired' in this sense, are any reactions besides mere metabolic processes like digestion and respiration beyond the reach of rational reflection?)

For Wittgenstein, as I read him, our form of life is the body of reactions natural to talkers. Whether you say that the human form of life is one thing or many depends on your perspective. You can regard the human form of life as a cultured nature; this is to attribute one form of life to all human talkers. Or you can talk about *a* human form of life, one of the particular cultural realizations of that nature, a particular repertoire of expressions of, for example, hope and grief. But in talking about many human forms of life, we still make implicit use of a notion of human nature, for it is what we see exemplified in all these different ways. We bring to our efforts to understand these different forms of life an assumption that they will exemplify concerns with birth, sex, death; with hope, grief, happiness; that they will have some way of distinguishing and relating the human, animate, and inanimate worlds, and so on. To say that there is one human form of life is to say that any speaker of a language will have natural reactions to such concerns and that these reactions are conceptualized. This account may seem to deliberately embrace an ambiguity in the notion *form of life*. But the ambiguity—or rather the two perspectives from which to describe a form of life—is inherent in a concept at such a high level of generality. (Consider the related ambiguity in the concept *culture*.)

There is an important objection to this concept of form of life that concerns my description of natural reactions as acquired and in particular my inclusion of concept use among the "natural" reactions. The worry is that this creates a philosophical muddle by running together two quite distinct things: our nature and our norms (including our conceptual norms). According to what goes under the rubric "philosophical naturalism," the human animal is to be understood in terms of, and human phenomena are to be explained by, our nature as described by natural science; what we are, in the most basic sense, is given by psychology (including cognitive science) and biology (including evolutionary theory and ecology) and perhaps ultimately by physics and chemistry. Naturalism tends to see norms (including those involved in one's grasp of concepts) as phenomena that present a prima facie mystery or puzzle; part of naturalism's project is therefore to show how norms could have emerged from interactions between beings that were initially just behaving in accordance with biological and other natural laws. From the point of view of naturalism, the idea that it is our nature to inhabit the realm of normativity merely introduces obscurity into the concept of nature, which should be kept as clear and as closely tied to science as possible;

for naturalism, the notion of form of life I have sketched (if it figures at all in an accurate description of human life) is a phenomenon to be explained by appeal to the scientific conception of nature.

There are at least three different questions about our normative capacities that philosophical naturalism can be concerned with. The first is: "How does an individual *homo sapiens*, whose natal capacities are describable in purely physiological terms, come to grasp norms and become capable of acting from respect for them?" The second is a parallel question for the species as a whole: "How did the species *homo sapiens* evolve its conceptual and linguistic capacities?" I think there is nothing wrong with these questions in themselves. Indeed, Wittgenstein's remarks regarding the enculturation of children can be understood as preliminary contributions to the first question. But these two legitimate questions tend to shade over into a question that Wittgenstein would find problematic—a question we could express as, "How are norms reducible to, or explainable in terms of, nature as described by science?" This is the question naturalistic philosophers are tempted to answer by citing such things as behavioral regularities or linguistic dispositions.[13] And it is from the point of view of this variety of naturalism that the objection to Wittgenstein's notion of form of life arises. This variety of naturalism is a major target of Wittgenstein's criticism in the *Investigations*. Wittgenstein's response to the naturalist's objection is a critique of the project from which the objection arises. I cannot explore that critique here, other than to note that it is ultimately a critique of the scientism that identifies of intellectually respectable explanations with those that contemporary natural science countenances.

WITTGENSTEIN VERSUS CONVENTIONALISM

If my elaboration of Wittgenstein's concept of form of life, or, as we could put it, the concept of the natural reactions of human talkers, is to be rendered tenable, we will have to see how it jibes with Wittgenstein's most notorious invocation of the term *"Lebensformen"* (a passage already cited in a quotation from Winch above): "What has to be accepted, the given, is—so one could say—forms of life" (*PI*, p. 226).

Many readers have taken this to be an endorsement of cultural and even political conservatism; they think Wittgenstein is saying that the forms of social life have to be taken as they are, and they think, moreover, that for Wittgenstein this conservatism is necessary as a matter of logic. Because things only have meaning for me against the background of my social and linguistic norms, I must, logically, accept those norms, or else lose my power of understanding. Rational criticism can be carried out only within my form of life; I cannot criticize my form of life itself; hence, it is "what has to be accepted, the given."[14]

But to gain a proper appreciation of this passage we have to pause over three questions about it that are typically not explicitly posed (because, I think, the answers are mistakenly taken to be obvious). (1) Who, according to Wittgenstein, has to accept "forms of life"? (2) With respect to what is a form of life given? (3) Why do "forms of life" have to be accepted, by whoever it is who has to accept them? Answers to these questions easily fall out of the conventionalist interpretation. According to it, (1) anyone who wishes to speak or act meaningfully has to accept one or another of the in principle unlimited number of forms of life. And (2) the form of life a person accepts is given with respect to assigning meaning to her utterances and behavior; furthermore, an individual's acceptance of a form of life provides the ultimate source of the bindingness of linguistic norms on her. Finally, (3) a person has to accept (one or more) forms of life in order to enter the domain of meaningfulness; it's the acceptance of a form of life that imparts meaning to the words, so if anyone wants to speak or act meaningfully, she has to accept a form of life. In other words, the conventionalist interprets Wittgenstein's remark as stating a requirement on all language speakers.

I think this remark should be interpreted in quite another way, as a piece of advice regarding philosophical method. Wittgenstein means to be pointing a way out of the philosophical fly-bottle. When he is talking about accepting a form of life, he means accepting that our life with words is the place to look to resolve philosophical perplexity. For a philosopher to reject forms of life is to turn away from the ordinary use of words. I don't mean to imply that Wittgenstein simply wants philosophers to talk about ordinary things in ordinary ways. It is not as if the solution to philosophical perplexity is simply to talk about apples and tables instead of meaning and language; nor does Wittgenstein assume that the way we ordinarily talk is beyond philosophical reproach. But his reminders about ordinary uses of words are supposed to draw our attention to how, in doing philosophy, words (e.g., "language," "understanding," "knowledge," "feeling," "sensation") drift from their everyday use, and to how this unmooring of our philosophical statements sometimes results in our not knowing what we mean by our words. An example (to which we shall return) of turning away from the use of language is assuming that a speaker's act of "inner ostensive definition" (a kind of inner pointing) can establish that a sign refers to a certain sensation, without considering the role that the sign has in the speaker's life.

Thus I would answer the above three questions this way: (1) It is philosophers (or the philosophical impulses within each of us) who have to accept forms of life. (2) Our form of life is that to which we should look to address philosophical perplexity. (3) We ought to look to our form of life because otherwise we will remain perplexed. In the discussion of Wittgenstein's private language argument I offer below, we see an example of the philosophical importance of accepting our form of life.

By way of developing the contrast between the reading I am offering of the *Investigations* and conventionalism, let's examine conventionalism's theses (1)–(3) in light of the concept form of life I have sketched.

Thesis (1), which asserts that a form of life is essentially arbitrary, in that any expressive vehicle could be used for any content, turns out, on my interpretation, to be true only in a limited way of a limited portion of what goes under the rubric "form of life." The natural reactions we acquire include linguistic responses. To be sure, it is a historical contingency that we use the vocable "red" for red and that we conjugate the verb "to be" as we do, and so on. Other words would do as well, and could be adopted by a group fiat. But the concept form of life also comprises naturally communicative behavior, such as writhing on the ground groaning (as we say) in pain. This behavior is expressive, but its expressiveness is in no way arbitrary or up to us. Regardless of conventions, writhing and groaning behavior expresses pain. (Even if the agent is feigning it, her groaning still expresses pain; that's what makes it *pain* that she is feigning.[15])

Another restriction on arbitrariness is the need for pattern. Although one could imagine assigning vocables to linguistic functions in a wholly arbitrary fashion, so that the past tense of the verb for swimming was "glick" and the present tense was "ho" and the future tense was "blitheragoo," and so on for all words without discernible pattern, the result would be a highly limited symbolic system. The problem would not simply be that, if it could express a range of meanings comparable to that expressible in our language, no human being could learn it.[16] More importantly, a language that lacked syntactic pattern, in which every expression was an idiom, would be impoverished in its expressive resources.[17]

Thesis (2) asserts that individuals *accept* their form of life. This, like thesis (1), is on my interpretation only a partial truth. I have noted the freedom that comes with conceptual capacities. An aspect of this freedom is that an individual can modify or reject her natural impulses and reactions. (Consider how one may conquer even the urge to eat.) We could thus say that you tacitly accept all the reactions in your form of life that you do not choose to reject.

But such tacit acceptance is quite different from the acceptance of conventions that conventionalists have in mind. In fact, it is not easy to make sense of their notion of acceptance. Conventionalists envision a neutral territory, free of commitment to any norms of communication, from which you can weigh the merits of accepting versus rejecting a body of conventions, acceptance of which will in turn render your behavior and utterances significant. A similar picture is very compelling in political philosophy, where the neutral territory may be understood as rational self-interest (perhaps operating behind a veil of ignorance); self-interest provides the ground for choosing among different imaginable sets of social institutions; that choice is in turn the ground of political obligation. Another similar picture also serves for deliberation about how best to express oneself: if I'm bilingual, I might have to decide whether to speak one language or another to a given audience.[18] But we cannot use this kind of picture for the adoption of a form of life, because what we are to adopt, on the conventionalist interpretation, is that which will make our behaviors and utterances significant. To be free of such conventions (to occupy the neutral ground from which the adoption of a system of conventions is to take place) is for our doings to be bereft of significance. And so, in particular, there is no possibility, from such a neutral ground, of doing something that would have the significance of adopting a convention.

Even if we were to make sense of a notion of the adoption of conventions that are the basis of meaningfulness, the resulting notion of agreement in conventions is different from the sharing of a form of life, as I understand it. When Wittgenstein says "We agree in the language we use" and calls that agreement "agreement in form of life," conventionalists hear him as saying that we come to agreements on the ways we will use words, which agreements (our "form of life") give us a shared language. I hear him as saying, not that we agree *on* what language we will use, but that we agree *in* or *through* language. Language is the medium in which we discover or form our agreements—and likewise our disagreements. (Wittgenstein could also have said, "We disagree in the language we use.") And our form of life is a label for those reactions and sensibilities on which we draw to find any agreement, or to express any disagreement.

Thesis (3) holds that the basis for the bindingness of the conventions of language is one's acceptance of a form of life. Since for Wittgenstein it is wrong to say that a form of life is accepted by those to whom it belongs, it follows that thesis (3) is not Wittgenstein's position. Indeed, one of Wittgenstein's aims is to undermine the question to which this thesis is an answer. This question is, what makes the norms of language binding? What makes me obliged to use language as my fellow English-speakers do? Thesis (3) proposes that we account for the normativity of language in terms of another layer of normativity, the normativity of agreement. If I have contracted with my neighbors to use a word in a certain way, then my use of the word in a different way is a violation of my contract with them, and is therefore forbidden.

Wittgenstein encourages us to question whether the proposed conventions could possibly do the task they are supposed to. Can we really make sense of the normative priority assigned to convention as opposed to language? Conventionalism presupposes that norms of agreement—roughly, the obligation to keep one's promises—logically precede the norms of language. But how do we achieve an agreement to act in a certain way, if we're not already talking intelligibly together? What we imagine at the state prior to language is, I think, uniformities of behavior; but these don't amount to normatively structured agreements until we interpret them in ways that can only find expression in language.

I will close this critique of conventionalism's theses (1)–(3) with a tentative explanation of the philosophical attraction of conventionalism. This is that it appears to satisfy a felt need to ground the norms of language. The felt need arises, I suspect, from a sense of alienation, or of the possibility of alienation, from one's language. In such a mood, one wonders, "Why do I have to talk as everyone else does? Why can't I use my *own* words? Why do I have to follow these rules of grammar?" These questions have their basis in the awareness of the contingencies that determine both the character of my language and the fact that that language (and not another) is mine. In the face of such anxiety, positing a moment of acceptance of conventions appears to offer a way to replace alienation with an authentic relationship to one's language. The criticisms I have been raising against conventionalism, however, should prompt a question as to just how effective this gambit can be.

Wittgenstein, on my interpretation, does not want to provide an answer to the questions that such alienation prompts. Instead, perhaps we should see in the concept *form of life* a means of eliminating the source of the alienation. If we see our linguistic norms as an array of natural reactions that are developments of our innate communicative abilities, then perhaps the recognition that our expressions might have been different need not produce a crisis about the bindingness of linguistic norms.

In the concluding section of this chapter I will examine another source of conventionalism's appeal, one arising from Wittgenstein's private language argument. This argument is notoriously difficult to interpret, and conventionalism (in its theses (4)–(6)) offers a plausible candidate explanation of why Wittgenstein should conclude (as he appears to) that it is impossible to have a language that can be understood by only one individual. So if I am to maintain that conventionalism is an untenable reading of Wittgenstein, I need to offer an alternative interpretation of the private language argument—one that will distance Wittgenstein from theses (4)–(6).

THE PRIVATE LANGUAGE ARGUMENT AND
THE PUBLIC CHARACTER OF LANGUAGE

The alleged possibility of a private language emerges in the *Investigations* immediately following the statement that humans' agreement in the language they use "is not agreement in opinions but in form of life." Since Wittgenstein is plainly concerned to challenge this alleged possibility, it can easily seem that his point is that the agreement in form of life that makes meaningful speech and action possible must be social. I will suggest that the resulting interpretation, to the effect that Wittgenstein thinks that meaningful language use must somehow be social, presupposes a mistaken clarity about what a private language is.

The usual interpretations of Wittgenstein in this area take him to be posing the question of whether language must be shared. Because of the intimate grammatical connections between speaking a language and following rules, the question of whether language must be shared can be recast as the question of whether an isolated individual can be said to follow rules. There are two main readings of Wittgenstein on this question. Conventionalism maintains and attributes to Wittgenstein the claim that in order for my behavior to count as following a rule, other people must be present to observe my behavior and to determine whether it is in conformity to the rule. Hence, an isolated individual cannot use language meaningfully. (This is captured in theses (4)–(6) above.) Other philosophers, in opposition to conventionalism, argue that the presence of others is too strong a requirement for behavior to count as following a rule. These philosophers describe a Robinson Crusoe figure who keeps a journal of, say, the flora and fauna he observes and who (these philosophers think) is surely using language meaningfully and hence is following rules, despite his isolation. They think that the correct construal of Wittgenstein's position is that for someone's behavior to qualify as rule-following (and so as meaningful) it must be *possible in principle* for others to verify that it conforms to the relevant rules; even if there are no other sapient beings on Crusoe's island to witness his behavior, others could in principle observe it and determine whether he is obeying rules for the use of his words. These commentators would say that Wittgenstein's claim is that any language must be *shareable*, but not that it must be actually *shared*.

Against both of these positions on the question of the role of others in making rule-following possible stand philosophers who think that whether an individual is following a rule is a question which requires no reference to what anyone else observes or is capable of observing. This position is often cast as a rejection of Wittgenstein's conclusions regarding the impossibility of a private language. Margaret Gilbert provides a good example of this position:

[A] person has a language or grasps a concept as long as he possesses a certain property, and whether or not he possesses that property can be ascertained by considering how it is with him considered in isolation from all other people. If on a certain occasion I use the term 'red' in the sense of *red*, then this is solely a matter of how it is with me now. It does not concern how it is or has been or will be with any other person. It seems to follow that in principle a being could use a word in a certain sense even if he has always been entirely alone in the world. For his doing so is, after all, only a matter of how it is with him. Whether or not a being possesses a concept is, one might say, a 'private' matter, though one others may be able to find out about in at least some instances. So let us call this the *privacy thesis*. (Gilbert 1989, p. 95)

On the view that Gilbert is here describing (which she defends under the label "the natural view"), others *may* be able to find out whether I possess a certain concept (or rule); but I could possess concepts even if others *cannot* find out that I do. For whether I'm using a given concept is a fact about me that makes no reference to connections (actual or notional) with others.

These three positions on the role of others in making rule-following possible are all responses to Wittgenstein's remarks about a private language. And they have an assumption in common, viz., that it is clear what it would be to have a private language. Philosophers of all three stripes think that Wittgenstein gives us a description of a private language, or, a language which "another person cannot understand" (*PI*, §243), and then argues (correctly or incorrectly, depending on which position you embrace) that the thing described is not possible. But as I read Wittgenstein's remarks concerning a language which another person cannot understand, his purpose is not to deny that such a thing is possible, but rather to question just what if anything philosophers are imagining when they (purport to) debate the status of what they call a private language. In other words, Wittgenstein is not trying to demonstrate that what philosophers describe as a private language is impossible; he is trying to get the parties to the debate to recognize that they haven't really offered a description of anything under the rubric "private language."[19]

This alternative reading of Wittgenstein is suggested in the way he frames the issue of a putative private language. He begins by describing something that *is* imaginable: "We could . . . imagine human beings who spoke only in monologue; who accompanied their activities by talking to themselves" (*PI*, §243). The discussion of this imaginable case is followed by the central question I will be examining:

> But could we also imagine a language in which a person could write down or give vocal expression to his inner experiences—his feelings, moods, and the rest—for his private use?—Well, can't we do so in our ordinary language?—But that is not what I mean. The individual words of this language are to refer to what can only be known to the person speaking; to his immediate private sensations. So another person cannot understand the language. (*PI*, §243)

This passage exemplifies the dynamic that I see at work throughout this part of the *Investigations*. The interlocutor wants to suppose (or is committed to the possibility of) a language for a person's "private use." Wittgenstein immediately offers him something answering to that description: "our ordinary language," which a person can of course use in a locked diary, say, to keep a record of his inner experiences for his private use. But the proffered language does not satisfy the interlocutor: "But that is not what I mean." The interlocutor rejects the language we have; he wants something else, something other than the genuine possibility Wittgenstein holds out in response to his demand.

In order to fully appreciate Wittgenstein's work in this stretch of the *Investigations*, we would need to understand the source of the interlocutor's desire, or demand, for something else. What makes him want (or think he has to make sense of) a private language? This is a question I cannot explore fully here, but one important reason for caring about private languages comes from empiricist conceptions of meaning, according to which words can only mean ideas in the mind of the speaker, or sense-data, or other items of direct awareness, where these are construed in empiricist terms. (Strikingly similar versions of this thesis can be found in Locke and Russell.[20]) Items of direct awareness, as Russell (for example) conceives them, are available only to the one individual directly aware of them, so on this conception of meaning it can easily appear that "the words of [any] language are to refer to what can only be known to the person speaking." The empiricist conception of meaning may have little appeal as a general theory of language nowadays, but it is still an attractive account of the meaningfulness of sensation-language. Since sensation-talk is the most plausible candidate for a private language, Wittgenstein focuses his critique on it.

The empiricist conception of meaning entails that I am trapped behind a veil of ideas, regarding not just what I can know, but also what I can mean. No matter how hard I try to make myself understood, I am always blocked by the nature of language: I can only mean or refer to items within my private field of meaning. In this scenario, the privacy of my language wears the aspect of tragedy. We may also imagine a scenario with an aspect closer to that of comedy: this is to think of someone struggling to guard his thoughts from the intrusions of a world that would pry into his private affairs. Here we imagine someone seeking secrecy, whose anxiety is that his thoughts and feelings will always be exposed to the understanding of others. Whether we imagine the interlocutor to be trying to overcome a privacy that is forced upon him by his philosophical commitments, or to be trying to secure a secret domain against public understanding, will affect the course of the argument at a later stage.

The interlocutor demands a language that another person cannot understand, either because such a language is required for the tenability of his philosophical theories of meaning and knowledge or because it provides him a secret domain. At first blush, it would seem easy to provide such a language: he can simply make up new words for his sensations. But, as before, the proffered possibility fails to satisfy the interlocutor. Such a language isn't private enough, he finds:

Now, what about the language which describes my inner experiences and which only I myself can understand? *How* do I use words to stand for my sensations?— As we ordinarily do? Then are my words for sensations tied up with my natural expressions of sensation? In that case my language is not a "private" one. Someone else might understand it as well as I. (*PI*, §256)

When Wittgenstein is talking about how we use words to stand for our sensations, he is alluding to an aspect of our form of life that I sketched above, viz., that human beings naturally make gestures and facial expressions and adopt physical attitudes all of which are naturally communicative. In maturing into our form of life, we learn linguistic expressions that in many ways replace natural ones. If the linguistic expressions the interlocutor invents for his inner experiences have this kind of etiology, then the connection between natural and linguistic expression would give others the means to interpret his supposedly private linguistic expressions. (They'll notice, say, that he makes the face expressive of tasting something bitter and so will be able to infer the reference of his expostulated "Plurf.")

To make sure that his invented sensation-language stays private in the sense he (thinks he) wants, the interlocutor will then have to focus on those sensations that have no natural expression:

But suppose I didn't have any natural expression for the sensation, but only had the sensation? And now I simply *associate* names with sensations and use these names in descriptions. (*PI*, §256)

Wittgenstein elaborates the kind of association needed in the following fuller description of this thought-experiment.

Let us imagine the following case. I want to keep a diary about the recurrence of a certain sensation. To this end I associate it with the sign "S" and write this sign in a calendar for every day on which I have the sensation. . . . I can give myself a kind of ostensive definition.—How? Can I point to the sensation? Not in the ordinary sense. But I speak, or write the sign down, and at the same time I concentrate my attention on the sensation—and so, as it were, point to it inwardly. (*PI*, § 258)

This "kind of ostensive definition" is supposed to establish the rule that makes "S" the sign for the sensation, that thereby renders it meaningful, and that thus enables the interlocutor to use it to express the sensation on which he has just concentrated his attention. But can this "ceremony" establish the rule? Wittgenstein suggests that the answer is no:

But "I impress it [the connexion between the sign and the sensation] on myself" can only mean: this process brings it about that I remember the connexion *right* in the future. But in the present case I have no criterion of correctness. One would like to say: whatever is going to seem right to me is right. And that only means that here we can't talk about "right." (*PI,* §258)

One can wonder here: why is there no criterion of correctness? Isn't the interlocutor's criterion for the correct use of "S" simply writing "S" when he has the associated sensation?

Conventionalism provides a not implausible argument for Wittgenstein's conclusion. For the interlocutor's inscribed "S" to be meaningful (to be a genuine sign), there must be a criterion for its correct use. But so long as we consider the interlocutor in isolation, it appears that we can find no criterion—the interlocutor has nothing to go on save "what seems right to [him]." Conventionalism says, "The required criterion of correctness must be supplied by others: others have to be able to evaluate your use of 'S' to ascertain its conformity to the rule that you impose on yourself. But since you stipulate that others cannot understand 'S,' they cannot ascertain whether you are following your alleged rule, and so you cannot be following a rule at all."

If others' enforcement of the rule were the only way to supply a criterion of correctness for it, then Wittgenstein's remarks would indeed imply conventionalism. But, as Wittgenstein presents the issue, what is lacking is not the presence (actual or potential) of others, but a *use* or function for "S."

> Then did the man who made the entry in the calendar make a note of *nothing whatever?*—Don't consider it a matter of course that a person is making a note of something when he makes a mark—say in a calendar. For a note has a function, and this "S" so far has none. (*PI,* §260)

This is an initially puzzling remark. Doesn't "S" plainly have the function of recording on what days the interlocutor has a particular sensation? Isn't this use of "S" just like my using a special symbol to note on the calendar those mornings on which I awake feeling anxiety, say? To understand Wittgenstein's remark, we have to recall the requirement of privacy that the interlocutor has imposed on his sign "S." It is to refer to a sensation, but unlike my feeling of anxiety, this sensation is to have no manifestation apart from the interlocutor's inscribing it in his diary. (For if the interlocutor's sensation had another mode of expression, observers could come to understand his inscribed "S.") The function of the inscribed "S" is supposed to be recording the sensation. But what is the point of creating that record? If the supposed sensation named by "S" plays some role in the interlocutor's life, then "S" becomes potentially intelligible to others. To safeguard the privacy he demands of his language, the interlocutor has to stipulate that his inscribing of "S" has no purpose save to record a sensation without natural expression or any other role in his life. The intelligibility of the interlocutor's demand for privacy now resolves itself into the question whether we can find this inscribing activity intelligible. Since to protect the privacy of his language the inter-locutor has had to stipulate that this activity has no connection with anything beyond itself, it becomes hard to see it as "recording the occurrence of a sen-sation."[21] But even if we find we can regard his behavior as *recording*, we should also pause to ask whether this supposed use of a sign, as attenuated as it is, really answers to the felt demand for privacy that motivated the in-terlocutor at the outset. Is *this* what the private meanings of our words come to? Is *this* the secret domain that had to be secured against prying eyes?

Suppose the interlocutor insists: "The absence of a wider role in my life for the sensation and its recording makes no difference to whether my inscrip-tions are meaningful. It is still the case that 'S' names a distinctive sensation, that my diary records its occurrences, and that you cannot understand what 'S' means." But why can't we understand "S"? Already knowing that it is a sensation without natural manifestations gives us a preliminary handle on it. And if the interlocutor describes it in more detail ("a subtle tingling in my right earlobe"), we get a still clearer, more definite understanding of what "S" means. One might argue here that no matter how thoroughly the interlocu-tor describes the sensation, I cannot understand what he means so long as I have not had the experience that "S" names; without that experience, I won't know what it is to feel "S." But this is not true in general. I don't have to have had a heart attack in order to understand what it is to feel a vise-like tight-ness in one's chest and numbness in one's left arm; I can refer to these sen-sations, and can recognize them in others or in myself (even the first time I suffer them). And even though the sensation supposedly named by "S" has no natural expression, unlike heart attack sensations, this need not impair my understanding of the interlocutor's inscriptions, provided that he gives a full enough description of his sensation.

In the preceding paragraph, I am supposing that the interlocutor is the kind of philosopher who is struggling to break through the barrier of privacy that seems to cut him off from mutual understanding. This philosopher will try to make himself understood: he will go beyond the bare inscribing of "S" in his diary; he will explain his sensation, describe it, make something of it. Wittgenstein's claim is that in doing this, he makes an understanding of "S" available to others. Of course the other kind of interlocutor, the philosopher who is out to guard his secret inner realm, will refrain from describing his al-leged sensation. Such an interlocutor can achieve privacy. But it is a philo-sophically uninteresting form of privacy, a privacy of inexpressiveness. Of course you can hide your thoughts and feelings from the world—simply by keeping silent. Others cannot discover the contours of your mind if you will not speak or act or manifest emotion.

But the privacy of inexpressiveness doesn't seem to be what our philo-sophical interlocutor wants; it isn't that he asserts the possibility of his having a language that no one else could understand for the reason that he refuses to speak it. The interlocutor's private language was supposed to be something in which he "could write down or give vocal expression to his inner experiences—his feelings, moods, and the rest—for his private use" (*PI*, §243). The sign "S" is to be an expression of a sensation that no one but the speaker can understand. As we have seen, this implies that it is the sign of a sensation that has no natural or other manifestations in the speaker's life. So what we have to imagine is this: on some days, he inscribes an S-shaped mark in a book that has the appearance of a diary, while on other days he does not; there is no other visible event or behavior with which we can correlate the marking. But if this is all we imagine, we are not entitled to say that the interlocutor is recording a sensation; so far, all we have in this imagined scenario is several disconnected inscribings; we have no basis for saying even that the "S"s have a logical connection among themselves, much less that they refer to a sensation. So the interlocutor adds to his description of the scenario: "'S' is the name of a sensation." To which we may reasonably ask, "Which one?" Now either (1) the interlocutor describes the sensation or provides some other way for us to recognize that "S" is the expression of a sensation, or (2) he lapses into the privacy of inexpressiveness. If he takes option (1), then, as before, this description makes the meaning of "S" available for others to understand and so undercuts the claim that the language is private. If he takes option (2), he refuses to provide a basis for his claim that "S" is the name of a sensation; that claim, however, stands in need of such a basis, since without it the interlocutor has not said enough about his imagined scenario to allow us to see "S" as expressing a sensation. So if the interlocutor takes option (2) he fails to make good his claim for the expressive function of the language that others cannot understand.

Wittgenstein captures the crucial movement of this dialectic as follows:

> What reason have we for calling "S" the sign for a sensation? For "sensation" is a word of our common language, not of one intelligible to me alone. So the use of this word stands in need of a justification which everybody understands.—And it would not help either to say that it need not be a sensation; that when he writes "S," he has something—and that is all that can be said. "Has" and "something" also belong to our common language.—So in the end when one is doing philosophy one gets to the point where one would like just to emit an inarticulate sound.—But such a sound is an expression only as it occurs in a particular language-game, which should now be described. (*PI*, §261)

The interlocutor wants (or believes he is saddled with) something that he calls "a private language." But his desire turns out to be incoherent. When he says, in describing this alleged language, "Another person cannot understand my use of the sign 'S'," he lapses into nonsense. For he needs to assert that the sign "S" has a use (e.g., to express a sensation), and so he makes a move in our public language game. This is ipso facto something that another can understand. If on the other hand he refrains from asserting that "S" has a use, he has not made the claim he (apparently) set out to affirm, namely, that it is possible for him to use a term that no one else understands. Perhaps then he tries to affirm that claim in a way that is meaningful for him but which no one else understands. That is when he produces an inarticulate noise; for that noise to be the expression of anything (let alone a philosophical claim) is for it to be part of a language-game, "which should now be described." But of course describing the language-game will land him back in the dilemma between wanting to enter a philosophical claim and needing to keep his meaning private. The incoherence of the desire for a language that no one else can understand lies in wanting on the one hand to assert that one is using one's invented signs meaningfully, while wanting on the other hand to evade the commitments that follow from saying that the signs are meaningful.

Perhaps this will seem unfair. We are requiring the interlocutor to describe what he purports to imagine in our common language, and then noting that whatever he says in that language is capable of being understood by others. You might wonder, "Why couldn't the interlocutor conduct all of his imagining in a language that no one else can understand, and not worry about providing the public with a description of what he imagines?" Here we should note that the desire or demand for a private language originates in philosophical reflection: it was an (apparent) possibility that emerged in the course of reflection conducted in our common language. But every attempt to describe this alleged possibility fails to satisfy the interlocutor, for what we describe never seems private enough. If the interlocutor then refrains from the demand to describe his alleged possibility in our common tongue, he is withdrawing from the discussion. Is this what he desires?

There may remain a kind of uneasiness about this argument. One might be inclined to suppose that what the interlocutor imagines outruns what can be described in our language. And if so, then perhaps the interlocutor does indeed imagine a private language, but describing it in the common currency of philosophical discourse inevitably falsifies what he imagines. Perhaps the philosophical debate, which (I argue) the interlocutor cannot meaningfully join, should be seen as a preliminary step towards his attaining the ineffable thoughts that we (misleadingly) call "imagining a private language."

I cannot here give a thorough critique of such a retreat into the realm of the ineffable. I will only suggest that this move still leaves the interlocutor in an untenable position. The possibility of a private language enters the dialectic as a philosophical thesis. The interlocutor that we now imagine appears to accept Wittgenstein's critique, and so says that one cannot describe a private language. But the interlocutor's retreat into the ineffable is meant to leave the impression that he still has a something that he cannot describe. (The interlocutor's gambit has to leave an "impression," not a claim, because Wittgenstein's critique— which the interlocutor appears to accept—would apply to any attempt to claim that he imagines a private language.) But what is gained by hanging on to that something (the "imagined private language") if not a basis for saying, *sotto voce*, "Still, there could be a private language"? The interlocutor retreats into the ineffable because he recognizes the cogency of Wittgenstein's critique, but he wants to hang onto an impression, a sense, a *something* that the critique should compel him to recognize as devoid of content.

The conclusion of Wittgenstein's private language argument is that philosophers exhibit a deep confusion when they purport to embrace the possibility of a private language. Nothing satisfies the demands the interlocutor places on the "S" he imagines inscribing. This conclusion is not that something (a private language) is logically or conceptually impossible, in opposition to those who assert that it *is* possible. Rather, this argument shows that when a philosopher tries to specify the *something* that is the supposed topic of debate, he fails. The things that he can describe (a secret code, or a language of invented terms for sensations, or silence) do not seem private in the way he thinks he wants; but to reject these specifications of his desires leads ultimately to his needing to make an inarticulate noise—which is not what he wants either.

The philosopher's failure to make a claim, the incoherence of his desires, does not license us to assert the denial of his purported claim. That is, from our inability to make sense of the philosopher's saying "There can be a language spoken by one person which no one else can understand," we may not conclude that a language understood by just one person is impossible. (One could construe the remark "A private language is impossible," not as the denial of the interlocutor's claim, but as an expression of the conclusion that the interlocutor fails to provide a sense for his words "a private language."[22] On this construal the only problem with the remark is that its form almost irresistibly suggests that there is something we mean by "a private language.")

Can we draw any conclusions regarding the social character of language from Wittgenstein's argument? One may restate the interlocutor's claim that it is possible for someone to speak a language that only she can understand as the claim that someone who is cognitively isolated may nonetheless possess a language. The conventionalist responds to this claim by arguing that, because the source of meaningfulness of language and action is social conventions, such a speaker is impossible. Wittgenstein, as I have interpreted him, is interested not in refuting the interlocutor's claim but rather in exploring what he could possibly mean by his words. Consequently, Wittgenstein's discussion of the purported possibility of a private language does not constitute an argument for the necessarily social character of meaningfulness.

But Wittgenstein does think that philosophers need to regard language as a social phenomenon. The failure to so regard language is common to the interlocutor and to the conventionalist who tries to refute him. Both the interlocutor and the conventionalist think that it makes sense to ask the question, "If an individual is using language meaningfully must others be able to understand her language?" This question, as the philosopher intends it, presupposes that the individual's use of language is conceptually distinct from her relations with others. It asks, "Are the latter necessary to the former?" In posing this question, the interlocutor and the conventionalist share too narrow a focus on the individual. As I read him, Wittgenstein argues that to see what it is to "speak a language" or "follow a rule" or "express a sensation" we must look at our shared life with words. When in doing philosophy we screen off our shared life with words so as to focus on the individual's supposed language, we shut ourselves off from that which we claim to want to see. This is not to say that an individual considered in isolation cannot possess language; it is instead a note about the grammar of these concepts that begins to explain why we cannot find a philosophically satisfactory meaning for the words "a speaker whose language cannot be understood by others."

These remarks allow us to locate the importance Wittgenstein assigns to philosophers' accepting our form of life. For a philosopher to reject the human form of life is to suppose that, to understand what it is to speak a language, follow a rule, or express a sensation, we need something other than an examination of our shared life with words. (Thus an appeal to conventions to explain what makes language meaningful is, on my reading, a rejection of our form of life.) To accept our form of life is (in part) to address philosophical questions about language, rule-following, expressing a sensation, and the like by examining and describing our shared life with words, the form of life of human talkers. This form of life lies right before our eyes, but we are constantly tempted to neglect it, as being too obvious, too unremarkable, to be relevant to our philosophical bemusement.

ACKNOWLEDGMENTS

For helpful comments on earlier drafts of this essay, I am grateful to Maudemarie Clark, Alice Crary, Hibi Pendleton, Jim Wetzel, and, especially, Fred Schmitt.

NOTES

1. Annette Baier (1997a) shows that, even in the modern period, social conceptions of reason (enunciated by Hume and Shaftesbury, among others) challenged the individualistic conception of reason held by Descartes and Locke.

2. See for example Giddens (1993, p. 57).

Edward Witherspoon

3. Winch draws the connection between the meaningfulness of action and that of language via the notion of rule-following:

> This notion of being committed by what I do now to doing something else in the future is identical in form with the connection between a definition and the subsequent use of the word defined. . . . It follows that I can only be committed in the future by what I do now if my present act is the *application of a rule*. (Winch 1990, p. 50)

Here Winch is implicitly identifying all normative constraint with being bound by rules. In the second edition of *The Idea of a Social Science*, Winch distances himself from this formulation in recognition of Wittgenstein's claim that "the application of a word is not everywhere bounded by rules" (*PI*, p. §84). Winch's original formulation is an over-simplified picture of normativity, but this weakness does not affect the issues I discuss.

4. Winch qualifies this assertion of the relative independence of distinct forms of life by noting that there can be areas of overlap between, for example, science and religion. In the preface to the second edition of *The Idea of a Social Science* he acknowledges that this qualification does not do enough to undo the overall impression the passage leaves, viz., that a form of life is autonomous, rationally independent of other forms of life, and so immune to criticism from outside. The alternative interpretation of the concept *form of life* that I develop does not occasion the worries about relativism that Winch faces.

5. As I indicated above, there is material in Winch (1990) and other writings for presenting Winch's interpretation of Wittgenstein in a different light. In particular, there is reason to believe Winch would not endorse the idea that one can adopt or reject a form of life at will. He also believes that there are universal human concerns (including at least birth, sex, and death (Winch 1970)), to which all cultures assign significance. Consequently, our talking about such matters is not purely conventional.

6. The function Kripke calls "quus" takes pairs of integers as input; if both integers are less than 57, the function's output is their sum; otherwise, its output is 5 (Kripke 1982, pp. 8–9).

7. See especially his chapter "Natural and Conventional" in Cavell (1979) and the essay "Declining Decline" in Cavell (1989).

8. Kripke develops a view not unlike this supposed convention. In his "skeptical solution," an individual, Smith, judges the arithmetical results of another individual, Jones, as correct based on whether they are the answers he (Smith) is inclined to give; if Jones diverges from him in inexplicable ways, Smith may regard him as not meaning addition by "plus." If Jones's divergence from Smith and others is severe enough, he will be regarded as not a (fully qualified) member of the community. This setting of the boundary of the community and the specification of the assertion conditions for saying "Jones is using addition" are conventional features of our community that foster agreement (within the community) on the results of arithmetical calculations (Kripke 1982, pp. 90–3).

9. Compare Cavell's remarks about the concept of logical inference (Cavell 1979, p. 118).

10. As I noted above regarding the connection between imagining a language and imagining a form of life, we should not assume that languages and forms of life stand in a one-to-one relation.

11. Recall that Wittgenstein answers the question, "But can he [a dog] also believe his master will come the day after to-morrow?" in the negative (*PI*, p. 174).

12. John McDowell elucidates the inseparability of concept-possession and the potential for critical reflection in his parable of rational wolves (McDowell 1998, pp.169–73).

13. See for example the dispositional account of what makes it correct to answer "125" to the question "What is 57 + 68?," which Kripke describes and powerfully criticizes (Kripke 1982, pp. 22–37).

14. For examples of this interpretation see Gellner (1985) and Giddens (1993, p. 57). Such interpretations are effectively criticized in Crary (2000).

15. Cf. Cavell's discussion of criteria at Cavell (1979, pp. 44–5).

16. I take this to be a lesson of Chomsky's explanation of language learning as the activation of an innate and highly structured language-processing capacity.

17. See Cavell's argument concerning what is lost if we imagine a different verb for every different context in which we would use our word "feed" (Cavell 1979, pp. 180ff).

18. Lewis's account of linguistic conventions in Lewis (1969) illuminates this sort of deliberation about expressive vehicles. It does not shed much light on the animating question of what I call conventionalism, which is the question of how the expressions among which I am choosing get their meaning.

19. The reading of the private language argument that I offer in this section takes its inspiration from Cavell (1979, pp. 343–54) and Diamond (1989).

20. See Locke's *Essay*, Book III, Chapter 2 (Locke 1975, pp. 404–408) and "Knowledge by Acquaintance and Knowledge by Description" at Russell (1959, p. 58).

21. For an elaboration of this moment in Wittgenstein's discussion, see Cavell (1979, p. 350).

22. It may be that Winch means his claims for the necessity of others for rule-following to be construed as notes on the meaninglessness of philosophers' descriptions of a private language. (This may be the point of his rather cryptic challenge to Strawson's and Ayer's arguments against Wittgenstein (Winch 1990: 33-36).) If so, theses (4)–(6) above do not express Winch's actual interpretation of Wittgenstein; they do, however, capture the essence of many interpretations.

9

Denotation and Discovery

Gary Ebbs

PRACTICAL JUDGMENTS OF SAMENESS OF DENOTATION

Speakers of the same natural language typically take each other's words at face value. If you show me a ring and say, "This ring is gold," I'll take you to have asserted that the ring is gold, without first thinking about whether this way of taking your words is justified. When I take your word 'gold' at face value in this way, I take it to be true of the ring just in case *my* word 'gold' is true of the ring, hence just in case the ring is gold. This way of taking your word is *like* a judgment in that I may revise it in light of new information, but *unlike* a judgment in that it is unreflective and may never come up for review. I call it a *practical judgment of sameness of denotation.*

Our practice of taking other English speaker's words at face value extends across time, from moment to moment and, in some cases, for centuries. For example, if we learn that in 1650 a jeweler showed John Locke a ring and said, "This ring is gold," we'll take the jeweler to have asserted that the ring is gold. When we take the jeweler's word 'gold' at face value in this way, we in effect take it to be true of an object x just in case *our* word 'gold' is true of x, hence just in case x is gold. We thereby make what I call a *practical judgment of sameness of denotation across time.*[1]

We express such judgments when we take ourselves to have made a discovery or to agree or disagree with other speakers. For instance, we take for granted that when chemists first accepted the sentence "Gold is the element with atomic number 79," they did not thereby introduce a new denotation for the word 'gold'. [2] Trusting our practical judgments of sameness of denotation for 'gold', and taking for granted that gold is the element with atomic number 79, we can *agree* with a jeweler who in 1650 showed John Locke a ring and said, "This ring is gold," only if the ring was (a bit of) the element with atomic number 79. We realize that perhaps the ring wasn't gold, even if it passed all of the jeweler's tests for being gold. In this practical way we acknowledge that truth is independent of belief.

There is a diverse group of philosophers, including David Chalmers, Michael Dummett, Frank Jackson, John McDowell, Christopher Peacocke, and (sometimes) Hilary Putnam, who think that if no theory of what determines the denotations of our words *justifies* (or shows that we are *entitled* to) our practical judgments of sameness of denotation, then our *impressions* that we can make discoveries, that we can agree or disagree, and that truth is independent of belief, are *illusory*.[3] Against this, I will emphasize that we trust our practical judgments of sameness of denotation more than any theory of what determines the denotations of our words. I will argue that the denotations of our words are not settled by *a priori* linguistic rules or by causal-historical facts, but that our practical judgments of sameness of denotation are of a piece with our pursuit of truth, so we should not reject them. Instead, we should build these judgments into a deflationary account of denotation and truth.

ANALYTICITY

To begin with, consider the relationship between our practical judgments of sameness of denotation and the thesis that some of our sentences are "analytic," in the sense that we cannot abandon them without changing the subject. One version of this thesis is that we *make* some of our sentences true by agreeing on how they are to be evaluated.[4] The main problem with this version of the thesis is that it conflates truth and belief. As Frege observed in a different connection, "Being true is different from being taken to be true, whether by one or many or everybody, and in no case is to be reduced to it. There is no contradiction in something's being true which everybody takes to be false" (1964, p. 13).

One way to support the thesis that some of our sentences are analytic without conflating truth and belief is to derive the thesis from a description of how we evaluate sentences. To see how this might be done, consider W. V. Quine's account of the deviant logician's predicament. Against the idea that deviant logicians may "reject the law of non-contradiction and accept an occasional sentence and its negation both as true," Quine argues as follows:

> [They] think they're talking about negation, '~', 'not'; but surely the notation ceased to be recognizable as negation when they took to regarding some conjunctions of the form 'p.~p' as true, and stopped regarding such sentences as implying all others. Here, evidently, is the deviant logician's predicament: when he tries to deny the doctrine he only changes the subject. (1986, p. 81)

The moral is that even though truth is not up to us, for some words, including '~', 'not', we can agree on criteria that settle whether or not a speaker is using them to talk about the same subjects that we talk about when we use them.

This is the truism behind what I call methodological analyticity—the idea that even though truth is not up to us, there are sentences we cannot reject without changing the subject. The least problematic version of the idea, due to Rudolf Carnap, makes sense only for sentences of an artificial language system.[5] If we accept Quine's textbook explanations of '~', sentences of the form '~(p.~p)' come close to being "analytic" in Carnap's strict sense of that troublesome word.

The sort of methodological analyticity I want to discuss is also supposed to be a feature of natural language sentences, such as 'Bachelors are unmarried adult males'. The idea is that we *tacitly* agree on criteria that settle whether or not a speaker is using 'bachelor' to talk about bachelors, 'adult' to talk about adults, and so on. We tacitly agree, for instance, that no one can reject 'Bachelors are unmarried adult males' without changing the subject. Moreover, the criteria on which we tacitly agree are in principle obvious to us—we can tell by reflecting on our own usage of the terms whether not an explicit statement of the criteria is correct. Natural language sentences that are analytic in the sense can play a methodological role in our inquiries that is analogous to the more strictly defined methodological role of analytic sentences in Carnap's artificial constructed language systems. That is why I call this sort of analyticity *methodological*.

One might be inclined to dismiss methodological analyticity (even the pure form of it that is restricted to artificial languages) with the claim that for any sentence we accept, we can imagine that it's false. This claim may seem to follow immediately from Frege's distinction between truth and belief. But that distinction has no direct bearing on whether we can imagine that a sentence we now accept is false. What would it be, for instance, to imagine that a sentence of the form '~(p.~p)' is false?

A better argument against methodological analyticity is that we may at one time feel confident that we could not reject a given statement without changing the subject, but later realize that we were wrong. This point is usually attributed to Quine, but Hilary Putnam was the first to present examples that make it convincing.[6] He observed, for instance, that in the eighteenth century, scientists had no idea how their theory that physical space is Euclidean could be false—no idea how one could reject the statement that physical space is Euclidean without changing the subject. After much theoretical work in mathematics and physics, scientists replaced that earlier theory of space with the theory that physical space is non-Euclidean. When scientists came to believe that physical space is non-Euclidean, they took themselves not to have *changed the topic*, but to have *discovered* that space is non-Euclidean.

To accept this description of the case, we must trust the later scientists' practical judgments of sameness of denotation for the phrase 'physical space' more than we trust the earlier scientists' speculation that one cannot reject the statement that physical space is Euclidean without changing the subject. The later scientists might be wrong about physical space— perhaps it's Euclidean after all. But we take them to have *discovered* that physical space is non-Euclidean, and so we accept their practical judgments of sameness of denotation for 'physical space'. These practical judgments are embodied in their use of that phrase to express what they take to be a discovery about physical space. Their use of that phrase links it to earlier uses of the phrase, and those earlier uses of the phrase are linked to even earlier uses of it. Taken together, these uses of 'physical space' constitute a transtemporal chain of practical judgments of sameness of denotation for 'physical space'. In a similar way, every inquiry brings with it some chain or other of practical judgments of sameness of denotation across time. In this sense, our practical judgments of sameness of denotation are of a piece with our pursuit of truth.

One might think that this reasoning only shows that we can be radically wrong about our own tacit criteria for applying our terms, not that methodological analyticity is incorrect. As I defined it above, however, methodological analyticity implies that we can tell just by reflecting on our own current usage of a term whether or not a given explicit statement of how it should be applied is correct. Putnam's counterexamples show that we can't tell just by reflecting on our own current usage of a term whether or not a given explicit statement about how it should be applied will survive a conflict with our practical judgments of sameness of denotation. In this way, Putnam's counterexamples undermine methodological analyticity.

PRIMARY INTENSIONS

One might grant that we *trust* our practical judgments of sameness of denotation, but think that if we cannot also *justify* them, then our impression that we can make discoveries is illusory. It is natural to think that for every word used by a given speaker, there are linguistic rules that determine the denotation of that word. If there are such rules, then, for instance, my practical judgment that another speaker's word 'gold' has the same denotation as my word 'gold' is correct if and only if the denotation determined by the linguistic rules for her word 'gold' is the same as the denotation determined by the linguistic rules for my word 'gold'. Can we identify linguistic rules that we can use to justify our practical judgments of sameness of denotation?

We cannot use disquotational rules to justify these judgments. A disquotational rule for applying a given word—a rule such as 'gold' denotes an object x if and only if x is gold—tells us nothing about the conditions under which a practical judgment of sameness of denotation for that word is true. A justification of such judgments therefore requires *more* than a disquotational specification of rules for applying our words.

Assuming that for every word w used by a given speaker S there are rules that determine the denotation of w, it is tempting to think that those rules are settled by S's *beliefs* about how w should be applied. Inspired by this thought, David Chalmers has recently proposed a theory of intensions (or concepts) that is meant in part to justify our practical judgments of sameness of denotation across time. He defines the *primary intension* of a word as a special sort of function from (agent-centered) worlds to extensions: in a given (agent-centered) world, the primary intension of a word picks out what the extension of the word would be if that (agent-centered) world turned out to be actual (Chalmers 1996, p. 57). To grasp the primary intension of 'water', for instance, we must grasp a function that yields the set of all and only portions of *water* as value if the actual (agent-centered) world has water in its rivers, lakes, and oceans, but yields the set of all and only portions of *twin-water* as value if the actual (agent-centered) world has twin-water in its rivers, lakes, and oceans.

What is distinctive of a primary intension, according to Chalmers, is that our grasp of it is independent of *all* our empirical beliefs. He argues that there *must be* a primary intension for any word that we can use to express a discovery. If we are to express a discovery about water that is based on our examination of a given sample of what we take to be water, he reasons, we must be able to say *why* it counts as a sample of *water* by appealing to rules that we can grasp without going through any empirical investigation or presupposing any empirical beliefs (p. 62).

This reasoning moves from a truism to a substantive epistemological claim. The truism is that we take ourselves to express a discovery about water by using the term 'water' only if we take for granted that the denotation of 'water' does not change as a result of our supposed discovery. The substantive epistemological claim is that we are entitled to take ourselves to express a discovery about water by using the term 'water' only if we can *justify* our practical judgments of sameness of denotation for 'water' by appealing to rules that we can grasp without going through any empirical investigation or presupposing any empirical beliefs.[7]

A primary intension is well-suited to this justificatory role, according to Chalmers. "The intension specifies how reference depends on the way the external world turns out, so does not itself depend on the way the external world turns out" (p. 57). By reasoning about "what our words *would* refer to if the actual world turned out in various ways," Chalmers thinks, we can simultaneously *see* that our words have primary intensions and *discover* what they are.

The main problem with this proposal is that what we *actually* say when we find ourselves in a previously imagined situation almost always trumps our earlier speculations about what we *would* say if we *were to* find ourselves in that situation. What we actually say when we find ourselves in a previously imagined situation reflects our best current judgment of what is true in that situation. When we are actually in the previously imagined situation, our best judgment of what is true in that situation brings with it practical judgments of sameness of denotation. If those practical judgments of sameness of denotation conflict with earlier speculations, then so much the worse for those speculations. A scientist in the eighteenth century might have confidently predicted that even if it turns out that there is some mathematically consistent non-Euclidean geometry, it *can't be* the description of what he calls physical space. But the actual history of our practical judgments of sameness of denotation for 'physical space' yields the opposite conclusion that when scientists came to accept that physical space is non-Euclidean, they did not thereby change the subject by tacitly defining a new denotation for the phrase 'physical space'. As I emphasized above, the later scientists' practical judgments of sameness of denotation are of a piece with their inquiry into the shape of physical space. We take the later scientists' practical judgments of sameness of denotation to trump the earlier scientists' speculations because we are confident that the later scientists have *discovered* that physical space is non-Euclidean.

This example shows that statements we can't imagine giving up without changing the subject are not thereby *guaranteed* to be true. But one might think that to accept Chalmers's claim that some of our words have primary intensions that we can know *a priori*, we need only suppose that some of the statements that we can't imagine giving up without changing the subject actually *are* true. The trouble is that Chalmers's primary intentions are supposed to "back *a priori* truths"—statements that are "true no matter how the actual world turns out" (p. 59). Hence to accept Chalmers's claim that some of our words have primary intensions that we can know a priori, it is not enough to suppose that some of the statements that we can't imagine giving up without changing the subject are true.[8]

Like Chalmers, Frank Jackson tries to defend the inference from "we don't understand how we could give up statement S without changing the subject" to "we could not give up statement S without changing the subject." "[S]urely it *is* possible to change the subject," Jackson reasons, "and how else could one do it other than by abandoning what is most central to defining one's subject? Would a better way of changing the subject be to abandon what is less central?" (Jackson 1998, p. 38). The mistake here is to suppose that our best *current* judgment about what counts as changing the subject is immune to future revisions. It is a truism that if we want to change the subject, we must rely on our understanding of what is most central to defining it. But this truism does not establish that our current understanding of what is most central to defining our subject cannot be revised without changing the subject. This claim is discredited by many actual cases in which we were once confident that we could not revise a given statement without changing the subject, but discovered later that we were wrong.

Both Jackson and Chalmers sometimes claim to be able to accommodate such discoveries (Chalmers 1996, pp. 55–6; Jackson 1998, pp. 46–55).[9] They do not seem to realize that to accommodate such discoveries is to concede that our practical judgments of sameness of denotations are more trustworthy than our explications of our own primary intensions. This concession undermines their thesis that our understanding of our own primary intensions justifies our practical judgments of sameness of denotation across time.[10]

THE CAUSAL-HISTORICAL THEORY OF DENOTATION

You may be convinced by these arguments against Chalmers and Jackson but hope to find a different sort of justification of our practical judgments of sameness of denotation. Saul Kripke and Hilary Putnam devised the causal-historical theory of denotation to explain and justify the practical judgments of sameness of denotation that led them to reject the description theory of proper names and natural kind terms. In outline, the causal-historical theory is that the denotation of a name or a kind term is *initially* determined by an "ostensive definition" that may partly rely on causal connections to samples or things that the name or term is to denote. Once the denotation of a word is established in this way, speakers of the language can be credited with using that word if and only if they are connected by an "appropriate" causal chain with other speakers who use the word, and they are "minimally competent" in its use. "Appropriate" and "minimally competent" are place-holders for specifications of the causal chains and competencies that explain and support our practical judgments of sameness of denotation.

There is no consensus about how to specify these supposed chains and competencies, and many philosophers concede that there are kind terms (such as names of biological species) that pose challenges for the causal-historical theory. Nevertheless, many philosophers still think that by citing causal-historical facts we can explain why the denotations of our word 'gold', for instance, did not change as a result of our discovery that gold is the element with atomic number 79. Even in this paradigm case, however, as I shall now try to show, we cannot justify our practical judgments of sameness of denotation by citing causal-historical facts.

A THOUGHT EXPERIMENT[11]

The historical background for my argument is that platinum was not discovered until the mid-eighteenth century, when chemists called it "white gold" because of its striking similarities to what they previously called gold.[12] Platinum has a higher melting point than gold. But like gold, platinum dissolves in aqua regia, which was named for its ability to dissolve gold.[13] In 1650, a chemist applying this "acid test" to a sample of platinum might have concluded that it should be called gold.[14] We now know that platinum and gold are different elements: platinum is the element with atomic number 78, and gold is the element with atomic number 79.

With this in mind, suppose that there is a Twin Earth that is indistinguishable from Earth up until 1651, when large deposits of platinum are uncovered in Twin South Africa, and that once it is established by Twin Earth chemists that the newly uncovered metal dissolves in aqua regia, members of the Twin English–speaking community call it 'gold,' treating it in the same way we treat gold: the platinum is mined as gold, hammered (and later melted) together with gold to produce coins and bars that are valued by Twin Earthlings just as we value gold. Everyone on Twin Earth trusts the Twin Earth chemists' judgment that the newly uncovered metal is properly called 'gold'.

Suppose also that on Twin Earth chemistry develops in almost exactly the same way in which it develops on Earth, except that when Twin Earth chemists investigate what they call 'gold', they conclude that there are two kinds of 'gold'—their word 'gold' denotes x if and only if x is (a bit of) the element with atomic number 78 or x is (a bit of) the element with atomic number 79.

Recall that Twin Earth is just like Earth with a slightly different future after platinum is first uncovered in Twin South Africa in 1651. To see the possibility of this Twin Earth scenario, it is enough to imagine a few accidental differences between the two communities that allow for the uncovering of large amounts of platinum on Twin Earth.[15]

The crucial point is that just as members of our English-speaking community take for granted that the denotation of the English word 'gold' did not change as a result of the discovery that it denotes x if and only if x is (a bit of) the element with atomic number 79, so members of the Twin English–speaking linguistic community take for granted that the denotation of their Twin English word 'gold' did not change as a result of their discovery that it denotes x if and only if x is (a bit of) the element with atomic number 78 or x is (a bit of) the element with atomic number 79. Members of the two communities have different beliefs about what their word form 'gold' denotes, and they take these beliefs for granted even when they are evaluating utterances made by using gold in 1650. For instance, suppose that in 1650 John Locke and his twin on Twin Earth both uttered the words 'There are huge deposits of gold in those hills', with Locke indicating South African hills and Twin Locke indicating the corresponding Twin South African hills, both of which contain platinum but no gold. We take Locke's word 'gold' to be true of an object x just in case x is gold, whereas our contemporaries on Twin Earth take Twin Locke's word 'gold' to be true of an object x just in case (as we would say it) x is either gold or platinum. We conclude that Locke's utterance is false, and our contemporaries on Twin Earth conclude that Twin Locke's utterance is true.[16]

A DILEMMA FOR THE CAUSAL-HISTORICAL THEORY OF DENOTATION

Let's see if we can give a causal-historical explanation of our entrenched practical judgment that the denotation of the English word 'gold' did not change since 1650. Suppose that in 1650 members of both linguistic communities affirmed the following "ostensive definition":

(A) x is gold if and only if for most things y that I and other speakers in my linguistic community have on other occasions called gold, x is (a bit of) the same substance as y.

The question is whether any such ostensive definition in 1650 actually *determined* that gold is true of x if and only if x is (a bit of) the element with atomic number 79. The answer is "no."

To see why, note first that to explain our practical judgment that the denotation of the English word gold did not change since 1650 by appealing to (A), we must assume that:

(B) For all x and y, if x and y are gold, then x is (a bit of) the same substance as y.

is true in English and Twin English. Even if we stipulate that (B) is true in these languages, we have no good reason to believe that 'x is (a bit of) the same substance as y' is true in *Twin* English of the ordered pair $<x, y>$ only if x has the same atomic number as y. The social (especially economic) practices in which the application of gold to gold or platinum is embedded in the Twin Earth community strongly suggest that if x is gold and y is platinum, for instance, then 'x and y are gold' and 'x is (a bit of) the same substance as y' are true in Twin English of $<x, y>$, even though x does not have the same atomic number as y. One might try to rule this out by stipulating that:

(C) For all x and y, if x is (a bit of) the same substance as y, then x has the same atomic number as y.

is true in both in English and Twin English. One problem with this strategy is that in 1650 no one was in a position to formulate (C), because analytical chemistry had not yet been developed. The crucial problem, however, is that even if we stipulate that (C) is true in English and Twin English, (B) may be false in Twin English. One may "ostensively define" 'gold' by affirming (A) without thereby guaranteeing that (B) is true.

One might think that to give a causal-historical justification of our practical judgment that the denotation of the English word 'gold' did not change since 1650, we need not suppose that an affirmation of (A) in 1650 could have *guaranteed* that (B) is true in English. One might think it is enough to suppose that (A) and (B) *are* true in English. But this is not enough. Even if (A) and (B) are true in English, as we all suppose, that does not show that our practical judgments of sameness of denotation across time for 'gold' are correct and the practical judgments of sameness of denotation across time for 'gold' in the Twin Earth community are incorrect.

This problem with Kripke-style ostensive "definitions" is similar to the problem with Chalmers's theory of primary intensions.[17] A Kripke-style ostensive definition of the denotation of a term can be part of a theory of what *determines* the denotation of the term, hence not just another entrenched *belief* that we express by using the term, only if we know that the ostensive definition *could not turn out to be false*. But we can know this only if, as Chalmers assumes, we can discover the rules for correctly applying our kind terms simply by reflecting on what we *would* say if the world turned out in various ways, without presupposing any empirical beliefs. As I emphasized earlier, however, what we *actually* say when we find ourselves in a previously imagined situation almost always trumps our earlier speculations about what we *would* say if we *were to* find ourselves in that situation. What we say when we find ourselves in a previously imagined situation reflects our best current judgment of what is true in that situation. When we are in the previously imagined situation, our best judgment of what is true in that situation brings with it practical judgments of sameness of denotation. If these practical judgments of sameness of denotation conflict with earlier speculations, we scrap the speculations, not the practical judgments of sameness of denotation. In our pursuit of truth, we trust our practical judgments of sameness of denotation across time, so we have no guarantee that a given "ostensive definition" of the denotation of a term is analytic, in the sense that we cannot revise it without changing the subject.[18]

The causal-historical theory of denotation therefore faces a dilemma: the more informative the supposed ostensive definitions are, the more likely it is that they will later be revised without changing the subject; but the less informative they are, the less likely it is that there is only one way of correctly applying them. I conclude that affirmations of (A) in 1650 do not rule out either the Earthlings' or Twin Earthlings' discoveries about what their word form 'gold' denotes and therefore do not justify the practical judgments of sameness of denotation for 'gold' in either linguistic community.

DISPOSITIONS

Suppose that Locke and Twin Locke *would have* accepted that gold is (a bit of) the element with atomic number 79 if they *had been* presented with the evidence we now have for this conclusion. One might think that an affirmation of (A) in 1650 rules out the Twin Earthlings' practical judgments of sameness of denotation for 'gold' if it is supplemented with a counterfactual of this kind.[19]

The problem with this strategy is that whether or not an individual would accept or reject certain sentences may depend on the *order* in which he is presented with evidence that supports those sentences.[20] It is plausible to suppose that Locke and Twin Locke would have affirmed the sentence 'x is gold if and only if x is (a bit of) the element with atomic number 79' if they had been presented with the same evidence that later English speakers encountered, *in the same order* in which they actually encountered it. But it is equally plausible to suppose that Locke and Twin Locke would have affirmed the sentence 'x is gold if and only if either x is the element with atomic number 79 or x is the element with atomic number 78' if they had been presented with the same evidence that later Twin English speakers encountered, *in the same order* in which they actually encountered it. We have no independent grounds for saying that one of these presentations of the evidence is correct and the other is incorrect, and so an appeal to dispositions cannot show that our community's practical judgments of sameness of denotation for 'gold' are correct and theirs are incorrect.[21]

METHODOLOGICAL INTERLUDE

Some causal theorists feel that the denotation relation is mysterious *unless* it is explained in causal-historical terms, so they are ready to reject our practical judgments of sameness of denotation if no causal-historical theory of denotation supports them. Various technical alternatives are open to someone who wishes to reject our practical judgments of sameness of denotation across time.[22] For present purposes, however, the question is why we should feel driven to reject these practical judgments.

As I noted earlier, Saul Kripke and Hilary Putnam devised the causal-historical theory of denotation to explain and justify the practical judgments of sameness of denotation that led them to reject the description theory of proper names and natural kind terms. It ought to seem puzzling that some philosophers who were persuaded by Kripke and Putnam to reject description theories of denotation because these theories conflict with our practical judgments of sameness of denotation are now inclined to reject those same practical judgments if they can't be justified by citing causal-historical facts. One can't have it both ways. No one who rejects description theories because they conflict with our practical judgments of sameness of denotation is in a position to reject these judgments just because they conflict with causal-historical theories of denotation.[23]

This should be enough to convince us to reject causal-historical theories of denotation. But there is a deeper and more illuminating reason for rejecting such theories: they conflict with practical judgments of sameness of denotation that are (in the sense I explained earlier) of a piece with our pursuit of truth.

A DEFLATIONARY ALTERNATIVE[24]

I have argued that we cannot justify our practical judgments of sameness of denotation by appealing to a priori rules or by citing causal-historical facts. I also explained why I think we should not reject our practical judgments of sameness of denotation just because we find that we are unable to justify them. I propose that we focus instead on *describing* our practice of disquoting our own words and taking other speakers' words at face value.

A disquotational specification of the denotation of our term 'gold' tells us nothing about what *determines* the denotation of 'gold' or how to *find out* whether or not something is gold. What then is the *point* of having such a thin account of denotation? One good reason for constructing a disquotational account of denotation is to define a truth predicate that we can use to specify the laws of logic schematically for regimented sentences of our own language.[25] A regimented first-order fragment of English, for example, may include such sentences as '(This ring is gold) → (This ring is gold)', '$\forall x((x$ is gold) → (x is gold))', and '$\exists x \forall y(x$ loves $y) \to \forall y \exists x(x$ loves $y)$'—instances, respectively, of the schemata 'p → p', '$\forall x(Fx \to Fx)$', and '$\exists x \forall y Gxy \to \forall y \exists x Gxy$', To specify logical laws schematically, we can say, for example, "every sentence of the form 'p → p' is true," "every sentence of the form '$\forall x(Fx \to Fx)$' is true," and "every sentence of the form '$\exists x \forall y Gxy \to \forall y \exists x Gxy$' is true."

To make such generalizations precise, we need to know which sentences of our regimented language are instances of a given logical schema, and what it means to say of one of these sentences that it is true. The first need is met by well-established syntactical criteria for admissible substitutions of regimented English sentences and predicates for schematic letters,[26] and the second need is met by a Tarski-style truth predicate that is defined recursively, using clauses that specify conditions under which English predicates are *satisfied* by sequences of objects.

If our metalanguage contains the object language, our accounts of satisfaction and denotation can be disquotational. Suppose that all the variables of the object language are numbered sequentially, and let the *i*th variable in this sequence be called var(*i*). A *sequence* of objects is a function from positive integers to objects; for any such sequence *s*, let s_i be the *i*th object in *s*. If the metalanguage contains the object language, we can say, for example, that for every sequence *s*, *s* *satisfies* 'gold' followed by var(*i*) if and only if s_i is gold.[27] Similarly, we can say that for every sequence *s*, 'gold' followed by var(*i*) *denotes* s_i if and only if s_i is gold.[28] More generally, we can accept the results of applying the following disquotational patterns to any of our one-place predicates:

(S) For every sequence *s*, *s* *satisfies* '____' followed by var(*i*) if and only if s_i is ____.

(D) For every sequence *s*, '____' followed by var(*i*) *denotes* s_i if and only if s_i is ____.

Each speaker who understands these patterns can apply them to his own words. For instance, if I affirm the results of writing 'gold' in the blanks of (D), I assert that (my predicate) gold followed by var(*i*) denotes an object s_i if and only if s_i is (a bit of) gold.

To *describe* our practice of disquoting our own words and taking other speakers' words at face value, it is enough to trust our practice of taking other speakers' words at face value and to find applications of the disquotational patterns (S) and (D) to our own words both obvious and useful.[29] For instance, if I affirm the result of writing my word 'gold' in the blanks of (D), I can see that when I take another English speaker's word 'gold' at face value, I in effect take for granted that her word 'gold' denotes something s_i just in case s_i is gold, and so her word 'gold' has the same *denotation* as my word 'gold', This result of combining my practice of taking other English speakers' words at face value with applications of (D) to my own words is a practical judgment of sameness of denotation.

We can describe our practical judgments of sameness of denotation in this way without justifying them. I propose that we trust these judgments unless we have some special reason to doubt or revise them.

But what counts as a special reason? Here is an example. I was surprised to read recently that there is a group of astronomers who now say, "Pluto is not a planet, it's just a big asteroid." At first I took the astronomers to be claiming that Pluto is not a planet. After I learned more about *why* these astronomers say, "Pluto is not a planet," however, I started to suspect that their sentence 'Pluto is not a planet' amounts to a stipulative new definition for their term 'planet', so that when they say, "Pluto is not a planet," they are not

claiming that Pluto is not a planet.[30] I have since learned that many astronomers have come to the same conclusion: the startling sentence 'Pluto is
not a planet' does not express a *discovery* but introduces a new denotation
for the term 'planet'.[31] I also learned that some of the astronomers who were
reported in the popular media to have said, "Pluto is not a planet," really
meant to say, "Pluto is not a *major* planet."[32] In short, I was wrong to take
the first, unqualified version of the claim at face value.[33]

There are no similar reasons to doubt or revise the practical judgments of
sameness of denotation across time in either linguistic community of my
thought experiment. I propose that we trust these practical judgments and
accept that the denotation of 'gold' has not changed since 1650 in either English or Twin English—chemists in both linguistic communities discovered
the underlying chemical properties of what they respectively call 'gold'.[34]

It may seem strange to suppose that the Twin English word 'gold' that was
used on Twin Earth in 1650 is true of x if and only if x is either gold or platinum, even though in 1650 that word was not yet *actually* applied to platinum. In contrast, it does not seem strange to suppose that the English word
'gold' that was used on Earth in 1650 is true of x if and only if x is gold. But
I have argued that nothing *rules out* the Twin Earthlings' practical judgments
of sameness of denotation for their word 'gold'. The only salient difference
is that our practical judgments of sameness of denotation for our word 'gold'
feel familiar to us and theirs don't. We should not mistake this feeling of familiarity for *evidence* that we are right and they are wrong.

To put our feeling of familiarity in perspective, it helps to note that there
are terms whose use on Earth resembles the use of 'gold' on Twin Earth. Our
word 'jade' is true of both jadeite and nephrite. The Chinese character called
yu that we translate as 'jade' was actually applied only to nephrite until the
eighteenth century, when the Chinese first encountered jadeite and started
carving it. The mineralogical differences between nephrite and jadeite were
discovered in 1863, a century after the Chinese practice of applying *yu* to
both nephrite and jadeite became entrenched (Hansford 1968, pp. 26–29).
They (and we) take for granted that the denotation of *yu* did not change
when it was applied to jadeite. Similarly, Twin English speakers take for
granted that the denotation of their term 'gold' did not change when it was
applied to the element with atomic number 78. We are therefore in no position to dismiss their practical judgments of sameness of denotation for 'gold'
just because these judgments seem strange to us.

POSSIBLE PASTS

Imagine a world in which the English-speaking linguistic community ceased
to exist in 1651. It might seem that in 1650 in such a world, the denotation of

the English word 'gold' must be *indeterminate*, because the use of the English word 'gold', described independently of its denotation, is compatible with both of the denotations described in the gold-platinum thought experiment. It might therefore seem that to accept the practical judgments of sameness of denotation for gold in both linguistic communities of the gold-platinum thought experiment, one must also accept the strange idea that the denotation of a word w at time t can be determined by the use of w at some time *after t*.[35]

This reasoning presupposes that the use of a word determines its denotation. In my view, however, the use of a word never determines its denotation, for the simple reason that even our most deeply entrenched beliefs about how our words are correctly applied may be false.[36] There is therefore no obstacle to making sense of the claim that in the world described in the previous paragraph, in 1650 the English word 'gold' denotes x if and only if x is a bit of the element with atomic number 79.

As Kripke explained in Kripke (1980), possible worlds are not discovered, they are stipulated. When we describe a world w in which the English-speaking community ceased to exist in 1651, we *stipulate* that we are talking about the English word 'gold'. If the English word 'gold' denotes x if and only if x is a bit of the element with atomic number 79, as we believe, then it follows from our description of world w that in w in 1650, the English word 'gold' denotes x if and only if x is a bit of the element with atomic number 79. Similarly, in a world in which the Twin English–speaking linguistic community ceased to exist in 1651, in 1650 the Twin English word 'gold' denotes x if and only if either x is a bit of the element with atomic number 78 or x is a bit of the element with atomic number 79.

These possible pasts will seem puzzling only if we assume that the use of a word, described independently of its denotation, determines its denotation. I recommend that we reject this assumption and trust our practical judgments of sameness of denotation across time.

ARE WE MAKING THINGS UP AS WE GO?

But if we cannot justify our practical judgments of sameness of denotation, are we always just *deciding* how to apply our words? One might worry that, like "locomotives . . . which unroll their tracks before them as they move through a terrain,"[37] we are just making things up as we go.

This worry may *seem* compelling, but I think it is confused. Our understanding of sameness of denotation is rooted in our practice of taking other speaker's words at face value. When we try to suspend all our practical judgments of sameness of denotation, the very idea of sameness of denotation seems to vanish into thin air.[38] We understand what it is to *decide* how to apply our words only by contrast with cases in which we apply them without reflection, as a matter of course, hence *without* deciding how to apply them. We understand what it is to *make up* new applications for our words only by contrast with cases in which we apply them without reflection, as a matter of course, hence *without* making up new applications for them. We can't doubt all our practical judgments of sameness of denotation at once, so we can't make sense of the worry that we just are making things up as we go.[39]

I noted at the start that we make practical judgments of sameness of denotation when we take ourselves to have made a *discovery* or to agree or disagree with other speakers. Many philosophers believe that we can trust these aspects of our linguistic practices only if we can *justify* our practical judgments of sameness of denotation. Against this I have emphasized that we trust these practical judgments more than any proposed philosophical justification of them. Our practical judgments of sameness of denotation are of a piece with our pursuit of truth, in the sense that our confidence that we have made a discovery always rests partly on our confidence in some chain or other of practical judgments of sameness of denotation across time. But our confidence that we have made a discovery typically trumps any conflicting prior speculations about the denotations of our words. A surprising result of these reflections is that the very trust in our practical judgments of sameness of denotation that initially led many to embrace ambitious justificatory projects ultimately undermines those projects and supports a new kind of deflationism about denotation and truth.[40]

To support this deflationism I have highlighted the methodological role of our practical judgments of sameness of denotation. I have tried to persuade you that we should evaluate any proposed account or theory of truth by comparing our confidence in it with our trust in practical judgments of sameness of denotation. This comparison convinces me, for the reasons I sketched above, that we should trust our practical judgments of sameness of denotation and doubt that there is a substantive theory that justifies them.

ACKNOWLEDGMENTS

This chapter is an expanded version of the paper I presented at the Central Division meetings of the APA in May 2000, with Mark Wilson as commentator, and at the University of Wisconsin, Milwaukee, in October 1999. For challenging and helpful comments on various versions of the chapter, I thank Hugh Chandler, Brie Gertler, Richard Heck, Mark Kaplan, John Koethe, Michael Liston, Patricia Marino, Fred Schmitt, Bill Taschek, Joan Weiner, and Mark Wilson.

NOTES

1. These two opening paragraphs are modifications of the two opening paragraphs of Ebbs (2000).

2. In Kripke (1980), on page 138, Saul Kripke stresses that scientific discoveries do not constitute a change of denotation.

3. For instance, in McDowell (1984), John McDowell argues that unless we possess some account of how it is possible for our words to conform to independent, objective, patterns of application, we cannot avoid the conclusion that our impression that we can make judgments is illusory. In "On Truth" (first published in 1983, reprinted in Putnam 1994a), Hilary Putnam uses a similar argument against W. V. Quine's deflationary view of truth. See also Chalmers (1996); Dummett (1978b, pp. 420–40); Jackson (1998); McDowell (1994); Peacocke (1999); and essays 13, 15, and 17 in Putnam (1994a).

4. This version of the thesis goes hand in hand with what Paul Horwich calls "the strategy of implicit definition," according to which "terms may be provided with their meanings by the assertion of statements containing them" in such a way that some of the asserted statements could not be abandoned without changing the denotations of the terms they contain. Horwich rejects this position, for reasons he explains in chapter 6 of Horwich (1998a). I am sympathetic with Horwich's objections, but I think he does not expose the deepest problem with the strategy of implicit definition—that it ignores the diachronic dimension of our pursuit of truth. My criticisms in this chapter of the methodological version of analyticity and of Chalmers's theory of primary intensions highlight the diachronic dimension of our pursuit of truth and indicate how I would argue against the stronger and even less plausible thesis that we *make* some of our sentences true by agreeing on how they are to be evaluated.

5. Carnap makes this explicit in the first sentence of his paper "Quine on Analyticity" (Creath 1990, pp. 427–32).

6. See Hilary Putnam, "The Analytic and the Synthetic" (1962), reprinted in Putnam (1975a).

7. Chalmers presupposes that for all we know without empirical investigation, we may actually be in any world in which all of our subjective experiences are the same as they are in the actual world. This presupposition is incoherent, in my view, for reasons I explain in Ebbs (1996, 2001), but I do not question it here.

8. One can define a function F from words and (agent-centered) worlds to extensions so that for any ordered pair of words and agent-centered worlds, the value of F for that ordered pair is the extension of the word as used by the agent in that agent-centered world. Suppose we know a priori that for each pair of words and agents, there exists such a function. It does not follow, as Chalmers seems to assume, that we can know *a priori* what the value of the function is for the world we are actually in. For a similar criticism of a related position, see Stalnaker (1990).

9. Jackson also sometimes agrees with Lewis (1994) that we should disregard practical judgments of sameness of denotation that conflict with our explications of our primary intensions. See Jackson (1998, p. 38n12). In this mood, Jackson explicitly concedes that the theory of primary intensions conflicts with a large number of our practical judgments of sameness of denotation.

10. My argument against Chalmers and Jackson suggests that "the syntactic construction of a quantity name may not reveal its actual ties to other quantities adequately," as Mark Wilson has stressed. See Wilson (1993 pp. 53-94); the quoted passage is on p. 82. I agree with Wilson that we may *discover* that many of our terms have what he calls honorable intensions. Unlike Chalmers's hypothetical primary intensions, *honorable* intensions are not known *a priori*.

11. I also use this thought experiment in Ebbs (2000).

12. See Crosland (1962 p. 97).

13. See the entries for "gold" and "platinum" in *the New Columbia Encyclopedia* (1975).

14. Crosland reports that in 1752, a Swedish chemist named Scheffer concluded that the close similarity of (what we now call) platinum to gold justifies the claim that (what we now call) platinum is white gold (1962, p. 97). Crosland also points out that "the distinct nature of new substances was not always easy to demonstrate by elementary analytical methods and the skeptics could always maintain that any apparent discovery was really a substance previously known." (p. 98).

15. This thought experiment is similar in structure to the Druid thought experiment that Mark Wilson presents in Wilson (1982):

> A B-52 full of regular American types landed on their uncharted island and the Druids exclaimed, "Lo, a great silver bird falleth from the sky." . . . [After this event] . . . the extension of the predicate 'is a bird' for the cosmopolitan Druidese is something like the set of flying devices (including animal varieties) . . . [But] . . . If the hapless aviators had crashed in the jungle unseen and were discovered by the Druids six months later as they camped discontentedly around the bomber's hulk, their Druid rescuers would have proclaimed, "Lo, a great silver house lieth in the jungle." . . . [In this alternative linguistic community] airplanes are no longer [read: are not] held to be 'birds.' . . . Which extension should be assigned to 'bird' in cosmopolitan Druidese thus depends upon the *history* of the introduction of B-52's to the island. (pp. 549–50)

A similar thought experiment is briefly sketched by Daniel Dennett on page 312 of Dennett (1987).

16. This way of illustrating the odd consequences of the first thought experiment is adapted from a similar thought experiment presented by Keith Donnellan in Donnellan (1983, p. 103).

17. The similarity is not accidental. Chalmers's theory of primary intensions is a development of Gareth Evans's interpretation (in Evans 1985) of Kripke's claim in *Naming and Necessity* that there are contingent a priori truths. A model theoretic framework for Evans's idea of contingent a priori truths is sketched in Davies and Humberstone (1980). A number of philosophers, including David Chalmers, take for granted that Kripke-style ostensive definitions of natural kind terms must be contingent a priori, even if the discoveries we make about the natural kinds thus defined are not a priori. Chalmers (following Davies and Humberstone) credits Stalnaker (1978) with helping to develop the formal framework for the idea of a primary intension. But Stalnaker himself doubts that we can know primary intensions a priori. See Block and Stalnaker (1999). For an earlier criticism of an epistemological assumption similar to Chalmers's, see Stalnaker (1990).

18. Similarly, we have no guarantee that a "recognitional capacity" that we associate with a given term determines the denotation of the term, in the sense proposed by Jessica Brown in Brown (1998). On any nonsemantic account of a "recognitional capacity," the members of the Earth and Twin Earth linguistic communities in my thought experiment associate the same "recognitional capacity" with the term 'gold' in 1650. Yet they later characterize the denotation of 'gold' differently and revise the "recognitional capacities" they respectively associate with the word form 'gold', without taking themselves to be changing the subject. If we take our practical judgments of sameness of denotation across time as our best guide to when we have changed the subject and when we haven't, then my thought experiment undermines Brown's theory of what determines the denotation of natural kind terms.

19. Hilary Putnam sometimes seems tempted by this idea. See, for example, "The Meaning of 'Meaning,'" reprinted in Putnam (1975); and Putnam (1988, pp. 30–37).

20. This formulation of the challenge my thought experiment poses for dispositional theories is due to Bill Robinson. The point was already implicit in Mark Wilson's druid thought experiment (see footnote 15).

21. The observations in this section suggest an argument against Paul Horwich's use theory of meaning. According to that theory, the meaning of a term is constituted by its possession of a certain "acceptance property" that can be specified independently of its meaning or denotation. Candidates for such properties are nonsemantic facts about a speaker's linguistic behavior, in particular, facts about which sentences the speaker is disposed to accept under various circumstances. For instance, according to Horwich, "the acceptance property that governs the speaker's overall use of 'and' is (roughly) his tendency to accept 'p and q' if and only if he accepts both 'p' and 'q'" (1998a, p. 45). Moreover, according to Horwich, two words express the same concept if they have the same basic acceptance property (p. 46), and any two words that express the same concept must have the same denotation (p. 69). Horwich is therefore committed to saying that the term 'gold' expresses the same concept and has the same denotation in 1650 in both of the linguistic communities of my thought experiment. This aspect of his use theory clearly conflicts with our confidence that we have not changed the denotation of our term 'gold' since 1650.

22. Of these alternatives, Hartry Field's method of defining partial denotation, presented in Field (1973), is the best known and, in my view, the most promising.

23. David Lewis is one proponent of a priori intensions who accepts this methodological point and embraces description theories of denotation. In Lewis (1994), he concedes that very often more than one denotation is compatible with the descriptions that we associate with a term. In such cases, Lewis recommends that we use Field's method of defining a partial denotation for the term (see Field 1973).

24. Some of the material in this section is adapted from Ebbs (2002).

25. As Quine has stressed. See Quine (1986, pp. 10–14, 35–46, 53–5). For more on this theme, see Leeds (1978), Field (1994), and Horwich (1998b).

26. See for instance Quine's syntactical criteria for substitution, presented in chapters 26 and 28 of Quine (1982).

27. The satisfaction clauses for predicates are needed to give inductive specifications of satisfaction conditions for sentences containing quantifiers. Suppose our

regimented language contains just negation (symbolized by '¬'), alternation (symbolized by '∨'), and a universal quantifier (symbolized by '∀'). (In this language there is no separate symbol for the extential quantifier; extential quantifications must be expressed in terms of negation and universal quantification. Other truth functional connectives, such as '→' and '∧' can expressed in terms of '¬' and '∨'.) Then the satisfaction clauses we need, in addition to those for the n simple predicates of the language, may be formulated as follows:

> (n+1) For all sequences s and sentences S: s satisfies the negation of S if and only if s does not satisfy S.

> (n+2) For all sequences s and sentences S and S': s satisfies the alternation of S with S' if and only if either s satisfies S or s satisfies S'.

> (n+3) For all sequences s, sentences S, and numbers i: s satisfies the universal quantification of S with respect to var(i) if and only if every sequence s' that differs from s in at most the ith place satisfies S.

Suppose that together with the satisfaction clauses for the n simple predicates of the language, these clauses inductively define satisfaction for all sentences of the language. Using this inductive definition of satisfaction, we can then define truth for this language as follows: a sentence of the language is *true* if and only if it is satisfied by all sequences. (The above satisfaction clauses are modeled on Quine's formulations in Quine 1986, chapter 3.)

28. Note that on this use of the term 'denote', a word does not denote its extension; the extension of a word is the *set* of objects that the word denotes. See Quine (1982, p. 94). Note also that to specify the denotation of a predicate it isn't necessary to identify objects as members of sequences; I do this here only to highlight the intimate connection between denotation and satisfaction.

29. I do not claim that applications of the disquotational patterns (S) and (D) yield analytic truths, or that the left and right sides of the resulting biconditionals are synonymous. If every deflationary view of truth entails such dubious claims, then the view of truth that I propose is not deflationary. Naturally I don't accept the antecedent of this conditional. But see Gupta (1993) for a defense of the antecedent and a criticism of the view that applications of the disquotational patterns (S) and (D) yield analytic truths.

30. Some astronomers maintain that Pluto is one of the many Kuiper Belt objects, and that if we had known of the existence of all of these objects when Pluto was first discovered, we would not have called Pluto a planet. The argument fails, however, for the same reason that the appeal to dispositions can't show that our practical judgments of sameness of denotation for 'gold' are correct, and those on Twin Earth in the gold-platinum thought experiment are incorrect (see §7 above). What we are disposed to accept depends in part on the order in which we are presented with the relevant evidence. There are no independent grounds for establishing that the actual order in which we were presented with the relevant evidence is the wrong order for settling whether or not Pluto is a planet.

31. For an argument that Pluto is a planet, see Stansberry (2001); for the opposing view, see Jewitt (2001).

32. For an explicit statement of this weaker claim, see Minor Planet Center (2001).

33. We can criticize particular practical judgments of sameness of denotation only against a background of practical judgments of sameness of denotation that we accept without justification. Such judgments cannot all come up for review at the same time. Hence the fact that our practical judgments of sameness of denotation are revisable does not imply that there are standards independent of all them relative to which they are justified or unjustified.

34. Their discoveries do not conflict because the denotations of their terms are different, even though the terms themselves are spelled in the same way. Although we might have been tempted at first to take the Twin English term 'gold' at face value, if we are convinced that it denotes an object x if and only if x is either gold or x is platinum, and we do not revise our judgment that platinum is not a type of gold, we will not take it at face value. If by some strange circumstance we were ever in a position to learn their language, we would be able say what the denotation of their term is disquotationally, but we still would distinguish their term 'gold' from ours, possibly by using subscripts that mark the difference.

Some superficially similar conflicts about the denotations of words cannot be resolved in this way. Suppose, for instance, that one linguistic community *actually* splits into two communities, C1 and C2, that become isolated from each other. Let *T* be an unambiguous term of the language used before the split, and assume that *after* the split

1. the use of *T* in C1 comes to differ from the use of *T* in C2,
2. the characterization of *T*'s denotation that is accepted in C1 is different from the characterization of *T*'s denotation that is accepted in C2, and
3. members of both communities take for granted that the denotation of their term *T* is the same as it was before the split.

If members of the two isolated communities later realize that their practical judgments of sameness of denotation across time for *T* lead back to a single unambiguous term of the language used before the split, they are not likely to relinquish their practical judgments of sameness of denotation across time for *T*. They will likely take themselves to *disagree* about the denotation of *T*, and so they will try to persuade each other of their views.

35. For a defense of the view that the denotation of a word w at time t can be determined by the use of w at some time *after t*, see Jackman (1999b).

36. See Ebbs (2000) for a detailed argument in defense of this claim.

37. This striking image is from Wilson (1982, p. 586). Wilson does not believe there is any real danger that we are just making things up as we go.

38. At one point in Kripke's exposition of Ludwig Wittgenstein's remarks on rule following, Kripke writes: "It seems that the entire idea of meaning vanishes into thin air" (1982, p. 22). In Ebbs (1997, chs. 1, 10), I reconstruct and criticize Kripke's skeptical argument.

39. This is an argument I first presented in Ebbs (2000).

40. In this short chapter, I have focused exclusively on explaining how we can incorporate our practical judgments of sameness of denotation within a deflationary view of truth. I have said nothing about how I would try to answer the many fundamental criticisms of deflationary views of truth that are now familiar in the literature

on truth. My answers to some of these criticisms agree with the answers of Field (1994), Horwich (1998b), Leeds (1978), and Quine (1986). But my way of describing practical judgments of sameness of denotation leads me to disagree with Field, Horwich, Leeds, and Quine about some key points. For a sketch of my answers to some of the central objections to deflationary views of truth, see Ebbs (2002).

10

Individual Autonomy and Sociality

Seumas Miller

This chapter is concerned with the relationship between the autonomy of the individual human agent and human sociality and specifically with an alleged problem for individual autonomy arising from sociality.[1] In the absence of specific characterisations of the key notions of individual autonomy and sociality, the precise nature of the problem is somewhat unclear.[2] However, at an intuitive level the problem is obvious enough and stems from the fact that individual agents are necessarily embedded in, and conditioned by, social processes, structures, and attitudes. Individual agents make choices within a preexisting framework of social forms, including hierarchical organizations. The attitudes of individual agents, including their desires and beliefs, are dependent on social attitudes, such as approval and disapproval. Moreover, the very abilities of individual agents to make appropriately autonomous responses to these social forms, structures, and attitudes—abilities such as the ability to reason or to imagine alternative possibilities to the ones socially presented to them—are themselves socially provided, conditioned, and constrained. In short, what and who an individual agent is, and which choices they make, is necessarily in large part a function of their past and present social environments. Does not this fact undermine the possibility of individual autonomy?

I argue that the answer is in the negative. Indeed, I argue that not only is sociality consistent with individual autonomy, sociality—or at least certain social forms—is an enabling condition for individual autonomy. In this connection consider the conventions of language. Linguistic conventions are necessary for the existence of (nonrudimentary) thought, and thought is necessary for autonomy.

On the other hand, it is evident that under certain conditions social forms are inconsistent with individual autonomy. In this chapter I consider three conditions under which social forms might pose an *in principle* threat to individual autonomy.

The first condition is that social forms might not be such that the agents who participate in them engage in *interdependent* action and do so as more or less *equal* partners. So hierarchical organizations constitute an in principle threat to individual autonomy.[3] Naturally, under certain conditions the in principle threat to individual autonomy posed by hierarchical organizations might cease to exist—for example, if participation is consensual.[4] On the other hand, regularities in action, such as conventions and social norms, do not constitute even an in principle threat.

The second in principle threat to individual autonomy is the absence in a community of certain specific, widely accepted, objectively valid, moral principles. Agents living in a community must be able to make, and act on, certain objectively valid moral judgments if their autonomy is not to be under threat. In this connection consider status hierarchies. Status hierarchies are an inevitable feature of social life, and a defining feature of such hierarchies is that they mobilize the basic human desire for approval by others in one's social group. Some status hierarchies are powerful, but not reflective of, or at least constrained by, objective moral principles and values. As such, they constitute an in principle threat to individual autonomy; the individual can find him/herself unable to make autonomous decisions as a result of their inability to resist powerful status driven values and imperatives. Consider the crippling loss of self-esteem, and consequent loss of autonomy, that members of an oppressed race group might suffer in a racist society, or that poor performers might suffer in an extreme meritocracy, or that the ugly might suffer in a society obsessed with physical beauty.[5] A key objective moral principle here is one that holds all human beings to be of equal moral worth, including by virtue of their capacity for autonomous decision making. This principle, if widely accepted, constrains the power of status hierarchies.

Social forms that are "addicted" to the past pose a third in principle threat to individual autonomy.[6] The nature and function of present social forms, including conventions, social norms, and institutions, are necessarily in large part dependent on the past social forms that they grew out of. However, if it turned out that social forms were so tradition bound that present participants in social forms could not over a reasonable period of time collectively act to transform them into viable new social forms, then present participants could not be said to have collective, or individual, autonomy. Doubtless, many societies are tradition bound in this sense, but I suggest that this is not necessarily the case.

Before proceeding further, we need a working account of the key notions of individual autonomy and sociality.

AUTONOMY

For the purposes of this chapter, I assume that an autonomous agent is a rational agent and also a moral agent.[7] Here I am also assuming that autonomy is principally a property of persisting agents rather than of discrete actions. In this respect there is a contrast with at least some notions of freedom—for example, the notion involved in expressions such as "a freely performed action." It does not make much sense to say that John was an autonomous agent for ten seconds of his life, or that some action was autonomously performed, even though the agent who performed it lacked autonomy.

Roughly speaking, a rational agent is possessed of a continuing, integrated structure of propositional attitudes, engages in practical and theoretical reasoning, and is disposed to make true judgments and valid inferences in so doing.[8] Moreover, a rational agent is disposed to intentionally act on the judgments that result from their practical reasoning. Further, in the case of human rational agents, they exist for a finite period of time. Being aware of their finitude, they rationally ought to make their plans—including their life plan—accordingly.

Here I assume that the notion of a rational agent admits of degrees; some rational agents are more rational than others by virtue of, for example, being disposed to make fewer invalid inferences.

Here I also take it that the reasoning procedures in question—for example, deduction and induction—are objectively valid procedures. In the case of human beings, a process of socialization is a necessary condition for acquiring such procedures. But socialization is not sufficient for such acquisition; unlike many subrational species, human beings have an innate capacity to grasp these procedures. Moreover, these procedures are objectively valid; they are not merely arbitrary "wired in" mental constructs, much less social constructions.[9]

Further, on this account of rational agency, it does not follow that a rational agent must be able to provide, let alone must actually provide, reasons for all their action-guiding beliefs or attitudes. For there might well be moral or rational principles grasped by an agent but principles that are such that there are no further principles that rationally justify them.[10] However, the notion of a rational agent does involve the notion of a being possessed of higher-order propositional attitudes, including higher-order beliefs that function as reasons for some of their lower order beliefs.[11]

A rational agent is not necessarily a moral agent. Roughly speaking, a human moral agent is a rational agent who is disposed to make true judgments and valid inferences in relation to the moral worth of human actions, attitudes, motivations, emotions, agents, and so on. Here the actions, attitudes, and so on in question, include those of others, as well as one's own. For human moral agents, at least, operate in an interpersonal and social world.

Moreover, the judgments of moral worth in question include reason-based judgments on ultimate ends; ends that are not themselves means to other ends.[12] Because a moral agent is also a rational agent, a moral agent is disposed to act intentionally on the judgments that result from their practical reasoning. As with rational agency, moral agency admits of degrees. Some moral agents are less moral than others.

The notion of moral worth is necessarily somewhat vague and is in any case in part relative to one's favored moral theory. Here I simply note that judgments of moral worth in relation to human actions, dispositions, emotions, or persons and so on not only are a species of value judgment, but also are judgments in relation to matters of great importance, at least from the perspective of the human agents making those judgments. Indeed, arguably matters of moral worth are by definition those matters taken to be of supreme importance in the life of an individual or collective.

In my characterization of rational and moral agents, it might seem that I have not left space for the distinction between nonrational and irrational agents, and between nonmoral and immoral agents. This is not so. By my lights, a nonrational agent is one who is not capable of making judgments or inferences; an irrational agent is one who is capable, but has some significant deficit in their rationality and thus makes a significant number of false judgments and/or invalid inferences or often fails to act on the results of their practical reasoning.[13] Similarly, a nonmoral agent lacks the capacity to make moral judgements and act on them; an immoral agent, by contrast, is merely (significantly) deficient in their moral judgment making or often fails to act on their correct moral judgments. That said, I accept that with respect to some agents, whether or not those agents are nonmoral agents—as opposed to immoral agents—might not be entirely determinate.[14]

Note that I have tied rationality to the achievement of truth as well as to (so to speak) valid reasoning, and I have assumed an objectivist conception of morality. Here I am not specifying any particular objectivist theory of moral claims. Moreover, I acknowledge that objectivism in relation to moral claims is not necessarily to be assimilated to objectivism in relation to (say) claims about ordinary middle sized physical objects, or claims about numbers. Perhaps moral claims necessarily involve processes of interpretation, including self-interpretation.[15] Further, objectivism in relation to moral claims may involve a greater extent of indeterminacy, inexactitude, and uncertainty than objectivism in other domains of knowledge.

Let me now turn directly to the notion of autonomy. Given the distinction between rational agents and moral agents, there might be a distinction between autonomous rational agents and autonomous (rational) *moral* agents. Certainly, there is a distinction between exercises of *freedom* in the sense of freely chosen actions of rational agents, and *autonomy* in the sense of autonomous (rational) moral agents; and between exercises of *freedom* in the sense of freely chosen actions of (rational) moral agents, and *autonomy* in the sense of autonomous (rational) moral agents. For there are freely chosen actions that have no moral significance, and there are moral and immoral agents who freely choose to perform actions that they know to be morally wrong. At any rate, my concern in this chapter is only with autonomous (rational) moral agents.[16] Here the property of being autonomous qualifies *moral agency* as opposed to action or rational agency.

From the fact that an agent is rational and moral (in the above-described senses) it does not follow that the agent is an autonomous moral agent. To see this imagine a moral agent who always acts on true moral judgments derived from correct moral principles, but nevertheless the agent's beliefs in the correctness of these moral principles is entirely dependent on the hypnotic power of some arch-manipulator.

So being rational and moral (in the above described senses) are necessary, but not sufficient, conditions for being autonomous. There is at least one further condition that is necessary for autonomy, or at least necessary for the autonomy of moral, including human, agents. This condition is the nonexistence of a certain kind of state of affairs external to the putatively autonomous human agent. These states of affairs are ones in which the decisions or actions of an external agent or agents is a sufficient condition for the agent in question performing the action that he performs, or believing in the moral principle that he believes in and acts on.[17] Autonomy involves a degree of independence.[18]

There are further necessary conditions for being autonomous—for example, self-mastery of the sort undermined by drug addiction.[19] However, such necessary conditions do not include being able to infringe the laws of physics or the laws of logic. The fact that a human agent cannot hope to fly when they jump off a tall building, or cannot both walk and not walk at the same time, does not undermine their autonomy.

And there are other constraints on human agents that do not undermine their autonomy. Some of these constraints are generated by psychophysiological features of humans. Consider the inability of humans to freely determine what their perceptual and bodily sensations will be, or the inability of most humans to withstand the pain of extreme torture for long periods. Other constraints are generated by psychomoral features, such as the basic desire to be approved of by at least some other human beings and the basic disposition to approve of oneself.

I assume that these logical, physical, and psychological constraints are just that: constraints. As such, they constrain what a human agent can be and what they can do; but they do not necessarily fully determine what such an agent is or does. So autonomy is not ruled out by this kind of weak determinism.[20]

Naturally, in accepting this weak determinism I have not resolved, what might be termed, the metaphysical problem of freedom. This is the kind of

Seumas Miller

freedom at issue in traditional philosophical debates regarding freewill, causation, and determinism. I take it that freedom in this sense is at most a necessary condition for autonomy. For the conceptual context for discussions of autonomy is one consisting of interacting human agents, rather than causal interactions broadly understood. At any rate, the problem of metaphysical freedom is usefully described by Thomas Nagel, albeit under the heading of autonomy.[21] Assume that either an action is causally explained or that it is unexplained. If the former, then arguably we are not autonomous, because the cause(s) provides the only sufficient condition(s) for the action being performed; any reason we might have for performing the action is impotent. But, if the action is unexplained then equally we are not autonomous. For, if an action is not explained, then presumably there is no reason for its performance; so it is not a rational action and, therefore, not the action of an agent acting autonomously.

One might respond to this as follows. First, reasons are, or can be, causes. Second, irrespective of whether an action had a cause or not, there might still be a reason for its performance; if so, then this reason provides an explanation—even if not a causal explanation—for the performance of the action. However, says Nagel, "an autonomous intentional explanation cannot explain precisely what it was supposed to explain, namely *why I did what I did rather than the alternative that was causally open to me*. It says I did it for certain reasons, but does not explain why I didn't decide not to do it for other reasons."[22] Nagel's thought here appears to be that the process of an agent's *autonomous reasoning* in relation to their performance of an optional course of action must terminate in a reason and terminate in a reason that is such that if one has that reason then necessarily one will perform the action. But there are no such reasons. For one can always ask why the agent did not decide—on the basis of other reasons—to perform the alternative action.[23]

Fortunately, it is not one of my ambitions in this chapter to solve the problem of metaphysical freedom. Rather, for the purposes of this chapter, I simply assume that we have metaphysical freedom, or that it is an open question whether or not we have it, or that we do not have it but, contra appearances, this does not undermine our individual autonomy. For my concern here is with the specific threat of sociality to individual autonomy. Let me now turn, then, to the notion of sociality, and specifically of social action. Here I rely heavily on the theory of social action that I have set forth in detail elsewhere.[24]

SOCIALITY

Many human actions are *individual* actions. Individual actions are the actions of individual human persons that are not performed in cooperation with, or otherwise directed at, other persons. As such, individual actions are not necessarily social actions. And there are other categories of human action that are not social actions.

Actions that are not necessarily social include, what might be termed *natural* actions. A natural action is one that is performed by virtue simply of needs and dispositions that the agent has through being a member of the human species as distinct from, say, some social group. Obvious examples are eating and drinking. Eating and drinking are not actions that *logically* presuppose, or logically imply, social forms.

Another important category of actions that are not necessarily social are what I will term *interpersonal* actions. An interpersonal action is an individual action that is interdependent with the action of some other single person or is otherwise directed to a single person.[25] Here the action is directed to the other person qua particular person, or qua member of the human species; it is not directed at the other person qua member of a social group or occupant of a social role or the like. Many cooperative or joint actions are of this sort. Here the contrast is with actions that are performed in accordance with a social form, or are directed to a number of other persons qua members of a social group, and actions directed to a single person qua member of some social group or occupant of a social role or the like. Typically, sexual acts or acts of intimate friendship or the behaviour of a newborn infant in relation to his mother are (predominantly) interpersonal actions in this sense, but institutional acts of conferring degrees or conforming to conventions of dress are not. Moreover, some of these natural, interpersonal actions are also moral actions. Consider actions motivated by an instinctual feeling of sympathy for a fellow human being, qua human being—as opposed to, qua member of one's social group.

Interpersonal actions presuppose the existence of that relationship that obtains when, so to speak, one mind confronts another mind. Such "confrontations" are everyday occurrences, but paradigmatic examples are situations in which one person is said to look the other in the eye. Here one person is aware of the other person, including being aware that the other person is aware of them. Such mind-to-mind interactions need to be distinguished from, on the one hand, mind-to-own-mind (introspective) and mind-to-material world (e.g., perceptual) interactions, and, on the other hand, from mind-to-social-world (social) interactions. Following C. D. Broad, I call such mind-to-mind interactions *extraspective* interactions.[26]

Roughly speaking, mind-to-*social-world* interactions take place when one or more individual actors interact with, or direct their actions to, other individual actors (who might, or might not, be copresent), but do so qua parties to a convention or social norm, qua occupants of an institutional role or qua members of a social group or other social form. In other words, social actions are human actions performed in accordance with social *forms* such as conventions, social norms, institutions, social groups, and the like.[27]

Note that while I have contrasted social actions with individual, natural, and interpersonal actions, the fact that an action is social does not preclude it from also being, at another level of description, individual, natural, or interpersonal. For most individual and interpersonal actions, and most natural actions (whether natural individual actions or natural interpersonal actions), are also, at least to some extent, social actions by virtue of being regulated to some extent by social forms, such as conventions, social norms, and the like. Indeed, the social dimension of human actions consists in the regulation of prior individual and interpersonal actions, many of which are prior natural actions.

Here there is a further important point. Most actions governed by social forms are, nevertheless, not fully determined by those forms. For example, the conventions of the English language dictate that strings of English words be ordered in certain ways and not in others. But these conventions do not determine which words will be used. Rather individuals can choose which sentence to utter and can choose from an infinity, or at least an indeterminately very large number, of possible sentences. Indeed, as mentioned earlier, the conventions of the English language are enabling conditions for (nonrudimentary) communication and thought. In this respect they are different from some other conventions that constrain—without fully determining—prior human action, but that do not in any profound sense *enable* higher-level activity (e.g., the conventions governing the use of a knife and fork).[28]

The picture of social action, and of sociality, that I have sketched is of a set of structures of social forms that constrain, but do not fully determine, prior human action. Moreover, some of these structures also enable various forms of higher level human activity to take place. Within this framework individuals can perform individual and interpersonal actions of their own choosing; they can do so while continuing to comply with the relevant social forms. To this extent social forms are like the principles of logic, of the physical sciences, and of psychology that I mentioned earlier.

On the other hand, there is an important difference between "constraining" social forms and the "constraining" principles of logic, physics, biology, psychology, and so forth. For the elements of the social framework—the conventions, social norms, and so on—are themselves "constructions out of," and therefore reflect collective choices in relation to, prior nonsocial— often natural—actions. (The terms *natural* and *social* are contrasting ones.) These nonsocial actions might be individual actions or they might be interpersonal actions. (The terms *individual* and *interpersonal* are contrasting ones, and both are qualified by the terms *natural* and *social*.) To take as an example a social action type that we discuss in the following section, conventions are regularities in a species of interpersonal action, namely, joint or cooperative action.

Even when social forms regulate prior *social* actions they reflect collective choices in relation to prior nonsocial actions; for at the core of any social action there is ultimately a nonsocial (often natural) action; and that nonsocial action is either an individual, or an interpersonal, action. Consider highly conventionalised banquets; there may well be a number of layers of conventions, but at the core, so to speak, there is the natural, individual action of eating.

Once constructed, social forms become a regulating, but not fully determining, framework within which higher-order individual and interpersonal human actions are performed. Accordingly, on this picture, there is no obvious inherent threat to individual autonomy posed by sociality. Naturally, specific social forms may under certain conditions pose a threat to individual autonomy; one of the main aims of this chapter is to unearth just such social forms and conditions.

Armed with the above characterisations of an autonomous agent, and of sociality, we are now in a position to directly address our central question—viz., whether individual autonomy is undermined by sociality.

SOCIAL REGULARITIES IN ACTION

Elsewhere I have argued in detail for the following claims concerning social regularities.[29] Here I simply put them forward as having intuitive plausibility.

The main categories of social regularity in action are conventions and social norms. Roughly speaking, conventions are regularities in action that realize shared ends. They are regularities in what is referred to as joint or cooperative action.[30] Thus conventions of language enable the shared end of communication to be achieved, monetary conventions greatly enhance economic exchanges, conventions of politeness facilitate social interaction, and so on.

By contrast, social norms are regularities in action that embody felt moral and related attitudes.[31] In most societies there are social norms proscribing murder, rape, theft, and so on.

On the above conception of conventions it is easy to see why conventions do not necessarily undermine individual autonomy. For on this conception conventions are simply regularities in joint action that enable shared ends, and thus individual ends, to be realized.

What of social norms? In so far as social norms embody objective moral principles, they embody the judgments that an autonomous moral agent would make, or more precisely, they embody the judgments that an *ideal* autonomous moral agent would make. In this connection recall my assumption that autonomous moral agents have a disposition to make objective moral judgments on the basis of valid inferences.

So far so good, but what if the shared ends that justify conventions were not themselves freely chosen? Would this not undermine the claim to autonomy of agents who were parties to those conventions?

And relatedly, what if the social norms that agents in a given society conformed to embodied objective moral principles, but nevertheless those agents, either did not freely choose those principles, or (in the case of some agents) did not judge them to be correct? Would not either of these considerations undermine the claim to autonomy of the agents in question?

Some ends realized by conventions are freely chosen by the agents who are parties to those conventions. Consider the collective end of each to be with one's friends; a collective end that is realized by the convention of meeting at bar A rather than bar B or bar C. And some of these freely chosen collective ends are means to other collective ends. Suppose that the collective end of meeting is itself a means to the further collective end of mutual exchange of business information.

Perhaps some moral principles are not objectively valid or invalid, but rather a matter for individual or collective choice. If so, then there would be plausibility in the claim of existentialists that autonomy is likely to be inconsistent with at least some socially accepted moral principles. After all, it would be extremely fortuitous if individual and collective choices always coincided.

But there are some ends realized by conventions, and there are many moral principles, that are not freely chosen.

Human beings do not, for the most part, freely decide whether or not to be the kinds of creatures that want to eat, or to have sex, or to communicate with one another; they must eat to live, and they are by nature sexually oriented and communicative.

The fact that human beings have a range of basic needs and natural inclinations does not undermine the possibility of their being autonomous; rather it places constraints on their decision making. Human beings need to eat, but what, when, how, how much, and so on, is very much a matter of individual and collective choice. And one element of collective choice is choice of conventions; it is a matter of (often rational) collective choice whether this convention rather than some alternative convention is established for the purpose of realizing a given end.[32]

Nor does the fact that some of these needs or inclinations are essentially interpersonal, such as communication and sex, mean that the shared ends that they give rise to somehow constitute a threat to the individual autonomy of the agents pursuing those ends. Once again, who one has sex with, when and what one communicates, and so on is very much a matter of individual, interpersonal, and collective choice. Moreover, an important element of collective choice in all this is the choice of conventions in relation to ends that derive from basic interpersonal needs and inclinations. Consider here the collective choice of linguistic conventions in relation to the interpersonal need for communication.

What of grasping the validity of objective moral principles? Human beings do not freely decide that murder or rape is morally wrong; rather they make a (correct) judgment that this is so. This judgment is truth aiming and can be said to be "free" only in this somewhat limited sense. The fact that judgments, including many if not all moral judgments, ought to be constrained by the truth, does not somehow compromise or diminish the autonomy of the person making those judgments—any more than the need to be constrained by scientific facts diminishes the autonomy of scientists engaged in scientific work.

Indeed, being able to make *correct* moral judgments is a necessary condition for moral agency and, therefore, for being an autonomous moral agent. By my lights, a being who was not disposed to make correct moral judgments—and act on them—would not be a moral agent and therefore would not be an autonomous moral agent.

Moreover, a rational, *moral agent* who, nevertheless, *frequently* infringed *fundamental* moral principles—either because he or she made incorrect moral judgments or because he or she chose to ignore their correct moral judgments—would not be acting as an *autonomous* moral agent. The autonomy of such an agent is significantly diminished by the fact that he or she frequently, and in fundamental ways, acts against his or her nature as a moral agent. Such an agent would be a grossly *immoral* agent, as opposed to a nonmoral agent. If an immoral agent is not acting freely but acting (say) under inner compulsion, then he or she is not acting autonomously. On the other hand, if an immoral agent is acting freely then he or she is, nevertheless, not necessarily acting autonomously. In particular, if they are *grossly* immoral agents, then they are not acting autonomously; rather they are acting, so to speak, with licence.

On the other hand, even autonomous moral agents make *some* false moral judgments and *sometimes* fail to act on their correct moral judgments. Suppose a moral agent makes an important false moral judgment that is inconsistent with a prevailing (objectively correct) social norm? Or suppose the agent makes the correct moral judgment, but nevertheless fails to act on it; he or she knowingly does wrong. Is there not now a conflict between the autonomy of the individual agent and compliance with morally correct social norms? No doubt there is a conflict; I am not suggesting that being autonomous entails making correct moral judgments all the time and always acting on one's correct moral judgments. Rather, the point I am making is that given the objective character of at least most important moral issues, there is no in principle inconsistency between individual autonomy and social norms.

In theory, they can, and ought to, coincide; autonomous individuals and reflective societies can, and ought to, agree on moral truths.

It might be responded to all this that the real problem with social norms, as distinct from objective moral principles grasped by autonomous moral agents, is that social norms—whether they embody *objective* moral principles or not—constitute a *coercive* imposition on the individual members of social groups.

The notion of coercion being used here is somewhat opaque, but there is no doubt that social norms can have a coercive function, for example, a social norm according to which blacks are treated as being inferior.[33] However, the question is whether this is necessarily the case. I suggest that it is not. Here we need to distinguish two different kinds of issue. The first issue pertains to *induction* into a moral community. It is a necessary—but not a sufficient—condition for an individual human being *initially* grasping the validity of moral principles that they are inducted as a child into some moral community. But it would not follow from this that the principles were coercively imposed on the individual; that the individual did not come to grasp the truth of the principles; or that he does not later in life freely conform to the principles. Rather the learning environment provided by the moral community is a necessary condition for the individual initially coming to grasp moral principles, as an initial grasp of mathematical principles might require a teacher.

Another kind of issue concerns the *continued* conformity of a rational, moral adult to the current social norms of the community to which they belong. With respect to many moral principles, it is plausible that a necessary (but not sufficient) condition for the continued conformity of one autonomous agent is the continued conformity—together with the persistence of the associated moral attitudes—of the other members of the social group. There are a number of reasons why this might be so, three of which I explain and illustrate below. However, the general point to be made is that from the fact that an agent's conformity to a moral principle is *in part* dependent on the conformity to that moral principle on the part of others, and/or on the existence of relevant associated moral attitudes in others, it does not follow that the moral principle has been coercively imposed on the agent and that therefore the agent's autonomy is diminished.

The first of the above-mentioned reasons is as follows. Sometimes the failure of others to conform to a moral principle provides a reasonable excuse, and perhaps an adequate moral justification, for one's own nonconformity. If others tell lies to me, or break promises to me, or steal from me, does not this give me an excuse for doing likewise? After all, if I continue to comply with principles of truth-telling, or promise-keeping, or respect for property when others do not, I will be exploited and I might even suffer great harm. Surely turning the other cheek is not in all such circumstances a moral requirement.

So with respect to some moral principles, it is necessary that others conform to them if I am reasonably to be expected to do so. Accordingly, when
I conform in a context of general conformity—and conform in part because
others conform—I may well be acting reasonably and (other things being
equal) autonomously. Certainly, there is no reason to think that my conformity to such moral principles is necessarily the result of coercion. I conclude that the fact that my continuing conformity to a social norm is *in part*
dependent on the continuing conformity of others does not necessarily diminish my autonomy.[34]

The second of the three reasons why the conformity and moral attitudes
of others might be a necessary condition for my own conformity can be explained and illustrated as follows. Sometimes *other agents' disapproval* of a
given moral agent's nonconformity to a moral principle is a necessary condition for the conformity of that moral agent to that moral principle. (Or at
least, other agents' disapproval of the agent's nonconformity *and approval
of his conformity*, is a necessary condition for the agent's conformity.) Assume that the agent in question generally acts in accordance with moral principles, and assume that he believes conformity to this particular moral principle is the right thing to do. Nevertheless, the agent might be tempted to
infringe this principle, and some other moral principles, and might actually
infringe all of these moral principles, were it not for the disapproving attitudes of other agents. Consider certain kinds of corruption.

Suppose the agent in question is given a very demanding position of great
political power, but one with a meagre financial reward. Suppose, further,
that he is occasionally offered bribes to ensure that government tenders on
offer go to one of a number of foreign contractors. He knows that it is
morally wrong, but he also knows that accepting foreign bribes is not unlawful—so he will go unpunished—and that his wrongful actions will go
undiscovered. Moreover, his life, and that of his family, will be made a great
deal easier if he accepts the bribe. He also resents having to work so hard
and under such great pressure for so little reward. He feels inclined to start
taking the bribes on offer, even though he believes it would be morally
wrong for him to do so. At this point, he remembers that others would
strongly disapprove of his accepting a bribe, and he does care what other
people think of him. Of course, since his actions will go undiscovered, he
will never in fact have to suffer their disapproval. However, he worries about
what they would think of him, if they *knew* what he had done. For he is not
seeking *misplaced* approval; nor is his fundamental concern to avoid *justified* disapproval. Rather he desires *justifiably* to be approved of and *justifiably* to avoid being disapproved of. Accordingly, he refuses the bribe.

In the above scenario, the agent's belief that accepting bribes is wrong,
taken in conjunction with his desire, both for the justified approval of others
and to avoid their justified disapproval, is sufficient to cause him to refuse

the bribe. Here, one contrast is with an agent who does what is morally right only because it is morally right and thus entirely independently of what the attitudes of others might be. What others might think or not think of its actions in itself makes no difference to its actions. (Of course, it cares what others might *do to it* as a result of their attitudes to it.) Perhaps such a moral agent is autonomous; however, I suggest that it is not a recognizable (autonomous) *human* agent.[35] Human beings are social animals and care deeply about what others think of them. Accordingly, obliviousness to the moral approval and disapproval of others cannot be a necessary condition for the moral autonomy of human beings.

Another contrasting agent to the one in the above-described scenario is an agent who cares about what others think of her, but who lacks a certain self-awareness. Assume that this second contrasted agent believes that taking bribes is morally wrong and is influenced by this consideration, but—like the agent in the original scenario—this agent is even more strongly influenced by the temptations afforded by the bribe, given bribe taking is not unlawful, she will go unpunished, and so on. However, assume that there is an important difference between this agent and the one in the original scenario. This agent decides to take the bribes. She does so because she thinks that her desire for the moral approval of others, and her aversion to their moral disapproval, will be satisfied, just so long as she is not found out; and she knows that she will not be found out.

Here we need to get clear what the precise nature of the attitude of moral approval and moral disapproval is. The whole point of the attitude of moral approval is that the person approved of has done what is morally right, and vice-versa for the attitude of moral disapproval. So person *A* morally approves of person *B* for the reason that person *B* does what is right. Accordingly, if *B* desires *A*'s moral approval, then *B* not only desires that *A* approve of *B* because *A* *believes* that *B* does what is right; but *B* also desires that *A* approve of *B* because *A* *knows* that *B* does what is right. Naturally, if *A* falsely believes that *B* does what is morally right, then *A* will morally approve of *B*. However, the point is that *B* will not have secured what *B* desired. For *B* knows that he, *B*, has not done what is right, and that therefore *A*'s attitude of approval is not the kind of approval that he, *B*, desires; *B* desires to be approved of because he has *in fact* done what was right.[36]

Now let us return to the second agent we contrasted with the agent in our original scenario. Recall that this second contrasting agent desires both moral approval and to avoid moral disapproval. However, on the basis of our discussion of the nature of moral approval and disapproval, we can now see that she will not fully or adequately realize her desire. For although she does not see this at the time of her decision to take the bribes, her desire is not simply to be an object of moral approval (and to avoid being an object of disapproval); rather it is a desire to be an object of moral approval (and to avoid being an object of moral disapproval) *because she has in fact done what is right, and avoided doing what is wrong*. So this agent, unlike the agent in the original scenario, lacks a certain reflective self-awareness in relation to the nature of her desire for moral approval and the avoidance of moral disapproval.

The agent in the original scenario cares about what others think of him; he desires their moral approval. But he is also reflectively self-aware in relation to this desire; he knows what it is that he *really* desires in this regard. What is the significance of this for the relationship between individual autonomy and the dis/approval of others?

I have described a certain kind of moral agent who is susceptible to corruption, but who, nevertheless, is able to resist corruption in part because of his belief that corruption is morally wrong and in part because of his desire justifiably to be morally approved of and justifiably to avoid being disapproved of. So this agent cares what others think of him to the extent of being influenced by their moral approval and disapproval; in this he is at one with most human beings. Yet the fact that this agent in this way cares what others think of him does not diminish his autonomy; and certainly it does not show that he has been coerced by others. For the moral attitudes of other agents constitute only a necessary, but not a sufficient, condition for his moral probity. Moreover, the performance of the morally significant action of refusing to take the bribes—the action in part motivated by his desire for others' moral approval and the avoidance of their moral disapproval—is actively mediated by his awareness of the nature of this desire of his. This kind of action-guiding self-awareness is indicative of *autonomous* moral agency.

I conclude that the existence of social norms sustained in part by the moral approval and moral disapproval of others is quite consistent with individual autonomy, and therefore that the individuals who conform to those norms are by no means necessarily coerced into so doing.

Let me now explain and illustrate a third and final reason why the conformity and moral attitudes of other agents might be a necessary condition for a given agent's conformity. The agent in question might not even reasonably have a *belief* in certain moral principles, in the absence of conformity to those principles by other agents, and in the absence of those agents' ongoing expressions of disapproval of nonconformity.

Consider a traditional community in which there is an abhorrence of engaging in homosexual practices. Everyone believes that engaging in homosexual practices is morally wrong, even the minority who feel inclined to engage in them. Now assume that the beliefs of the community in relation to homosexual practices are incorrect; there is nothing morally wrong with these practices. Further, assume that over time these beliefs will be challenged on the basis of rational scrutiny, and indeed will eventually be overturned. Naturally, mutual belief in, and continued conformity to, a set of moral principles may at times require reflection, explicit widespread discussion, and public communication; what might be required from time to time is a kind of explicit collective reaffirmation of the group's moral principles. Likewise, the abandonment of certain hitherto accepted moral principles may involve such ongoing processes of collective discussion and decision.

At any rate, in the antihomosexual practices phase it does not even occur to most heterosexually inclined persons to question their abhorrence of homosexual practices. For although that abhorrence is partly socially instilled, it is also in part sustained by the fact that it is psychologically conducive— they themselves find the sexual advances of members of the same sex somewhat repellent. No doubt the majority should question their moral beliefs in regard to homosexual practices, but they do not; and it is understandable why they do not. In our example a necessary, but not sufficient, condition for the (incorrect) moral belief of almost any individual member of the community is the (incorrect) moral beliefs of most of the other members of the community. Nevertheless, the autonomy of the majority (heterosexually inclined) members of the community is not diminished by virtue of their incorrect moral beliefs about homosexual practices. To see this consider the homosexual minority. By contrast with the heterosexual majority, the autonomy of the homosexual minority *is* diminished by the prevailing social norms. Specifically, the social norms are an obstacle to the sexual self-expression of the minority homosexually inclined group.

The basic point to be extracted from our explanatory discussions and illustrations is that social norms *taken individually* do not necessarily threaten individual autonomy. For any given social norm need only be such that the moral attitudes and conformity of others is a necessary, but not a sufficient condition, for one's own moral attitude and conformity. I deal with the question as to whether an individual's autonomy is threatened by the set of social norms to which he or she adheres, *the set of social norms taken as a whole*, in the final section of this chapter.

ORGANIZATIONAL HIERARCHIES

Individuals realize their ends not only by performing joint actions directed to shared ends, including repetitive joint actions, but also by *specialization*. Assume agent A performs task x, and agent B task y, and agent C task z. Assume also that: A cannot y or z (or at least cannot y or z without difficulty); B cannot x or z; and C cannot x or y. Assume finally that if A dies or leaves, B and C will identify some D to replace A; similarly if B or C leaves or dies, then some E or F will be found as a replacement. What we have is an organization, albeit a primitive one.

So organizations consist of an (embodied) formal structure of interlocking roles.[37] And these roles can be defined in terms of specialized tasks governed by procedures and conventions. Moreover, unlike social groups, organizations are individuated by the kind of tasks that their members undertake and also by their characteristic functions or ends. So we have governments, universities, business corporations, armies, and so on. Perhaps governments have as an end or goal the ordering and leading of societies, universities the end of discovering and disseminating knowledge, and so on.

Most societies at most times have made use of, and been comprised in part of, organizations. Moreover, the structure of organizations has varied enormously. Some are extremely hierarchical with an emphasis on controlling individual behaviour and attitudes. Military organizations have traditionally been of this kind. It is often claimed that Japanese organizations, including corporations and government departments, are also of this sort, though with the qualification that employees are looked after and treated well so long as they conform to prevailing conventions and norms and obey their superiors. Other organizations, such as western universities, have been more collegial in character.

Here my concern is with hierarchical organizations, organizations that involve relations of authority, and therefore power relations. Such organizations constitute an in principle threat to individual autonomy. Such organizations include governments.

However, while institutional authorities wield power, they are also dependent on collective acceptance.[38] Consider Peter Sellars in the movie, *Being There*. Sellars plays the role of a gardener who for various reasons begins to be treated by the staff of the president, and ultimately by everyone, as if he were the president of the USA. Eventually, he can even have run for office and be elected. Unfortunately, he has no understanding of the political system, or of relevant policies, and has no leadership qualities whatsoever. Nevertheless, it seems to be the case that the gardener can become the president by virtue of collective acceptance.

Institutional *authorities* are vulnerable to a degree that other institutions, such as the English language, are not. As Searle points out, the communist government of Russia turned out to have clay feet.[39] Once people chose not to obey its directives, it was finished; it simply ceased to function or exist as a government. However, it is difficult to see how the English language could go out of existence in such spectacular fashion; for it depends on millions of often-disconnected communicative interactions between millions of different people, and languages are in any case more essential to human beings than governments are.[40]

However, there is a particular reason for the vulnerability of institutional authorities. The rights of institutional authorities are dependent on collective acceptance. The point here is not simply that (say) rulers cannot *exercise* their right to rule, if their right to rule is not collectively accepted; though this is in fact the case. Rather a ruler does not even *possess* a right to rule unless she is able to exercise authority over her subjects. This seems to be a general feature of the deontic properties of those in authority.

Accordingly, the rights possessed by institutional authorities are not only rights to exercise powers in the narrow sense of a right that might not actually be able to be exercised; rather these rights are ones that, if not able to be exercised, are not possessed. In short, these rights are de facto *powers*. Indeed, the actions of those in authority constitute in large part the *exercise of power*. As such, these actions of authorities are an *in principle* threat to individual autonomy. Naturally, this in principle threat might cease to exist under certain conditions—for example, if the institutional authority is subject to consensual democracy.

As we have seen, the power of institutional authorities is dependent on collective acceptance. To this extent institutional power is potentially constrained by autonomous individuals acting collectively. However, collective acceptance might be passive in a sense of passivity consistent with the nonexistence of autonomy. Moreover, even if a majority actively accepts some authority—that is, they exercise their autonomy in accepting the authority—it might still be the case that a minority does not.

As is well known, institutional mechanisms have been developed to deal with this problem of respect for individual autonomy in the context of hierarchical organizations. Democratic processes are perhaps the most important category of such institutional mechanisms. The basic idea is a very familiar one. It involves each individual autonomously participating in the democratic process, and deciding to abide by the outcome of that democratic process—for example, voting for a particular leader and accepting the outcome of the vote.

In so far as an individual autonomously chooses to participate in organizational hierarchies, or in so far as individuals autonomously accept (say) democratic decision procedures, and those democratic decision procedures permeate organizational hierarchies, then organizational hierarchies are not necessarily inconsistent with individual autonomy. However, in contemporary societies, at least, organizational hierarchies, such as large public and private-sector bureaucracies are unavoidable, and are not subject to pervasive democratic decision-making procedures. Accordingly, individual autonomy is compromised. Moreover, individual autonomy is also compromised in nondemocratic nation-states, and even in democratic nation-states, because in the contemporary world, at least, there is no real option but to live in a nation-state and thereby to be subject to governmental control.

HIERARCHIES OF STATUS

Status hierarchies do not necessarily rely on organizational power or on authority more generally. Certainly, status hierarchies, like organizational hierarchies, are dependent on collective acceptance. However, the collective acceptance in question tends to be different in nature. Specifically, status hierarchies, but not necessarily organizational hierarchies, depend on mobilizing the desire to be approved. The notion of approval here used is a generic one embracing the desire to be admired, to be respected, and even to be envied; it is not simply the narrower notion of moral approval. This (generic) desire for social approval is at the core of status hierarchies.

Some theorists regard social approval as the linchpin of all social norms.[41] Let us dub such an account the *social approval theory*.[42]

The social approval theory is consistent with our intuition that social norms involve social attitudes of approval and disapproval and that these attitudes function as a motivating factor in our conformity. So, by the lights of the social approval theory, conformity to a social norm by one agent is dependent on the other members of the social group.

However this dependence is not interdependence of action. One agent does not perform action x on condition the other agents perform action x. Nor on this account is there interdependence of attitude. One agent does not dis/approve of an action on condition the other agents dis/approve of that action. Rather the dependence is between the *action* of one agent and the *attitudes* of the other agents. An agent performs an *action x* on condition the other agents *approve of him/her x-ing.*

It is important to note that this kind of dependence of action on attitude needs to be distinguished from the kind in which an agent x's on condition *everyone, including himself,* approves of his x-ing—the agent conforms but is motivated by a desire to meet his own expectations of himself, as well as the expectations of others. The social approval theory of social norms ought to be rejected. For one thing, on this account each agent conforms to a social norm on condition that other agents approve of his/her conformity; his/her own approval is not necessary. So individual autonomy is immediately at risk. Conformity is completely dependent on social pressure; truth-aiming judgments in relation to moral worth have no role to play. The reason we conform is because others disapprove of us if we do not, and we desire to be approved of.

For another thing, the social approval theory confuses social norms with fashions and other status-driven behavior. In the case of a fashion each agent does what others approve of, largely because they approve of it. So each wears flared trousers this week largely because others approve of it and drain pipe trousers the week after because that is what others approve of at that time.

The social approval theory of social norms is not correct. Nevertheless, social approval is a powerful and pervasive social force, and one that maintains a large number of regularities in action, including fashions and other forms of social conformity.

One of the most important aspects of the desire for social approval is the desire for status, whether it be the individually held status of a pop star, sports star, or academic star, or the collectively held status of a member of the ruling class or a dominant racial group.[43] I take myself to have demonstrated that the concept of a regularity in action sustained by the desire for status is not to be identified with the concept of a social norm—a regularity in action sustained by moral beliefs. However, it is conceivable that a desire for status, and a corresponding adulation of those with status, comes to assume such importance that it overrides hitherto accepted moral considerations; perhaps this was the case with kings and emperors in the past and is now the case with pop stars and sports stars in contemporary societies. That is, among the members of some social group the desire for, and adulation of, status may come to assume the role and substance of a moral belief. In that case, the regularities sustained by these beliefs in the importance of status would be in effect social norms.

However, such regularities would not be *objectively* morally valid. Indeed, their existence might well be cause for moral concern. One important ground for concern would be the threat they pose to individual autonomy. Untrammelled pursuit of status, and corresponding adulation of status—whether status of the individually held, or collectively held, type—amounts to servility on the part of the individual to the approval of the group. As such, it is inconsistent with individual autonomy. The decisive mode of protection is a commitment to certain objective moral principles on the part of the individuals that comprise the group or—in the case of collectively held status—groups. More specifically, there needs to be a commitment to the principle of the equal worth of human beings, including by virtue of their capacity for autonomous decision making. This, and related objective moral principles, if adhered to by members of the social group, constitute objectively valid social norms that function to constrain status hierarchies and thereby to protect individual autonomy.

THE THREAT OF THE PAST

The social forms and objects that condition the actions of individual persons predate and postdate the actions, interactions, and indeed lives of particular generations of individual persons. Moreover, social forms and objects undergo change by virtue of the *joint* participation in them over long periods of time of different particular individuals and different sets of interpersonally connected individuals, by virtue of changes to other *connected* social forms and objects, and by virtue of the different nonsocial conditions, including physical conditions, through which they persist. Accordingly, individual persons are not simply inducted into a social world; they are inducted into a socio*historical* world.[44] Does the historicity of social actions threaten individual autonomy?

Individuals are inducted into the social forms and other social ideas of the past—including socially communicated theories, quasi-theories, and moral narratives. But these social forms and social ideas do not constitute a monolithic structure; rather they comprise a miscellany of sometimes competing conventions, norms, institutions, and socially conditioned theories and narratives. Moreover, the residue of the past consists in more than social forms and social ideas; it also contains the ideas, memories, and handed-down skills that derive from the individual—as opposed to collective—lives of past generations. For example, a mother might have had personal moral experiences particular to herself, which she might make known to her daughter but not to others. Or the unique ideas of a great philosopher might become known to future generations of thinkers.

And there is this further point. Individuals do not confront the residue of the social forms of the past as atoms; they confront it—or rather participate in it—*jointly*. It does not follow from this that any given generation of individuals can simply abandon these social forms; far from it. However, it does follow that these social forms are to a greater or lesser extent subject to change and in some instances rejection; and that they are often changed and rejected in accordance with more or less rational processes. At any rate, these processes of change do not involve actions other than the actions of individual human beings. Further, these processes consist in large part of the *joint* activity of individual actors.

An important corollary of this conception is that much joint activity takes place over an extended period of time, and specifically, *intergenerationally*. The building of the Great Wall of China and the development of the literary form of the novel are in each case *intergenerational joint* projects. More generally, most important institutions involve intergenerational joint projects. Consider universities or governments or hospitals.

The historicity of social action, and specifically of social forms, does not seem, at least in principle, to threaten individual autonomy, any more than the existence of present social action and social forms threatens it; social actions and social forms, whether residues of the past or newly arrived, are essentially manifestations of joint activity. As such, they do not constitute an in principle threat to autonomy. But here we need to take a closer look at the impact of past decisions on present ones.

In this connection, I want to draw attention to two constraints on practical reasoning in accordance with historically established social forms and, therefore, on the actions of autonomous moral agents.[45]

The first constraint on practical reasoning arises in relation to participation in long-term projects, including historically established institutional enterprises.

An agent living in a moral community[46] typically contributes to a variety of long-term projects that: (1) realize *collective*, and not simply individual, ends[47]; and (2) are historically established and *intergenerational* in character. Notable among such long-term projects are historically established institutional enterprises that realize not only individual ends, but more importantly, collective ends that are pursued (at least in part) because they are believed to be morally worthy ends; such ends include collective goods. Consider in this connection a school teacher, a doctor in a hospital, a police officer, or a worker in the clothes industry. And consider a taxpayer or a voter or a parent.

Michael Bratman has considered rationality in relation to long-term projects, albeit not *collective* long-term project, and, therefore, not *intergenerational* collective projects. Bratman has successfully argued in relation to the future-directed intentions involved in long-term projects, that it might be rational for an agent with such intentions not to reconsider one of those intentions, even though it might be rational to reconsider that intention, and indeed change it, from an all-things-considered external viewpoint.[48] The general point here is that finite agents that are long-term planners need to build in a degree of stability into their future-directed intentions or ends, if they are to achieve them; they need to focus on the means to the end, rather than constantly questioning the rationality or wisdom of the long-term end itself, or embarking on a different project that would realize a different end. So there is a presumption in favor of maintaining, rather than abandoning, long-term ends and projects.

In the light of Bratman's point, and given that *historically established* institutional enterprises are a species of long-term project, there is a presumption in favor of an agent who is participating in an historically established institutional enterprise not to abandon that enterprise.

However, there will be restrictions on the choices of participants in (intergenerational) institutional enterprises that might not exist, or exist to the same extent in individual, long-term projects. In the case of collective projects, the participation of any given agent is dependent of the participation of the other agents; so if the other agents abandon the project, then typically the given agent has no choice but also to abandon it. Moreover, in the case of institutional enterprises, in particular, usually a would-be participant necessarily embarks on the project after it is already in progress; she participates in a project that is at a stage, and in a condition, not of her own choosing. In addition, since an institutional project is a collective project, typically any given agent cannot determine the precise nature and direction of the project; for the agent is only one among a possibly very large number of contributors.

These above-mentioned general points seem to hold for intellectual institutions as well as other institutions. On the other hand, intellectual institutions need to allow greater individual freedom within them than is the case for some other institutions. On the institution of science it is worth quoting Michael Polanyi at length:

> The existing practice of scientific life embodies the claim that freedom is an efficient form of organisation. The opportunity granted to mature scientists to choose and pursue their own problems is supposed to result in the best utilisation of the joint efforts of all scientists in a common task. In other words: if the scientists of the world are viewed as a team setting out to explore the existing openings for discovery, it is assumed that their efforts will be efficiently coordinated if only each is left to follow his own inclinations. It is claimed in fact that there is no other efficient way of organising the team, and that any attempts to coordinate their efforts by directives of a superior authority would inevitably destroy the effectiveness of their cooperation. (1951, p. 34)

Prior to embarking on a long-term *individual* project, a *rational* individual agent will go through an intensive process of reason-based decision making and specifically a process that looks at the *individual* actions that she will be performing and the *individual* ends that she will realize. However, as we have seen above, once a single agent has decided to embark on such a project, the agent ought to have a presumption in favour of not abandoning it. This presumption in favor of continued participation in any such project or enterprise can be offset by rational and moral considerations, for example, the end or goal of the project can no longer be achieved, the end or goal of the project has come to be seen to be less important than some other ends that would be realized by other projects; but there is, nevertheless, a presumption to be offset.[49]

Moreover, for the same reasons as apply in the case of a *single*, rational agent, a given *set* of individual agents, once they have embarked on a long-term *collective* project ought to have a presumption in favor of not abandoning the project. Accordingly, each of the member agents of the set of agents ought to have a presumption *qua member of the set of agents participating in that collective project*, in favor of not abandoning the project. Thus, members of an historically established institutional enterprise, such as a legal system, ought to have a presumption against abandoning that institution. This presumption in favor of continued participation can be offset by rational, including moral, considerations; but there is, nevertheless, a presumption to be offset.[50]

The existence of this presumption amounts to a constraint on each agent's practical reasoning in relation to his or her continued participation in both long-term individual and long-term joint projects, including historically established institutional enterprises.

But notice that we have now identified two aspects of the presumption in favor of agents not abandoning long-term collective projects, including institutional enterprises. For the presumption is possessed by any given participating individual agent *qua individual agent performing individual actions in pursuit of individual ends*, albeit in the context of a collective enterprise; but it is also possessed by each participating individual agent *qua member of the set of agents participating in the collective enterprise.* The presumption against an individual agent—qua individual agent pursuing individual ends—abandoning the collective project, might be offset by some other consideration particular to her, for example, she has a personally rewarding individual project to pursue. However, it would not follow from this that the collective project ought to be abandoned; far from it. More specifically, it would not even follow from this that the individual agent in question ought to abandon the collective project. For qua member of the set of participating agents perhaps she ought *not* to abandon the collective project; perhaps she is making a valuable contribution to an important collective end. In that case the individual would find herself in a dilemma. There is no reason to think that she would not be able to resolve the dilemma; after all, she remains *one agent*, albeit one agent who functions as an agent performing actions in the service of individual ends, as well as an agent performing (sometimes the same) actions in the service of collective ends. Nevertheless, there may well be a dilemma to resolve.

This first constraint on an agent's practical reasoning does not threaten his or her individual autonomy. To be sure, individual autonomy is diminished if the range of historically established institutions that individuals can choose from is highly restricted. Consider a simple society without art, music, or any developed intellectual traditions or institutions. Moreover, agents who want to engage in long-term joint projects, including historically established institutions, will have to pay a price of sorts; they will not at all times be in possession of an all-things-considered good and decisive rational justification for their participation in any given project—indeed, from an all-things-considered external viewpoint it might be that they should abandon the project; they will be dependent on the contributions of others; they will have to join the institution when it is at a stage and in a condition not of their choosing; and any given individual cannot determine the nature and direction of an institutional enterprise. But for this price they receive the benefit of being able to complete and contribute to larger projects and thereby realize, and contribute to the realization of, much greater ends than would otherwise be the case.

Indeed, it is typically in the context of long-term joint enterprises, especially historically established institutional enterprises, that the greatest achievements are made. Consider the cathedrals built in Europe in the Middle Ages. Or consider the contribution of a notable scientist to the understanding of problems in (say) physics. Surely, when agents participate in such enterprises their autonomy is often thereby enhanced, rather than necessarily diminished. For, on the one hand, they may well achieve individual ends beyond what they would otherwise have been able to achieve, for example, the exercise of their creative ability as a craftsman or physicist; and on the other hand, they may well contribute to a collective end of enormous significance, for example, the construction of one of the highest expressions of collective aesthetic, moral, and spiritual value, namely a famous cathedral or a theoretical framework that illuminates a range of profound and long-standing intellectual questions in relation to the nature of the physical universe.

The second constraint on practical reasoning that I wish to draw attention to arises in connection with whole structures of historically established social norms. This constraint arises from the fact that any given agent's conformity to a given set of social norms is by definition to a considerable extent dependent on the conformity, and the moral attitudes, of the past and present others who conform, or conformed, to those social norms. Here it is important to stress that any given moral agent involved in diverse interactions with other moral agents conforms not simply to one or two social norms, but rather to a large and complex structure of social norms. Moreover, for finite creatures such as human beings, such a structure of social norms is necessarily in large part intergenerational in character; when it comes to the establishment of a complete, or near complete, structure of social norms governing individual and interpersonal actions, each new generation cannot simply begin anew.

Nevertheless, this conformity to an historically established structure of social norms might still seem to be an irrational addiction to the past and, therefore, a threat to individual autonomy. So it is important to get clear what exactly the constraints on autonomy are in this regard. Here a number of points need to be made.

First, a single rational agent (at least in theory) could reconsider with a view to revision, or even abandonment, *any one* of the moral principles s/he adheres to, while continuing to conform to the other principles.[51] However, she or he could not revise and abandon *all* or most of these principles *at the same time* on pain of losing her or his individual self-identity—moral identity being a necessary condition for the self-identity of most human beings.[52] The same point holds for a set of rational agents *jointly* reconsidering the moral principles that they adhere to as members of a moral community; in theory *any one* principle could be revised, and even abandoned, but not the totality simultaneously.

Second, a single, rational, human agent could *not—even over a significant period of time—individually* reconsider and revise, let alone abandon *all*, or even most, of the moral principles that he or she originally adhered to, on pain of not being able to continue to cooperatively interact with the fellow members of his or her moral community.

Third, the members of the moral community (at least in theory) could—over a significant period of time—*jointly* (rationally) reconsider, revise, and even abandon large fragments of the structure of moral principles that they adhere to.

In short, an historically established framework of social norms in a moral community operates as a (multifaceted) *constraint* on the practical reasoning of the rational members of that community. On the other hand, within that constraint, or those constraints, individuals, especially individuals acting jointly, are free to make significant changes over time to this historically established framework. Naturally, specific structures of social norms may well undermine individual autonomy—for example, structures of norms in slave societies.[53] However, it seems that there are other actual, or at least possible, societies in which the structures of social norms embody a high degree of individual freedom, egalitarianism, reflective rationality, and so on, and that in these societies at least, individual autonomy is alive and well. Accordingly, it seems reasonable to conclude that historically established frameworks of social norms are not *in principle* inconsistent with individual autonomy.

If it is still insisted that *any* historically established framework of social norms necessarily diminishes individual autonomy, then the following response is available. Given that individual human beings (1) have to be inducted into some structure of moral principles, and (2) desire to live in communities, and need, therefore, to conform to some structure of social norms, the only coherent notion of autonomy for human agents is one that takes an historically established framework of social norms as a background condition for their individual and interpersonal action. Such a framework of social norms is an enabling condition for the existence of an autonomous human moral agent seeking to engage in individual and interpersonal action; it is not necessarily a threat to it. Immanuel Kant uses the image of a bird to make this kind of point: "The light dove cleaving in free flight the thin air, whose resistance if feels, might imagine that her movements would be far more free and rapid in airless space" (1943, p. 6).[54] Just as air is necessary for birds to fly, so a structure of historically established social norms is necessary for autonomous human beings to live as human beings.

ACKNOWLEDGMENTS

Thanks to the editor, Fred Schmitt, and to Andrew Alexandra for helpful comments on this chapter.

NOTES

1. On this general issue see: Benn (1988, pp. 169, 179, 194–98, ch. 12); Dworkin (1988, ch. 10); Benson (1991); Christman (1991); Kekes (1989, pp. 111–12f); May (1996, p. 18f); Mackenzie (2001).
2. For a detailed recent account of individual autonomy see Mele (1995).

3. Naturally, hierarchical institutions with specific oppressive cultures are especially problematic. See May (1996, ch. 4).

4. I take it that the contractarian tradition in moral and political philosophy is in large part an attempt to deal with this in principle threat to individual autonomy posed by hierarchical structures, especially governments.

5. For an elaboration of this kind of point, see Mackenzie (2001).

6. John Kekes (1989, p. 112) argues for a balance between individuality and tradition. In this he is surely right.

7. Sometimes I use the terms *rational agent* and *moral agent* in contrast with *nonrational agent* and *nonmoral agent* (respectively); sometimes I use them in contrast with *irrational agent* and *immoral agent* (respectively). I trust the context will make clear which sense of rational agency and of moral agency is in play. Note also that the dividing line between moral agency and immoral agency, and between rational agency and irrational agency, is indeterminate.

8. By valid inferences I do not simply mean formally valid deductive and inductive inferences; rather I have in mind rationally valid inferences more broadly and informally understood.

9. Naturally, the use of these procedures involves specific social forms—for example, a deductive argument might be presented using the English language. Nonetheless, deduction per se is not a social construction. The objectivist view of rational/logical procedures has a long history. For a plausible objectivist account see Pap (1958).

10. Moreover, the process of reasoning for finite beings must stop somewhere. Indeed, rational, finite beings sometimes need to make judgments in relation to the time that ought to be spent on providing reasons for a given putative belief. In addition, there are generic sources for many beliefs which generate efficiencies in this regard. Consider the huge number of beliefs based on observation or memory or the testimony of others (or some combination of these). (On issues to do with testimony see Coady 1992.) Presumably, I have reasons to believe in the reliability of (say) my eyesight, or (say) my short-term memory, or the testimony of (say) my immediate friends and family in relation to a wide range of issues. Such reasons include the coherence of the beliefs received from these sources with my other beliefs, and the fact that intentions based on these beliefs are successful. Accordingly, I do not need to check each belief emanating from these sources on an individual basis. (These reasons will not assuage Cartesian skepticism; but they are not intended to do so.)

11. See Frankfurt (1971).

12. On the importance to autonomy of higher order attitudes see Frankfurt (1971), Dworkin (1988). For the elaboration of a view that stresses the moral evaluation of higher order attitudes see Taylor (1977).

13. So for the purposes of this chapter weakness of the will is a species of irrationality. Alfred Mele (1995) provides a detailed elaboration of weakness of the will and its relation to autonomy.

14. Perhaps it is indeterminate whether someone like Adolf Hitler was a nonmoral agent, or a grossly immoral agent. If he did not have the capacity to make correct moral judgements and act on them in a fairly wide range of morally significant situations, then perhaps he was a nonmoral agent. And if he was a nonmoral agent, and even one free to do what he did, it does not make sense to ascribe

moral responsibility to him. On the other hand, if he simply made a wide range of important false moral judgments (or refused, or otherwise failed, to act on his correct moral judgments) in relation to (say) Jews, then perhaps it is more accurate to describe him as a grossly immoral person. Grossly immoral persons can be ascribed *moral* responsibility.

15. See Taylor (1989).

16. As with rational agency and moral agency, autonomy admits of degrees. Moreover, an autonomous agent might be more autonomous in relation to one sphere of his or her life (e.g., his or her career) than another (e.g., relationship with his or her spouse). Andrew Alexandra reminded me of this latter point.

17. In this respect, the conditions for the ascription of autonomy appear to be different from the conditions for the ascription of moral responsibility for the outcomes of actions. For I can be held morally responsible for an outcome that was overdetermined in that I caused it (I provided a sufficient condition for its existence) simultaneously with someone else causing it (they also provided a sufficient condition for its existence).

18. This is the condition most stressed by theorists of autonomy. However, as noted by a number of theorists, autonomy cannot simply be equated with independence. See Dworkin (1988); Benn (1988, ch. 12). In relation to independence and other conditions—notably "internal" conditions—for intellectual and academic autonomy, see Miller (2000a).

19. See Stanley Benn (1988, chs. 8–11) for a comprehensive account of the conditions for autonomy, including regarding the absence of inner compulsions. Strictly speaking, an agent with an inner compulsion might be a rational moral agent on my account of the latter. This might be so if the compulsion—say, a compelling desire to avoid a painful state—was neither objectively immoral nor irrational in the light of the agent's other attitudes, and yet the compelling desire was induced by, for example, one's physiological addiction to drugs. On the other hand, this might not be so if autonomy is itself an objective moral principle that must be grasped and acted on—including in relation to the compulsive desire in question—if an agent is to be regarded as both moral and rational. Drug addicts whose lives are consumed by their "habit" are not rational moral agents, but so-called recreational users might be. The "addiction" of the latter might be both rational and moral and also sufficiently contained so as not to threaten their autonomy overall.

20. Stanley Benn (1988) argues against accounts of freedom and autonomy in terms of possibility. He opts for a theory in terms of eligibility/ineligibility according to which one is not free to x if the costs of doing so are higher than a rational person could reasonably be expected to pay. Suffice it to say here that in my view autonomy presupposes freedom, and that freedom (but not autonomy) can be largely accounted for in terms of possibility. That is—roughly speaking—you are free to x (but not necessarily autonomous) if you have the ability and opportunity to x, and there is nothing to prevent you from x-ing. Thus (perhaps contra Benn 1988, p. 138) if a robber demands your wallet at gunpoint, then you are still free not to give it to him, notwithstanding the costs of not doing so. Naturally, because he will shoot you dead if you do not hand the wallet over, and he will take the wallet over your dead body, you are not free to retain your wallet. So the person who was robbed was free not to hand over their wallet, but his or her autonomy has been diminished irrespective of

whether he or she handed it over or was killed after he or she failed to do so. Further, the freedom of the bank robber is compromised by the existence of an effective criminal justice system. Perhaps he or she is free to commit one act of robbery. However, he or she is not free to commit many such acts. For once caught, convicted, and imprisoned, he or she will not be free to commit these further planned robberies. In my view freedom is necessary for autonomy, so a rational moral agent who is imprisoned has diminished autonomy.

21. Nagel (1986, pp. 113–20). See also Williams (1995b).

22. Nagel (1986, p. 116).

23. It is not entirely clear to me why this is a problem in cases where a rational agent has a good and decisive reason to perform an action and has *no reasons* whatsoever to perform the only alternative action. Here I am thinking of a situation in which I have a good and decisive reason to *x*, and the only alternative is to refrain from *x*-ing. But perhaps I have misunderstood Nagel.

24. Miller (2001a).

25. I use the term *interpersonal* for cases in which two or more agents actually perform distinct, but interdependent actions; or, more precisely, for cases in which one agent performs an action with the intention that the other agent (or other agents) perform a second action by way of response (Miller 2001a, p. 5.) Actions that are not interpersonal are individual actions.

26. Broad (1928, p. 328).

27. Here I am assuming that the notion of a social action is, at least in part, ostensively defined, and I offer accounts (Miller 2001a) of the various categories of social action thus defined.

28. Thanks to Andrew Alexandra for reminding me of this point.

29. Miller (2001a, chs. 3, 4).

30. Miller (2001a, ch. 2).

31. Miller (2001a, ch. 4).

32. I do not mean to imply that a choice between conventions is necessarily an arbitrary choice. Sometimes such collective choices are arbitrary, but this is by no means necessarily the case. See Miller (2001a, ch. 3). Nor do I mean to imply that rational choices always result from explicit—as opposed to implicit—processes of reasoning.

33. See Stanley Benn (1988, ch. 12) for a taxonomy of social groups in relation to degrees of social control.

34. Naturally, if nonconformity to social norms is such that the very existence of a moral community is called into question, then it might no longer be possible to function as a moral agent and, therefore, as an autonomous moral agent. In this respect individual autonomy, at least for social beings, is dependent on general conformity to central moral principles. See the last section of this chapter.

35. Perhaps it is something like what those of a Kantian persuasion have in mind when they speak of rational, moral agents.

36. Perhaps there are desires for approval (and to avoid disapproval) that are possessed, irrespective of whether or not the approval (or disapproval) is justified. (In my view, these would not be desires for *moral* dis/approval.) If so, and if the desire of the agent in our scenario were this kind of desire, then the realization of this agent's desire would not be affected by his belief that he had done wrong; for such

a desire is realized if, and only if, the agent is approved of by others. If the agent in our scenario had this kind of desire then it may well be rational for him to take the bribes on offer. For he would not have a conflict between taking the bribes and acting on his desire to be approved of. (There would still be a conflict with his belief not to do wrong, but that was outweighed, in our scenario, by other considerations.) On the other hand, if the agent in our scenario had a genuine desire for *moral* approval (and to avoid moral disapproval) then there would be a conflict between this desire and his taking the bribes. For this desire could not be adequately and fully realized, if he takes the bribes. Rather his taking of the bribes would sour the enjoyment he used to experience as a result of the moral approval of others. Accordingly, it may well be rational for him to refuse the bribes.

37. See Rom Harre (1979, pp. 37–43) for an account of structure. See also Miller (2001a, ch. 5).

38. Language does not in this way depend on collective acceptance. For an account of the dependence of language on "collective acceptance," and specifically on conventions, see Miller (2000c).

39. Searle (1995, p. 91).

40. Thanks to the editor for reminding me of this latter point.

41. See, for example Pettit (1990b). There is a tendency not to distinguish social approval in the generic sense from moral approval.

42. See Miller (2001a, pp. 130–38).

43. Status is of course often reinforced by institutional power and wealth, for example, the status of whites by the government in apartheid South Africa and the status of sports and pop stars by large media corporations in contemporary Australia.

44. Miller (2001a, Intro).

45. Miller (2001a, pp.151–59).

46. My use of the term *moral community* in this chapter is in contrast with non-moral community, as opposed to immoral community.

47. Roughly speaking, a collective end is an individual end more than one agent has, and that is such that, if it is realized, it is realized by all, or most, of the actions of the individuals involved (Miller 2001a, p. 57).

48. Bratman (1987, ch. 6). The notion of an all-things-considered external viewpoint is by no means unproblematic, even when we are speaking of a single agent at a particular time and in respect of a specific future project. When we consider collective projects then we have multiple agents, and therefore multiple all-things-considered external viewpoints; and when we consider intergenerational collective projects, then we have multiples of multiple agents and external viewpoints. Moreover, with such projects we have multiple agents, both at a given time, and over intergenerational time, all of whom are engaged in interdependent decision making with at least some of the other agents. Accordingly, we have multiple all-things-considered external viewpoints, each of which has to take into consideration the things being taken into consideration by the other external viewpoints. At this point, we start to lose our grip on the notion of an all-things-considered external viewpoint. At any rate, for my purposes here all I need to do is gesture at the intuitive and vague *idea* of an all or most or many-things-considered external viewpoint.

49. So from time to time during the course of a long-term project a rational agent will engage in a reconsideration of the project and his or her participation in the proj-

ect. At such reconsiderations one of the questions raised would be whether or not the presumption in favor of not abandoning the project has been offset. Such reconsiderations ought to be relatively infrequent, given the costs they incur.

50. And, of course, the institution, over time, can be transformed in sometimes very significant ways, if that is desirable.

51. I say "in theory" because I am assuming that the consistent infringement of one moral principle might not necessarily impact on an agent's capacity to comply with other moral principles. But this is doubtful, at least in relation to many moral principles—for example, refraining from killing people.

52. So I take it that if a functioning human person was able to abandon all their moral principles today, then tomorrow they would no longer be a functioning human being; moral principles are central to a moral agent's identity, and like the planks on Aristotle's ship, they cannot be replaced all at once. Naturally, a person could move from one moral community to another, and there could be important differences between the two communities. However, if the differences between the two communities are too profound then the person may not be able to make the switch. On the other hand, if the switch was gradual—given a good deal of overlap between possible human moral communities—then a switch might be relatively painless.

53. For many people in such "moral" (i.e., immoral) communities, individual autonomy may well be impossible.

54. This point is not undermined by Robinson Crusoe scenarios. The point about Robinson Crusoe is that he continued to desire social interaction (e.g., with Man Friday or with his former society), and he continued to rely on social forms (e.g., language) and social activities (e.g., reading) in order to maintain his existence.

11

Social Construction: The "Debunking" Project

Sally Haslanger

INTRODUCTION

The term *social construction* has become a commonplace in the humanities. Its shock value having waned and its uses multiplied, the metaphor of construction has, as Ian Hacking puts it, "become tired" (Hacking 1999, p. 35). Moreover, the variety of different uses of the term has made it increasingly difficult to determine what claim authors are using it to assert or deny and whether the parties to the debates really disagree.

In his book *The Social Construction of What?*, Hacking offers a schema for understanding different social constructionist claims along with a framework for distinguishing kinds or degrees of constructionist projects. Hacking's efforts are useful, but his account leaves many of the philosophical aspects of social construction projects obscure, as are the connections, if any, with more mainstream analytic philosophy projects. My goal in this chapter is to argue that although Hacking's approach to social construction is apt for some of those working on such projects, it does not adequately capture what's at issue for an important range of social constructionists, particularly many of us working on gender and race. Moreover, a different way of understanding social construction reveals interesting connections and conflicts with mainstream analytic projects.

I agree with Hacking that it isn't useful to try to determine what social construction "really is" because it is many different things, and the discourse of social construction functions differently in different contexts. So instead I focus on a particular kind of social constructionist project, one I call a "debunking project," to consider how exactly it is supposed to work, how it differs from other constructionist projects, and what, if any, meta-physical implications it has.

Given the multiple uses of the term "social construction," one might won-der why it matters whether this or that project is properly characterized as a form of social constructionism. And of course, in the abstract it matters very little. But in the current academic context, the classification of some view as social constructionist can mean that it is not worth taking seriously or, alter-natively, that it is one of the views to be taken seriously. Insofar as the label carries such weight, it is useful to differentiate some of the various construc-tionist projects so that their intellectual affiliations and incompatibilities can be clarified.

HACKING ON SOCIAL CONSTRUCTION

Hacking suggests that in order to understand social construction, we should ask first: What is the point of claiming that something is socially constructed? He offers this schema for understanding the basic project:

> Social construction work is critical of the status quo. Social constructionists about X tend to hold that:
> (1) X need not have existed, or need not be at all as it is. X, or X as it is at pres-ent, is not determined by the nature of things; it is not inevitable.
> They often go further, and urge that:
> (2) X is quite bad as it is.
> (3) We would be much better off if X were done away with, or at least radically transformed. (Hacking 1999, p. 6)

In order for a claim of social construction to have a point, however, there is a precondition to be satisfied: "(0) In the present state of affairs, X is taken for granted, X appears to be inevitable" (Hacking 1999, p. 12).

In this schema, X can range over very disparate kinds of things, includ-ing ideas, concepts, classifications, events, objects, persons. Allegedly so-cially constructed things include: child abusers, the self, quarks, the con-cept of the economy, the classification "woman refugee." Especially important to Hacking is the distinction between constructing *ideas* (which includes concepts, categories, classifications, etc.) and constructing *ob-jects* (e.g., Hacking 1999, pp.10–11, 14, 21–22, 28–30, 102, etc.). (Note that Hacking's understanding of "objects" is broad and includes: people, states, conditions, practices, actions, behavior, classes, experiences, rela-tions, material objects, substances [i.e., stuffs], unobservables, and funda-mental particles (Hacking 1999, p. 22).) Although X in the schema above ranges over both ideas and objects, he urges us to be clear which we are talking about in order to avoid confusion.

Condition (0), on Hacking's account, is a necessary condition for a work to be considered "social constructionist" at all. Cases that don't appear to satisfy (0), for example, the "invention" of Japan (Hacking 1999, pp. 12–13) and the construction of "obvious" social kinds, don't qualify as genuine social constructionist projects. Hacking offers a framework for classifying the variety of constructionist views (given (0)), with respect to their acceptance of claims (1)–(3):

> *Historical constructionist:* Contrary to what is usually believed, X is the contingent result of historical events and forces, therefore (1): X need not have existed, is not determined by the nature of things, etc.
>
> *Ironic constructionist:* Historical constructionism PLUS: at this stage we cannot help but treat X as "part of the universe," but our way of thinking may evolve so that X is no longer viewed in this way.
>
> *Reformist constructionist:* Historical constructionism PLUS (2): X is quite bad as it is. Although we cannot at this stage see how to avoid X, we should try to improve it.
>
> *Unmasking constructionist:* Historical constructionism PLUS if we understand the function of X socially, we will see that it should have no appeal for or authority over us.
>
> *Rebellious constructionist:* Historical constructionism PLUS (2): X is quite bad as it is. And (3), we would be much better off if X were done away with or radically transformed.
>
> *Revolutionary constructionist:* Historical constructionism PLUS (2): X is quite bad as it is. And (3), we would be much better off if X were done away with or radically transformed. In addition, the revolutionary constructionist acts to do away with X. (Hacking 1999, pp. 19–20)

It is important to note that it is common to all of Hacking's constructionists that they use a claim about the contingent causes or historical source of the phenomenon X to support the idea that X need not have existed or need not have been "at all as it is." He says explicitly, for example, that "construction stories are histories" (Hacking 1999, p. 37; also p. 48); and the point, as he sees it, is to argue for the contingency or alterability of the phenomenon by noting its social or historical origins. So, if one were to argue, on Hacking's account, that the idea of refugee were socially constructed, then the point would be that the idea of refugee is the result of historical events, that we might have lacked that idea and have had other ideas instead.

Idea-Construction

In keeping with Hacking's account, let's distinguish the "idea-constructionist" project and the "object-constructionist" project, and focus for the time being on idea-constructionist projects. Given the account so far, it isn't clear how any idea-constructionist project should be able to get off the

ground, for it seems implausible that they satisfy condition (0). *Of course*
what concepts and so what ideas we have is the result of social-historical
events; who is in the business of denying that? (Hacking seems to agree—
1999, p. 69.) It would seem to be a matter of common sense that concepts
are taught to us by our parents through our language; different cultures have
different concepts (that go along with their different languages); and concepts evolve over time as a result of historical changes, science, technologi-
cal advances, and so on.[1] Let's (albeit contentiously) call this the "ordinary
view" of concepts and ideas.[2] Moving to more theoretical domains, even the
most arch realist who believes that our concepts map "nature's joints" allows
that groups come to have the concepts they do through social-historical
processes. So what could possibly be the excitement in claiming that any
particular concept emerges as a result of historical events and forces? If
Hacking feels free to deny that a book such as *Inventing Japan* is a social
constructionist project because it is too obvious that Japan is a social entity
and so condition (0) is not satisfied (Hacking 1999, p. 13), why should we
not similarly rule out all attempts to reveal the historical origins of a particular idea or concept, that is, all purportedly idea-constructionist projects?

To answer this we need to elaborate Hacking's account further. Let's begin by considering what, on Hacking's view, is supposed to be controversial
or interesting in the claim that some idea or other is constructed Hacking
identifies three "sticking points"—presumably implicit in (1) or in the inference to (1)—that arise in debates between constructionists and noncon-
structionists. (Although his discussion of these sticking points focuses on
constructionist debates concerning natural science, it appears at various
points he intends them to be characteristic of constructionist debates more
generally, so I'll articulate them in more general terms.)

On his account, constructionists with respect to a domain *D*, for example,
the natural world, mental illness, rocks, are sympathetic to (a) the contingency of our understanding of *D*; (b) nominalism about kinds in *D*, or more
precisely, a denial that the domain *D* has an inherent structure; and (c) an explanation of the stability of our understanding of *D* in external rather than internal terms. Letting the domain be the natural world, the constructionist
claims (or tends to claim) that a scientific theory different from current scientific theory might nonetheless have emerged and been as successful in its
own terms as ours is in our terms (Hacking 1999, pp. 68–80); that the natural world does not have an "inherent structure" (Hacking 1999, pp. 80–4);
and that the best explanation of the stable elements of current scientific theory relies on factors external to science, for example, the educational system
that instills in aspiring scientists the practices and the background assumptions that give rise to the dominant theory (Hacking 1999, pp. 84–95). So on
Hacking's view the idea-constructionist thesis is not simply that our ideas
have a history, or that what concepts we have is influenced by social forces.

Rather, the idea-constructionist holds a cluster of theses opposing what is taken to be a standard explanation of the origins of our ideas or theories and why we retain them. (Henceforward I'll use the term *idea-constructionism* for this cluster of theses, not just the simpler claim that our ideas are the contingent result of social/historical events and forces.)

Let's take a moment to spell out the idea-constructionists' adversary a bit further. The question on which the debate hinges seems to be: are the origin and stability of our ideas/classifications determined by "how the world is," more specifically, by the domain they purport to describe? As Hacking sees it, the constructionist says "no," and the adversary says "yes." But the suggestion that the domain of inquiry "determines" our classifications of it is a bit puzzling. Hacking clearly states that the kind of determination at issue is causal determination: the nonconstructionist maintains that the domain D has an inherent structure, that our understanding of D is in some sense inevitable because the inherent structure of D causally determines how to understand it, and that our understanding of D is stable because the stable structure of the world sustains it. Hacking's idea-constructionist claims, in contrast, that the results of our inquiry into D "are not predetermined," in particular that they are "not determined by how the world is" (Hacking 1999, p. 73), and that we remain stably committed to the results, not because the content of our theories supports them, but due to social and psychological forces at work. Hacking explicitly claims that the constructionist's point is "not a logical one" (Hacking 1999, p. 73) and emphasizes later that the real issue for constructionists is not semantics, but the dynamics of classification (Hacking 1999, p. 123). Although there is a metaphysical issue lurking behind the debate, viz., whether the world has an inherent structure, this is at issue only because the nonconstructionist invokes such a structure in explaining the origins and stability of our beliefs.

Let's call the constructionist's adversary Hacking has described a "world-idea determinist" to contrast it with Hacking's idea-constructionist who is trying to show that the results of our inquiry into D are not only not determined by the inherent structure of the world, but in fact "are not determined by anything" (Hacking 1999, p. 73). Within a debate between these opposing sides, it might seem interesting to claim that some idea of ours has social-historical origins, for the alternative seems to be that the world's inherent structure, by itself, determines what ideas we use to describe it. There may well be, as Hacking strives to show, some scientists who maintain something as extreme as world-idea determinism, so the point is worth making. But casting social constructionism in general in these terms has several serious drawbacks:

First, the target world-idea determinism is not plausible on its face, and one does not need anything as strong as idea-constructionism to defeat it. To claim that our ideas and the classifications we use to frame them (pick any domain you want) are not in any way influenced by social conditions but are inevitable and stable because they map the relevant domain's inherent structure rules out even a minimal fallibilism.[3] Surely even good scientific method requires one to allow that new data may defeat one's best theory, and conceptual innovation will be called for; certainly ordinary nonscientists, philosophers and the like don't take themselves to be infallible about any domain except perhaps the contents of their own consciousness and simple arithmetic.

Second, although the claim that our ideas are conditioned by social and historical events is plausible, Hacking has expanded idea-constructionism into something quite implausible. In the end, idea-constructionism rejects normative epistemology altogether and opts instead for sociology: reasons for belief are replaced by causes, justifications with explanations, semantics with dynamics (Hacking 1999, pp. 90–2, 121–24). It's one thing to acknowledge that the causal routes responsible for our way of thinking travel through and are influenced by the contours of our contingent social structures; it's another thing to entirely replace questions of justification with questions of causation. Although some social constructionists take this line, it is a quite radical position that hardly seems supported by the core idea-constructionist observation that our ideas are the product of social and historical forces.[4]

Third, the world-idea determinist position Hacking describes as the target of social constructionists is not a common view in philosophy and is not the sort of thing that is likely to be accepted by anyone who accepts what I've claimed is an ordinary view about ideas and concepts, namely that what ones we have are conditioned by our culture. If world-idea determinism is the social constructionists' target, it isn't surprising that philosophers in general and metaphysicians in particular have paid little attention to the social constructionist literature. But more important, Hacking's constructionist doesn't have much to say to the nonspecialist or nonacademic, for it rejects the "ordinary view" of concepts. This is a problem, for as Hacking himself claims, "most people who use the social construction ideas enthusiastically want to criticize, change, or destroy some X that they dislike in the established order of things" (Hacking 1999, p. 7). We constructionists are, on the whole, a politically motivated bunch. But what a waste of breath and ink it would be if our target is a view that most people would find quite bizarre.

Determinism??

If world-idea determinism is not a worthy target of the social constructionist, then is there something nearby that we should be considering? There are three separate issues concerning the relationship between our classifications and the world that lie in the background of Hacking's discussion: (1) what *causes* us to use certain classifications/concepts, (2) by virtue of what is a concept or classification *apt*, and (3) what, if anything, *justifies* our use of one classification scheme as opposed to another? If one is primarily interested in the origins of our ideas, then the debate between Hacking's idea-constructionist and the world-idea determinist seems to represent two ends of a spectrum of possible views. Plausibly our ideas and classifications are the product of some combination of worldly input from perception and experience and social input from language, practices, and the like. The debate as presented by Hacking is not very interesting because neither extreme view is plausible and very little is offered to cover the more interesting middle-ground.

However, if, for example, one is interested in what makes a particular scheme apt, then the issues look quite different. In a telling passage, Hacking describes the constructionist's nominalism as follows:

> If contingency is the first sticking point [between the constructionist and the non-constructionist], the second one is more metaphysical. Constructionists tend to maintain that classifications are not determined by how the world is, but are convenient ways in which to represent it. They maintain that the world does not come quietly wrapped up in facts. Facts are the consequences of the ways in which we represent the world. The constructionist vision here is splendidly old-fashioned. It is a species of nominalism. It is countered by a strong sense that the world has an inherent structure that we discover. (Hacking 1999, p. 33)

Here, as mentioned before, the broad background question seems to be: are our classifications determined by how the world is or not? If the question is, what causes us to have the classifications we do, then we have simply returned to the old world-idea determinist question: are we caused to have the classification scheme we have by the structure of the world itself? And we can agree that social-historical factors play a role. But nominalism and its adversaries aren't about what causes our classifications but what determines their correctness or aptness. The question is: is the aptness (correctness, fittingness) of our classifications determined by the structure of the world, or is their aptness determined by our choice? In other words, which way does the direction of fit run: are our classifications apt because they fit the world, or are they apt because the world fits them? In either case, aptness is not a matter of causal determination. The "inherent structurist" (Hacking's substitute term for *realist* in the debate with the "nominalist") doesn't think that the world *causes* our classifications to be apt, neither does the nominalist think that our acts of classifying *cause* the world to have a structure. If the idea-constructionist and the inherent structurist are going to have a debate about nominalism, questions about the causal origins of our beliefs aren't really relevant.

If any part of the idea-constructionist project were to have metaphysical implications, one would expect them to show up in the constructionist's commitment to nominalism. But on Hacking's account there is no basis in the constructionist arguments for denying that the domain of our inquiry, whatever it may be, has an inherent structure. The main constructionist premise is that our concepts and ideas are the product of historical forces and could have been different. As suggested above, this is entirely consistent with the most arch realism, or "inherent structurism" about kinds (as Hacking would seem to agree—1999, p. 80). We're left, then, with nothing of metaphysical interest in the idea-constructionist project (assuming that a bald denial of a metaphysical thesis is not metaphysically interesting).

A third question in this general area (in addition to what causes us to use certain classifications and what makes them apt) is what justifies our use of the classifications we've chosen. This issue seems to lie in the background behind Hacking's "third sticking point" between the idea-constructionist and the world-idea determinist. This sticking point, as characterized by Hacking, concerns the causes of the stability of our ideas, or the results of our inquiry. Why, for example, do Maxwell's Equations or the Second Law of Thermodynamics remain stably entrenched in our physics (Hacking 1999, p. 86)? Why do we continue to use the periodic table of the elements in our chemistry? The idea-constructionist maintains that this stability is due entirely to "external factors." Hacking is frustratingly unclear where he intends to draw the line between "internal" and "external" factors, but the discussion as a whole suggests that the world-idea determinist is supposed to think that the inherent structure of our domain of inquiry is somehow causally responsible, ruling out the influence of ordinary human interests, contingent facts about the point of our inquiry, or what technology we have available to test our hypotheses.[5]

But the problem is that again the issue has been framed in causal terms for the benefit of Hacking's constructionist. It should be obvious that the results of any inquiry are at least partly conditioned by the circumstances of inquiry, the kind of technology that is available to the inquirer, the attitudes'and biases of the inquirers, and the like, and should the circumstances, technology, resources, and so on change, this is likely to influence what conclusions we draw. Again, one need not be a social constructionist to grant this. It may be that there are scientists who believe that natural laws are "facts we run up against"(Hacking 1999, p. 86) as if their effect is then to write themselves in our notebooks. But again, if this is the constructionist target, it is hard to understand why it should be interesting to philosophers or the general public.

A nearby question that the constructionist rhetoric often seems to be addressing is: what justifies us in our ongoing commitment to a theory, classification scheme, and so on. This isn't, or isn't obviously, a causal question. Many different factors contribute to the justification of a theory, including coherence, supporting evidence, simplicity, fruitfulness, and so on. These are sometimes called "constitutive values" of inquiry. Feminists have also argued that contextual values are relevant to justification, for example, whether the question motivating the theory is legitimate, whether the methods allow for certain evidence to emerge, whether the community of researchers exhibits a certain diversity (Longino 1980; Anderson 1995). With the distinction between "constitutive" and "contextual" values in mind, it is possible to identify several views that seem to be floating around in the discussion. One extreme view is that nothing *justifies* our use of a particular classification scheme; the best we can do is *explain* why we use this or that classification scheme by doing sociology, or Foucauldian genealogy, perhaps. An opposing extreme view is that the world itself—its inherent structure—justifies us: because our ideas are caused by the inherent structure of the world, they're justified. But the more philosophically interesting options concern what norms—contextual, constitutive, or some combination of both—are the basis for justification. But this last set of options aren't seriously considered in the discussion.

Unfortunately, the debate Hacking has described between the social constructionist and the world-idea determinist seems to frame it either as entirely concerned with the causes of the stability of our ideas, or as a debate between the two most radical and implausible of the views regarding justification. So again his idea constructionist seems to be of little interest to the philosopher or anyone but a few radicals in the science wars.

CONSTRUCTED OBJECTS

Having devoted considerable attention to Hacking's account of the idea-constructionist project, we should now turn to consider object-construction. Hacking's work on the social dynamics that produce certain kinds of people is important; his historically nuanced discussion of social categorization in, for example, the "helping professions," provides rich resources for thinking about how the social world comes to be as it is (Hacking 1986, 1991, 1992, 1995b, 1999). This work finds a place in his discussion of social construction under the rubric of "object construction." Moreover, object constructionism has, I believe, more to offer the metaphysician than we found in the idea-constructionist project.

According to Hacking's account of object-construction, some objects, in particular some objects that we might not expect to be, are the product of social-historical forces. What are some examples? Possibly the self (Hacking 1999, pp. 14–16); more plausibly, on Hacking's view, people *of certain kinds*. What kinds? Women refugees, child viewers of television, child abusers, schizophrenics. The key to understanding this claim is what Hacking calls *interactive kinds* (Hacking 1999, pp. 32, 102–105).

> The "woman refugee" [as a kind of classification] can be called an "interactive kind" because it interacts with things of that kind, namely people, including

individual women refugees, who can become aware of how they are classified and modify their behavior accordingly."(Hacking 1999, p. 32)

The classification "quark," in contrast, is an *indifferent kind*: "Quarks are not aware that they are quarks and are not altered simply by being classified as quarks" (Hacking 1999, p. 32). As Hacking elaborates the idea of an interactive kind it becomes clear that the interaction he has in mind happens through the awareness of the thing classified, though is typically mediated by the "larger matrix of institutions and practices surrounding this classification" (Hacking 1999, p. 103; also pp. 31–2, 103–106).

So, for example, the idea or classification "woman refugee" is a socially constructed idea (along the lines we considered in the previous sections); but this classification occurs within a matrix of social institutions that has a significant effect on individuals. Thus, Hacking argues, the individuals so-affected are themselves socially constructed "as a certain kind of person" (Hacking 1999, p. 11). For example, if a particular woman is not classified as a woman refugee,

> she may be deported, or go into hiding, or marry to gain citizenship. . . . She needs to become a woman refugee in order to stay in Canada; she learns what characteristics to establish, knows how to live her life. By living that life, she evolves, becomes a certain kind of person [a woman refugee]. And so it may make sense to say that the very individuals and their experiences are constructed within the matrix surrounding the classification "women refugees." (Hacking 1999, p. 11)

To understand Hacking's view of "object construction," the first point to note is that our classificatory schemes, at least in social contexts, may do more than just map preexisting groups of individuals; rather our attributions have the power to both establish and reinforce groupings that may eventually come to "fit" the classifications. In an earlier essay, drawing on Hacking's work, I referred to this as "discursive" construction:[6]

> *discursive construction:* something is discursively constructed just in case it is (to a significant extent) the way it is because of what is attributed to it or how it is classified (Haslanger 1995, p. 99).

Admittedly, the idea here is quite vague (e.g., how much is "a significant extent"?). However, social construction in this sense is ubiquitous. Each of us is socially constructed in this sense because we are (to a significant extent) the individuals we are today as a result of what has been attributed (and self-attributed) to us. For example, being classified as an able-bodied female from birth has profoundly affected the paths available to me in life and the sort of person I have become.

Note, however, that to say that an entity is "discursively constructed" is not to say that language or discourse brings a material object into existence de novo. Rather something in existence comes to have—partly as a result of having been categorized in a certain way—a set of features that qualify it as a member of a certain kind or sort. My having been categorized as a female at birth (and consistently since then) has been a factor in how I've been viewed and treated; these views and treatments have, in turn, played an important causal role in my becoming gendered a woman. Having been categorized as a "widow," Christiana was forced to endure harsh rituals that disrupted her family (her children were hired out as servants) and caused her to become seriously ill.[7] Widows in many parts of the developing world are denied basic human rights, for example, they are often stripped of property, subjected to violence, and face systematic discrimination in custom and law. In a context where widowhood is associated with certain material and social conditions that are imposed after the death of one's husband, it is plausible to say that widows constitute a social group or kind, and that one's being a widow, that is, being a member of that social kind or sort, is a result of social forces: Christiana's being a widow (in a sense that entails suffering the social and material deprivations), is a result of her having been categorized as a widow in a matrix where that categorization carries substantial weight.

One might resist this description of things on several counts. To begin, one might object that Christiana's fate was caused not by being *categorized* as a widow but by her husband's death. Admittedly, it is misleading to say that it was the *categorization* alone that made her a widow; but likewise it is misleading to suggest that it was the death alone. (Note that if the husband didn't actually die, but is thought to have died, the effects of being categorized as a widow might be the same as if he actually died.) The cause of her misfortune was his death in a social matrix where the death, or presumed death, of one's husband signals, at least ordinarily, a debilitating change in social status. Can we be clearer on both the source and the product of the construction?

Hacking is especially interested in a certain kind of object construction, namely, construction works by the social context providing *concepts* that frame the *self-understanding* and *intentions* of the constructed agent. In cases like this, agents incorporate (often consciously) socially available classifications into their intentional agency and sense of self; but as their self-understanding evolves, the meaning of those classifications evolves with them. This forms a "feedback loop" (hence the term: *interactive kinds*) between what we might think of as objective and subjective stances with respect to the classification. Hacking's paradigm examples concern the labeling of various mental illnesses: multiple personality disorder, autism, and posttraumatic stress disorder. Individuals are diagnosed with such illnesses; treatment plans are developed; their self-understanding is modified. In some cases groups of those diagnosed develop support groups, communities, and political movements. As their self-understanding and behavior changes, however, the diagnosis and patient profile must evolve to take this into account.

To emphasize the importance of the agent's active awareness in this process, we might call this "discursive *identity* construction." This is a construction of *kinds* of people because (at least according to Hacking) people fall into certain kinds depending on their identities, where "identity" is understood as a psychological notion intended to capture one's self-understanding and the intentional framework employed in action. Through being categorized as a widow, Christiana comes to think of herself as a widow, to act as a widow, to live as a widow, that is, she becomes a certain kind of person. Hacking would have us say that she has been constructed "as a widow." We might unpack this as: her self-understanding as a widow (and pattern of her actions conforming to this understanding) is the result of having been classified as a widow. No doubt this is an important claim: that certain identities and ways of life come into existence and evolve in response to social and theoretical categorization (especially categorization that emerges in psychology and social work) has important social and political implications (Hacking 1995, esp. chs. 14–15). But at the same time it isn't entirely surprising that how people think about themselves is influenced by what vocabularies they are given. Is there something more behind the idea of object construction?

Reflecting on Christiana's widowhood reveals that Hacking's emphasis on the construction of "identities" is overly narrow in several respects. Note first that the notion of *kind* in philosophy has several different uses. On one use it is meant to capture a classification of things by essence: things fall into kinds based on their essence, and each thing falls only into one kind. On this view, horses constitute a kind because they share an equine essence, but red things don't constitute a kind because apples, t-shirts, and sunsets don't share an essence. However, on a more common use, the term *kind* is used as equivalent to "type" or "sort" or "grouping." So far I've been using the term kind in the latter sense and will continue to do so. Of course, there are many ways to sort people into groups. One way is in terms of their (psychological) "identity." Other ways include: by appearance, ancestry, religion, neighborhood, income, nationality, parental status, even by insurance carrier or long distance phone service. If we are exploring the ways in which categorization can have an impact on what sort of person we are, then its impact on our "identities" is one thing to look at. But if we are concerned with the ways in which categorization can cause or perpetuate injustice, then it will be useful to look at effects that aren't necessarily internalized in the way that Hacking suggests, that is, effects of classifications that aren't used to frame our intentions and don't come to be part of our self-understandings. In moving away from an emphasis on the psychological we are also in a position to rethink the sources of construction and to expand them beyond a narrow range of "discourse" that focuses on concepts and language to other aspects of the social matrix.

Christiana's husband dies. The death, at some level, is a biological event. That it was Christiana's *husband* who died, is, of course, a social matter, for marriage is a social institution. What about Christiana's becoming a widow? This is more complicated still, for the meaning of "widowhood" varies across social groups. Social constructionists interested in the impact of categorization on individuals are usually interested not only in the nominal classification "widow" or "wife" (etc.), but also in the system or matrix of practices and institutions that create "thick" or "robust" social positions, that is, social positions that entail a broad range of norms, expectations, obligations, entitlements, and so on. It is one thing to have one's husband die; it is another thing to be socially positioned as a "widow" in a community where widowhood is a subordinated status.

The distinction between "thick" and "thin" social positions I'm relying on deserves more attention than I can devote to it here. However, the basic idea is that some social positions carry with them more demanding norms, expectations, and obligations than others; some carry more privileging entitlements and opportunities than others. "Thin" social positions carry very little social weight. "Thick" social positions can empower or disempower the groups standing in those positions. Being a widow in the contemporary United States is a much thinner social position than being a widow in, say, the region where Christiana lives.

Given the norms and expectations that constitute the position of widow in some contexts, women who lose their husbands are disempowered. Typically in contexts where a group is systematically mistreated, there are explanations and rationalizations of the mistreatment. For example, in some traditions, because a widow has special connection to the deceased she is considered unclean and must go into ritual seclusion. She may not touch herself, even to bathe or feed herself. She relies on older widows to care for her. Initially she may be given no clothes or only "rags"; eventually she must wear special clothes of mourning. If she refuses (as some Christians do) to participate in the rituals, she is, in effect, "excommunicated" from the village: the villagers are prohibited from communicating with her or engaging in any commerce with her (Korieh 1996, chs. 2, 3).

Needless to say, someone whose belongings are taken from her, is dressed in rags, and is denied the opportunity to bathe and feed herself will likely appear "unclean." In this case, the widow's supposed metaphysical uncleanliness is the justification for the rituals that result in her physical uncleanliness and social alienation (she may not touch herself, even to bathe, *because* she is unclean). Although her eventual condition may itself seem evidence for the rightness of the treatment, of course it is simply evidence for its effectiveness.

In such contexts the social constructionist is concerned to argue that the thick social position of "widow," is not naturally or metaphysically justified, that her appearance is not evidence of the rightness of the rituals, that the practices structured apparently as a response to the condition of "widow-hood" actually create the condition. (On this sort of self-fulfilling ideology more generally, see Geuss 1981, pp. 14–15.) Although there may be independent social reasons, to maintain rituals in spite of false natural or metaphysical assumptions underlying them, usually the social constructionist's point is to argue that the rituals or practices in question are unjust and should not be maintained in their current form and that the supposed metaphysical or natural justification for them is misguided.

This example of widowhood is intended to show that there is something wrong with seeing object construction as a process that primarily works with and on ideas. On Hacking's account, object construction starts with a socially available concept or classification that is incorporated into an individual's self-understanding. The concept is then modified as her self-understanding evolves and ultimately the changes force a reconceptualization of the classification by others. This is an important and interesting phenomenon. But focusing on this process makes it seem that the impact of social forces on us and the locus of social change is primarily cognitive: social categories are offered to us that we internalize and modify, offering back a revised classification that others then adjust to (or not). Disrupt the classifications and you disrupt the social structure.

Hacking of course allows that ideas occur in matrices, so there are structural and material elements playing a role in making the classification concrete. But a matrix is a complex, usually unwieldy, and somewhat haphazard collection of institutions and practices together with their material manifestations. Narratives and scripts accompany the practices; rules are part of the institutions. But one may be profoundly affected by the matrix without accepting the narrative, following the script, or even knowing the rules. A Christian widow in a non-Christian context may refuse to "identify" as a widow or to participate in the local widowhood practices. Nevertheless, the status of widow is, without her acquiescence, imposed upon her. I would propose that she is, as much as the more compliant woman, socially positioned as a widow, that is, a member of the social kind *widow*.

Moreover, the matrix may shape one's life without one's falling into any of its articulated classifications. Consider Christiana's children who were sent to live with others as servants after she was widowed. There may be no named category or social classification: "child of a widow," but there is nonetheless a social position created by widowhood practices for the fatherless children. And it might be an important political move to make this category explicit, to name it, to argue that the severe economic consequences of a father's death are not "necessary" or "natural," to empower the children within it, and lobby for a reconceptualization of their entitlements.

So although language and explicit classification can play an important role in identifying groups and organizing social practices around groups, and although group membership can become an important part of one's self-understanding, it is also important to note how social matrices have an impact on groups of individuals without the group being an explicit or articulated category and without the members of the group internalizing the narrative and the norms associated with it. In other words, we need a way of thinking about "object construction" or better, the formation of social kinds, that acknowledges the causal impact of classification, but also gives due weight to the unintended and unconceptualized impact of practices.

In summary, in thinking about the ways that classification can make a difference (pun intended) it is important not to focus so narrowly on "identities" that we lose sight of the ways that classification can affect us without influencing our self-understanding or without our even being aware of it. We need also to account for the ways that social practices can constitute "thick" social positions without explicit categorization being, at least in the first instance, a primary factor in creating or maintaining the position. This suggests at least a two-dimensional model is required to understand this form of social construction: one dimension represents the degree to which explicit classification is a causal factor in bringing about the features that make for membership in the kind (as opposed to the features being an unintended byproduct of social practices); the other dimension represents the degree to which the kind in question is defined by "identification" with the social position.[8] For example, widowhood in some parts of the world is an explicit category that has an impact on creating and maintaining a "thick" social position; yet one need not identify with that position in order to be positioned as a widow (one might be positioned as a widow while rebelling against it). Child of a widow is an implicit category, though again one need not identify with that position in order to occupy it. Other positions, however, involve greater agency in conformity to the practices defining them. For example, the category of student, refugee, or voter. Even here, though, we should distinguish conformity to the practices, and acceptance of the assumptions behind them. For example, a refugee may conform to the rules defining refugee status, without coming to think of herself *as a refugee*, or intentionally acting *as a refugee*.

In the previous section we saw how the social world had a causal impact on our ideas; in this section we've considered how the social world (including our ideas and classifications) have an impact on things to form them into kinds. The—perhaps by now obvious—point is that ideas and objects interact in complex ways and transform each other over time. Broadly speaking, social construction is about this complex interaction. Thus far it may appear that social construction is all about causation (this, after all, seems to be Hacking's view); but there remain questions about kinds and classification that have not yet been addressed.

SOCIAL KINDS

One of the important messages of Hacking's work on social construction is that we must distinguish *what* is allegedly being constructed, namely ideas or objects, in order to avoid confusion. In other words, he has focused on distinguishing different *products* of construction, but in every case construction is a causal *process*. But we should also be careful to distinguish different ways in which things are constructed, in particular, different ways things might "depend for their existence" on a social context.

Hacking believes that gender is a perfect example of a case in which the idea and the object are both socially constructed:

> There are many examples of this multi-leveled reference of the *X* in "the social construction of *X*." It is plain in the case of gender. What is constructed? The idea of gendered human beings (an idea), and gendered human beings themselves (people); language; institutions; bodies. Above all, "the experiences of being female." One great interest of gender studies is less how any one of these types of entity was constructed than how the constructions intertwine and interact. (Hacking 1999, p. 28)

Here Hacking suggests that "gender" (in different senses) is both an idea construction and an object-construction. Gender is an idea-construction because the *classification* men/women is the contingent result of historical events and forces and does not correspond to and is not stable due to the world's inherent structure. And yet the classifications "woman" and "man" are interactive kinds: gender classifications occur within a complex matrix of institutions and practices, and being classified as a woman (or not) or a man (or not) has a profound effect on an individual, both in terms of the social consequences for her and in terms of her experience and self-understanding. That is, women and men are constructed *as gendered kinds of people*.

Although on Hacking's view the claim that gender is constructed has more than one sense, on both senses it is a causal claim: the point is either a causal claim about the source of our "ideas" of man or woman or a claim about the causes of gendered traits. However, there are contexts in which the claim that gender is socially constructed is not a causal claim; rather the point is constitutive. The point being made is that gender is not a classification scheme based simply on anatomical or biological differences, but should be understood as a system of social categories that can only be defined by reference to a network of social relations. In this case, the concept of gender is introduced as an analytical tool to explain a range of social phenomena, and we evaluate the claim by considering the theoretical usefulness of such a category (Scott 1986).[9] There is room for much debate, not only over the question whether we should employ such a category, but if we do, how we should define it, that is, what social relations (or clusters of social relations) constitute the groups *men* and *women*. The debates here parallel others in social theory: One might debate whether the category "underclass" is useful to explain a wide range of social and cultural phenomena and, if so, how we should define it.

Although Hacking is generous in suggesting that feminist theorists, following Beauvoir, have been important in developing the notion of construction, he suggests that the claim that gender is socially constructed is redundant, and not, at least at this point in time, particularly useful (Hacking 1999, p. 39). Gender is, on any definition, a social phenomenon: "no matter what definition is preferred, the word ['gender'] is used for distinctions among people that are grounded in cultural practices, not biology" (Hacking 1999, p. 39). The point seems to be that if one means by the claim that gender is socially constructed the constitutive claim that gender is a social category, then one's point is no better than a tautology. That the social classifications *men* and *women* are social classifications is redundant. "If gender is, by definition, something essentially social, and if it is constructed, how could its construction be other than social?" (Hacking 1999, p. 39).

It is odd that Hacking should frame his rhetorical question this way, for as we've seen, on his view, to say that something is socially constructed is to say that it is, in some way, socially caused. But we should avoid conflating social kinds with things that have social causes. Sociobiologists claim that some social phenomena have biological causes; some feminists claim that some anatomical phenomena have social causes, for example, that height and strength differences between the sexes are caused by a long history of gender norms concerning food and exercise.[10] It is an error to treat the conditions by virtue of which a social entity exists as causing the entity. Consider, for example, what must be the case in order for someone to be a husband in the contemporary United States: A husband is a man legally married to a woman. Being a man legally married to a woman does not *cause* one to be a husband; it is just what being a husband consists in.

It is also significant that not all social kinds are obviously social. Sometimes it is assumed that the conditions for membership in a kind concern only or primarily biological or physical facts. Pointing out that this is wrong can have important consequences. For example, the idea that whether or not a person is White is not simply a matter of their physical features, but concerns their position in a social matrix, has been politically significant, and to many surprising.

To help keep distinct these different ways in which the social can function in construction, let's distinguish:

X is socially constructed causally as an F iff social factors (i.e., *X*'s participation in a social matrix) play a significant role in causing *X* to have those features by virtue of which it counts as an *F*.

X is socially constructed constitutively as an F iff X is of a kind or sort *F*
such that in defining what it is to be *F* we must make reference to social
factors (or: such that in order for *X* to be *F*, *X* must exist within a social
matrix that constitutes *F*s).

In summary, social constructionists are often not just interested in the
causes of our ideas and the social forces at work on objects, but are interested in how best to understand a given kind, and in particular whether it is
a natural or social kind. Because on Hacking's view social constructionisms
are concerned with causal claims, it doesn't capture what's interesting in
claiming that something is, perhaps surprisingly, a social kind.

NATURAL STRUCTURES AND SOCIAL STRUCTURES

How should we construe the constructionist project of arguing that a particular kind is a social kind? What could be interesting or radical about such a
project? Is Hacking right that it is not useful to point out that a social kind is
a social kind?

I am a White woman. What does this mean? What makes this claim apt?
Suppose we pose these questions to someone who is not a philosopher,
someone not familiar with the academic social constructionist literature. A
likely response will involve mention of my physical features: reproductive
organs, skin color, and so on. The gender and race constructionists will reject this response and will argue that what makes the claim apt concerns the
social relations in which I stand. In effect, the constructionist proposes a different and (at least in some contexts) surprising set of truth conditions for the
claim, truth conditions that crucially involve social factors. On this construal,
the important social constructionist import in Beauvoir's claim that "one is
not born but rather becomes a woman," is not *pace* Hacking (Hacking 1999,
p. 7) that one is caused to be feminine by social forces; rather, the important
insight was that being a woman is not an anatomical matter but a social matter; for Beauvoir in particular "Here is to be found the basic trait of woman:
she is the Other in a totality of which the two components are necessary to
one another" (Beauvoir 1989, p. xxii; also 1989, pp. xv–xxxiv).

This project of challenging the purported truth conditions for the application of a concept I call a "debunking" project. A debunking project typically
attempts to show that a category or classification scheme that appears to
track a group of individuals defined by a set of physical or metaphysical conditions is better understood as capturing a group that occupies a certain
(usually "thick") social position. Hacking is right that the goal is often to challenge the appearance of inevitability of the category, to suggest that if social
conditions changed, it would be possible to do away with the category. But

an important first step is to make the category visible *as a social category*. This sometimes requires a rather radical change in our thinking. For example, elsewhere, following in Beauvoir's now long tradition, I have argued for the following definitions of man and woman:

S is a woman iff

i) *S* is regularly and for the most part observed or imagined to have certain bodily features presumed to be evidence of a female's biological role in reproduction;

ii) that *S* has these features marks *S* within the dominant ideology of *S*'s society as someone who ought to occupy certain kinds of social position that are in fact subordinate (and so motivates and justifies *S*'s occupying such a position); and

iii) the fact that *S* satisfies (i) and (ii) plays a role in *S*'s systematic subordination, i.e., *along some dimension*, *S*'s social position is oppressive, and *S*'s satisfying (i) and (ii) plays a role in that dimension of subordination.

S is a man iff

i) *S* is regularly and for the most part observed or imagined to have certain bodily features presumed to be evidence of a male's biological role in reproduction;

ii) that *S* has these features marks *S* within the dominant ideology of S's society as someone who ought to occupy certain kinds of social position that are in fact privileged (and so motivates and justifies *S*'s occupying such a position); and

iii) the fact that *S* satisfies (i) and (ii) plays a role in *S*'s systematic privilege, i.e., *along some dimension,* *S*'s social position is privileged, and *S*'s satisfying (i) and (ii) plays a role in that dimension of privilege.

(Haslanger 2000)

These definitions are proposed, not as reconstructions of our commonsense understanding of the terms *man* and *woman* but as providing a better explanation of how gender works.

What does this mean? There are two clusters of questions that should be distinguished. The first is whether employing a classification *C* (e.g., a distinction between the two groups as defined above) is theoretically or politically useful. The second is whether the theoretical understanding of *C* captures an ordinary social category, and so whether it is legitimate or warranted to claim that the proposed definitions reveal the commitments of our ordinary discourse. Those who hold the view that we have privileged access to the meanings of our terms will be suspicious of any attempt to provide radical analyses of our discourse. However, such semantic confidence is not warranted. It is broadly recognized that we often don't know exactly what we are talking about—at least not in all senses of "what we're talking about"—and that reference can be successful even under circumstances of semantic ignorance. I, like Putnam, cannot distinguish between beeches and elms. But that does not prevent my words "beech" and "elm" from referring to the correct species of tree (Putnam 1975b, 1973). If, however, there is no avoiding some form of semantic externalism, then it is perfectly reasonable to suppose that familiar terms that we ordinarily think capture physical kinds in fact capture social kinds.

To see how this might work, consider an early (simplified) version of scientific essentialism (Putnam 1975b, 1973; Kripke 1980). The term *water* may refer to the natural kind *water* even in contexts where no one is in a position to say what all and only instances of water have in common, for reference can be fixed by ostending certain paradigm instances with the intention to refer to the kind shared by the paradigms. The ordinary speaker might not be in a position to say what the kind in question is, or even identify the paradigms (I cannot point out a beech tree). Rather, we rely on a "semantic division of labor": I intend to mean by "beech" what others who are familiar with the paradigms mean, and it is up to the "experts" to determine what kind the paradigms share. Putnam and others assumed that the relevant "experts" would be *natural scientists* (the issue was framed as a question about the use of natural kind terms), and that the kind sought by the experts would be the *essence* of the paradigms.[11] However, we need not accept these naturalistic and essentialist assumptions. In my mouth, the term *underclass* refers to a social kind even though I am not in a position to define the kind. I defer to certain social scientists to refine the relevant range of paradigms and to provide a social theory that gives explanatory weight to this category and determines its extent. If I come to learn the currently accepted definition of 'underclass' and believe that it has problematic implications or presuppositions, then I may need to stop using the term. Note, however, that although in the examples thus far I have supposed that the speaker intends to participate in the semantic division of labor, semantic externalism does not depend on my intention to defer. Even if I think I know perfectly well what arthritis is, when I believe that I have arthritis in my thigh, the content of my belief is determined by experts on joint disorders (Burge 1979).

Debunking constructionists can be understood as relying on a kind of semantic externalism. We use the terms *Black, White, Hispanic,* and *Asian*. But can an ordinary speaker say what it is that all and only White people have in common? We can identify a range of quite different cases. Contemporary race theorists have argued that the cases don't fall within a meaningful biological kind. One conclusion, then, is to maintain that the term *White race* is vacuous, that the predicate "is a White person" has no extension (Appiah 1996). The social constructionist about race will claim, however, that the cases share membership in a social kind. This is not to claim that they all share an essence, so are all essentially White, but that our best social theory finds the category useful and provides an account of what the cases have in common (Haslanger 2000). The goal is not *just* to find something that all and only the cases have in common. Rather, it is to find a theoretically valuable kind that captures more or less the usual range of samples or paradigms. Both scientific and social theory can tell us that what we thought was a paradigm case of something doesn't fall within the kind it proposes as the best extension of our term. Whether we go with the theory or our pretheoretic beliefs about the extension is a judgment call of the sort made in the process of finding reflective equilibrium.

Of course, social constructionists often make great efforts to distance themselves from the kind of realism that is commonly associated with scientific essentialism. Scientific essentialism is associated with many views in metaphysics, epistemology, and philosophy of language that are not part of the debunking constructionist's agenda. For example, it is open to the constructionist to maintain that theoretical commitment to certain kinds or categories is at least partly a political choice, especially in the context of social theory. This brings us back to some of the issues raised in the discussion of object construction.

Recall the widow Christiana and her children. As noted above, there may not be an explicit or named social category *child of widow*, yet in developing a social theory for the society in question, it may be important to introduce such a category in order to understand the social and economic forces that result in the outcomes one is concerned to explain. What outcomes one is interested in explaining, what social forces one postulates, what form of explanation one seeks, are matters that are influenced by constitutive and contextual values (Anderson 1995). Moreover, the theoretical decisions may have political repercussions. One may, for example, introduce a category for *child of widow* in order to point out injustice and argue for changes to existing practices and institutions.

More complicated are decisions about how to theorize social categories for which there are explicit terms, for example, widow, Hispanic, woman, middle-class. There will be many cases in which what is common to the range of paradigms could be captured by several different theoretical models or several different classifications within a model. For example, consider 'widow.' In considering widows where widowhood is a "thick" social position and involves practices of subordination, one might choose to define the term 'widow' (or the corresponding term in the native language) thinly to mean simply "woman whose husband has died," and to argue that widows need not and should not be treated as they are. Alternatively, one might choose to define the term 'widow' to capture the thick social position—with its associated rituals and deprivations—and to argue that there should be no more widows. A third option would be to seek a middle-ground: to define 'widow' so it is not so tightly bound to the practices of a particular society that we cannot consider the fate of widows across cultures but theorize the category (roughly) as a site of subordination grounded in the loss of standing provided by one's husband, due to his death. Each of these options (and others) will not only have theoretical advantages and disadvantages, but will also have political advantages and disadvantages both locally and more globally.

There are two points to be drawn from this example. First, although typically debunking constructionists will want to "debunk" the assumption that a social category is grounded in or justified by nonsocial (natural or metaphysical) facts, there may also be cases in which the project is to "debunk" the assumption that a thick social category is grounded in and justified by thinly social facts (possibly in conjunction with natural or metaphysical facts). So, one might argue that ("thick") widowhood is a social construct, where the point is that it is wrong to see widows as the social kind consisting of women whose husbands have died, and who for some reason or other come to be poor, childless, and filthy. Rather, the claim would be that the ("thick") condition of widows as poor, childless, and so on, is something that "we"—our institutions and practices—have created. The purpose here would not be to suggest that the ordinary notion of "widow" is wrongly thought to be a natural category, but that the social position of widow is more robustly social than ordinarily thought.

Second, the debunking constructionist may need to respond to the two questions raised above in different ways depending on context: (1) is the classification C useful politically and/or theoretically useful, and (2) should we take the theoretical classification C to capture the commitments of ordinary discourse? How one answers these questions will depend on many factors, including of course theoretical and empirical concerns. But it will also depend on one's broader purposes in theorizing, the political context of one's theorizing, and one's particular position within that context.

CONCLUSION

Although Hacking's discussion of social construction is valuable and provides insight into the ways in which the notion of construction is often used and misused, there are important constructionist projects he neglects. In particular, he tends to ignore or dismiss the kind of project I've been calling the "debunking" project in which constructionists argue that there is a theoretically important social kind or category that has not been adequately acknowledged, or not been adequately acknowledged to be social. Debunking constructionists may seem to be offering radical and implausible "analyses" of our ordinary concepts, in fact they can be better understood as working within a semantic externalist model that looks to social theory to provide us with an account of our social terms, just as scientific essentialism looks to the physical sciences to provide an account of our naturalistic terms. Debunkers sometimes surprise us, however, in suggesting that what we thought were natural terms are in fact social terms.

There are of course many philosophical issues the debunking constructionist needs to address; the project raises interesting philosophical questions about the relationship between, for example our everyday understandings of social phenomena and social theory, our everyday understandings of what we mean and what might make our terms apt, the epistemic demands/constraints on theorizing and the political demands/constraints on theorizing. But in raising these questions, debunking constructionism, in contrast, say, to Hacking's "idea-constructionism," is much more philosophically palatable and meaningfully engaged with ongoing work in philosophy in general and metaphysics in particular.

ACKNOWLEDGMENTS

Thanks to Roxanne Fay, Rae Langton, Ishani Maitra, Agustin Rayo, Ásta Sveinsdóttir, Kayley Vernallis, and Stephen Yablo for discussion of earlier versions of this chapter. Thanks also to Frederick Schmitt for comments on an earlier draft.

NOTES

1. Ideas are similar, but perhaps less conditioned by language and more specific to the individual.
2. Hacking more often speaks of the social construction of "ideas" and sometimes of the social construction of "the idea of X (in its matrix)" where the matrix is the social setting "within which an idea, a concept or kind, is formed" (Hacking 1999, pp. 10–11). The emphasis on ideas and matrices rather than concepts doesn't change the ordinary view, for if on the ordinary view concepts are influenced by society and concepts are generally thought to play a role in any idea, then ideas will be too. Given that the matrix is the social context for the idea, including, for example, in the case of woman refugee: "a complex of institutions, advocates, newspaper articles, lawyers, court decisions, immigration proceedings" (Hacking 1999, p.10) the ordinary view would certainly hold that the idea in its matrix is conditioned by social forces.
3. Different sorts of fallibilism may be relevant here because Hacking uses the term *idea* to cover both concepts/classifications and theses or propositions. My point is that it is rare to find someone who holds that *either* their concepts/classifications are inevitable, given how the world is, determined by the inherent structure of the world, and so on, or that their beliefs/theoretical commitments are.
4. It should be noted that Hacking allows idea-constructionism to come in degrees, so plausibly world-idea determinism does too. So the adversary for a moderate constructionist may be someone who allows that reasons and justification, not just causes and explanation, are appropriate considerations in discussing a theory. But as I suggest below, the interesting moderate cases deserve more attention than Hacking accords them.

5. Sometimes Hacking represents the issue of stability as a question of whether, given the methods we've embraced, the technology available to us, and so on, we could have come up with different results. Of course if we allow that we could have used the methods or the technology better or worse than we actually did, we could have reached different results. The more serious question is whether using the technology to its limits and following the methods perfectly could yield different and incompatible results. It's hard to see how one could give a general answer to this question, for it would depend crucially on what methods and what technology one had in mind.

6. Note that a discourse, and so discursive construction, will involve more than spoken language. See Fraser (1992). For a clear explanation of one feminist appropriation of Foucault's notion of "discourse," see also Scott (1988).

7. For Christiana's story, see: http://www.womenforwomen.org/ourstories/stories.htm.

For more information on Widowhood Practices, see also EWD (Empowering Widows in Development): http://www.oneworld.org/empoweringwidows/history.html.

According to the FWD literature, "In widowhood, a woman joins a category of women among the most marginalized, and invisible. There is little research to inform public opinion or goad governments and the international community to action. Widows hardly figure in the literature on poverty or development.

Certainly in India and in many countries in Africa, and probably elsewhere, irrespective of religion, tribe, income, class, education, or geographical location, millions of widows are deprived of their universally acknowledged human right to shelter, food, clothing, and discriminated against in relation to health, work, dignity, and participation in the community life." (See: http://www.oneworld.org/empoweringwidows/patp_widow.html).

For a conference on widow's rights, and in particular, a presentation by Dr. Eleanor Nwadinobi, President of the Widows' Development Organization (WiDO), Nigeria http://www.widowsrights.org/ctuesam3.htm.

See also the Association of African Women Scholars (AAWS):

However, harsh treatment of and ritualized oppression of widows is not specific to Africa: http://www.womenaction.org/ungass/caucus/windows.html.

Statement to UN General Assembly Beijing + 5 Special Session: http://www.womenaction.org/ungass/caucus/widows.html.

8. Thus far I've been assuming that the kinds we're concerned with correspond with "thick" social positions, that is, positions defined within a network of social relations and typically entail a range of norms, expectations, obligations, entitlements, and so on. But one might argue that not all social kinds are like this and, more significantly, our classifications and practices can have a significant impact on the world that extends well beyond this. Hacking himself has used the example of classifying some microbes as pathogenic; this classification can have a profound effect on the kinds of microbes so classified. One might argue, then, that certain bacteria are socially, even discursively, constructed insofar as they are the result of mutations in previous bacteria that we classified as pathogenic and treated with antibiotics. Those interested in the subtle (and not so subtle!) effects of humans on ecosystems might have use for speaking of social construction in this broad sense.

9. There are moments when Hacking seems to acknowledge that some forms of construction are not causal but constitutive. I discuss one such passage below (Hacking 1999, p. 39), but his discussion does not reveal an understanding of the distinc-

tion. For example, constitutive constructions are treated as "add-on" entities, "the contingent product of the social world" (Hacking 1999, p. 7). This misses the point that a social construction claim may function to challenge the presumed content of our conceptual repertoire and not simply its origins. More on this later.

10. For example, recent race theorists such as Lucius Outlaw suggest that race is a social category but caused by natural forces (Outlaw 1996). Hacking himself also mentions Hirschfeld, but really muddles the debates over race and essentialism (Hacking 1999, pp. 16–18).

11. Note that Hacking himself relies on a version of scientific essentialism in clarifying the sense in which, for example, "autism" is a social construct. He argues:

> Now for the bottom line. Someone writes a paper titled "The Social Construction of Childhood Autism." The author could perfectly well maintain that (a) there is probably a definite unknown neuropathology P that is the cause of prototypical and most other examples of what we now call childhood autism; (b) the idea of childhood autism is a social construct that interacts not only with therapists and psychiatrists in their treatments, but also interacts with autistic children themselves, who find the current mode of being autistic a way for themselves to be.
>
> In this case we have several values for the X in the social construction of X = childhood autism; (a) the idea of childhood autism, and what that involves; (b) autistic children, actual human beings, whose way of being is in part constructed. But not (c) the neuropathology P, which ex hypothesi, we are treating as an indifferent kind. A follower of Kripke might call P the essence of autism. For us, the interest would not be in the semantics but the dynamics. How would the discovery of P affect how autistic children and their families conceive of themselves; how would it affect their behavior? (Hacking 1999, p. 121)

Hacking, however, inherits the naturalistic bias of the early scientific essentialists in allowing that there may be an underlying kind that the natural scientist discovers, but in ignoring the possibility that in other cases there are social kinds underlying our discourse that the social scientist discovers.

12

Social Construction, Social Roles, and Stability

Ron Mallon

Social constructionist claims are ubiquitous in the social sciences and humanities. Even a cursory scan of the titles of academic books or journal articles will suggest that, among other things, race, gender, sexual orientation, the emotions, and mental illness are socially constructed.[1] While many philosophers and academics associate the term "social constructionism" with radical antirealism, a careful study of at least some constructionist claims suggests a different interpretation. Here I have in mind claims about what Ian Hacking calls human kinds: "kinds of people, their behaviour, their condition, kinds of action, kinds of temperament or tendency, kinds of emotion, and kinds of experience" (1995a, pp. 351–52). On this alternative interpretation, many of these constructionist claims about human kinds are attempts to undermine what I call *human nature* explanations of behavior or other facts about persons by appeal to what I call *social role* explanations. Understood in this way, constructionist explanations are a variety of causal explanation.[2] Roughly, human nature explanations appeal to biological facts about persons to explain other facts about them. In contrast, social role explanations appeal to the social role that a person occupies to explain the same facts. For example, a social constructionist might try explaining racial difference by simultaneously undermining explanations of racial difference that appealed to biological differences among members of different races, and instead explaining what differences there are in terms of the different social roles occupied by members of different races in a racialized society.

We can juxtapose human nature and social role explanations of individual behaviors and social facts by considering Hilary Kornblith's broader question, "what is the world, that we might know it?"[3] That is, what must the world be like such that we are able to have knowledge of it? The answer Kornblith gives is that it is a world made up of natural kinds—mind-independent property clusters in the world that support our attempts at induction and explanation.[4] Such clusters support these inductive enterprises because they are *stable*: they recur across instances and through time. They therefore allow us to induce from observed instances to others. But what about the social world? Our day-to-day world is a social world, a world made up of people, groups of people, conventions, and institutions with which we interact, and must interact, in order to survive and flourish. Such interactions are exquisitely complex, and so it is remarkable that we are able to interact with such astonishing success. Echoing Kornblith, we can ask, "what is the *social world* that we might know it?" The answer provided by human nature explanations allows a straightforward extension of Kornblith's answer because human nature explanations may proceed by invoking natural kinds that human beings instantiate.[5] Stable features of the social world may be explained as the products of stable features of human nature. For example, the evolutionary psychologists Margo Wilson and Martin Daly (1992) explain human sexual jealousy (and differential jealousy patterns between the sexes) as the result of evolved mechanisms that serve to promote particular reproductive strategies. Sexual jealousy, they claim, is exhibited cross-culturally, and the need to manage such emotions also provides a partial explanation of the existence and structure of other social institutions concerned with marriage and child care. So, if we want to understand the stability of the social world, human nature advocates have a ready answer: the stability of the social world is explained by stable features of human nature.

What can the social constructionist say? One variety of social constructionist wants to explain various features of social life by reference to differential social roles. But, the question is, do such social roles have the stability to explain the constancy and predictability of the social world and our success within it? One possibility—the one I pursue in this chapter—is to claim that social roles are natural kinds or are analogous to natural kinds in the ways they structure the social world and reference to them figures in our successful inductive and predictive enterprises.[6] If this is correct, then the stability of the social world (and our knowledge of it) might also be explained by the presence of stable, causally efficacious social roles.

But this approach runs contrary to long-running strands of the philosophy of social sciences and social theory that say that social roles do not have such stability. One source of doubt about the stability of social roles arises from the camp of constructionist social theory itself. Constructionist social theorists routinely assert the instability of social categories. For example, in their widely read book *Racial Formation in the United States*, Michael Omi and Howard Winant argue that the "effort must be made to understand race as *an unstable and 'decentered' complex of social meanings constantly being transformed by political struggle*."[7] Omi and Winant are not speaking here only of the *meanings* or *concepts* of race but of the social roles structured by such meanings or concepts. And the reason such social roles are unstable, they believe, is that they are not grounded in biological facts, but rather are created via a "social and historical process" (1994, p. 55). And the point of constructionist work (or at least one point) is to destabilize the phenomena further by drawing attention to this instability. Another source of pessimism about social roles is found in the general view that all regularities of the social sciences are constituted partly by the intentional states of actors and that because of this, phenomena such as social roles will be highly volatile. This worry takes many forms. First, that human choices constitute an open-ended causal system that is susceptible to many forms of interference and may exhibit a highly sensitive dependence on initial conditions.[8] Or that, in particular, because of conceptual innovation and conceptual diversity, types structured by human intentional states will be highly volatile and local.[9] A more recent source of such skepticism—and the one on which I focus—is Ian Hacking's (1995a) thesis of "the looping effect of human kinds." This phenomenon occurs when persons classified in a certain way come to change in response to the labels placed upon them. According to Hacking, this looping effect dramatically destabilizes knowledge of human kinds, and it marks a fundamental difference between the social sciences and the natural sciences. If these philosophers and social theorists are right, then it would seem that social roles do not have the stability to ground our inductive, predictive, and practical success in the social world. And insofar as we take our social success to require such a ground, some other alternative—perhaps that provided by human nature explanations—must be found.

While human action may be usefully individuated by the intentional states of the actors, and human institutions may be structured by the intentions of the actors that comprise them, neither of these facts undermines the possibility of understanding social roles on the model of stable natural kinds. So, I maintain that social roles of the sort invoked by some constructionists may be property-cluster kinds of the same sort Kornblith invokes to explain our cognitive success in understanding the natural world. One part of the explanation of our social success is that we live in a world made up of social role kinds that we simultaneously know and maintain by our epistemic and practical activities. If this is correct, a scientific approach to social life may also take account of social roles in the explanation of individual behavior or group difference. Note that social role kinds are explanatory kinds in two senses. First, they are kinds in that there is a kind of thing, the social role, that has a variety of manifestations but can be characterized in a general way. Second, they are kinds in that particular sorts of social role may be explanatory kinds within a social milieu. So for example, if gender is a social role, then the property of having one or another gender may be an explanatory kind.

A few caveats are in order. First, to call social role kinds "natural" kinds would be, for many, to stress the meaning of "natural" beyond its breaking point. So, I alternately call them *property-cluster* kinds, *explanatory* kinds, or *relevant* kinds. Second, to claim that social roles may be property-cluster kinds is not to say that every social role amounts to such a kind. Because the account of social roles is independent of the account of cluster-kinds presented, the discussion leaves open which—and to what extent—particular social roles count as explanatory kinds. So, for example, to say that race or gender is a social role is not by itself to say that race or gender counts as a robust enough social role to be a relevant kind. Third, even if, for example, race or gender social roles are robust enough to be relevant property-cluster kinds, this should not be taken to deny that there are important differences between human nature and social role explanations of racial or gender difference. Finally, my explanation and defense of social role kinds does not imply that I hold that human nature explanations are bankrupt or seldom appropriate. In fact, the simplistic division between human nature and social role explanations I have employed cannot be sustained across a great variety of behavioral phenomena. Instead, most behavioral phenomena will require complex explanations invoking both biological (or psychological) and sociocultural causes, and both situational and developmental factors.[10] I take it that discovering what explanation (or combination of explanations) is true of any particular case will require answering a difficult set of empirical questions.

My present aim is not to explore these complexities, but rather to come to a better understanding of social roles and social role explanations as understood by social constructionists and other social theorists. This project is important both because social roles are implicitly invoked in widespread talk of social construction, but also because they are claimed to have an important role to play in both social and psychological explanation. An adequate theory of social roles also ought to have application in a variety of other discourses. For example, among moral and political philosophers, social roles are also invoked with some frequency and are widely held to raise questions about moral obligation and social and political identity. I won't delve into these accounts here, except to say that a complete working out of these accounts ought to provide a theory of social roles, and I hope that the present account can be adapted and extended to suit these purposes.

Here's how I will proceed. In the first section, A Preliminary Account of Social Roles, I set out an account of social roles. The account is general so as to cut a broad swath across a variety of apparently very different sorts of social roles. Then, in the second section, Social Roles as Property-Cluster Kinds, I argue that social roles may be property-cluster kinds and thus figure in our successful inductive and explanatory projects. In the final section, Hacking and Instability, I focus on the challenge to this idea posed by Hacking's claim that knowledge of human kinds is fleeting because of the instability created by a "looping effect." My strategy is to show that the very mechanisms that Hacking suggests lead to instability, may instead be sources of stability for the social role in question. By sketching a plausible account of stability, I hope to answer Hacking and provide a partial answer to other critics of stable social roles as well.

A PRELIMINARY ACCOUNT OF SOCIAL ROLES

Let us distinguish a social role from a *niche*. A *niche* is simply a causal role that may be occupied by a thing. This causal role is distinguished by the causal effects on the occupant and by the causal effects of the occupant. The number of niches is indefinitely large (as large as the number of ways of carving up causal roles), but some niches may have characteristics that make them particularly interesting or explanatory within a given investigation. One example of a niche is what Frank Sulloway (1996) calls *functional birth order*. Sulloway defends the claim that birth order is a predictor of personality traits, including the "big five" personality traits—openness to experience, conscientiousness, agreeableness/ antagonism, neuroticism (or emotional instability), and extraversion.[11] His explanation of the source of these differences is developmental: younger siblings must pursue different strategies than older siblings to acquire resources because they are smaller and less capable of achieving their ends by force.

A *social role*, as I use the term, is a particular sort of niche, distinguished by its occupant being acted upon by special sorts of conceptual or linguistic causes. Social roles in this sense are part of the apparatus that coordinates and structures social life within a community. Such social roles may be characterized as follows:

1. Social role niches are associated with a term, label, or mental representation that picks out a class of persons and a *conception* of the role—a set of beliefs about the persons so picked out.
2. Many elements of the conception of the role are widely shared by members of the community in which the role exists.
3. At least some of these beliefs are typically *action-guiding*, specifying particular forms of behavior and courses of action for one so labeled.
4. The beliefs are also typically action-guiding for members of the community who engage in labeling.
5. The actions structured by the conception give the role its causal power.

Social roles, but not necessarily important niches, are conceptualized by those whose lives the social roles order, and it is because they are so conceptualized that the role has causal power. Notice that a shared label or conception of the niche is no part of the causal explanation of Sulloway's birth-order effects. Thus, birth-order niches are not social roles in the sense considered here. This characterization of social roles is general enough to encompass several importantly different cases. First, sometimes persons may be labeled because they instantiate a biological natural kind, for example, *diabetic*. On the account in question, such persons may also count as occupying the social role of the diabetic. Other social roles operate without the associated concept or conception picking out a biological natural kind. As we noted at the outset, race and certain mental illnesses are sometimes understood as social roles, but if constructionist or eliminativist skeptics are correct, race and these mental illnesses are not biological natural kinds. The account also encompasses a third sort of role: institutional social roles like being a U.S. Senator or being a licensed bass fisherman. Clearly the question of whether social roles can be invoked to ground our knowledge of the social world is concerned primarily with the second and third sorts of cases. In these cases, according to the constructionist, the differences among occupants of varying social roles are to be explained at least primarily by reference to the fact that they occupy the social role. In the second sort of case, differential features of category members are widely believed to result from natural (for example, biological) differences. Call such roles *covert* roles. In contrast, roles of the third sort—institutional social roles—are *overt* because the differentiation of members of these roles is widely recognized within a community to be the result of that community's practices.[12] While it is a necessary feature of social roles in the sense considered here that they be locally conceptualized, it is not necessary that they be known to be social roles (i.e. they may be believed to be natural categories).

It might seem as though the conditions on being a social role are too weak. It is counterintuitive and to some extent misleading to think of *diabetic* as a social role. Moreover, the conditions on offer are so loose that even mildly explanatory properties like *being tall, wearing clown make-up,* or *having a last name that begins with the letter "A"* would be accompanied by social roles on the characterization offered above. In each of these cases, there is a conception of appropriate behavior toward the person and of the person that structures a social role.[13] Perhaps we should add additional conditions that restrict the class of social roles further, ruling out instances like *diabetic* and *being tall*.

I prefer the weaker characterization of social roles. It is useful to think about recognized biological kinds of persons like *diabetic* as occupying social roles, because in some cases there may be a question as to whether a feature typical of such a person (e.g., a characteristic symptom) stems from their biological make-up or from the social role they occupy. Such is often the case in disputes over whether particular gender differences result from biological sex differences or social role differences. Allowing that recognized biological natural kinds that persons instantiate may be accompanied by social roles thus avoids prejudging particular explanatory questions. It is also useful to offer a characterization of social roles that includes weakly explanatory social roles like *being tall, wearing clown make-up,* or *having a last name that begins with the letter "A."* While we could strengthen the requirements on being a social role to require that bona fide social roles must be explanatorily important, that would be a step toward confusing the requirements on being a social role with those on being a relevant, explanatory kind. I prefer to retain a weaker conception of social roles in order to keep these issues separate. This is in part because I think the conception of social roles may characterize interesting phenomena even if those phenomena are not explanatorily important enough for us to consider them genuine kinds within a particular investigation.[14]

Remember that social roles are explanatory kinds in two senses. First, there is a sort of thing—the social role—with a variety of manifestations. In this section, I've characterized this sort of thing in a general way that draws together a great deal of social theory and the metaphysics of social institutions. It is a feature of the account that it provides a unified story about the structure of overt and covert roles by appealing to widely held beliefs, and actions structured by those beliefs, to explain both sets of phenomena. In the next section, I argue that particular sorts of social roles may be property-cluster kinds, and such arguments apply both to covert and overt social roles.

SOCIAL ROLES AS PROPERTY-CLUSTER KINDS

Paradigmatic natural kinds for philosophers are species and elements. But over the last twenty years philosophical work in, for example, the philosophy of mind and psychology has led to relatively wide acceptance of the view that categories from the special sciences that are useful in explanation and prediction count as natural kinds from the point of view of those sciences (e.g., Fodor 1981b, Griffiths 1999). Richard Boyd (1988, 1991, 1992, 1999a) develops an account of the metaphysics of such natural kinds that captures the idea that such kinds support our attempts at induction and explanation. Boyd suggests that in our attempts to understand the world we want concepts or terms that pick out causally homeostatic property clusters, the elements of which are (as a matter of contingent fact) instantiated in the world.[15] Boyd, and as I noted at the outset, Kornblith, build upon this foundation to provide a general explanation of our success in understanding the natural world. In this section, I set out Boyd's account of natural kinds as homeostatic property-cluster kinds. I then argue that social roles of the sort discussed in the first section may be property-cluster kinds of this sort.

Expanding the Franchise: The Liberalization of Natural Kinds

Central to Boyd's account of natural kinds is what he calls *causal home-ostasis*: "Either the presence of some of the properties . . . tends (under appropriate conditions) to favor the presence of the others, or there are underlying mechanisms or processes that tend to maintain the presence of the properties . . . or both" (1999a, p. 143). Such a kind is characterized by both (1) the properties in the property cluster and (2) the mechanism of causal homeostasis—the mechanism that is the source of the properties' continued co-occurrence in the cluster.

As Robert Wilson (1999a, p. 198) notes, Boyd's account is a cluster account twice over. First, because an individual does not have to instantiate all the properties in the cluster in order to be a member of the kind. (Manx cats do not have tails, but they are cats all the same.) Kind membership, on this view, may be a partial affair. Second, because the properties of a cluster kind actually "cluster" in the world. The world is lumpy in that properties are not instantiated evenly throughout space and time, but instead occur in clumps.

Let's try to spell out Boyd's account more carefully by employing a paradigmatic philosophical natural kind: water. Instances of water share a variety of superficial properties (e.g. liquidity, freezing point, etc.) and these superficial properties are clustered because they are caused by the microstructural properties of H_2O. The mechanism of H_2O's microstructural properties thus explains the clustering of the superficial properties. This picture of natural kinds leads Kripke (1980) and Putnam (1975b) to view the chemical structure of water as giving its essence. On this view it is sufficient for some stuff to be water (in any possible world) that it be an instance of H_2O, *whether or not it has the superficial properties*.[16] And conversely, nothing is water unless it is H_2O. H_2O, it seems, is a property-cluster kind in Wilson's second sense only, because instantiating the property of water looks to be an all-or-nothing affair.[17]

Such property clusters support our inductive enterprises because they allow us to draw successful conclusions about all instances of a kind on the basis of examining a few instances. For example, on the basis of examining very few instances of water, we can successfully infer lots of things about other instances of water. And this success is supported by the fact that the properties of water are tightly clustered and causally homeostatic.

But, as Boyd points out, natural kinds in some sciences may be causally homeostatic categories that lack the kind of simple "essence" that chemical compounds like water have. By way of example, he writes,

> The appropriateness of any particular biological species for induction and explanation in biology depends upon the imperfectly shared and homeostatically related morphological, physiological and behavioral features which characterize its members. (1991, p. 142)

In biological species, the instances of a kind instantiate (more or less) property clusters of various sorts of features, but such instantiation is imperfect (remember Manx cats). Nonetheless, kind terms picking out species can also figure in successful inductive enterprises. Because species exhibit a variety of properties that are clustered and causally homeostatic, we can—imperfectly—induce facts about all the instances of a cluster kind from the few that we actually examine.

Boyd's account is thus a principled liberalization of the idea of natural kinds. This is first, because the property-cluster account of kinds moves from all or nothing accounts of kind membership to a cluster view on which kind membership need not involve satisfying interesting necessary and sufficient conditions. But there is also a second sense in which Boyd's account liberalizes the notion of natural kinds: it expands the sorts of properties that may be contained in the property cluster. While examples like water might lead us to believe that properties that characterize natural kinds or their mechanisms of causal homeostasis must be intrinsic features of members of the kind, reflection on, for example, species suggests that relational properties may be included as well.[18] While disputes over the *correct* species concept or concepts are contentious and ongoing, it is widely accepted that an adequate species concept will take into account relational or historical features of the organisms to be classified. So for example, according to Mayr's classic *biological species concept*, species are groups of populations that "respond to one another as potential mates and seek one another for the purpose of reproduction" (1984, p. 533).[19] The stability of species property clusters is thus sustained by (a variety of) barriers to genetic flow. In contrast, according to phylogenetic accounts, species depend for their identity on relations to historically situated speciation events (on their location in a phylogenetic tree). Thus these accounts, too, incorporate relational features into species definitions. Boyd's account thus incorporates his insight that these developments in the species debate have more general implications for the theory of natural kinds. Allowing relational features to figure as components of causally homeostatic property clusters is a *principled* liberalization of the notion of natural kinds because it is guided by attempts to pick out kinds of great explanatory and predictive importance. What is relevant to the ability of the kind to support induction is that there is some stable mechanism or set of mechanisms that causes properties to cluster in a regular way, not whether the properties in the cluster or the mechanisms of causal homeostasis are intrinsic to the kind members.[20] To recap: what emerges from Boyd's discussion of causally homeostatic kinds is that properties in a cluster may be imperfectly shared and also that there need be no restriction on the sorts of properties that may be included in the cluster or the mechanisms of homeostasis, as long as the clusters are doing the inductive and explanatory work required of them.

Opening the door to relational properties in property-cluster kinds also opens up the door to properties that result from human convention. Boyd says as much:

> It . . . follows that there should be kinds and categories whose definitions combine naturalistic and conventional features in quite complex ways. . . . It follows that extensions of the traditional account of natural kinds should be appropriate just to the extent that the kinds in question are employed for induction and explanation. (1992, p.140)

There is simply no a priori reason why social roles of the sort discussed in the first section cannot figure among the important property-cluster kinds that structure our social world. Instead, whether a particular social role type does count as explanatory is an empirical question. We may not want to call such kinds "natural" kinds, but insofar as social kinds are property-cluster kinds, they may support induction and explanation, and thus deserve a place in our best theories of the social world.

Social Roles as Homeostatic Property Clusters

Boyd's account of property-cluster kinds allows us to see quite clearly why social roles may be explanatory, relevant kinds. Occupants of robust social roles will share a variety of interesting and important properties worthy of notice in social life and social theory, and the mechanism by which they share these properties is the social role that they occupy. These clustered properties are of at least four kinds:

1. Social role occupants may have greater propensity to act in certain ways, in virtue of their currently being in a particular social role.[21] (These propensities will be intentionally mediated by an occupant's beliefs about their situation.)
2. They may also share various causal effects of occupying the social role that do not depend on the concurrent existence of the social role. For example, if social role occupation causes individuals to develop skills, capacities, proclivities, or character traits, these would presumably persist in those individuals even after the social institutions that caused them to develop have passed away.[22]
3. Social role occupants may also share dispositional properties to cause responses in others (i.e., they may share secondary qualities). Consider a dispositional property to be one that is manifested in certain conditions, thus: x has disposition P iff x manifests P in situation C. A person occupying the social role of "man" may have a disposition to cause others to respond to the person in particular ways. The property is dispositional, because it is manifested only in a particular social milieu, and

it is a response-dependent property in that being in a "man" social role depends on the dispositions of others to treat one as a man. In general, social role occupants may have lots of dispositions to produce various kinds of reactions (judgings, approvings, disapprovings, etc.) in members of the community that participate in the practices that constitute the social role.

4. Finally, social role occupants will share various properties that comprise the basis of ascription to the category. For example, Senators will share the property of having been appropriately elected, and occupants of a masculine social role will (by and large) share characteristic male sexual features.

These sorts of properties may be relevant to understanding social life. They are clustered in individuals occupying social roles precisely in virtue of their occupation of those social roles. Thus, social role occupants instantiate property-cluster kinds where the mechanism controlling the clustering of those properties is the social role they occupy.[23]

We noted above that homeostatic property-cluster kinds support induction. Because various mechanisms cause explanatorily relevant properties to cluster in the world, and because our own conceptual apparatus leads us to pick out these kinds with concepts and seek to reason inductively about them, we can achieve extremely useful knowledge about the mind-independent world. For similar reasons, social role kinds also support induction. To the extent social roles involve a thick cluster of interesting properties that are tightly correlated, you can successfully infer things about one social role occupant from facts about another. Among the properties you can engage in induction about are even those properties that are conventionally assigned (3. above). For example, if you know that Senator Lenkiewicz served six years between elections (and you treat "Senator" as a kind term), you can infer from that that Senator Fitzpatrick will probably serve six years as well. Thus, knowledge of facts about overt social role occupants comes to us in at least two ways: first, by checking the rules to which we collectively defer (e.g., the U.S. Constitution says that Senators serve six-year terms), but also, and importantly, by induction.

Are Social Role Kinds Scientific Kinds?

The sorts of mechanisms that underlie many paradigmatic natural kind property clusters are not the same sorts of mechanisms underlying social kind property clusters. For many important natural kinds, the mechanisms that result in property clusters are themselves independent of human actions and thoughts. But the present point is that this difference, as important as it is, makes no difference at all to the capacity of social kinds to be explanatory and to support induction about the social world, or to the capacity of the concepts of social kinds to be projectable within a certain social context that includes such social role occupants. But there remain questions about whether social role kinds of the sort suggested here are appropriately scientific to figure in genuine law-like regularities. Paul Griffiths draws a useful distinction between *scope* and *force*. Scope indicates the size of the domain over which a law-like generalization is applicable. Force, in contrast, is a measure of the "reliability of predictions made using that generalization." (1999, p. 217). Social role kinds might be thought to fail on both counts. Their scope is limited, since they apply only within a particular cultural milieu (or subcultural milieu), and their reliability in prediction is weak.

Law-like generalizations employing social role kinds do lack the sort of scope that laws of the basic sciences have. Such social role kinds are what Ruth Millikan (1999) has called "historical kinds." They are kinds the "predicates for which are non-accidentally projectable: there are good reasons in nature why one member of an historical kind is like another, hence why inductions are successful over the kind" (p. 55). But such inductions will be limited in scope because the "good reasons" will obtain only in a cultural setting that is structured by a conception of the kind in question. This limitation is at least one reason why humanist social scientists and philosophers of social science have come to view the project of finding social kinds as bankrupt. Taylor, for example, writes:

> The success of prediction in the natural sciences is bound up with the fact that all states of the system, past and future, can be described in the same range of concepts. . . . This conceptual unity is vitiated in the sciences of man by the fact of conceptual innovation, which in turn alters human reality. (1971, p. 209)

The problem, according to Taylor, is that since human reality differs fundamentally from time to time, place to place, the concepts that accurately describe kinds in one cultural location will be inadequate to another. But such limitations do not rule out social role kinds any more than they rule out other historical kinds like biological species. The test of whether a particular social role amounts to an important kind is not whether it obtains universally, but whether making reference to the kind is useful in explanation and prediction. And if what you are trying to explain or predict is itself local to a historical or spatial social setting, then limitations on scope are unproblematic. There is also the additional possibility that scientists or critical theorists may be able to recognize social role types that exist across various cultural milieus. In order to be "nonaccidentally" grouped together as members of the same projectable kind, such social roles would have to have a common cause. Such a cause could take the form of an older social role that caused two modern descendents. Alternatively, social roles of the same type might come about as the result of constraints imposed by human psychology,[24] or of some more general facts about human relations. To the extent that such cross-cultural roles exist, we can expect the scope of generalizations involving such role kinds to be larger.

As for the reliability of predictions made using law-like generalizations employing social role terms, they will vary. Recall that both philosophers of social science and social theorists routinely emphasize the instability of social kinds and implicitly cast doubt on the possibility of reliable generalizations. Interpreting such instability within the idiom of Boyd's account of kinds, we can say that these theorists maintain that the properties of social role kinds are not causally homeostatic—that is, the mechanisms that are responsible for such clustering are themselves insubstantial or transient, and so the reliability of predictions employing social role terms is very weak. It is true that the strength of a cluster—that is, the probability of the elements of the cluster covarying in an instance of the kind—can be a source of variation in the strength of causal generalizations making reference to the cluster-kind. And as with any special science, generalizations employing social role terms can be expected to be at best true, *ceteris paribus*. But there seems no reason to believe, a priori, that predictions that rely on such generalizations must be especially weak. We should expect to find causally homeostatic mechanisms exhibiting a continuum of different strengths. At one extreme, we can find the property clusters of the basic sciences that have extraordinary explanatory power and that may be characterized as having simple necessary and sufficient conditions. At the other end of the continuum, we can find clusters with quite transient mechanisms that maintain weak and quite imperfect property clusters. The variability in strength of these mechanisms may mean variability in the reliability of predictions making reference to the kinds they underlie. But what I have been suggesting is that social role kinds may be more tightly clustered than philosophers and social theorists often claim. In the next section, I scrutinize one such claim more closely.

HACKING AND INSTABILITY

Understanding social roles as stable property-cluster kinds helps us understand both how constructionists could be right that our social world is structured by social roles in ways we do not always recognize and how it could be the case that our social world is nonetheless stable. But the view that social roles could be stable kinds is seen as problematic by both philosophers of social science and many social theorists. In fact, such claims are so widespread so as to make a survey of all of them impossible here. Instead, I consider one influential account of instability: Hacking's account of the "looping of human kinds" (1995b). Hacking's account has the virtue of being both philosophical and social theoretical—concerned both with the metaphysics of kinds and the nature of social identities. I argue, contra Hacking, that the looping of human kinds shows how the mechanisms involved in creating social roles may act to stabilize those social roles. Thus, my aim is both to critique Hacking's account of the looping effect of human kinds and to sketch an account of the stability of social roles. To the extent the account of stability I provide is viable, it may also provide an answer other critics of the stability of social roles.

The Looping Effect and the Instability Thesis

Hacking's "looping effect" occurs when persons interact with the systems of classification they fall under. The effect of this looping, according to Hacking, is that knowledge of human kinds is difficult to get and harder to keep. He writes, "People classified in a certain way tend to conform to or grow into the ways that they are described; but they also evolve in their own ways, so that the classifications and descriptions have to be constantly revised" (1995b, p. 21). Writing of child abuse, he is even less sanguine: "The concept of child abuse may . . . be so made and molded by attempts at knowledge and intervention, and social reaction to these studies, that there is no stable object, child abuse, to have knowledge about" (p. 61). While Hacking's discussion is often framed in terms of particular kinds (e.g., child abuse, multiple personality disorder, etc.), he frames his thesis quite generally, as one about "the looping of human kinds." Recall that he defines these quite broadly as "kinds of people, their behaviour, their condition, kinds of action, kinds of temperament or tendency, kinds of emotion, and kinds of experience" (1995a, pp. 351–52).[25] This broad characterization thus includes many things we might think of as biological kinds. For example, having an O-positive blood type or being diabetic counts as a human kind on this characterization. But if all human kinds are as unstable as Hacking says child abuse is, then his position amounts to a general skepticism about the possibility of successful medical science, psychiatry, psychology, social science, and basic social knowledge.

A more charitable interpretation of Hacking limits the claim that human kinds (and our knowledge of them) are unstable to social role kinds—kinds of person whose differentiation is the result of the application and internalization of culturally local conceptions of the kind.[26] This would include both what we earlier called "overt" and "covert" social roles. But the kind of instability of most interest to us is that which threatens the constructionist claim that our social world is to be explained by reference to covert social roles rather than biological nature—the instability of *covert* social roles. In fact, Hacking's own work focuses upon covert social roles (without explicitly limiting himself to them) in making his case about the looping effects of human kinds. For example, Hacking believes that most or all of the symptoms of most sufferers of multiple personality disorder are to be explained by appeal to the social roles occupied by multiples and not by some underlying biological dysfunction. So, for the purpose of focusing the discussion, I limit the discussion of the "looping effect" even further to include just covert roles. In doing this, I am considering the very class of roles that are of most interest to the constructionist, and the very class of roles that Hacking utilizes to make his case.

On this more limited interpretation of Hacking, attempts at knowledge of covert roles are doomed to inadequacy because the study of the phenomena will cause them to change.[27] On this reading of Hacking's view, the social world is a Heraclitean river, and knowledge of it is fleeting at best. Even though Hacking limits his discussion of looping effects to *covert* kinds, he clearly sees his view as radical. He writes that looping effects mark "a cardinal difference between the traditional natural and social sciences" because "the targets of the natural sciences are stationary" while "the targets of the social sciences are on the move" (1999, p. 108). For present purposes, if looping effects are as pervasive and destabilizing as Hacking suggests, then it suggests that social role kinds cannot be part of the metaphysical basis that supports our knowledge of the social world. At the outset, I said that social roles were explanatory and relevant kinds in two senses. First, I said there is a general kind of thing, the social role, that may be manifested in a variety of particular ways, either overtly or covertly. Second, I said that particular sorts of social roles such as being mentally ill or being a man may be explanatory kinds within a social setting. Hacking's view threatens the second of these claims, since it suggests that the differential features of occupants of social roles will not remain stable enough for terms associated with social roles to play a useful part in explanatory and predictive theories.

Let's try to get more clear on just what is the "looping effect of human kinds." The looping occurs when a theory held by a community (I'll call them the *labelers*) interacts with the properties of those described by the theory (I'll call them the *labeled*). Since we are all theorists of our social world, the labeled may be labelers as well. We can visualize the loop like this:

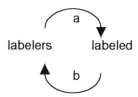

The "b" arrow—the arrow from those who are labeled to the labelers—is an arrow of epistemic constraint. As the labeled class changes, the labelers will attempt to track those changes in their theories of the class (on

pain of having a false theory). What about the "a" arrow that links the labelers to the labeled? This arrow represents the labeling and differential
treatment of the labeled class. Call this broad set of actions undertaken by
labelers vis-à-vis the labeled class the *regime of labeling*. The a arrow represents the regime of labeling directed at the labeled class. We can now
more carefully state Hacking's view as the Instability Thesis:

> (IT) For (covert) human kinds, changes in the labeled class caused by the
> regime of labeling cause the beliefs guiding the regime of labeling to become
> untrue.

If Hacking is correct, human kinds may be relatively stable across instances
at a particular time, but over time the kind will be destabilized by changes
caused by the regime of labeling. What sorts of changes are relevant? In discussing the looping of human kinds, Hacking has in mind changes in persons' intentional states and behaviors (or changes that are mediated by
changes in intentional states and behaviors). Changes in the regime of labeling cause intentional reactions on the part of those who are labeled. (This is
what distinguishes looping effects from just any old causal effects.) But what
is the mechanism of this causation, and how does it occur so rapidly? Work
in social psychology, cognitive science, anthropology, and sociology review
a variety of ways in which persons may be affected by their social roles, and
this is hardly the place to review this literature. Instead, I want to concentrate
on the set of mechanisms that are central to Hacking's own account—and
much work in philosophy of social science and social theory as well—those
mechanisms involving intentional action and practical agency.[28]

Identifications

A key element of the mechanisms in question is what K. Anthony Appiah
calls *identification*: "the process through which an individual intentionally
shapes her projects—including her plans for her own life and her conception of the good—by reference to available labels, available identities" (1996,
p. 78). By "label," Appiah means here a term that is associated with a concept and a conception of the thing picked out by the term—just the elements
I suggested characterized a social role. So identification is an avenue via
which social role memberships may shape persons' projects and behaviors.
And crucially, that avenue operates via the construction of intentions from
available concepts.

Appiah's notion of identification involves two unclear ideas: the idea that
labels play a "shaping role" in intentional projects, and the idea that some labels or identities are available. Let me say something first about availability.
In developing his account of identification, Appiah follows earlier work by

Hacking (1986, 1995), in which Hacking notes that Elizabeth Anscombe's insight that "all action is action under a description" has the important consequence that,

> When new descriptions become available, when they come into circulation, or even when they become the sorts of things that it is all right to say, to think, then there are new things to choose to do. When new intentions become open to me, because new descriptions, new concepts, become available to me, I live in a new world of opportunities. (1995, p. 236)

So, for example, the possibility of acting "as black" or "as a man" or "as a plumber" presupposes the availability of the concepts *black, man,* and *plumber.*[29] Geoffrey Chaucer could not have chosen to *write a Beat poem* at least in part because the concept of a Beat poem was not available to Chaucer. Since these concepts are only available in certain cultural milieus, the actions that they play a role in describing are also available only those same milieus. The meaning of "available" here is something like *conceptually available,* and a concept is conceptually available if it is part of the conceptual repertoire of the actor.[30]

What does it mean for available concepts to shape our intentional projects? One way in which the available terms or concepts shape our intentional projects is by constituting the descriptions under which our intentional actions occur. Thus, if James chooses not to cry in public, because it is a instance of his general project of being a macho man, the concept *macho* is a proper part of the description *being a macho man* under which his action occurs. Call this sort of shaping *minimal shaping.* Minimal shaping occurs whenever there is an action, because all actions are under some or another description and thus minimally shaped by that description.

Both Hacking and Appiah seem to have more than minimal shaping in mind, though. Both are concerned not just with minimal shaping, but with the way in which a conception associated with a concept can affect one's choice of projects and behaviors. So, for example, Hacking discusses both the ways in which people may act according to the label and conception they fall under. How do such effects occur? There are at least two sorts of avenues via which the conception may act on labeled persons. First, the conception may make some behaviors *causally salient.* Second, the conception may structure the social world so as to make some behaviors *strategically salient.* Earlier in his discussion of identification, Appiah alludes to both sorts of effects when he writes,

> Once the racial label is applied to people ideas about what it refers to, ideas that may be much less consensual than the application of the label, come to have their social effects. But they have not only their social effects but psychological ones as well; and they shape the ways people conceive of themselves and their projects. (1996, p. 78)

Labels express concepts that figure in a causal theory of the world. And, insofar as the concepts pick out explanatory kinds in the world, the labels one falls under will have some explanatory force, and this force constrains one's choice of projects. How does this constraint occur? According to the causal salience account of shaping, some labels pick out putatively natural categories, and if one falls under that label, engaging in the "natural" behavior is likely to meet with less resistance than engaging in "unnatural" behavior. Appiah seems to have something like this in mind in his discussion of psychological effects. Explaining this idea, Sally Haslanger writes:

> in practical decision making we ought to be attentive to things' natures. It won't do to try to fry an egg on a paper plate; there's no point in trying to teach a rock how to read. Because the world is not infinitely malleable to our wants and needs, reasonable decision making will accommodate "how things are," where this is understood as accommodating the natures of things, the background conditions constraining our actions. (1993, p. 105)

Haslanger is writing about the way conceptions of gender serve to regulate behavior because of the putatively natural character of gender. And it's easy to see how other human kind concepts and labels might work the same way. For example, if when someone falls under a racial concept it suggests that some projects are natural and others unnatural, then practical reason (together with Haslanger's suggestion about avoiding conflict with the natures of things) dictates that one should take one's natural category memberships into account. In short, a concept and conception of a kind of person makes some sorts of projects and behaviors *causally salient* to the labeled. Note that the claim is not that a person's projects are directly shaped by their intrinsic nature, but rather that their projects are shaped by the local theory of what their intrinsic nature entails—a local theory embodied in a conception that makes certain projects or behaviors salient. Thus the shaping of intentional projects is itself intentionally mediated.

By itself, such causal salience is an incomplete account of the way in which regimes of labeling affect individual projects. It's incomplete because it is not merely the perceived natures of things (understood as presocial features of the world) that guide our identifications but *all* features of the world that seem relatively intransigent, including social features. To put it in a Durkheimian way, we need to understand social facts as things—as exhibiting coercive power over individual choice. It is a central feature of everyday human life that we attempt to coordinate our actions with others. In other words, we attempt to decide what others will do, given various things we might do, and we choose our actual actions accordingly. Recognizing that the social world places strong constraints on our actions allows us to understand a second mechanism by which social roles shape their occupants' projects. Insofar as a person is a union leader, *garçon de café*, gang member, prom queen, or is gay, white, a man, joyful, or mentally ill, that person will have certain permissions and expectations as well as restrictions and prohibitions placed upon her by others. What's more, some of these social strictures may be enforced, with social disapproval or even violence. Because such categories often come with a policy on the part of a community to treat certain people in a certain way, they create a range of socially available options from which labeled persons may choose. (Such social transformation is what Appiah refers to as the "social effects" of labeling.) Thus, behaviors may also be *strategically salient*. In many contexts, strategic salience radically affects one's choices of intentional projects. If, for example, you are a member of a race in a highly racialized society, or a member of a sex in a highly gendered society, you may have little choice but to choose your intentional projects from among those that are socially permitted.

So, social roles affect individuals' projects and intentions by delimiting the space of what is conceivable (because one can only act in ways one can conceive), and constraining the space of causally and strategically salient actions. How does this lead to instability? While Hacking discusses a number of forces that may result in the instability of a social role, he discusses only two that bear on the instability thesis.[31] The first possibility he considers is that members of a labeled class will organize in response to a regime of labeling and attempt to alter it. Those classified as homosexuals, for example, have organized and systematically agitated to alter the regime of labeling (including the practices of discriminatory treatment) that go with the label (e.g., Hacking 1986). Hacking documents a similar phenomena occurring with multiple personality sufferers (1995a), and sufferers (and the relatives of sufferers) of childhood autism (1995b, 1999). We must be careful here. A conception can change not for epistemic reasons, but because of political pressure placed upon those who count as experts about a category. But the instability thesis posits a particular sort of problem that occurs when a labeled class actually changes, rendering the old conception obsolete. So, insofar as the agitation of a labeled class takes the form of exhibiting alternative sorts of behaviors (acting against the dominant conception of the type), such agitation has the effect of undermining the accuracy of the conception of the labeled class and is a genuine source of the sort of instability relevant to assessing the looping effect of human kinds. Michael Walzer provides an example of such instability from the caste systems of ancient India, "A certain kind of collective mobility is possible, for castes or subcastes can cultivate the outward marks of purity and (within severe limits) raise their position in the social scale" (1983, p. 27). A second possibility is that a new conception of a labeled class may alter those conditions that gave rise to the behavior described by the conception. This is Hacking's view of child abuse. As new theories of abuse become disseminated, they create a new social context in which agents may choose different actions (1986, 1995a, ch. 4,

1999, ch. 5). Abuse statistics may then rise or shift as new people (and sorts of people) decide to abuse or as new forms of abuse take hold. These two possibilities form the core of what Hacking calls the looping effect of human kinds, and both are genuine sources of instability for a social role.

Instability and Stability

Although the ways in which conceptions of a kind of person may change the causal and strategic salience of particular sorts of act are undoubtedly only part of the causal story of social role effects on persons, they seem the best interpretation of what Hacking thinks is creating instability. But now we are in a position to see the Instability Thesis as unmotivated and probably wrong. Hacking provides little reason to think that such regimes of labeling must always be so causally efficacious as to undermine the associated conception or theory as an instrument of explanation and prediction. Hacking gives us a picture of how instability might work, but no illumination to why it should always work, or in what cases it does work. To recognize that social roles may be unstable is not even to show that they usually are.

Begin with causal salience. Suppose the going conceptions of x do make some actions and life options causally salient for those who fall under the associated concept of x. Then a person who falls under a particular concept might choose to pursue one project rather than another because they believe it would be more natural for someone like them. But this should have the effect of making those who fall under such a label *conform* to the conception, rather than deviate from it. And thus, the conception might come to describe accurately a world that is of its own making. Thus, the possibility that conceptions make certain actions causally salient provides no reason to believe the Instability Thesis.

What about strategic salience? Hacking's own arguments for instability resulting from the looping of human kinds stem from shifts in the strategic salience of certain actions. But strategic salience may also result not in deviance but conformity. This mechanism affects labeled individuals via the community's behavior towards the labeled class. And this behavior will be guided by the conception of the labeled class. To choose a simple example, if Norton were to wear a skirt to his workplace at the bank, instead of trousers, he would likely face snickers, jokes, jeers, and perhaps even disgust on the part of some. This communal behavior would be guided by a conception of gender appropriate clothing for a bank teller. And on the street outside the bank, he might face worse yet. These are facts about the social world Norton inhabits, and they conspire to keep him in trousers. Because Norton plans his dress against the background of his other preferences and the stable social world he inhabits, he seldom seriously thinks about deviating from even this minor norm. Moreover, because deviance from this minor norm is rare, false or unreflective beliefs about this gender-marked behavior (and the gender category it is associated with) face little pressure for revision. Such characteristics may amount to elements of property-cluster kinds to the extent that whole sets of such behavioral (or behaviorally mediated) characteristics are associated in a conception, and are reliably preferred under prevailing social conditions. For example, if this one gender norm is associated with many others, including other norms for how to dress, speak, walk, think, and more generally act, and if these norms are enforced on those who fall under gender labels, then they could have the effect of causing a variety of properties to cluster in social role occupants.

The idea is that social roles may be maintained by the strategic individual choices of actors in a community. This may seem surprising, but once we consider that the relevant mechanisms operate via individual actors' choices, it should not be. For what I am suggesting is that social roles might be sustained by a sort of equilibrium common in examples from game theory. Game theory makes clear the way elaborate, multiperson games may be sustained by the rational choice of individuals. The present suggestion is that we can understand certain effects of social roles (e.g., systematic behaviors on the part of social role occupants) as being in equilibrium with the actions of labelers that sustain the social role. Each party participates in the acts as they do because to deviate unilaterally from doing so would result in lower expected utility, given what every other person is doing.[32] That such game theory can be drawn upon to provide a theory of stable conventions is something David Lewis's pioneering work established decades ago.[33] Unfortunately, there is not room here to consider in detail how game theory or Lewis's theory can be applied social roles, but we can at least state a sufficient condition for the stability of a particular feature of the social world caused by the presence of a social role:

> *F* is a stable feature of members of labeled group *L* in a community *C* that employs a regime of labeling *R* if:
> 1. Members of *C* prefer to employ *R* as long as they believe the conception that figures in *R* picks out *L* and correctly ascribes *F* to members of *L*.
> 2. Members of *C* do believe that the conception that figures in *R* correctly ascribes *F* to members of *L*.
> 3. Members of group *L* prefer to act so as to maintain *F* as long as members of community *C* employ *R*.

Thus, to return to our earlier example, trouser wearing among men is stable as long as:

> T1. Members of the community prefer to maintain that men wear trousers and punish exceptions, as long as they believe it is the case that men generally wear trousers and exceptions are unusual and punishable.

T2. Members of the community do believe that men generally wear trousers and exceptions are unusual and punishable.

T3. Men prefer to wear trousers as long as deviance from this regularity is punished.

Strictly speaking, this sufficient condition isn't met, because not all men wear trousers, and not all nontrouser wearing by men is treated as abnormal. (I assume the condition can be modified to be a more plausible description of an equilibrium in the real world.) But what the condition does is show the way that a social role and its causal effects may be kept in equilibrium by the preferences and approximate rationality of participants in the society. It shows how conceptions of particular kinds of persons may stabilize the behavior they describe, even when behaviors in question have no presocial link to the kinds of person in question. And this shows a quite general way in which even relatively superficial effects of labeling practices may be stable, and thus gives us good reason to doubt the Instability Thesis.

Other Sources of Stability

The two mechanisms that I have examined are central to Hacking's own account of the looping effect, but I have argued they may lead to stabilized rather than destabilized social roles. Of course, the discussion here is far from complete, and there are other sources of both stability and instability for social role kinds. In particular, I limited my discussion of instability to Hacking's looping thesis, and thereby concentrated on mechanisms of stability and instability that are intentionally mediated. There is, however, another important model of social constructionist thought that emphasizes social role explanations that are not necessarily intentionally mediated. I have in mind what Paul Griffiths (1997) has called a *reinforcement model* of social construction. Here I briefly sketch this alternative model and consider a way in which it too could give rise to a stable relationship between the conception of the social role and the properties of the occupants of the role.[34]

The reinforcement model of social construction is a diachronic, developmental account. It emphasizes nonintentionally mediated changes in a person brought by social role occupation, explaining variant behaviors as resulting from variations in patterns of developmental reinforcement. Griffiths suggests that the conceptions of appropriate behavior in the social role establish norms that create "something akin to a pattern of reinforcement which shapes people's behavior so that it conforms to the norms" (p. 143). The patterns of reinforcement in question don't cause the agent to represent propositionally certain patterns of behavior as desirable. Rather, once the person is ascribed to a particular social role, the reinforcement shapes particular cognitive mechanisms such that the individual components of the ascribed social role become nearly reflexive, and together these components comprise the role behaviors.[35]

Griffiths provides an interesting example of this model that emerges from research on basic affects. Over the last thirty years, an impressive body of research has accumulated documenting the existence of near universal correlations between certain facial expressions and emotions. Paul Ekman, the leading researcher in this field, summarized the state of the art in 1992:

> There is consistent evidence, across investigators, of universal facial expressions for at least five emotions [happiness, surprise/fear, sadness, anger, and disgust/contempt]. More research is needed to resolve questions about whether there are three or four more. (pp. 550–51; cf. Griffiths 1997, ch. 3 for a review)

These robust correlations lead Griffiths to remark that the emergence of these expressions in infants "conforms to the classical biological determinist model, in which almost any environment that supports survival to adulthood supports development of the trait" (p. 156). But drawing on work by Ekman (1972), Griffiths notes that even these "biologically determined" motor responses can be shaped by cultural reinforcement:

> In studies of facial expression in Japanese and American students, Ekman and his collaborators found that the Japanese suppressed their facial expressions in the presence of authority figures. They superimposed voluntary muscle movements so as to produce a polite smile. These voluntary movements were initiated so quickly that the initial emotional expressions could be detected only by using frame-by-frame analysis of videotapes. (p. 156)

In this case, a pattern of reinforcement in the social environment of the Japanese students leads them to develop an alternative, reflexive expression in the presence of authority figures. The pattern of reinforcement was likely the result of the community's norms about what counts as appropriate behavior towards others in the social hierarchy. And these norms are presumably part of the community's conceptions of the social role of subordinate in a hierarchy.

How do such effects created by reinforcement bear on the instability thesis? Once a regime of labeling actually creates new properties of persons, those effects are really there in the world. They are a stable part of the world that we are epistemically pulled to describe in our theories of it. In fact, such effects are more stable than the strategic responses of role occupants discussed in the last subsection, since reflexive dispositions will continue to be manifested—at least for a time—even when the regime of labeling is removed. Any conception of hierarchical behavior among Japanese college students that failed to mention differential facial expressions would be importantly incomplete. But a complete conception may itself contribute to the continued reinforcement of hierarchically "appropriate" behavior. As with intentionally mediated responses, reinforced behaviors may come to be in equilibrium with the conceptions that created and describe them.

Hacking's general statements about the looping of human kinds are too broad to be plausible. But the more limited Instability Thesis is still a threat to viewing social roles as cluster kinds that underwrite our knowledge of the social world. What I've tried to show here is that the Instability Thesis is still much too general, and that there's every reason to expect the forces that contribute to the "looping of human kinds" to result in stability as well as instability. If what I have said is correct, then we also have an answer to social constructionist critics of stability. Such critics, as I noted in the introduction, often emphasize the instability of social kinds because such kinds are not rooted in biological facts. Such categories have, in the words of the critical sociologist Stuart Hall, "no guarantees in Nature" (1996, p. 166). But having no guarantees in nature, is not the same as having no guarantees at all. A particular social setting, structured by the conception in question, may be guarantee enough for a particular social role to create a stable, explanatorily relevant property-cluster kind.

CONCLUSION

The preceding discussion offers an interpretation of a broad class of social constructionist claims about human kinds. On this interpretation, to say that x is socially constructed (where x is replaced by the term for a human kind) is to offer a substantive empirical hypothesis that the differential properties of instances of x are produced by the occupation of a social role. When a social role differentiates its occupant to the extent that a cluster of important properties regularly co-occur, I have suggested we ought to regard those occupants as instances of social kinds. Moreover, I have suggested that we do and should employ those kinds in reasoning about our social world. Because the theory of social roles set out makes only quite general assumptions about human nature (e.g., that humans may act in ways that are approximately rational and that they may experience behavioral reinforcement), it is compatible with humanist approaches to the philosophy of social science. But it differs sharply from hermeneutic, critical, and constructionist approaches to the social sciences in emphasizing the stability of social kinds. It is no surprise that the social world can be extremely volatile. But by excessively emphasizing this volatility, theorists in philosophy and the social sciences have threatened to make it a mystery how we manage to negotiate our social world successfully every day, and it leaves us without a clear understanding of the intransigence of social roles. Understanding mechanisms of stability, in contrast, not only offers an explanation of our social knowledge, but also presumably focuses our attention on those mechanisms that must be addressed in the attempt to disrupt social roles and effect the transformation of social life.

ACKNOWLEDGMENTS

I am grateful to Lori Alward, Robin Andreasen, Frankie Egan, Aaron Meskin, Elijah Millgram, Dominic Murphy, Ram Neta, Cindy Stark, Shaun Nichols, Frederick Schmitt, Stephen Stich, Jonathan Weinberg, and Charlotte Witt, and audiences at Washington University, Hong Kong University, and Texas Tech University, for numerous helpful comments on earlier drafts of this chapter.

NOTES

1. For a catalog of constructionist claims, see Hacking (1999, ch. 1). For some important accounts, see Mills (1998) or Outlaw (1996) on race; Kessler and McKenna (1977) on gender; Foucault (1978), McIntosh (1992), or Padgug (1992) on sexual orientation; Griffiths (1997, ch. 6) or Averill (1980a, 1980b) on the emotions; and Hacking (1995b), Showalter (1997), or Scheff (1984) on mental illness. Note that many of these authors do not describe themselves using talk of "social construction."

2. While some constructionists appeal to social role explanations, this is not the only thesis underlying constructionist claims. Recently Mallon and Stich (2000) have shown that some constructionists claims (and some disputes over constructionism) are motivated by the implicit assumption of a particular thesis about the meanings of terms. This chapter explores a more substantive interpretation of constructionist claims, but one that is compatible with that explored by Mallon and Stich.

3. Kornblith (1993). Kornblith adapts his question from McCulloch (1965).

4. Kornblith may be primarily concerned with understanding how we have *scientific* knowledge, rather than everyday knowledge. I think there is good reason to think there is no sharp divide between scientific and folk knowledge.

5. Consider, for example, the emphasis of evolutionary psychologists on the "psychological foundations of culture" (e.g., Tooby and Cosmides 1992).

6. Richard Boyd (1999a, pp. 153–54), for example, says social roles may be natural kinds, but it is unclear whether Boyd means social roles in the sense discussed here or something closer to a niche (see below).

7. (1986, p. 68). Italics in original. (Also occurs in 1994, pp. 54–5, sans italics).

8. For example, Taylor (1971).

9. For example, Fay (1983), Taylor (1971).

10. See Mallon and Stich (2000) for a sketch of some of the complex interactions of evolved and acquired elements in emotion phenotypes.

11. Sulloway's thesis is controversial. In the present context, it serves only as an illustration.

12. Paul Griffiths was here first. His illuminating discussion of constructionism (1997, ch. 6) introduces these terms. My employment of them here is a bit different than Griffiths's, but it picks out a similar distinction.

13. For example, our conception of *tall* suggests that tall people need more room to be comfortable, make better basketball players, must be looked up to in order to make eye contact, and so on.

14. I am grateful to Aaron Meskin and Frederick Schmitt for helpful discussion on this issue.

15. A full characterization of what makes a property "methodologically important" is beyond the scope of the present discussion, but it is sufficient that the property figure in other useful and explanatory theories.

16. It might be H20 and lack the paradigmatic superficial properties because conditions are bizarre.

17. This may overstate the case. Lots of examples of things called "water" are not pure H20. On the other hand, they are probably not pure water either.

18. The explanatory importance of relational properties has also found many defenders in the philosophy mind, in the debate over broad and narrow content. For example, Burge (1986), Jackson and Pettit (1988), and Stalnaker (1989).

19. Mayr quite explicitly notes the importance of relational properties to his account: "It is, however, irrelevant and misleading to define species in an essentialistic way because the species is not defined by intrinsic, but by relational properties" (1984, p. 535).

20. All this may seem rather quick to those immersed in the ongoing disputes over the species concept in the philosophy of biology. There, a central portion of the debate has centered around whether species are historical individuals or spatiotemporally unrestricted classes. The point for the present discussion is that both relational and historical accounts of species incorporate relational elements into species definitions. Recognizing this, combined with the position of species as a paradigmatic philosophical natural kind, serves to liberalize the notion of a natural kind. For discussion of property-cluster accounts and species, see Hull (1999), Boyd (1999a). For a more general discussion of historical kinds, see Millikan (1999), Boyd (1999b).

21. The situationist tradition of social psychology has produced quite dramatic demonstrations of situational pressures altering individual behaviors. For example, Latané and Darley (1968) on the bystander effect, Darley and Batson's (1973) Good Samaritan study, and Milgram's (1963) obedience experiments. See Ross and Nisbett (1991) for an opinionated introduction to the situationist literature.

22. There is a long history of concern with this sort of effect among various sorts of feminists. Mary Wollstonecraft argued in the eighteenth century that women were made vain, ignorant, and capricious by their lack of education. She went on to charge that it was these same qualities that were put forward to justify denying education to women (1995, chs. 2–3). Portions of Catherine MacKinnon's (1989) analysis of gender can be read in a similar way.

23. These four sorts of properties are not mutually exclusive.

24. I think it is too early to assess the form such metacultural constraints will take, but work by Scott Atran (1998), Alan Page Fiske (1993), Laurence Hirshfeld (1994, 1996), and Dan Sperber (1996) are very suggestive of ways in which facts about cognition may impose defeasible constraints on conceptual and social systems.

25. Despite this broad characterization, Hacking seems wary of extending the looping account, for example to race (1995a, pp. 355–56).

26. I am not sure if, or to what extent, Hacking would endorse this limitation.

27. Hacking introduces the distinction between interactive and indifferent kinds to distinguish kinds that are affected by their representation of, and interaction with, systems of representation from those that do not engage in such intentionally mediated interaction (1999, pp. 109ff).

28. In the second section (in the subsection entitled "Social Roles as Homeostatic Clusters"), I mentioned four sorts of effects that social role occupation might have on the occupant. The sorts of effects Hacking is concerned with are primarily those falling in the first or second group.

29. The philosophical idiom of the passages I am quoting renders things in terms of linguistic entities like labels and descriptions. I pass from this idiom to talk of mental entities like concepts and conceptions. While I take it that the latter talk is more accurate, for present purposes nothing hangs on this shift.

30. Notice that conceptual availability poses little restriction. It is, for example, possible for a person to identify in a way that it is metaphysically impossible for him to be. For example, I could identify as a denizen as of the fictional planet Krypton in the sense that I allowed Kryptonian ideals to shape my intentional projects. But I take it nothing could make me a Kryptonian.

31. Hacking discusses a number of other sources of instability that are orthogonal to the instability thesis and the looping of human kinds. For example, instability can occur when the conception of a kind of person is altered for general theoretical reasons (or for political or social reasons). Because the conception structures the regime of labeling, changes in the conception may disrupt the regime of labeling and the behavior of the labeled. Hacking claims that the linking of fugue to hysteria in late nineteenth-century France, and the subsequent skepticism about hysteria as a medical category in the early twentieth century, helped undermine the social conditions that made individuals undertake fugue behavior (1998, pp. 71ff). In addition, a social role kind may be unstable because other elements of the niche that support it—elements not directly structured by the conception (and not part of the regime of labeling)— change, thus altering the context in which agents choose their actions. Thus, for example, Hacking (1998) thinks that fugue arose among the working class against the background of emerging middle-class tourism. If he is correct, it suggests that changing economic circumstances (e.g., the extension of wealth and leisure to the working class) might have been enough to undermine fugue. While I think these are genuine sources of instability, they do not merit a general skepticism about the possibility of knowledge of social role kinds.

32. That is, the social role practice could be a Nash equilibrium. A Nash equilibrium for an n-person game is one such that every person is acting so as to maximize his or her expected utility, given the way every other person is acting.

33. Lewis (1969).

34. Griffiths contrasts this reinforcement model with what he calls the "social role" model of social construction. The latter model is similar to the one I have attributed to Hacking.

35. These sorts of effects would fall in group 2 of the classification introduced above in "Social Roles as Homeostatic Clusters."

Socializing Metaphysics:
A Bibliography

Kevin Kimble and Frederick F. Schmitt

This is a selective bibliography of recent work on the metaphysics of the social world, the social nature of individual human beings, and the social construction of nature. Included here as well are all additional references in the articles in this collection. See also the bibliography of collective intentionality at www.valt.helsinki.fi/kfid/codi/ (accessed February 2003). For a bibliography of social issues in epistemology, see Frederick F. Schmitt and James Spellman, "Socializing Epistemology: A Bibliography," in *Socializing Epistemology: The Social Dimensions of Knowledge*, edited by Frederick F. Schmitt (Rowman & Littlefield, 1994).

Aboulafia, Mitchell. 1986. *The Mediating Self: Mead, Sartre, and Self-Determination.* New Haven, Conn.: Yale University Press.

Alanen, L., S. Heinämaa, and T. Wallgren, eds. 1997. *Commonality and Particularity in Ethics.* New York: St. Martin's.

Alexander, J. and S. Seidman, eds. 1990. *Culture and Society: Contemporary Debates.* Cambridge: Cambridge University Press.

Anderson, Elizabeth. 1995. "Knowledge, Human Interests, and Objectivity in Feminist Epistemology." *Philosophical Topics* 23: 27–58.

———. 2001. "Unstrapping the Straightjacket of 'Preference': A Comment on Amartya Sen's Contributions to Philosophy and Economics." *Economics & Philosophy* 17: 21–38.

Anderson, C. Anthony and Joseph Owens, eds. 1990. *Propositional Attitudes.* Stanford, Calif.: Center for the Study of Language and Information.

Anscombe, G. E. M. 1963. *Intention.* 2d ed. Ithaca, N.Y.: Cornell University Press.

Antony, Louise and Charlotte Witt, eds. 1993. *A Mind of One's Own: Feminist Essays on Reason and Objectivity.* Boulder, Colo.: Westview.

Appiah, K. Anthony. 1996. "Race, Culture, Identity: Misunderstood Connections." In *Color Conscious: The Political Morality of Race*, edited by K. Anthony Appiah and Amy Guttman. Princeton, N.J.: Princeton University Press.

Appiah, K. Anthony and Amy Guttman. 1996. *Color Conscious: The Political Morality of Race*. Princeton, N.J.: Princeton University Press.

Archard, David, ed. 1996. *Philosophy and Pluralism*. Cambridge: Cambridge University Press.

Archer, Margaret. 1995. *Realist Social Theory: The Morphogenetic Approach*. Cambridge: Cambridge University Press.

———. 1996. *Culture and Agency: The Place of Culture in Social Theory*. Rev. ed. Cambridge: Cambridge University Press.

Argyle, M. 1991. *Cooperation: The Basis of Sociality*. London: Routledge.

Arrazola, X., K. Korta, and F. Pelletier, eds. 1998. *Discourse, Interaction, and Communication*. Dordrecht: Kluwer.

Atran, Scott. 1998. "Folk Biology and the Anthropology of Science: Cognitive Universals and Cultural Particulars." *Behavioral and Brain Sciences* 21: 547–609.

Austin, John. 1875. *Lectures on Jurisprudence, or the Philosophy of Positive Law*. London: J. Murray.

Averill, J. R. 1980a. "A Constructivist View of Emotion." In *Emotion: Theory, Research and Experience*. Vol. 1: *Theories of Emotion*, edited by R. Plutchik and H. Kellerman. New York: Random House.

———. 1980b. "Emotion and Anxiety: Sociocultural, Biological, and Psychological Determinants." In *Explaining Emotions*, edited by Amelie Rorty. Berkeley: University of California Press.

Axelrod, Robert. 1984. *The Evolution of Cooperation*. New York: Basic Books.

———. 1997. *The Complexity of Cooperation: Agent-Based Models of Competition and Collaboration*. Princeton, N.J.: Princeton University Press.

Bach, Kent. 1995. "Terms of Agreement." *Ethics* 105: 604–12.

Baghramian, M. and A. Dunlop, eds. 2000. *Dealing with Diversity*. London: Routledge.

Baier, Annette C. 1970. "Act and Intent." *The Journal of Philosophy* 67: 648–58.

———. 1997a. *The Commons of the Mind*. Chicago: Open Court.

———. 1997b. "Doing Things with Others: The Mental Commons." In *Commonality and Particularity in Ethics*, edited by L. Alanen, S. Heinämaa, and T. Wallgren. New York: St. Martin's.

Baker, H. A. Jr., M. Diawara, and R. H. Lindeborg, eds. 1996. *Black British Cultural Studies*. Chicago: University of Chicago Press.

Baker, Judith, ed. 1994. *Group Rights*. Toronto: University of Toronto Press.

Ball, T., J. Farr, and R. Hansen, eds. 1989. *Political Innovation and Conceptual Change*. Cambridge: Cambridge University Press.

Balzer, Wolfgang. 1990. "A Basic Model of Social Institutions." *Journal of Mathematical Sociology* 17: 1–29.

———. 1993. *Soziale Institutionen*. Berlin: de Gruyter.

Balzer, Wolfgang and Raimo Tuomela. 1997a. "A Fixed Point Approach to Collective Attitudes." In *Contemporary Action Theory*. Vol. 2: *Social Action*, edited by G. Holmström-Hintikka and R. Tuomela. Dordrecht: Kluwer.

———. 1997b. "The Structure and Verification of Planbased Joint Intentions." *International Journal of Cooperative Information Systems* 6: 3–26.

———. 2002a. "Collective Intentions and the Maintenance of Social Practices." Forthcoming in *Autonomous Agents and Multi-Agent Systems*.

———. 2002b. "Social Institutions, Norms, and Practices." Proceedings of the Workshop on Social Norms. Barcelona.

Barkow, Jerome H., Leda Cosmides, and John Tooby, eds. 1992. *The Adapted Mind*. New York: Oxford University Press.

Baron, Reuben M., Polemnia G. Amazeen, and Peter J. Beck. 1994. "Local and Global Dynamics of Social Relations." In *Dynamical Systems in Social Psychology*, edited by Robin R. Vallacher and Andrzej Nowak. San Diego: Academic Press.

Baxter, Don. 1988a. "Identity in the Loose and Popular Sense." *Mind* 97: 575–82.

———. 1988b. "Many-One Identity." *Philosophical Papers* 17: 193–216.

———. 1999. "The Discernibility of Identicals." *Journal of Philosophical Research* 24: 37–55.

———. 2001. "Instantiation as Partial Identity." *Australasian Journal of Philosophy* 79: 449–64.

———. 2002. "Altruism, Grief, and Identity." *Ms*.

Beauchamp, Thomas and Norman Bowie, eds. 1978. *Ethical Theory and Business*. Englewood Cliffs, N.J.: Prentice-Hall.

Belzer, Marvin. 1986. "Intentional Social Action and We-Intentions." *Analyse & Kritik* 8: 86–95.

Benhabib, Seyla. 1987. "The Generalized and the Concrete Other." In *Feminism as Critique*, edited by Seyla Benhabib and D. Cornell. Minneapolis: University of Minnesota Press.

———. 1992. *Situating the Self: Gender, Community, and Postmodernism in Contemporary Ethics*. London: Routledge.

Benhabib, Seyla and D. Cornell. 1987. *Feminism as Critique*. Minneapolis: University of Minnesota Press.

Benjamin, Martin. 1976. "Can Moral Responsibility Be Collective and Nondistributive?" *Social Theory and Practice* 4: 93–106.

Benn, S. I. 1988. *A Theory of Freedom*. Cambridge: Cambridge University Press.

Benson, Paul. 1991. "Autonomy and Oppressive Socialization." *Social Theory and Practice* 17: 385–408.

Berger, P. and T. Luckmann. 1967. *The Social Construction of Reality*. Harmondsworth: Penguin.

Bhargava, Rajeev. 1992. *Individualism in Social Science: Forms and Limits of a Methodology*. Oxford: Oxford University Press.

Bicchieri, Cristina. 1993. *Rationality and Coordination*. Cambridge: Cambridge University Press.

Bittner, Rudiger. 2002. "An Action for Two." In *Social Facts and Collective Intentionality*, edited by Georg Meggle. Frankfurt: Dr. Hänsel-Hohenhausen.

Blackburn, Simon. 1984. *Spreading the Word*. Oxford: Basil Blackwell.

Block, Ned and Robert Stalnaker. 1999. "Conceptual Analysis, Dualism and the Explanatory Gap." *Philosophical Review* 108: 1–46.

Bloor, David. 1997. *Wittgenstein, Rules, and Institutions*. London: Routledge.

Bogdan, Radu, ed. 1986. *Belief: Form, Content, and Function*. Oxford: Clarendon Press.

Bohman, James. 1991. *New Philosophy of Social Science*. Cambridge, Mass.: MIT Press.

Bourdieu, Pierre. 1977. *Outline of a Theory of Practice*. Cambridge: Cambridge University Press.

Boyd, Richard. 1988. "How to Be a Moral Realist." In *Essays on Moral Realism*, edited by G. Sayre-McCord. Ithaca, N.Y.: Cornell University Press.

———. 1991. "Realism, Anti-Foundationalism and the Enthusiasm for Natural Kinds." *Philosophical Studies* 61: 127–48.

———. 1992. "Constructivism, Realism, and Philosophical Method." In *Inference, Explanation, and Other Frustrations: Essays in the Philosophy of Science*, edited by John Earman. Berkeley: University of California Press.

———. 1999a. "Homeostasis, Species, and Higher Taxa." In *Species: New Interdisciplinary Essays*, edited by Robert A. Wilson. Cambridge, Mass.: MIT Press.

———. 1999b. "Kinds, Complexity and Multiple Realization." *Philosophical Studies* 95: 67–98.

Brandom, Robert B. 1994. *Making It Explicit: Reasoning, Representing, and Discursive Commitment*. Cambridge, Mass.: Harvard University Press.

Bratman, Michael. 1987. *Intentions, Plans and Practical Reason*. Cambridge, Mass.: Harvard University Press.

———. 1992. "Shared Cooperative Activity." *Philosophical Review* 101: 327–41.

———. 1993a. "Shared Intention." *Ethics* 104: 97–113.

———. 1993b. "Shared Intention and Mutual Obligation." *Cahiers d'Epistemologie*, no. 9319.

———. 1996. "Planning and Temptation." In May, Friedman, and Clark (1996).

———. 1997. "I Intend That We J." In Holmström-Hintikka and R. Tuomela (1997).

———. 1999a. *Faces of Intention: Selected Essays on Intention and Agency*. Cambridge: Cambridge University Press.

———. 1999b. *Intention, Plans, and Practical Reason*. Stanford, Calif.: CSLI Publications.

Braybrooke, David. 1987. *Philosophy of Social Science*. Englewood Cliffs, N.J.: Prentice-Hall.

———, ed. 1996. *Social Rules: Origin; Character; Logic; Change*. Boulder, Colo.: Westview.

Braybrooke, David, Bryson Brown, and Peter K. Schotch. 1995. *Logic on the Track of Social Change*. Oxford: Oxford University Press.

Brennan, G. 2001. "Collective Coherence?" *International Review of Law and Economics* 21: 197–211.

Broad, C. D. 1928. *The Mind and Its Place in Nature*. London: Kegan Paul.

Brodbeck, May, ed. 1968. *Readings in the Philosophy of Social Science*. New York: Macmillan.

Brooks, D. H. M. 1981. "Joint Action." *Mind* 90: 113–19.

———. 1986. "Group Minds." *Australasian Journal of Philosophy* 64: 456–70.

Broome, John. 2001. "Are Intentions Reasons? And How Should We Cope with Incommensurable Values?" In *Practical Rationality and Preference: Essays for David Gauthier*, edited by Christopher W. Morris and Arthur Ripstein. Cambridge: Cambridge University Press.

Brown, J. R. 1989. *The Rational and the Social*. London: Routledge.

Brown, Jessica. 1998. "Natural Kind Terms and Recognitional Capacities." *Mind* 107: 275–303.

Brown, S. C., ed. 1979. *Philosophical Disputes in the Social Sciences*. Sussex: Harvester Press.

Burge, Tyler. 1977. "A Theory of Aggregates." *Nous* 11: 97–117.

———. 1979. "Individualism and the Mental." In *Midwest Studies in Philosophy* 4: *Studies in Metaphysics*, edited by P. A. French, T. E. Uehling, and H. Wettstein. Minneapolis: University of Minnesota Press.

———. 1986. "Individualism and Psychology." *The Philosophical Review* 95: 3–45.

———. 1998. "Reason and the First Person." In *Knowing Our Own Mind*, edited by Crispin Wright, Barry C. Smith, and Cynthia Macdonald. Oxford: Clarendon.

Buschlinger, Wolfgang and Christoph Lütge, eds. 2003 (in press). *Festschrift* for Gerhard Vollmer. Stuttgart: Hirzel Verlag.

Campbell, Colin. 1996. *The Myth of Social Action*. Cambridge: Cambridge University Press.

Campbell, Keith, John Bacon, and L. Rhinehart, eds. 1992. *Ontology, Causality, and Mind: Essays on the Philosophy of David Armstrong*. Cambridge: Cambridge University Press.

Caporeal, L. R. and R. M. Baron. 1997. "Groups as the Mind's Natural Environment." In *Evolutionary Social Psychology*, edited by Jeffry A. Simpson and Douglas Kenrick. Mahwah, N.J.: Lawrence Erlbaum.

Carnap, Rudolf. 1956. *Meaning and Necessity*. 2d ed. Chicago: University of Chicago Press.

Carr, David. 1986. *Time, Narrative, and History*. Bloomington: Indiana University Press.

Carroll, Lewis. 1895. "What the Tortoise Said to Achilles." *Mind* 4: 278–80.

Cartwright, D. and A. Zander. 1968. *Group Dynamics: Research and Theory*. New York: Harper and Row.

Casati, R. and G. White, eds. 1993. *Philosophy and the Cognitive Sciences*. Kirchberg: Austrian Ludwig Wittgenstein Association.

Castaneda, Hector-Neri and George Nakhnikian, eds. 1963. *Morality and the Language of Conduct*. Detroit: Wayne State University Press.

Cavell, Stanley. 1976. *Must We Mean What We Say?* New York: Cambridge University Press.

———. 1979. *The Claim of Reason*. New York: Oxford University Press.

———. 1989. *This New Yet Unapproachable America*. Albuquerque, N.M.: Living Batch Press.

Chalmers, D. 1996. *The Conscious Mind*. Oxford: Oxford University Press.

Chapman, B. 1998. "More Easily Done Than Said: Rules, Reason and Rational Social Choice." *Oxford Journal of Legal Studies* 18: 293–329.

Christman, John. 1991. "Autonomy and Personal History." *Canadian Journal of Philosophy* 21: 1–24.

Clark, Austen. 1994. "Beliefs and Desires, Incorporated." *The Journal of Philosophy* 91: 404–25.

Coady, C. A. J. 1992. *Testimony: A Philosophical Study*. Oxford: Oxford University Press.

———, ed. 2000. *Why Universities Matter*. Sydney: Allen and Unwin.

Cohen, Philip R. and Hector Levesque. 1991. "Teamwork." *Nous* 25: 487–512.

360   *Kevin Kimble and Frederick F. Schmitt*

Cohen, Philip R., Hector J. Levesque, and Ira A. Smith. 1997. "On Team Formation." In *Contemporary Action Theory.* Vol. 2: *Social Action*, edited by G. Holmström-Hintikka and R. Tuomela. Dordrecht: Kluwer. In Holmstrom-Hintikka and Tuomela (1997).

Cohen, Philip, Jerry Morgan, and Martha E. Pollak, eds. 1990. *Intentions in Communication.* Cambridge, Mass.: MIT Press.

Cole, J. K., ed. 1972. *Nebraska Symposium on Motivation 1972*, vol. 4. Lincoln: University of Nebraska Press.

Cole, P., ed. 1978. *Syntax and Semantics: Pragmatics 9.* New York: Academic Press.

Coleman, Jules S. 1974. Power and the Structure of Society. New York: Norton.

————. 1990. *The Foundations of Social Theory.* Cambridge, Mass.: Harvard University Press.

Collin, Finn. 1997. *Social Reality.* London: Routledge.

Columbetti, M. 1993. "Formal Semantics and Mutual Belief." *Artificial Intelligence* 62: 341–53.

Conant, James and Urszula M. Zeglen, eds. 2002. *Hilary Putnam: Pragmatism and Realism.* London: Routledge.

Conte, R. and C. Castelfranchi. 1995. *Cognitive and Social Action.* London: UCL Press.

Cook, Gary. 1993. *George Herbert Mead: The Making of a Social Pragmatist.* Urbana: University of Illinois Press.

Copp, David. 1979. "Collective Actions and Secondary Actions." *American Philosophical Quarterly* 16: 177–86.

————. 1980. "Hobbes on Artificial Persons and Collective Actions." *Philosophical Review* 89: 579–606.

————. 1984. "What Collectives Are, Agency, Individualism and Legal Theory." *Dialogue* 23: 249–69.

————. 1992. "The Concept of a Society." *Dialogue* 31: 183–212.

————. 1995. *Morality, Normativity, and Society.* New York: Oxford University Press.

Coulter, Jeff. 1979. *The Social Construction of Mind.* London: Macmillan.

Crary, Alice. 2000. "Wittgenstein's Philosophy in Relation to Political Thought." In *The New Wittgenstein*, edited by Alice Crary and Rupert Read. London: Routledge.

Crary, Alice and Rupert Read, eds. 2000. *The New Wittgenstein.* London: Routledge.

Creath, R. 1990. *Dear Carnap, Dear Van.* Berkeley: University of California Press.

Crosland, Maurice P. 1962. *Historical Studies in the Language of Chemistry.* London: Heinemann Educational Books Ltd.

Cullity, Garrett and Berys Gaut, eds. 1997. *Ethics and Practical Reasoning.* Oxford: Oxford University Press.

Currie, G. 1984. "Individualism and Global Supervenience." *British Journal for the Philosophy of Science* 35: 345–58.

————. 1989. "Metaphysical Individualism." In *Freedom and Rationality: Essays in Honor of John Watkins*, edited by Fred D'Agostino and Ian C. Jarvie. Dordrecht: Kluwer.

Curtler, Hugh, ed. 1986. *Shame, Responsibility, and the Corporation.* New York: Haven Publishing.

D'Agostino, Fred and Ian C. Jarvie, eds. 1989. *Freedom and Rationality: Essays in Honor of John Watkins.* Dordrecht: Kluwer.

Danielson, P., ed. 1998. *Modeling Rationality, Morality, and Evolution.* Oxford: Oxford University Press.

Darley, J. M. and C. D. Batson. 1973. "From Jerusalem to Jericho: A Study of Situational and Dispositional Variables in Helping Behavior." *Journal of Personality and Social Psychology* 27: 100–119.

Davies, M. and Humberstone, L. 1980. "Two Notions of Necessity." *Philosophical Studies* 38: 1–30.

Dawes, R., A. van Kragtvan, and J. Orbell. 1990. "Cooperation for the Benefit of Us—Not Me, or My Conscience." In *Beyond Self-Interest*, edited by J. Mansbridge. Chicago: University of Chicago Press.

De Beauvoir, Simone. 1989. *The Second Sex*. Translated by H. M. Parshley. New York: Vintage.

Dennett, Daniel. 1987. *The Intentional Stance*. Cambridge, Mass.: MIT Press.

Dewey, John. 1927. *The Public and Its Problems*. New York: Henry Holt and Company.

Diamond, Cora. 1989. "Rules: Looking in the Right Place." In *Wittgenstein: Attention to Particulars*, edited by D. Z. Phillips and Peter Winch. New York: St. Martin's.

Donaldson, T. and E. Freeman, eds. 1994. *Business as a Humanity*. New York: Oxford University Press.

Donnellan, K. 1983. "Kripke and Putnam on Natural Kind Terms." In *Knowledge and Mind*, edited by Carl Ginet and Sydney Shoemaker. Oxford: Oxford University Press.

Douglas, M. and D. Hull, eds. 1992. *How Classification Works: Nelson Goodman among the Social Sciences*. Edinburgh: Edinburgh University Press.

Downie, R. S. 1969. "Collective Responsibility." *Philosophy* 44: 66–9.

Dretske, Fred. 1981. *Knowledge and the Flow of Information*. Cambridge, Mass.: MIT Press.

———. 1986. "Misrepresentation." In *Belief: Form, Content, and Function*, edited by Radu Bogdan. Oxford: Clarendon Press.

———. 1988. *Explaining Behavior*. Cambridge: MIT Press.

Dummett, Michael. 1978a. *Truth and Other Enigmas*. Cambridge, Mass.: Harvard University Press.

———. 1978b. "The Social Character of Meaning." In *Truth and Other Enigmas*, edited by Michael Dummett. Cambridge, Mass.: Harvard University Press.

Durkheim, Emile. 1951. *Suicide*. Translated by J. A. Spaulding and G. Simpson. Glencoe, Ill.: Free Press.

———. 1953a. *Sociology and Philosophy*. Translated by D. F. Pocock. Glencoe, Ill.: Free Press.

———. 1953b. "Individual and Collective Representations." In *Sociology and Philosophy*. Translated by D. F. Pocock. Glencoe, Ill.: Free Press.

———. 1982. *The Rules of Sociological Method*. Translated by W. D. Halls. New York: Free Press.

Dworkin, Gerald. 1988. *The Theory and Practice of Autonomy*. Cambridge, Mass.: Cambridge University Press.

Earman, John, ed. 1992. *Inference, Explanation, and Other Frustrations: Essays in the Philosophy of Science*. Berkeley: University of California Press.

Ebbs, Gary. 1996. "Can We Take Our Words at Face Value?" *Philosophy and Phenomenological Research* 56: 499–530.

———. 1997. *Rule-Following and Realism*. Cambridge, Mass.: Harvard University Press.

———. 2000. "The Very Idea of Sameness of Extension across Time." *American Philosophical Quarterly* 37: 245–68.

———. 2001. "Is Skepticism about Self-Knowledge Coherent?" *Philosophical Studies* 105: 43–58.

———. 2002. "Truth and Trans-Theoretical Terms." In *Hilary Putnam: Pragmatism and Realism*, edited by James Conant and Urszula M. Zeglen. London: Routledge.

Ekman, Paul. 1972. "Universals and Cultural Differences in Facial Expressions of Emotion." In *Nebraska Symposium on Motivation 1971,* vol. 4, edited by J. K. Cole. Lincoln: University of Nebraska Press.

———. 1992. "Are There Basic Emotions?" *Psychological Review* 99: 550–53.

Elster, Jon. 1985. "Rationality, Morality, and Collective Action." *Ethics* 96:136–55.

———. 1989. *The Cement of Society: A Study of Social Order.* Cambridge: Cambridge University Press.

Emmett, D. 1966. *Rules, Roles, and Relations.* London: Macmillan.

Evans, Gareth. 1985. *Collected Papers.* Oxford: Clarendon Press.

———. 1985b. "Reference and Contingency." In *Collected Papers*, edited by Gareth Evans. Oxford: Clarendon Press.

Fay, Brian. 1983. "General Laws and Explaining Human Behavior." In *Changing Social Science*, edited by D. R. Sabia and J. Wallulis. Albany: State University of New York Press.

———. 1996. *Contemporary Philosophy of Social Science: A Multicultural Approach.* Oxford: Blackwell.

Field, Hartry. 1973. "Theory Change and Indeterminacy of Reference." *The Journal of Philosophy* 70: 462–81.

———. 1994. "Deflationist Views of Meaning and Content." *Mind* 103: 249–85.

Fiske, Alan Page. 1993. *The Structures of Social Life: The Four Elementary Forms of Human Relations.* New York: Free Press.

Flew, Antony. 1985. *Thinking about Social Thinking.* Oxford: Blackwell.

Fodor, Jerry. 1981a. *Representations: Philosophical Essays on the Foundations of Cognitive Science.* Cambridge, Mass.: MIT Press.

———. 1981b. "Special Sciences." In *Representations: Philosophical Essays on the Foundations of Cognitive Science*, edited by Jerry Fodor. Cambridge, Mass.: MIT Press.

———. 1992. *A Theory of Content and Other Essays.* Cambridge, Mass.: MIT Press.

Foucault, Michel. 1972. *The Archaeology of Knowledge* and *The Discourse on Language.* Translated by A. M. Sheridan Smith. New York: Pantheon Books.

———. 1978. *The History of Sexuality.*Vol. 1: *An Introduction.* Translated by Robert Hurley. New York: Pantheon.

———. 1981. *Power/Knowledge*, edited by Colin Gordon. New York: Pantheon.

Frankfurt, Harry. 1971. "Freedom of the Will and the Concept of a Person." *The Journal of Philosophy* 68: 5–20.

Fraser, Nancy. 1992. "The Uses and Abuses French Discourse Theories for Feminist Politics." In *Revaluing French Feminism*, edited by Nancy Fraser and Sandra Bartky. Bloomington: Indiana University Press.

Fraser, Nancy and Sandra L. Bartky, eds. 1992. *Revaluing French Feminism.* Bloomington: Indiana University Press.

Frege, Gottlob. 1964. "Introduction." In *The Basic Laws of Arithmetic.* Translated by Montgomery Furth. Los Angeles: University of California Press.

French, Peter A., ed. 1972. *Individual and Collective Responsibility*. New York: Schenkman.

———. 1975. "Types of Collectivities and Blame." *Personalist* 56: 160–69.

———. 1977. "Institutional and Moral Obligations (or Merels and Morals)." *The Journal of Philosophy* 74: 575–87.

———. 1978. "Corporate Moral Agency." In *Ethical Theory and Business*, edited by Thomas Beauchamp and Norman Bowie. Englewood Cliffs, N.J.: Prentice-Hall.

———. 1979. "The Corporation as a Moral Person." *American Philosophical Quarterly* 16: 207–15.

———. 1982. "Crowds and Corporations." *American Philosophical Quarterly* 19: 271–78.

———. 1983. "Kinds and Persons." *Philosophy and Phenomenological Research* 44: 241–54.

———. 1984. *Collective and Corporate Responsibility*. New York: Columbia University Press.

———. 1986. "Principles of Responsibility, Shame, and the Corporation." In *Shame, Responsibility, and the Corporation*, edited by Hugh Curtler. New York: Haven Publishing.

———. 1991. *The Spectrum of Responsibility*. New York: St. Martin's.

———. 1994. "Responsibility and the Moral Role of Corporate Entities." In *Business as a Humanity*, edited by T. Donaldson and E. Freeman. New York: Oxford University Press.

———. 1995. "Action Theory, Rational-Choice Theory, and Ethics." *Business Ethics Quarterly* 5: 621–27.

———. 1996. "Integrity, Intentions, and Corporations." *American Business Law Journal* 34: 141–55.

French, P. A., T. E. Uehling, and H. Wettstein, eds. 1979. *Midwest Studies in Philosophy* 4: *Studies in Metaphysics*. Minneapolis: University of Minnesota Press.

———. 1990. *Midwest Studies in Philosophy* 15: *The Philosophy of the Human Sciences*. Notre Dame: University of Notre Dame Press.

Gadamer, Hans-Georg. 1992. *Truth and Method*. New York: Crossroad.

Gambetta, D. 1988. *Trust: Making and Breaking Cooperative Relations*. Oxford: Blackwell.

Garfinkel, Alan. 1981. *Forms of Explanation: Rethinking the Questions in Social Theory*. New Haven, Conn.: Yale University Press.

Gauthier, David. 1975. "Coordination." *Dialogue* 14: 195–221.

Gellner, Ernest. 1973. *Cause and Meaning in the Social Sciences*. London: Routledge and Kegan Paul.

———. 1985. *Relativism and the Social Sciences*. New York: Cambridge University Press.

Gergen, Kenneth. 1985. "The Social Constructionist Movement in Modern Psychology." *American Psychologist* 40: 266–74.

Geuss, Raymond. 1981. *The Idea of a Critical Theory*. Cambridge: Cambridge University Press.

Giddens, Anthony. 1976. *New Rules of Sociological Method*. New York: Basic Books. Reprinted 1993, Stanford, Calif.: Stanford University Press.

Gierke, Otto von, Ernst Troeltsch, and Ernest Barker. 1950. *Natural Law and the Theory of Society, 1500–1800*. Cambridge: Cambridge University Press.

Gilbert, Margaret. 1981. "Game Theory and *Convention.*" *Synthese* 46: 41–93.
———. 1983. "Agreements, Conventions, and Language." *Synthese* 54: 375–407.
———. 1987. "Modelling Collective Belief." *Synthese* 73: 186–204.
———. 1989. *On Social Facts.* London: Routledge. Reprinted 1992, Princeton, N.J.: Princeton University Press.
———. 1990. "Walking Together: A Paradigmatic Social Phenomenon." In *Midwest Studies in Philosophy* 4: *Studies in Metaphysics,* edited by P. A. French, T. E. Uehling, and H. Wettstein. Minneapolis: University of Minnesota Press.
———. 1993a. "Group Membership and Political Obligation." *The Monist* 76: 119–33.
———. 1993b. "Is an Agreement an Exchange of Promises?" *Journal of Philosophy* 90: 627–49. Reprinted in Gilbert, Margaret. 1996. *Living Together: Rationality, Sociality, and Obligation.* Lanham, Md.: Rowman & Littlefield.
———. 1993c. "Agreements, Coercion, and Obligation." *Ethics* 103: 679–706.
———. 1994. "Remarks on Collective Belief." In *Socializing Epistemology: The Social Dimensions of Knowledge,* edited by Frederick F. Schmitt. Lanham, Md.: Rowman & Littlefield.
———. 1996. *Living Together: Rationality, Sociality, and Obligation.* Lanham, Md.: Rowman & Littlefield.
———. 1997a. "Characterizing Sociality: The Plural Subject as Paradigm." In Greenwood (1997).
———. 1997b. "Group Wrongs and Guilt Feelings." *Journal of Ethics* 1: 65–84.
———. 1997c. "What Is It For *Us* To Intend?" In *Contemporary Action Theory.* Vol. 2: *Social Action,* edited by G. Holmström-Hintikka and R. Tuomela. Dordrecht: Kluwer. Reprinted in Gilbert , Margaret. 2000. *Sociality and Responsibility: New Essays in Plural Subject Theory.* Lanham, Md.: Rowman & Littlefield.
———. 1998. "In Search of Sociality." *Philosophical Explorations* 1: 233–41.
———. 1999a. "Obligation and Joint Commitment." *Utilitas* 11: 143–63. Reprinted in Gilbert, Margaret. 2000. *Sociality and Responsibility: New Essays in Plural Subject Theory.* Lanham, Md.: Rowman & Littlefield.
———. 1999b. "Reconsidering the 'Actual Contract' Theory of Political Obligation." *Ethics* 109: 236–60. Reprinted in Gilbert, Margaret. 2000. *Sociality and Responsibility: New Essays in Plural Subject Theory.* Lanham, Md.: Rowman & Littlefield.
———. 1999c. "Reasoning about Us." Paper presented at the expert seminar "Rationality and Intentions." Amsterdam, 1999.
———. 2000. *Sociality and Responsibility: New Essays in Plural Subject Theory.* Lanham, Md.: Rowman & Littlefield.
———. 2001a. "Collective Remorse." In War *Crimes and Collective Wrongdoing,* edited by A. Jokic. Oxford: Basil Blackwell.
———. 2001b. "Considerations on Collective Guilt." In *From History to Justice: Essays in Honor of Burleigh Wilkins,* edited by A. Jokic. New York: Peter Lang.
———. 2002a. "Collective Wrongdoing: Moral and Legal Responses." *Philosophy and Social Theory.*
———. 2002b. "Considerations on Joint Commitment: Responses to Various Comments." In *Social Facts and Collective Intentionality,* edited by Georg Meggle. Frankfurt: Dr. Hänsel-Hohenhausen..
———. 2001c. "Philosophy and the Social Sciences." In *The Scope of Logic, Methodology, and Philosophy of Science,* edited by P. Gärdenfors, J. Wolénski, and K. Kijania-Placek. Dordrecht: Kluwer.

Ginet, Carl and Sydney Shoemaker, eds. 1983. *Knowledge and Mind.* Oxford: Oxford University Press.

Glock, Hans-Johann. 2001. *Wittgenstein: A Critical Reader.* Oxford: Blackwell.

Goldman, Alvin. 1972. "Towards a Theory of Social Power." *Philosophical Studies* 23: 221–68.

Greenwood, John D., ed. 1997. *The Mark of the Social: Discovery or Invention?* Lanham, Md.: Rowman & Littlefield.

Griffiths, Paul E. 1997. *What Emotions Really Are.* Chicago: University of Chicago Press.

———. 1999. "Squaring the Circle: Natural Kinds with Historical Essences." In *Species: New Interdisciplinary Essays,* edited by Robert A. Wilson. Cambridge, Mass.: MIT Press.

Gruner, R. 1976. "On the Action of Social Groups." *Inquiry* 19: 443–54.

Gupta, Anil. 1993. "A Critique of Deflationism." *Philosophical Topics* 21: 57–81.

Guttenplan, Samuel, ed. 1994. *A Companion to the Philosophy of Mind.* Oxford: Basil Blackwell.

Haaparanta, L., M. Kusch, and I. Niiniluoto, eds. 1990. *Acta Philosophica Fennica* Special Issue on Language, Knowledge, and Intentionality: Perspectives on the Philosophy of Jaakko Hintikka 49. Helsinki: The Philosophical Society of Finland.

Habermas, Jürgen. 1971. *Knowledge and Human Interests.* Boston: Beacon Press.

———. 1988. *On the Logic of the Social Sciences.* Cambridge, Mass.: MIT Press.

Hacking, Ian. 1986. "Making Up People." In *Reconstructing Individualism: Autonomy, Individuality, and the Self in Western Thought,* edited by T. C. Heller, M. Sosna, and D. E. Wellbery. Stanford, Calif.: Stanford University Press.

———. 1991. "The Making and Molding of Child Abuse." *Critical Inquiry* 17: 253–88.

———. 1992. "World-Making by Kind-Making: Child Abuse for Example." In *How Classification Works: Nelson Goodman among the Social Sciences,* edited by M. Douglas and D. Hull. Edinburgh: Edinburgh University Press.

———. 1995a. "The Looping Effects of Human Kinds." In *Causal Cognition,* edited by Dan Sperber. New York: Clarendon Press.

———. 1995b. *Rewriting the Soul: Multiple Personality and the Sciences of Memory.* Princeton, N.J.: Princeton University Press

———. 1998. *Mad Travelers: Reflections on the Reality of Transient Mental Illnesses.* Charlottesville: University Press of Virginia.

———. 1999. *The Social Construction of What?* Cambridge, Mass.: Harvard University Press.

Haddadi, A. 1995. *Communication and Cooperation in Agent Systems: A Pragmatic Theory.* Berlin: Springer-Verlag.

Hager, M. M. 1989. "Bodies Politic: The Progressive History of Organizational 'Real Entity' Theory." *University of Pittsburgh Law Review* 50: 575–654.

Hall, Stuart. 1996. "New Ethnicities." In *Black British Cultural Studies,* edited by H. A. Baker Jr., M. Diawara, and R. H. Lindeborg. Chicago: University of Chicago Press.

Hansford, S. H. 1968. *Chinese Carved Jades.* London: Faber and Faber.

Hanson, Karen. 1986. *The Self Imagined: Philosophical Reflections on the Social Character of Psyche.* London: Routledge and Kegan Paul.

Hardin, Russell. 1982. *Collective Action.* Baltimore: Johns Hopkins University Press.

Harman, Gilbert. 1976. "Practical Reasoning." *Review of Metaphysics* 79: 431–63.

———. 1986. *Change in View*. Cambridge, Mass.: MIT Press.

Harre, Rom. 1979. *Social Being: A Theory for Social Psychology*. Oxford: Blackwell.

———. ed. 1986. *The Social Construction of Emotions*. Oxford: Basil Blackwell.

Harre, R. and P. F. Secord. 1972. *The Explanation of Social Behaviour*. Oxford: Blackwell.

Haslanger, Sally. 1993. "On Being Objective and Being Objectified." In *A Mind of One's Own: Feminist Essays on Reason and Objectivity*, edited by Louise Antony and Charlotte Witt. Boulder, Colo.: Westview.

———. 1995. "Ontology and Social Construction." *Philosophical Topics* 23: 95–125.

———. 2000. "Gender and Race: (What) Are They? (What) Do We Want Them To Be?" *Nous* 34: 31–55.

Heal, Jane. 1978. "Common Knowledge." *Philosophical Quarterly* 28: 116–31.

Hegel, G. W. F. 1977. *The Phenomenology of Spirit*. Translated by A. V. Miller. Oxford: Oxford University Press.

Held, Virginia. 1970. "Can a Random Collection of Individuals Be Morally Responsible?" In *Collective Responsibility*, edited by Larry May and Stacey Hoffman. Lanham, Md.: Rowman & Littlefield.

Heller, T. C., M. Sosna, and D. E. Wellbery, eds. 1986. *Reconstructing Individualism: Autonomy, Individuality, and the Self in Western Thought*. Stanford, Calif.: Stanford University Press.

Hendrick, C., ed. 1987. *Group Processes*. Newbury Park, Calif.: Sage.

Hiley, David R., James F. Bohman, and Richard Shusterman, eds. 1991. *The Interpretive Turn*. Ithaca, N.Y.: Cornell University Press.

Hinde, R. and J. Groebel, eds. 1991. *Cooperation and Prosocial Behavior*. Cambridge: Cambridge University Press.

Hirschfeld, L. A. 1994. "Is the Acquisition of Social Categories Based on Domain-Specific Competence or on Knowledge Transfer?" In *Mapping the Mind: Domain Specificity in Cognition and Culture*, edited by L. A. Hirschfeld and S. A. Gelman. New York: Cambridge University Press.

———. 1996. *Race in the Making: Cognition, Culture, and the Child's Construction of Human Kinds*. Cambridge, Mass.: MIT Press.

Hirschfeld, L. A. and S. A. Gelman, eds. 1994. *Mapping the Mind: Domain Specificity in Cognition and Culture*. New York: Cambridge University Press.

Hollis, Martin. 1998. *Trust within Reason*. Cambridge: Cambridge University Press.

Hollis, Martin and Stephen Lukes, eds. 1982. *Rationality and Relativism*. Oxford: Basil Blackwell.

Holmström-Hintikka, G. and R. Tuomela, eds. 1997. *Contemporary Action Theory*. Vol. 2: *Social Action*. Dordrecht: Kluwer.

Horwich, P. 1998a. *Meaning*. Oxford: Oxford University Press.

———. 1998b. *Truth*. 2d ed. Oxford: Oxford University Press.

Hughes, Justin. 1984. "Group Speech Acts." *Linguistics and Philosophy* 7: 379–96.

Hull, David.1999. "On the Plurality of Species: Questioning the Party Line." In *Species: New Interdisciplinary Essays*, edited by Robert A. Wilson. Cambridge, Mass.: MIT Press.

Hume, David. 1965. *A Treatise of Human Nature*, edited by L. A. Selby-Bigge. Oxford: Clarendon Press.

Hurley, S. 1989. *Natural Reasons*. New York: Oxford University Press.

Jackman, H. 1999a. "Convention and Language." *Synthese* 117: 295–312.

——. 1999b. "We Live Forwards but Understand Backwards: Linguistic Practices and Future Behavior." *Pacific Philosophical Quarterly* 80: 157–77.

Jackson, Frank. 1987. "Group Morality." In *Metaphysics and Morality: Essays in Honour of J. J. C. Smart*, edited by P. Pettit, R. Sylvan, and J. Norman. Oxford: Blackwell.

——. 1992. "Block's Challenge." In Campbell, Bacon, and Rhinehart (1992).

——. 1998. *From Metaphysics to Ethics: A Defence of Conceptual Analysis*. Oxford: Oxford University Press.

Jackson, Frank and Philip Pettit. 1988. "Functionalism and Broad Content." *Mind* 97: 381–400.

James, Susan. 1984. *The Content of Social Explanation*. Cambridge: Cambridge University Press.

Jarvie, Ian C. 1972. *Concepts and Society*. London: Routledge and Kegan Paul.

Jennings, N. and G. O'Hare, eds. 1996. *Foundations of Distributed Artificial Intelligence*. New York: Wiley.

Jewitt, Dave. 2001. "Pluto and the Pluto-Kuiper Express." www.ifa.hawaii.edu/kb /pluto.html (accessed February 2002).

Joas, Hans. 1997. *G H. Mead: A Contemporary Re-examination of His Thought*. Translated by Raymond Meyer. Cambridge, Mass.: MIT Press.

Jokic, A, ed. 2001a. *From History to Justice: Essays in Honor of Burleigh Wilkins*. New York: Peter Lang.

——. ed. 2001b. War *Crimes and Collective Wrongdoing*. Oxford: Basil Blackwell.

Jones, O. R., ed. 1971. *The Private Language Argument*. New York: Macmillan.

Kant, Immanuel. 1943. *Critique of Pure Reason*. Translated by J. Meiklehohn. New York: Wiley.

Kekes, John. 1989. *Moral Tradition and Individuality*. Princeton: Princeton University Press.

Kessler, Suzanne J. and Wendy McKenna. 1977. *Gender: An Ethnomethodological Approach*. Chicago: University of Chicago Press.

Kiikeri, M. and P. Ylikoski, eds. 2001. *Explanatory Connections: Electronic Essays in Honor of Matti Sintonen*. www.valt.helsinki.fi/kfil/matti/ (accessed August 2002).

Kim, U., H. C. Triandis, C. Kagitcibasi, S-C. Choi, and G. Yoon. 1994. *Individualism and Collectivism: Theory, Method and Applications*. Newbury Park, Calif.: Sage.

Kincaid, Harold. 1990. "Eliminativism and Methodological Individualism." *Philosophy of Science* 57: 141–48.

Kollock, P. 1998. "Transforming Social Dilemmas: Group Identity and Co-operation." In *Modeling Rationality, Morality, and Evolution*, edited by P. Danielson. Oxford: Oxford University Press.

Korieh, Chima Jacob. 1996. "Widowhood among the Igbo of Eastern Nigeria." www.uib.no/hi/korieh/chima.html (accessed September 2002).

Kornblith, Hilary. 1993. *Inductive Inference and Its Natural Ground: An Essay in Naturalistic Epistemology*. Cambridge, Mass.: MIT Press.

Kornhauser, Lewis A. 1996. "Conceptions of Social Rule." In *Social Rules: Origin; Character; Logic; Change*, edited by David Braybrooke. Boulder, Colo.: Westview.

Kornhauser, Lewis A. and L. G. Sager. 1993. "The One and the Many: Adjudication in Collegial Courts." *California Law Review* 81: 1–59.

Kripke, Saul. 1980. *Naming and Necessity*. Cambridge, Mass.: Harvard University Press.

———. 1982. *Wittgenstein on Rules and Private Language*. Oxford: Basil Blackwell.

Kutz, Christopher. 2000a. *Complicity: Ethics and Law for a Collective Age*. New York: Cambridge University Press.

———. 2000b. "Acting Together." *Philosophy and Phenomenological Research* 61: 1–31.

Lagerspetz, Eerik, Heikki Ikäheimo, and Jussi Kotkavirta, eds. 2001. *On the Nature of Social and Institutional Reality*. Jyväskylä: University of Jyväskylä Press.

Latané, B. and J. M. Darley. 1968. "Group Inhibition of Bystander Intervention in Emergencies." *Journal of Personality and Social Psychology* 10: 215–21.

Latour, Bruno and Steven Woolgar. 1979. *Laboratory Life: The Social Construction of Scientific Fact*. Beverly Hills, Calif.: Sage.

LeBon, Gustav. 1960. *The Crowd*. New York: Viking Press.

Leeds, S. 1978. "Theories of Reference and Truth." *Erkenntnis* 13: 111–29.

Lehrer, Keith and Carl Wagner. 1981. *Rational Consensus in Science and Society*. Dordrecht: Reidel.

Leiser, B. and T. Campbell, eds. 2001. *Human Rights in Philosophy and Practice*. Burlington, Vt.: Ashgate Press.

Lemert, Charles, ed. 1993. *Social Theory: The Multicultural and Classic Readings*. Boulder, Colo.: Westview.

LePore, Ernest and Robert Van Gulick, eds. 1991. *John Searle and IIis Critics*. Oxford: Basil Blackwell.

Levesque, H. J., P. R. Cohen, and J. H. T. Nunes. 1990. "On Acting Together." *Proceedings of Eighth National Conference on Artificial Intelligence,* vol.1. Cambridge, Mass.: MIT Press.

Levine, David P. and Lynn S. Levine. 1975. "Social Theory and Social Action." *Economy and Society* 4: 173–93.

Lewis, David K. 1969. *Convention: A Philosophical Study*. Oxford: Basil Blackwell.

———. 1994. "Reduction of Mind." In Guttenplan (1994).

Lewis, H. D. 1948. "Collective Responsibility." In *Collective Responsibility*, edited by Larry May and Stacey Hoffman. Lanham, Md.: Rowman & Littlefield.

List, Christian and Philip Pettit. 2002a. "Aggregating Sets of Judgments: Two Impossibility Results Compared." *Synthese*.

———. 2002b. "The Aggregation of Sets of Judgments: An Impossibility Result." *Economics and Philosophy* 18: 89–110.

Little, Daniel. 1991. *Varieties of Social Explanation*. Boulder, Colo.: Westview.

Lloyd, Genevieve. 1993. *Being in Time: Selves and Narrators in Philosophy and Literature*. New York: Routledge.

Locke, John. 1975. *An Essay Concerning Human Understanding*. Oxford: Oxford University Press.

Loewer, Barry, ed. 1985. *Synthese*. Special Issue on Consensus 62.

Londey, D. 1978. "On the Action of Teams." *Inquiry* 21: 213–18.

Longino, Helen. 1980. *Science as Social Knowledge*. Princeton, N.J.: Princeton University Press.

Lorber, J. and S. A. Farrell, eds. 1991. *The Social Construction of Gender*. Beverly Hills: Sage.

Lukes, Stephen. 1973a. *Emile Durkheim: His Life and Work*. London: Allen Lane.

———. 1973b. *Individualism*. New York: Harper Torchbooks.

———. 1973c. "Methodological Individualism Reconsidered." In *The Philosophy of Social Explanation*, edited by Alan Ryan. Oxford: Oxford University Press.

Lynch, Aaron. 1996. *Thought Contagion: How Belief Spreads Through Society*. New York: Basic Books.

Macdonald, G. and P. Pettit. 1981. *Semantics and Social Science*. London: Routledge & Kegan Paul.

Macdonald, Michael ed. 1991. *Canadian Journal of Law and Jurisprudence*. Special Issue on Collective Rights 4.

Mackenzie, Catriona. 2001. "On Bodily Autonomy." In *Philosophy and Medicine: Handbook of Phenomenology and Medicine*, edited S. K. Toombs. Dordrecht: Kluwer.

MacKinnon, C. A. 1989. *Toward a Feminist Theory of the State*. Cambridge, Mass.: Harvard University Press.

Mackor, Anne Ruth. 1998. "Rules are Laws." *Philosophical Explorations* 3: 215–32.

Mäkelä, P. and R. Tuomela. 2002. "Group Action and Group Responsibility." *Protosociology* 16: 195–214.

Mäki, Uskali, ed. 2002. *Fact and Fiction in Economics: Models, Realism, and Rhetoric*. Cambridge: Cambridge University Press.

Mallon, Ron and Stephen P. Stich. 2000. "The Odd Couple: The Compatibility of Social Construction and Evolutionary Psychology." *Philosophy of Science* 67: 133–54.

Mandelbaum, Maurice. 1973. "Societal Facts." In *Modes of Individualism and Collectivism*, edited by J. O'Neill. London: Heinemann.

Mansbridge, J., ed. 1990. *Beyond Self-Interest*. Chicago: University of Chicago Press.

Marmor, Andrei. 1996. "On Convention." *Synthese* 107: 349–71.

Martin, Michael and Lee McIntyre, eds. 1994. *Readings in the Philosophy of Social Science*. Cambridge, Mass.: MIT Press.

May, Larry. 1983. "Vicarious Agency and Corporate Responsibility." *Philosophical Studies* 43.

———. 1987. *The Morality of Groups: Collective Responsibility, Group Based Harm, and Corporate Rights*. Notre Dame: University of Notre Dame Press.

———. 1989. "Mobs and Collective Responsibility." In *Freedom, Equality, and Social Change: Problems in Social Philosophy Today*, edited by James Sterba and Creighton Peden. New York: Edwin Mellen.

———. 1990. "Collective Inaction and Shared Responsibility." *Nous* 24: 269–77.

———. 1992. *Sharing Responsibility*. Chicago: University of Chicago Press.

———. 1995. "Social Responsibility." *Midwest Studies in Philosophy* 20: 400–15.

———. 1996. *The Socially Responsible Self*. Chicago: University of Chicago Press.

May, Larry and Stacey Hoffman, eds. 1991. *Collective Responsibility*. Lanham, Md.: Rowman & Littlefield.

May, Larry, Marilyn Friedman, and Andy Clark, eds. 1996. *Mind and Morals: Ethics and Cognitive Science*. Cambridge, Mass.: MIT Press.

May, Larry, Christine Sistare, and Leslie Francis, eds. 2000. *Groups and Group Rights*. Lawrence: University of Kansas Press.

Mayr, Ernst. 1984. "Species Concepts and Their Application." In *Conceptual Issues in Evolutionary Biology: An Anthology*, edited by Eliot Sober. Cambridge, Mass.: MIT Press.

McCulloch, Warren. 1965. "What Is a Number That a Man May Know It, and a Man, That He May Know a Number?" *Embodiments of Mind*. Cambridge, Mass.: MIT Press.

McDougall, William. 1920. *The Group Mind*. New York: Putnam.

McDowell, John.1984. "Wittgenstein on Following a Rule." *Synthese* 58: 325–63.

———. 1989. "One Strand in the Private Language Argument." *Grazer Philosophische Studien* 33: 287–303.

———. 1991. "Intentionality and Interiority in Wittgenstein." In *Meaning Scepticism*, edited by K. Puhl. Berlin: Walter de Gruyter.

———. 1994. *Mind and World*. Cambridge: Harvard University Press.

———. 1998. *Mind, Value, and Reality*. Cambridge, Mass.: Harvard University Press.

McGeer, Victoria and Philip Pettit. 2001. "The Self-Regulating Mind." *Language and Communication* 22: 281–99.

McIntosh, Mary. 1992. "The Homosexual Role." In *Forms of Desire: Sexual Orientation and the Social Constructionist Controversy*, edited by Edward Stein. New York: Routledge.

McIntyre, Lee. 1996. *Laws and Explanation in the Social Sciences*. Boulder, Colo.: Westview.

McLean, J. 1999. "Personality and Public Law Doctrine." *University of Toronto Law Journal* 49: 123–49.

McMahon, Christopher. 1989. "Promising and Coordination." *American Philosophical Quarterly* 16: 239–47.

———. 1995. "The Ontological and Moral Status of Organizations." *Business Ethics Quarterly* 5: 541–54.

———. 2000. "Collective Rationality." *Philosophical Studies* 98: 321–44.

———. 2001. *Collective Rationality and Collective Reasoning*. Cambridge: Cambridge University Press.

Mead, George Herbert. 1962. *Mind, Self, and Society from the Standpoint of a Social Behaviorist, Works of George Herbert Mead*, vol. 1. Edited by Charles W. Morris. Chicago: University of Chicago Press.

Meijers, A. 1994. *Speech Acts, Communication and Collective Intentionality: Beyond Searle's Individualism*. Utrecht: de Jonge.

Mele, Alfred. 1995. *Autonomous Agents: From Self-Control to Autonomy*. Cambridge: Cambridge University Press.

Mellor, D. H. 1982. "The Reduction of Society." *Philosophy* 57: 51–75.

Milgram, S. 1963. "Behavioral Study of Obedience." *Journal of Abnormal and Social Psychology* 67: 371–78.

Miller, Kaarlo and Raimo Tuomela. 2001. "What are Collective Goals?" In *Explanatory Connections: Electronic Essays in Honor of Matti Sintonen*, edited by M. Kiikeri and P. Ylikoski. www.valt.helsinki.fi/kfil/matti/ (accessed August 2002).

Miller, Richard W. 1994. "Methodological Individualism and Social Explanation." In *Readings in the Philosophy of Social Science*, edited by Michael Martin and Lee McIntyre. Cambridge, Mass.: MIT Press.

———. 1996. "Worries about Quandries." In *Social Rules: Origin; Character; Logic; Change*, edited by David Braybrooke. Boulder, Colo.: Westview.

Miller, Seumas. 1982. "Lewis on Conventions." *Philosophical Papers* 11: 1–9.

———. 1986. "Conventions, Interdependence of Actions and Collective Ends." *Nous* 20: 117–40.

———. 1987. "Conventions and Social Contracts." *Philosophical Papers* 16: 85–106.

———. 1990. "Rationalising Conventions." *Synthese* 84: 23–43.

———. 1992a. "Joint Action." *Philosophical Papers* 21: 275–99.

———. 1992b. "On Conventions," *Australasian Journal of Philosophy* 70: 435–45.

———. 1995. "Intentions, Ends, and Joint Action." *Philosophical Papers* XXIV: 51–66.

———. 1997a. "Individualism, Collective Responsibility and Corporate Crimes." *Business and Professional Ethics Journal* 16: 19–46.

———. 1997b. "Social Norms." In *Contemporary Action Theory*. Vol. 2: *Social Action*, edited by G. Holmström-Hintikka and R. Tuomela. Dordrecht: Kluwer.

———. 998. "Collective Responsibility, Armed Intervention and Rwandan Genocide." *International Journal of Applied Philosophy* 12: 223–38.

———. 1999. "Collective Rights." *Public Affairs Quarterly* 13: 331–46.

———. 2000a. "Academic Autonomy." In *Why Universities Matter*, edited by C. A. J. Coady. Sydney: Allen and Unwin.

———. 2000b. "Collective Rights and Minorities." *International Journal of Applied Philosophy* 14: 241–57.

———. 2000c. "Speech Acts and Conventions." *Language Sciences* 22: 155–66.

———. 2001a. *Social Action: A Teleological Account*. New York: Cambridge University Press.

———. 2001b. "Collective Moral Responsibility." In *Human Rights in Philosophy and Practice*, edited by B. Leiser and T. Campbell. Burlington, Vt.: Ashgate Press.

———. 2001c. "Collective Responsibility." *Public Affairs Quarterly* 15: 65–82.

———. 2001d. "Collective Moral Responsibility for Omissions." *Business and Professional Ethics Journal* 20: 5–24.

———. 2001e. "Social Institutions." In *Realism in Action: Festschrift for Raimo Tuomela*, edited by M. Sintonen, P. Ylikoski, and K. Miller. Dordrecht: Kluwer.

———. 2002. "Against Collective Agency." In *Social Facts and Collective Intentionality*, edited by Georg Meggle. Frankfurt: Dr. Hänsel-Hohenhausen.

Millikan, Ruth Garrett. 1984. *Language, Thought, and Other Biological Categories*. Cambridge, Mass.: MIT Press.

———. 1998. "Language Conventions Made Simple." *The Journal of Philosophy* 95: 161–80.

———. 1999. "Historical Kinds and the 'Special Sciences.'" *Philosophical Studies* 95: 45–65.

Mills, C. 1998. *Blackness Visible: Essays on Philosophy and Race*. Ithaca, N.Y.: Cornell University Press.

Minor Planet Center. 2001. cfa-www.harvard.edu/icq/ICQPluto.html (accessed August 2002).

Mischel, T., ed. 1977. *The Self*. Oxford: Blackwell.

Morris, Christopher W. and Arthur Ripstein, eds. 2001. *Practical Rationality and Preference: Essays for David Gauthier*. Cambridge: Cambridge University Press.

Moser, Paul. 1992. "Beyond the Private Language Argument." *Metaphilosophy* 23: 77–89.

Nagel, Thomas. 1986. *The View from Nowhere*. Oxford: Oxford University Press.

Neier, Aryeh. 1998. *War Crimes: Brutality, Genocide, Terror, and the Struggle for Justice*. New York: Random House.

Nelson, Alan. 1994. "How *Could* Scientific Facts Be Socially Constructed?" *Studies in the History and Philosophy of Science* 25: 535–47.

New Columbia Encyclopedia. 1975. New York: Columbia University Press.

Nida-Rümelin, J., ed. 1999. *Analyomen 3: Perspektiven der Analytischen Philosophie.* Berlin: Walter de Gruyter.

North, Douglass C. 1996. "Institutional Change: A Framework Analysis." In *Social Rules: Origin; Character; Logic; Change,* edited by David Braybrooke. Boulder, Colo.: Westview.

Nye, Judith L. and Aaron M. Brower, eds. 1996. *What's Social about Social Cognition? Research on Socially Shared Cognition in Small Groups.* London: Sage.

Olafson, Frederick. 1979. *The Dialectic of Action.* Chicago: University of Chicago Press.

Olson, Mancur. 1965. *The Logic of Collective Action.* Cambridge, Mass.: Harvard University Press.

Omi, Michael and Howard Winant. 1986. *Racial Formation in the United States: From the 1960s to the 1980s.* New York: Routledge & Kegan Paul.

———. 1994. *Racial Formation in the United States: From the 1960s to the 1990s.* New York: Routledge and Kegan Paul.

O'Neill, J., ed. 1973. *Modes of Individualism and Collectivism.* London: Heinemann.

Outlaw, Lucius. 1996. *On Race and Philosophy.* New York: Routledge.

Padgug, Robert. 1992. "Sexual Matters: On Conceptualizing Sexuality in History." In *Forms of Desire: Sexual Orientation and the Social Constructionist Controversy,* edited by Edward Stein. New York: Routledge.

Pap, Arthur. 1958. *Semantics and Necessary Truth.* New Haven: Yale University Press.

Papineau, David. 1987. *Reality and Representation.* Oxford: Blackwell.

Parsons, Talcott 1951. *The Social System.* Glencoe, Ill.: Free Press.

Peacocke, C. 1999. *Being Known.* Oxford: Clarendon Press.

Perry, John. 1979. "The Essential Indexical." *Nous* 13: 3–21.

Pettit, P., R. Sylvan, and J. Norman, eds. 1987. *Metaphysics and Morality: Essays in Honour of J. J. C. Smart.* Oxford: Blackwell.

Pettit, Philip. 1977. *The Concept of Structuralism.* Berkeley: University of California Press.

———. 1990a. "The Reality of Rule Following." *Mind* 99: 1–21.

———. 1990b. *"Virtus Normativa:* Rational Choice Perspectives." *Ethics* 100: 725–55.

———. 1993. *The Common Mind: An Essay on Psychology, Society and Politics.* Oxford: Oxford University Press.

———. 1997. *Republicanism: A Theory of Freedom and Government.* Oxford: Oxford University Press.

———. 1998. "Defining and Defending Social Holism." *Philosophical Explorations* 1: 169–84.

———. 2000. "A Sensible Perspectivism." In *Dealing with Diversity,* edited by M. Baghramian and A. Dunlop. London: Routledge.

———. 2001. *A Theory of Freedom: From the Psychology to the Politics of Agency.* Cambridge: Polity.

Pettit, Philip and Michael Smith. 1996. "Freedom in Belief and Desire." *The Journal of Philosophy* 93: 429–49.

Phillips, D. Z. and Peter Winch, eds. 1989. *Wittgenstein: Attention to Particulars.* New York: St. Martin's.

Pink, Thomas. 1996. *The Psychology of Freedom.* Cambridge: Cambridge University Press.

Pinkard, Terry. 1996. *Hegel's Phenomenology: The Sociality of Reason.* Cambridge: Cambridge University Press.

Plutchik, R. and H. Kellerman.1980. *Emotion: Theory, Research and Experience.* Vol. 1: *Theories of Emotion.* New York: Random House.

Polanyi, Michael. 1951. *The Logic of Liberty: Reflections and Rejoinders.* London: Kegan Paul.

Power, R. 1984. "Mutual Intention." *Journal for the Theory of Social Behavior* 14: 85–100.

Pratt, Michael. 2001. "Scanlon on Promising." *The Canadian Journal of Law and Jurisprudence* 14: 143–54.

Price, Huw. 1988. *Facts and the Function of Truth.* Oxford: Basil Blackwell.

Puhl, K., ed. 1991. *Meaning Scepticism.* Berlin: Walter de Gruyter.

Putnam, Hilary. 1973. "Meaning and Reference." *The Journal of Philosophy* 70: 699–711.

———. 1975a. *Mind, Language and Reality.* Cambridge: Cambridge University Press.

———. 1975b. "The Meaning of 'Meaning.'" In *Mind, Language and Reality.* Cambridge: Cambridge University Press.

———. 1988. *Representation and Reality.* Cambridge, Mass.: MIT Press.

———. 1994a. *Words and Life.* Cambridge, Mass.: Harvard University Press.

———. 1994b. "On Truth." In *Words and Life.* Cambridge, Mass.: Harvard University Press.

Quine, W. V. 1982. *Methods of Logic.* 4th ed. Cambridge, Mass.: Harvard University Press.

———. 1986. *Philosophy of Logic.* 2d ed. Cambridge, Mass.: Harvard University Press.

Quinton, Anthony. 1975–76. "Social Objects." *Proceedings of the Aristotelian Society* 75: 1–27.

Rawls, J. 1971. *A Theory of Social Justice.* Cambridge, Mass.: Harvard University Press.

———. 1993. *Political Liberalism.* New York: Columbia University Press.

Reicher, S. 1987. "Crowd Behaviour as Social Action." In *Rediscovering the Social Group: A Self-Categorization Theory,* edited by J. C. Turner, M. A. Hogg, P. J. Oakes, S. D. Reicher, and M. S. Wetherell. Oxford: Blackwell.

Rescher, Nicholas. 1993. *Pluralism: Against the Demand for Consensus.* Oxford: Clarendon.

Ricoeur, Paul. 1992. *Oneself as Another.* Translated by Kathleen Blamey. Chicago: University of Chicago Press.

Robins, Michael. 1984. *Promising, Intending, and Moral Autonomy.* Cambridge: Cambridge University Press.

———. 2002. "Joint Commitment and Circularity." In *Social Facts and Collective Intentionality,* edited by Georg Meggle. Frankfurt: Dr. Hänsel-Hohenhausen.

Rorty, Amelie, ed. 1980. *Explaining Emotions.* Berkeley: University of California Press.

Rosenberg, Alexander. 1988. *Philosophy of Social Science.* Boulder, Colo.: Westview.

Ross, Lee and Richard E. Nisbett. 1991. *The Person and the Situation.* New York: McGraw-Hill.

Roth, Abraham Sesshu. 2002. "Sharing Intentions and Contralateral Commitments." *Ms.*

Roth, Paul. 1987. *Meaning and Method in the Social Sciences.* Ithaca, N.Y.: Cornell University Press.

Rouse, Joseph. 1987. *Knowledge and Power: Toward a Political Philosophy of Science*. Ithaca, N.Y.: Cornell University Press.

Rousseau, Jean-Jacques. *On the Social Contract*. Translated by D. A. Cress. Indianapolis: Hackett Publishing Company.

Rovane, Carol. 1997. *The Bounds of Agency: An Essay in Revisionary Metaphysics*. Princeton, N.J.: Princeton University Press.

———. 2000. "Not Mind-Body But Mind-Mind." *Journal of Consciousness Studies* 7: 82–92.

Rowe, Nicholas. 1989. *Rules and Institutions*. New York: Philip Allan.

Ruben, David-Hillel. 1985. *The Metaphysics of the Social World*. London: Routledge.

Rudner, Richard. 1966. *Philosophy of Social Science*. Englewood Cliffs, N.J.: Prentice-Hall.

Runciman, D. 1997. *Pluralism and the Personality of the State*. Cambridge: Cambridge University Press.

Russell, Bertrand. 1959. *The Problems of Philosophy*. Oxford: Oxford University Press.

Ryan, Alan, ed. 1973. *The Philosophy of Social Explanation*. Oxford: Oxford University Press.

Sabia, D. R. and J. Wallulis, eds. 1983. *Changing Social Science*. Albany: State University of New York Press.

Sandu, Gabriel and Raimo Tuomela. 1996. "Joint Action and Group Action Made Precise." *Synthese* 105: 319–45.

Saunders, John Turk and Donald F. Henze. 1967. *The Private Language Problem: A Philosophical Dialogue*. New York: Random House.

Sayre-McCord, G., ed. 1988. *Essays on Moral Realism*. Ithaca, N.Y. Cornell University Press.

Schatzki, Theodore R. 1996. *Social Practices: A Wittgensteinian Approach to Human Activity and the Social*. Cambridge: Cambridge University Press.

Scheff, Thomas. 1984. *Being Mentally Ill: A Sociological Theory*. New York: Aldine Publishing Co.

Schiffer, Stephen. 1972. *Meaning*. Oxford: Oxford University Press.

Schmitt, Frederick F., ed. 1994a. *Socializing Epistemology: The Social Dimensions of Knowledge*. Lanham, Md.: Rowman & Littlefield.

———. 1994b. "The Justification of Group Beliefs." In *Socializing Epistemology: The Social Dimensions of Knowledge*, edited by Frederick F. Schmitt. Lanham, Md.: Rowman & Littlefield.

———. 1998. "Realism, Antirealism, and Epistemic Truth." *Social Epistemology* 12: 267–87.

Schmitt, Frederick F. and James Spellman. 1994. "Socializing Epistemology: A Bibliography." In *Socializing Epistemology: The Social Dimensions of Knowledge*, edited by Frederick F. Schmitt. Lanham, Md.: Rowman & Littlefield.

Schmitt, Richard. 1989. "Methodological Individualism, Psychological Individualism and the Defense of Reason." In *Analyzing Marxism: New Essays on Analytical Marxism*, edited by Robert Ware and Kai Nielsen. Calgary: University of Calgary Press.

———. 1995. *Beyond Separateness: The Social Nature of Human Beings—Their Autonomy, Knowledge, and Power*. Boulder, Colo.: Westview.

Schroeder, Severin. 2001. "Private Language and Private Experience." In *Wittgenstein: A Critical Reader*, edited by Hans-Johann Glock. Oxford: Blackwell.

Schroeder, William R. 1984. *The Self and Its Other: Sartre and His Predecessors.* London: Routledge.

Schurz, G. and G. Dorn, eds. 1991. *Advances in Scientific Philosophy.* Amsterdam: Rodopi.

Schutz, Alfred.1962. *Collected Papers.* Vol. 1: *The Problem of Social Reality.* The Hague: Nijhoff.

——. 1967. *The Phenomenology of the Social World.* Translated by George Walsh and Frederick Lehnert. Introduction by George Walsh. Evanston, Ill.: Northwestern University Press.

Scott, Joan. 1986. "Gender: A Useful Category of Historical Analysis." *American Historical Review* 91: 1053–75.

——. 1988. "Deconstructing Equality-versus-Difference: Or, The Uses of Poststructuralist Theory for Feminism." *Feminist Studies* 14: 33–50.

Searle, John R. 1969. *Speech Acts.* Cambridge: Cambridge University Press.

——. 1983. *Intentionality.* Cambridge: Cambridge University Press.

——. 1984a. *Minds, Brains and Science.* Cambridge, Mass.: Harvard University Press.

——. 1984b. "Prospects for the Social Sciences." In *Minds, Brains and Science*, edited by John Searle. Cambridge, Mass.: Harvard University Press.

——. 1990. "Collective Intentions and Actions." In *Intentions in Communication*, edited by Philip Cohen, Jerry Morgan, and Martha E. Pollak. Cambridge, Mass.: MIT Press.

——. 1991. "Response: Explanation in the Social Sciences." In *John Searle and His Critics*, edited by Ernest LePore and Robert Van Gulick. Oxford: Basil Blackwell.

——. 1995. *The Construction of Social Reality.* New York: Free Press.

——. 2001. *Rationality in Action.* Cambridge, Mass.: MIT Press.

Seebass, Gottfried and Raimo Tuomela, eds. 1985. *Social Action.* Dordrecht: Reidel.

Seidman, Steven, ed. 1994. *The Postmodern Turn: New Perspectives on Social Theory.* Cambridge: Cambridge University Press, 1994.

Sellars, Wilfrid. 1963a. *Science, Perception and Reality.* London: Routledge.

——. 1963b. "Imperatives, Intentions, and the Logic of 'Ought.'" In *Morality and the Language of Conduct*, edited by Hector-Neri Castaneda and George Nakhnikian. Detroit: Wayne State University Press.

——. 1968. *Science and Metaphysics.* London: Routledge & Kegan Paul.

——. 1969. "Language as Thought and as Communication." *Philosophy and Phenomenological Research* 29: 506–27.

——. 1981. "Mental Events." *Philosophical Studies* 39: 325–45.

Sen, Amartya K. 1970. *Collective Choice and Social Welfare.* New York: Holden-Day.

Shapiro, Ian and Will Kymlicka, eds. 1997. *Ethnicity and Group Rights.* New York: New York University Press.

Shaw, M. 1981. *Group Dynamics: The Psychology of Small Group Behavior.* New York: McGraw-Hill.

Showalter, Elaine.1996. *Hystories: Hysterical Epidemics and Modern Media.* New York: Columbia University Press.

Shubik, Martin. 1982. *Game Theory in the Social Sciences: Concepts and Solutions.* Cambridge, Mass.: MIT Press.

Shwayder, David. 1965. *The Stratification of Behavior.* London: Routledge and Kegan Paul.

Simmel, Georg. 1950. *The Sociology of Georg Simmel.* Translated and edited by Kurt H. Wolff. New York: Free Press.

———. 1971a. *Georg Simmel: On Individuality and Social Forms*, edited by D. N. Levine. Chicago: University of Chicago Press.

———. 1971b. "How is Society Possible?" In *Georg Simmel: On Individuality and Social Forms*, edited by D. N. Levine. Chicago: University of Chicago Press.

Simpson, Jeffry A. and Douglas Kenrick, eds. 1997. *Evolutionary Social Psychology.* Mahwah, N.J.: Lawrence Erlbaum.

Sintonen, M., P. Ylikoski, and K. Miller, eds. 2003 (in press). *Realism in Action: Festschrift for Raimo Tuomela.* Dordrecht: Kluwer.

Skinner, Q. 1989. "The State." In *Political Innovation and Conceptual Change*, edited by T. Ball, J. Farr, and R. Hansen. Cambridge: Cambridge University Press.

Smith, N., ed. 1982. *Mutual Knowledge.* London: Academic Press.

Sober, Eliot, ed. 1984. *Conceptual Issues in Evolutionary Biology: An Anthology.* Cambridge, Mass.: MIT Press.

Sober, E. and D. Wilson. 1998. *Unto Others: The Evolution and Psychology of Unselfish Behavior.* Cambridge, Mass.: Harvard University Press.

Sperber, Dan, ed. 1995. *Causal Cognition.* New York: Clarendon Press.

———. 1996. *Explaining Culture: A Naturalistic Approach.* Oxford: Blackwell.

Stalnaker, R. 1978. "Assertion." In *Syntax and Semantics: Pragmatics* 9, edited by P. Cole. New York: Academic Press.

———. 1989. "On What's in the Head." In *Philosophical Perspectives* 3: *Philosophy of Mind and Action*, edited by James Tomberlin. Atascadero, Calif.: Ridgeview.

———. 1990. "Narrow Content." In *Propositional Attitudes*, edited by C. Anthony Anderson and Joseph Owens. Stanford, Calif.: Center for the Study of Language and Information.

Stansberry, John. 2001. "Pluto Is a Planet." http://mips.as.arizona.edu/~stansber/Planet.html.

Stein, Edward, ed. 1992. *Forms of Desire: Sexual Orientation and the Social Constructionist Controversy.* New York: Routledge.

Sterba, James and Creighton Peden, eds. 1989. *Freedom, Equality, and Social Change: Problems in Social Philosophy Today.* New York: Edwin Mellen.

Stoljar, S. J. 1973. *Groups and Entities: An Inquiry into Corporate Theory.* Canberra: Australian National University Press.

Stoutland, Frederick. 1997. "Why Are Philosophers of Action So Anti-Social?" In *Commonality and Particularity in Ethics*, edited by L. Alanen, S. Heinemaa, and T. Walgren. New York: St. Martin's.

Sugden, Robert. 1993. "Thinking as a Team: Towards an Explanation of Nonselfish Behavior." *Social Philosophy and Policy* 10: 69–89.

———. 2000. "Team Preferences." *Economics and Philosophy* 20: 175–204.

Sulloway, Frank. 1996. *Born To Rebel.* New York: Pantheon Books.

Sunstein, Cass. 1999. *One Case at a Time.* Cambridge, Mass.: Harvard University Press.

Sverdlik, Sven. 1987. "Collective Responsibility." *Philosophical Studies* 51: 61–76.

Tarde, Gabriel. 1903. *The Laws of Imitation.* Translated by E. Parsons. New York: Henry Holt.

Taylor, Charles. 1971. "Interpretation and the Sciences of Man." *Review of Metaphysics* 25: 3–51.

———. 1977. "What Is Human Agency?" In *The Self,* edited by T. Mischel. Oxford: Blackwell.

———. 1989. *Sources of the Self.* Cambridge, Mass.: Harvard University Press.

———. 1991. "The Dialogical Self." In *The Interpretive Turn,* edited by David R. Hiley, James F. Bohman, and Richard Shusterman. Ithaca, N.Y.: Cornell University Press.

Tollefsen, Deborah. 2000. "Organizations as True Believers." Paper presented at the American Philosophical Association Meetings, Eastern Division, New York.

Tomberlin, James. 1989. *Philosophical Perspectives* 3: *Philosophy of Mind and Action.* Atascadero, Calif.: Ridgeview.

Tooby, John and Leda Cosmides. 1992. "The Psychological Foundations of Culture." In *The Adapted Mind,* edited by Jerome H. Barkow, Leda Cosmides, and John Tooby. New York: Oxford University Press.

Toombs, S. K., ed. 2001. *Philosophy and Medicine: Handbook of Phenomenology and Medicine.* Dordrecht: Kluwer.

Triandis, Harry. 1995. *Individualism and Collectivism.* Boulder, Colo.: Westview.

Trigg, R. 1985. *Understanding Social Science.* Oxford: Basil Blackwell.

Tuomela, Raimo. 1984. *A Theory of Social Action.* Dordrecht: Reidel.

———. 1985. "Social Action." In *Social Action,* edited by Gottfried Seebass and Raimo Tuomela. Dordrecht: Reidel.

———. 1989a. "Actions by Collectives." *Philosophical Perspectives* 3: 471–96.

———. 1989b. "Collective Action, Supervenience, and Constitution." *Synthese* 80: 243–66.

———. 1989c. "Ruben and the Metaphysics of the Social World." *British Journal of Philosophy of Science* 40: 261–73.

———. 1989d. "What Does Doing One's Part of a Joint Action Involve?" *Analyse and Kritik* 11: 197–207.

———. 1990a. "Can Collectives Have Beliefs?" In *Acta Philosophica Fennica.* Special Issue on Language, Knowledge, and Intentionality: Perspectives on the Philosophy of Jaakko Hintikka 49, edited by L. Haaparanta, M. Kusch, and I. Niiniluoto.

———. 1990b. "What Are Goals and Joint Goals?" *Theory and Decision* 28: 1–20.

———. 1990c. "Methodological Individualism and Explanation." *Philosophy of Science* 57: 133–40.

———. 1991a. "Intentional Single and Joint Action." *Philosophical Studies* 62: 235–62.

———. 1991b. "Mutual Beliefs and Social Characteristics." In *Advances in Scientific Philosophy,* edited by G. Schurz and G. Dorn. Amsterdam: Rodopi.

———. 1991c. "On Searle's Argument Against the Possibility of Social Laws." In *John Searle and His Critics,* edited by Ernest LePore and Robert Van Gulick. Oxford: Basil Blackwell.

———. 1991d. "Supervenience, Collective Action, and Kelsen's Organ Theory." *Archive fur Rechtsund Sozialphilosophie* 40: 35–40.

———. 1991e. "The Social Dimension of Action Theory." *Revista de Filosofia* 3: 165–78.

———. 1991f. "We Will Do It: An Analysis of Group Intentions." *Philosophy and Phenomenological Research* 51: 249–77.

378   *Kevin Kimble and Frederick F. Schmitt*

—. 1992a. "Group Beliefs." *Synthese* 91: 285–318.

—. 1992b. "On the Structural Aspects of Collective Action and Free-riding." *Theory and Decision* 32: 165–202.

—. 1993a. "Corporate Action: A Reply to Coleman." *Analyse und Kritik* 15: 216–18.

—. 1993b. "Corporate Intention and Corporate Action." *Analyse und Kritik* 15: 11–21.

—. 1993c. "What Are Joint Intentions?" In *Philosophy and the Cognitive Sciences*, edited by R. Casati and G. White. Kirchberg: Austrian Ludwig Wittgenstein Association.

—. 1993d. "What Is Cooperation?" *Erkenntnis* 38: 87–101.

—. 1995. *The Importance of Us: A Philosophical Study of Basic Social Notions.* Stanford: Stanford University Press.

—. 1996. "Philosophy and Distributed Artificial Intelligence: The Case of Joint Intention and Joint Action." In *Foundations of Distributed Artificial Intelligence*, edited by N. Jennings and G. O'Hare. New York: Wiley.

—. 1997. "Searle on Social Institutions." *Philosophy and Phenomenological Research* 57: 435–41.

—. 1998a. "Collective Goals and Cooperation." In *Discourse, Interaction, and Communication*, edited by X. Arrazola, K. Korta, and F. Pelletier. Dordrecht: Kluwer.

—. 1998b. "Mutual Belief." In *Filosofisia Iskuja*, edited by P. Mäkelä et al. Technical Reports 65. Tampere: Department of Philosophy, Tampere University.

—. 1999. "Private Versus Collective Attitudes." In *Analyomen 3: Perspektiven der Analytischen Philosophie*, edited by J. Nida-Rümelin. Berlin: Walter de Gruyter.

—. 2000a. *Cooperation: A Philosophical Study.* Philosophical Studies Series 82. Dordrecht: Kluwer Academic Publishers.

—. 2000b. "Collective and Joint Intention." *Mind & Society* 1: 39–69.

—. 2001a. "Collective Acceptance and Social Reality." In *On the Nature of Social and Institutional Reality*, edited by Eerik Lagerspetz, Heikki Ikäheimo, and Jussi Kotkavirta. Jyväskylä: University of Jyväskylä Press.

—. 2001b. "Collective Intentionality and Social Agents." In *Explanatory Connections: Electronic Essays in Honor of Matti Sintonen*, edited by M. Kiikeri and P. Ylikoski. www.valt.helsinki.fi/kfil/matti/ (accessed August 2002).

—. 2002a. *The Philosophy of Social Practices: A Collective Acceptance View.* Cambridge: Cambridge University Press

—. 2002b. "Collective Acceptance, Social Institutions, and Social Reality." *Journal of Economics and Sociology.*

—. 2002c. "Collective Goals and Communicative Action." *Journal of Philosophical Research* 27: 29–64.

—. 2002d. "Joint Intention and Commitment." In *Social Facts and Collective Intentionality*, edited by Georg Meggle. Frankfurt: Dr. Hänsel-Hohenhausen.

—. 2002e. "Searle, Collective Intentionality, and Social Institutions." In *Speech Acts, Mind, and Social Reality*, edited by G. Grewendorf and G. Meggle. Dordrecht: Kluwer.

—. 2003 (in press). "Collective Acceptance, Social Institutions, and Group Beliefs." In Buschlinger and Lütge.

Tuomela, R. and Balzer, W. 1999. "Collective Acceptance and Collective Social Notions." *Synthese* 117: 175–205.

———. 2002. "Collective Acceptance and Collective Attitudes: On the Social Construction of Social Reality." In Mäki (2002).

Tuomela, R. and M. Bonnevier-Tuomela. 1995. "Norms and Agreement." *European
Journal of Law, Philosophy, and Computer Science* 5: 41–6.

———. 1997. "From Social Imitation to Teamwork." In *Contemporary Action Theory.*
Vol. 2: *Social Action*, edited by G. Holmström-Hintikka and R. Tuomela. Dordrecht:
Kluwer.

Tuomela, R. and K. Miller. 1985. "We-Intentions and Social Action." *Analyse und Kritik* 7: 26–43.

———. 1988. "We-Intentions." *Philosophical Studies* 53: 367–89.

———. 1992. "We-Intentions, Free-Riding and Being in Reserve." *Erkenntnis* 36: 25–52.

———. 2001. "What are Collective Goals?" In *Explanatory Connections: Electronic
Essays in Honor of Matti Sintonen*, edited by M. Kiikeri and P. Ylikoski.
www.valt.helsinki.fi/kfil/matti/ (accessed August 2002).

Tuomela, R. and M. Tuomela. 2002. "Acting as a Group Member and Collective Commitment." *Protosociology* 18: (in press).

Turner, J. C. and H. Giles, eds. 1981. *Intergroup Behavior.* Oxford: Blackwell.

Turner, J. C., M. A. Hogg, P. J. Oakes, S. D. Reicher, and M. S. Wetherell. 1987. *Rediscovering the Social Group: A Self-Categorization Theory.* Oxford: Blackwell.

Turner, Stephen. 1994. *The Social Theory of Practices.* Cambridge: Polity Press.

Ullman-Margalit, Edna. 1977. *The Emergence of Norms.* Oxford: Oxford University
Press.

———. 1978. "Invisible-hand Explanations." *Synthese* 39: 263–91.

Vallacher, Robin R. and Andrzej Nowak, eds. 1994. *Dynamical Systems in Social Psychology.* San Diego: Academic Press.

Van Inwagen, Peter. 1990. *Material Beings.* Ithaca, N.Y.: Cornell University Press.

Van Vugt, M., M. Snyder, T. Tyler, and A. Biel. 2000. *Cooperation in Modern Society.*
London: Routledge.

Velleman, J. David. 1997a. "Deciding How to Decide." In *Ethics and Practical Reasoning*, edited by Garrett Cullity and Berys Gaut. Oxford: Oxford University Press.

———. 1997b. "How to Share an Intention." *Philosophy and Phenomenological Research* 57: 29–50.

Wagner, Steven J. and Richard Warner, eds. 1993. *Naturalism: A Critical Appraisal.*
Notre Dame, Ind.: University of Notre Dame.

Walzer, Michael. 1983. *Spheres of Justice: A Defense of Pluralism and Equality.* New
York: Basic Books.

Ware, Robert. 1988. "Group Action and Social Ontology." *Analyse und Kritik* 10:
48–70.

Ware, Robert and Kai Nielsen, eds. 1989. *Analyzing Marxism: New Essays on Analytical Marxism.* Calgary: University of Calgary Press.

Wartenberg, Thomas. 1990. *The Forms of Power: An Essay in Social Ontology.*
Philadelphia: Temple University Press.

Watkins, J. W. N. 1968. "Methodological Individualism and Social Tendencies." In
Readings in the Philosophy of Social Science, edited by May Brodbeck. New York:
Macmillan.

———. 1973a. "Historical Explanation in the Social Sciences." In *Modes of Individualism and Collectivism*, edited by J. O'Neill. London: Heinemann.

———. 1973b. "Methodological Individualism: A Reply." In *Modes of Individualism and Collectivism*, edited by J. O'Neill. London: Heinemann.

Weber, Max. 1949. *The Methodology of the Social Sciences*. Translated and edited by Edward Shils and Henry Finch. New York: Free Press.

———. 1987. *The Theory of Social and Economic Organization*. New York: Free Press.

———. 1993. *Basic Concepts in Sociology*. Translated by H. P. Secher. New York: Citadel Press.

Werhane, Patricia. 1985. *Persons, Rights, and Corporations*. Englewood Cliffs, N.J.: Prentice-Hall.

Wertsch, James V. 1997. *Mind as Mediated Action*. Oxford: Oxford University Press.

Williams, Bernard. 1988. "Formal Structures and Social Reality." In *Trust: Making and Breaking Cooperative Relations*, edited by D. Gambetta. Oxford: Blackwell.

———. 1995a. *Making Sense of Humanity*. Cambridge: Cambridge University Press.

———. 1995b. "How Free Does the Will Need to Be?" In *Making Sense of Humanity*, edited by Bernard Williams. Cambridge: Cambridge University Press.

Wilson, Brian, ed. 1970. *Rationality*. Oxford: Blackwell.

Wilson, Mark. 1982. "Predicate Meets Property." *The Philosophical Review* 91: 549–89.

———. 1993. "Honorable Intensions." In Wagner and Warner (1993).

Wilson, Margo and Martin Daly. 1992. "The Man Who Mistook His Wife for a Chattel." *The Adapted Mind: Evolutionary Psychology and the Generation of Culture*. In *The Adapted Mind*, edited by Jerome H. Barkow, Leda Cosmides, and John Tooby. New York: Oxford University Press.

Wilson, Robert A.. 1999a. "Realism, Essence, and Kind: Resuscitating Species Essentialism?" In *Species: New Interdisciplinary Essays*, edited by Robert A. Wilson. Cambridge, Mass.: MIT Press.

———. 1999b. *Species: New Interdisciplinary Essays*. Cambridge, Mass.: MIT Press.

———. 2001. "Group-Level Cognition." *Philosophy of Science* 68: 262–273.

Winch, Peter. 1970. "Understanding a Primitive Society." In *Rationality*, edited by Brian Wilson. Oxford: Blackwell.

———. 1990. *The Idea of a Social Science*. 2d ed. London: Routledge and Kegan Paul.

Wittgenstein, Ludwig. 1958. *Philosophical Investigations*. New York: Macmillan.

———. 1978. *Remarks on the Foundations of Mathematics*. Rev. ed. Cambridge, Mass.: MIT Press.

Wollstonecraft, M. 1995. "A Vindication of the Rights of Woman." In *A Vindication of the Rights of Man with A Vindication of the Rights of Woman and Hints,* edited by S. Tomaselli. New York: Cambridge University Press.

Wright, Crispin. 1991. "Wittgenstein's Later Philosophy of Mind: Sensation, Privacy, and Intention." In *Meaning Scepticism*, edited by K. Puhl. Berlin: Walter de Gruyter.

———. 1998. "Self-Knowledge: The Wittgensteinian Legacy." In *Knowing Our Own Mind*, edited by Crispin Wright, Barry C. Smith, and Cynthia Macdonald. Oxford: Clarendon.

Wright, Crispin, Barry C. Smith, and Cynthia Macdonald, eds. 1998. *Knowing Our Own Minds*. Oxford: Clarendon.

Yi, Byeong-Uk. 2002. "Is There a Plural Object?" *Ms.*

———. forthcoming. "The Language and Logic of Plurals." *Journal of Philosophical Logic*.

Zimmerman, Michael J. 1985. "Sharing Responsibility." *American Philosophical Quarterly* 22: 115–22.

Index

Contributors

Gary Ebbs is associate professor of philosophy at the University of Illinois at Urbana-Champaign. He previously taught at Harvard University and the University of Pennsylvania. He is the author of *Rule-Following and Realism* (1997) and articles in philosophy of language, philosophy of logic, philosophy of mind, and the history of analytic philosophy. A unifying goal of his research is to describe the methodology of rational inquiry from an engaged, practical point of view.

Margaret Gilbert is professor of philosophy at the University of Connecticut, Storrs. She has been a visiting professor of philosophy at Princeton University and elsewhere. She frequently lectures in the United States, Canada, and Europe on topics in the philosophy of social science, social and political philosophy, and related fields. Her publications include *On Social Facts* (1989), *Living Together* (1996), and *Sociality and Responsibility* (2000).

Sally Haslanger is associate professor in the MIT department of linguistics and philosophy. Her publications have addressed topics in metaphysics, epistemology, and feminist theory, with a recent emphasis on accounts of the social construction of race and gender. In metaphysics, her work has focused on theories of substance—for example, on the problem of persistence through change and on Aristotle's view that substances are composites of matter and form. In connection with these issues, she has also published articles on pragmatic paradox and supervenience. Her work in feminist theory takes up issues in feminist epistemology and metaphysics, with a special interest in feminist critiques of objectivity and the distinction between natural and social kinds.

Kevin Kimble is a doctoral student in philosophy at Indiana University. His areas of interest include metaphysics, philosophy of mind, philosophy of religion, and ethics.

Ron Mallon is assistant professor of philosophy at the University of Utah and research assistant professor at the University of Hong Kong. His interests are in the philosophy of mind, philosophy of social science, and social and political philosophy.

Seumas Miller is professor of social philosophy and director of the Centre for Applied Philosophy and Public Ethics (an Australian Research Council–funded Special Research Centre) at Charles Sturt University, Canberra, Australia. His areas of interest are social philosophy, professional and applied ethics, and philosophy of language (pragmatics). He is the author or coauthor of numerous academic articles and a number of books, including *Rethinking Theory: A Critique of Literary Theory and an Alternative Account* (1992), *Police Ethics* (1997), *Social Action: A Teleological Account* (2001), and *Corruption and Anti-Corruption: An Applied Philosophical Study* (forthcoming).

Philip Pettit teaches political theory and philosophy at Princeton University where he is William Nelson Cromwell Professor of Politics. He previously taught at the Australian National University, Canberra. He is the author of *A Common Mind: An Essay on Psychology, Society and Politics* (1993), *Republicanism: A Theory of Freedom and Government* (1997), and *A Theory of Freedom: From the Psychology to the Politics of Agency* (2001). A collection of his papers, *Rules, Reasons and Norms*, appeared in 2002.

Abraham Sesshu Roth is assistant professor at the University of Illinois, Chicago, and has been a member of the philosophy department at UCLA. He has published several articles in the philosophy of action and in the interpretation of Hume, including "Reasons Explanation of Action: Causal, Singular, and Situational" in *Philosophy and Phenomenological Research* (December 1999). His current research in the theory of action focuses on shared agency; "Sharing Intentions and Contralateral Commitments," is a forthcoming paper.

Frederick F. Schmitt is professor of philosophy at Indiana University. He previously taught at the University of Illinois at Urbana-Champaign. His areas of specialization are epistemology and the history of epistemology. He is the author of *Knowledge and Belief* (1992) and *Truth—A Primer* (1995) and the editor of *Socializing Epistemology: The Social Dimensions of Knowledge* (1994).

John R. Searle was born in Denver, Colorado, and educated at the University of Wisconsin and Oxford University, where he was a Rhodes Scholar. He has all of his degrees from Oxford and taught there for three years before going to the University of California, Berkeley, in 1959 where he has been a professor since. He has lectured at universities throughout the world. He is the author of fourteen books and his works have been translated into twenty-one languages. He is married and has two sons and one granddaughter.

Raimo Tuomela is professor of philosophy at the department of philosophy, University of Helsinki, Helsinki, Finland. His main field of research is the philosophy of social action. He is the recipient of several grants and awards, including the von Humboldt Foundation Research Award. His recent books include *The Importance of Us: A Philosophical Study of Basic Social Notions* (1995), *Cooperation: A Philosophical Study* (2000), and *The Philosophy of Social Practices: A Collective Acceptance View* (2002).

Edward Witherspoon is assistant professor in the department of philosophy and religion at Colgate University. His main interests are the history of analytic philosophy, points of contact between analytic and continental philosophy, and the problem of skepticism. His publications include "Conceptions of Nonsense in Carnap and Wittgenstein," in Alice Crary and Rupert Read, eds., *The New Wittgenstein* (2000); "Logic and the Inexpressible in Frege and Heidegger," *The Journal of the History of Philosophy* (January 2002); "Houses, Flowers, and Frameworks: Mulhall and Cavell on the Moral of Skepticism," *The European Journal of Philosophy* (August 2002); and "Much Ado about the Nothing: Carnap and Heidegger on Logic and Metaphysics," forthcoming in C. G. Prado, ed., *A Dubious Estrangement*.